BEHIND YESTERDAY

BOOKS BY THE AUTHOR

TARGET LONDON
Thomas Watson Thriller Book 2
A new German secret weapon. A high-stakes battle for survival

THE GENEVA INTRUSION
Kate Adler thriller #1
Iran attacks the world's financial markets to start a war.

PRIMARY PROTOCOL
Kate Adler thriller #2
Kate and the cartel uncover a terrorist plot on French soil.

ISLANDS OF PEACE
Kate Adler thriller #3
Things are never what they seem.

BRIMSTONE OFFENSIVE
Kate Adler thriller #4
Never underestimate your enemy.

AT RANDOM
"Thoughts From a Marginal Mind."

BEHIND YESTERDAY

History, romance, and intrigue
in a time of war.

Richard D. Taylor

Pacific Grove Press

Behind Yesterday

Pacific Grove Press

Printed in the United States of America

For more information on this and other books by Mr. Taylor:

RichardDtaylor@gmail.com

I would love to hear from you.

Version V2025.11

To my father, Harold Taylor, who fought in the Pacific,
and to all those who fought for today's freedom in WWII.

BEHIND YESTERDAY'S COMPANION PIECE

This is a work of historical fiction, a genre of literature that tells stories set in a specific historical period. Two renowned examples are " War and Peace " by Leo Tolstoy and " Gone with the Wind " by Margaret Mitchell. These novels aim to entertain and deliver compelling stories rather than serve as documentaries. Certain events have been adapted or altered to align with the fictional narrative and enhance the storytelling experience.

Writing a historical novel requires extensive research, but not all ends in the final book. For readers who wish to learn more about the time period, the people featured, and any adaptations, I've created a companion piece at the back of this book. The piece provides additional historical context, insights into the story, descriptions of period-relevant items, and comments on individual chapters.

JUMP TO COMPANION PIECE

History 'tis but bottom sand in the hourglass,
Turned only at the will of the master,
Aloft for now, and beneath for then,
Save for the point of passing,
When at once there is neither and …

-- Richard D. Taylor

I don't understand the mystery of my being here, but just because we don't know how or why doesn't mean there isn't a significant reason for it occurring.

Thomas Watson

Chapter One

Caribbean Sea

Cruise Liner: Voyager of the Sea
10:15 pm New Year's Eve, 1989

Thomas Watson paused before the mirror in the ship's restroom, catching sight of his bloodshot eyes. He placed his drink glass on the marble counter and leaned closer to scrutinize his reflection. His eyes, reddened from days spent in the sun on the cruise, looked quite sorry. Thankfully, the New Year's Eve party upstairs was held in a dimly lit ballroom.

Thomas lingered for reasons he couldn't explain, staring into his eyes. Maybe it was the alcohol. He'd tried this strange habit before—locking eyes with his reflection—and noticed that if he stared long enough, his face seemed to change in unsettling ways. He had always dismissed it as an old parlor trick.

Just as he was about to turn away, the strange sensation intensified, shifting from peculiar to distinctly alarming. The mirror seemed to gain a gentle depth as if it were less a surface and more a portal. He slowly lifted his right hand, pressing a finger to the glass, expecting his reflection to duplicate the gesture. His reflection, however, raised two fingers to meet his.

"Good heavens," he exclaimed, startled back to reality. Dropping his hand, he felt relieved to see everything return to its natural state. His gaze wandered again, landing again on his tired eyes, only to catch the faintest hint of movement in the reflection behind him. He blinked. No, it wasn't just a movement—but a change, a subtle yet unmistakable transformation.

Turning around, Thomas found himself in an entirely different restroom. As he turned, his hand brushed against the drink he had placed on the counter—though, curiously, it was no longer a drink but a small bottle. He watched, almost detached, as it fell from the discolored counter toward a well-worn hardwood floor. The sound of shattering glass froze him in place.

Chapter Two

Cruise Liner: Voyager of the Sea
TWENTY MINUTES BEFORE THE MIRROR.

A light ocean spray drifted onto Thomas Watson's face as the Caribbean waves parted around the cruise ship. The history professor, tall and fit, presented himself as a striking and confident figure. Leaning on the railing, the wind tossed his light brown hair while he gazed over the open sea.

Thomas had excused himself from the lively New Year's Eve celebration in the Explorer Lounge behind him, seeking a moment of solitude and fresh air. Another gust of wind pressed the left lapel of his tuxedo jacket against his cheek. Taking a steady breath, he prepared to return to the merriment inside.

Only recently had Thomas begun to realize that he could no longer evade the prospect of a serious relationship without risking solitude for the rest of his life. Determined to change, he resolved to find what, to date, had seemed almost impossible—a true lifelong companion. This holiday cruise, shared with a few close friends, felt like a fresh start. The constant social engagements were exactly the sort of rejuvenation he sought.

As he ventured back inside, Thomas became aware of another pressing issue: he needed to find a restroom. Weaving through the bustling crowd, he made his way toward the grand entrance of the ballroom, where the ship's captain held court, graciously kissing the hands of ladies and greeting passengers.

"What a splendid job," Thomas mused as he navigated through the throng. Ducking to avoid an exuberant gesture, he unexpectedly bumped into a young woman. His hand shot out in a belated attempt to save her drink as it fell onto the carpet.

"My apologies," he said, feeling both embarrassed and utterly captivated by her beauty. She was, without a doubt, remarkable.

"Where on earth has she been all week?" he wondered.

He said, "Oh dear, that was terribly clumsy of me. Did any spill on you?"

Looking down at her dress, she replied with a British accent, "No... no, thankfully not," and, brushing a strand of hair behind her right ear, added with a smile, "What's a party without bumping into a few people... quite literally, it would seem?"

Her remark was met with a captivated silence. She appeared in her late twenties, slightly taller than average, with a graceful, well-proportioned figure. Her wavy auburn hair, styled in a WWII victory wave, shimmered under the ballroom lights. Her greenish-blue eyes sparkled as they held his, undeterred by the surrounding commotion. Her fine features—a delicate nose, high cheekbones, and fair complexion—hinted at an Irish lineage, while a slender gold necklace with a small diamond glimmered at her neck. Thomas found himself completely smitten, admiring her almost Vogue-like elegance.

He stared, entranced until the pause urged him to speak. "Then... why didn't I see you earlier this week?" he ventured, hardly the most poetic line, but the first thought that came to mind.

"Well, that's a curious question. Perhaps it just wasn't time for our paths to cross," she replied with a playful glint. "More likely, I tend to avoid crowds. But tonight, here I am!" she said, placing her hands on her hips and striking a lighthearted pose.

"Yes, well, I'm quite pleased that our paths crossed," Thomas replied awkwardly yet sincerely.

She met his gaze with a keen, appraising look that seemed to assess more than just his outward appearance. "How terribly rude of me," he continued, regaining his composure. "I'm Thomas Watson."

"Lovely to meet you, Thomas Watson. I'm Margaret..."

Before she could finish, the band started again, and someone who was clearly a friend came rushing over in a full top hat, a bright blue cummerbund, and flowing tails.

"This is the one you promised me, dearie," he said, gently pulling her onto the dance floor by the hand. "Ladies and gentlemen," he declared to their group at the table, "watch closely; the master shall now demonstrate the art of dancing with a beautiful woman." She laughed and told her friend, "A promise is a promise."

She looked back at Thomas while addressing her friend and added, "But I insist you return me to this most intriguing gentleman here."

"Agreed, my lady," he said with an exaggerated feigned bow, one hand holding his hat at his waist and the other raised high in the air. He narrowly avoided the nearest elegantly dressed couple, who responded with an icy glare. Recalling his earlier plan, and while she was still looking at him, Thomas said, "I'll be back when the song is over," pointing directly to a spot on the floor. "I'll be right here."

Stepping onto the dance floor, she placed one hand on her hip, extended her other arm in an elegant arch, and, with a playful wag of her finger, replied, "Right here, then! You promise, do you?" Her eyes sparkled with laughter as she twirled away.

Thomas could only manage a helpless nod, transfixed. Her long satin gown flared out as she spun across the dance floor, catching the light and creating the illusion of her gliding away. Her sultry, confident smile lingered in his memory as she vanished into the crowd, casting one last glance over her shoulder that ignited a fierce desire to know her better.

"So," Thomas thought, "that's what they mean by instant attraction." A deep yearning emerged within him to learn more about this woman.

Recognizing the urgency of his task, he hurried toward the restroom outside the main door of the ballroom. He bent down, scooped up Margaret's empty glass, and tossed it into an overflowing bin on the way. Given the difficulty of obtaining cocktails that evening, he chose to keep his own firmly in hand.

Chapter Three

IN A DIFFERENT PLACE.
London Suburbs 1940
Town of Amersham

When the glass hit the floor, Thomas realized he was in a very different place. The space transformed from stark commercial to something resembling a small bathroom in an old house. He saw an imposing, old-fashioned claw-foot tub filling the area behind him, complemented by wide-mouthed brass taps. Two bath oil bottles rested alongside a glass bowl filled with talcum powder on a nearby shelf. The walls were adorned with busy, patterned floral wallpaper, and several plants hung from the ceiling. In the corner stood a toilet with a small wooden cabinet mounted high on the wall. Thomas stared at the pull chain.

Thomas remained frozen as if any movement might upset the fragile reality around him. He took a deep breath and held it, gripped by a growing sense of unease. Just then, a woman's voice called out from beyond the closed door.

"Thomas, what was that noise? Are you all right, love? Whatever are you doing in there?"

Her voice was smooth, refined, and unmistakably British. Through the mottled glass of the door, he saw a shadow move closer. The doorknob turned, and a woman entered, dressed in a bra and garter belt beneath an opaque slip. Upon noticing his gaze, she paused, quickly adjusting her slip to cover her legs. She pointed a finger at him, half-playful, half-exasperated, "We've talked about this, Thomas. Stop staring. It won't do you any good."

But it wasn't her exposed leg that had caught his attention; it was her striking face, framed by waves of auburn hair cascading over her bare shoulders. Green eyes that sparkled with life enhanced her pale, delicate features. A slender gold necklace rested at her throat with the glint of a small diamond, and for a moment, Thomas thought he recognized her.

Even in his confusion, he couldn't help but note how remarkably beautiful she was. But—who was she?

She smoothed her slip, still eyeing him with mild annoyance as she pulled her hair behind her ear. Her gaze fell on the broken glass at his feet. "Good thing it was nearly empty, or I'd be denying you supper for this!" she said with a laugh, bending to pick up the largest shard of the bottle. Holding it up between them, she teased, "You brute! This was the last bit of my favorite face cream, and now it's ruined. I can't get this anymore."

Thomas, still leaning against the counter, looked at her, bewildered. Noticing his silence, her expression softened with concern. "Thomas… are you all right?" she asked gently. Despite her earlier reproach, her tone now conveyed genuine warmth as she placed a hand on his chest, searching his face.

"What's wrong?" she asked, her green eyes fixed on him. But he couldn't muster a reply, only staring back, his mind a tangled web of questions.

After a few silent seconds, she took his hand, gently guiding him out of the bathroom and into the adjoining bedroom. She dropped the shard of glass into a dustbin and eased him down onto the bed, sitting close beside him with one arm around his waist.

The room was modest, with two windows, several large armoires, and a small wind-up clock on the nightstand, which read 11:15. Thomas assumed it was nighttime, though heavy blackout curtains covered the windows, giving no hint of the world outside. He glanced down the short hallway connected to other rooms, realizing this was indeed a house, but whose?

"Thomas?" she prompted softly.

He looked at her, managing only, "I… I'm not sure. Just a bit… confused." What could he possibly say? "Where am I? And who are you?" Her tenderness hinted at a deep affection for him, though her modesty over her state of dress suggested she was not entirely at ease. Frustrated, he tried to recall what he had been doing just before staring into the mirror, but his thoughts slipped through his mind like water. Could this all be a dream?

Before he could ponder further, the sudden sound of sirens split the air—long, ominous, escalating into a steady, relentless drone.

"Oh no, not another drill," she muttered, springing to her feet. "Thomas, get your coat!"

Her urgency cut through his fog of confusion. "Thomas, quickly!" she urged, pulling a dress over her head.

He stood, catching her eye as her head emerged from the fabric. She nodded toward the armoire. "In there," she directed, and he opened the doors, spotting a long, black man's overcoat, which he pulled out.

"Now mine," she said, glancing at him expectantly.

"I don't see it," he said, searching for something resembling a woman's coat.

"Thomas! Not there—try my armoire, love. We must hurry."

Opening the other armoire, he found a dark green coat hanging inside the door. He handed it to her, and she swiftly threw it over her shoulders. She grabbed a silk scarf in the hallway and retrieved two small boxes with handles from a hall tree.

"Where are we going?" he asked, his voice tinged with rising unease.

She turned slowly, her gaze piercing, and he sensed the beginnings of worry in her expression. "Thomas, just come with me. We'll talk later."

Chapter Four

London Suburbs 1940

Town of Amersham—Amersham Shelter

They stepped out through the front door of the brick house, followed the short path to the gate, and emerged onto the street. Thomas glanced up and down the row of identical brick houses. The night was black and slightly cool. As he looked around, unsettled in his thoughts, a British cab sped past, its narrow headlights mere slits in the darkness.

"A British cab?" he wondered, pausing, though the sight added nothing of value. Around them, people were moving—some walking, others running—all in the same direction. Sirens wailed in the distance, accompanied by a low, ominous roar. Thomas and Margaret picked up their pace, covering three blocks before turning right at a corner.

They passed The Stags Pit pub with its imposing doorway; he could see a man emerge, closing it. Ahead at the shelter, Thomas saw groups descending below street level from all directions. Across the road, an elderly couple was hurriedly locking up their bakery. The roar grew louder and closer. Children, some in nightclothes hastily covered with jackets, hurried along, their worried mothers ushering them forward. It wasn't panic but rather deep concern.

Suddenly, the sky lit up—not with fireworks but with gunfire. Every sixth bullet traced a bright path through the dark, crossing in patterns from a mile off. Shafts of light pierced the blackness, illuminating the undersides of high clouds. The dull roar had become deafening, and the crowd broke into a slow run.

"Oh, God, it's not a drill!" Margaret shouted. "Thomas, follow me! We can make sense of it later if we're still alive."

"If we're still alive?" Thomas thought, shaken.

They ran faster toward the shelter entrance, joining the last stragglers as they reached the wide concrete steps. Thomas paused on the steps when he caught sight of the words "Amersham Station" painted above the opening and paused while Margaret continued forward. Beside the entrance was the familiar tricolor Underground logo, and beneath it, a yellow and black sign reading, "Air Raid Shelter, Night Only, Max.

Persons 125." Neatly stacked sandbags surrounded the entrance, arranged precisely as though their effectiveness depended on it.

A sudden explosion two blocks away threw a wave of hot air that swept down the street in a fiery blast. Stunned, Thomas covered his ears, realizing he'd felt the pressure wave of a bomb. His teeth had slammed together, narrowly missing his tongue. He was flung against the sandbags. "Thomas!" Margaret screamed, rushing back up the steps. She grabbed his coat sleeve, pulling him down toward the shelter. "Get in—now!"

They both heard the groans of an older man sprawled on the stairs, dressed in what appeared to be a police uniform. He was the ARP (Air Raid Precaution) warden, thrown by the blast. Thomas gently rolled him onto his back.

"Go on ahead," Thomas urged Margaret. "I'll follow."

"There isn't time!" she called over the increasing noise from above.

"Please, go now. *Please*," Thomas insisted. With one last look, she continued down the stairs. Thomas turned back to the warden, who lay covered in debris—roof tiles, bricks, dirt, and burning wood scattered around him. Thomas tossed aside a large piece of furniture and knelt beside the man, checking for serious injuries.

"Sir, can you get up?" Thomas asked.

The man groaned and lifted himself onto all fours. "Can you walk?" Thomas asked again, but the warden seemed too dazed to respond. After a moment, his head began to clear, and he reached for his tin hat lying nearby.

"Much obliged, lad," the warden managed. "Just a hand, if you would." Thomas doubted the man could hear much, having taken the blast's full force without the sandbags' protection. He helped the warden to his feet and, supporting his weight, guided him down the stairwell. The man's steps grew steadier when they neared the station door, though he was still breathless. A tall figure held the door open, and once inside, Thomas helped the warden sit against the wall.

"Close the doors!" the warden called out. The tall man was already shutting one door, and Thomas moved to close the other.

Margaret appeared beside him. "Thomas, darling, were you hurt?"

"Me? No, I think I'm all right," he assured her.

Margaret knelt beside the warden, loosening his collar and wiping the dirt from his face with her scarf. "I'm fine, Margaret," the warden said slowly. "Jus' need a bit ter gather me thoughts."

The man reached out an arm, waving her back, and ordered, "Take places, everyone, jus' like the drills. There's no need ter gettin in a fret now. You too, Margaret."

Margaret helped Thomas deeper into the station, slipping her arm through his. "Are you sure you're okay? Weren't you thrown against the wall?"

"A bit dizzy, like the warden, but I'm fine."

After a few steps, she asked again, glancing at her dirt-streaked scarf. "Are you certain? Did you hit your head?"

"You mean from the blast?" he replied.

"No, Thomas, before the blast. I've asked you twice now."

His ears still ringing, he managed, "I don't think so."

They passed groups of people settling down on the floor, families huddled close, mothers tending to children. Some people, looking like they'd been there for hours, lay on cots with belongings stashed neatly beneath.

"Here's our spot," Margaret directed him to a spot beside the ticket counter. "Sit here. All those drills about shelters finally have their use. I can't believe they're actually doing it."

"Doing what?" he asked.

"Bombing civilians. The Geneva Convention forbids it, but when did they ever care about conventions?"

Thomas thought to ask, "Who are 'they'?" but held back, feeling larger questions brewing.

"Good evening, Professor," greeted an elderly woman settling nearby with a blanket. "Margaret, didn't you bring your blanket?"

"No, Mrs. Somerville," Margaret replied, holding Thomas's arm. "We barely had time to grab our coats."

Mrs. Somerville smiled, noting Margaret's miss buttoned coat and missing stocking. Thomas helped Mrs. Somerville settle down on her blanket.

"Well, Professor," she remarked with surprise, "that's a kindness I didn't expect." She held his hand briefly, an unexpected warmth passing between them.

Upon releasing it, she added, "As to you, young lady, I quite understand your tardiness. Wish I were young again. In our younger days when Charles and I were courtin'," she said with a wink his way, "we were late for everything." She laughed, obviously enjoying the memory.

Thomas stepped away, perplexed by his surroundings. "What is going on here?" he thought. "Is this a London Underground station used as a bomb shelter?" The British cab, the beams of light, the accents—

everything spoke of England, but how? Across the station, a billboard advertised Chesterfield cigarettes beside a French Gauloises ad, each with vintage art, as if plucked from an old Life magazine. The situation was as confusing as it was intriguing.

He picked up a copy of *The Illustrated London News at a nearby newsstand.* The date stopped him: Saturday, 24 August 1940.

"1940?" he murmured. "What happened to 1989? What am I doing here?" His mind scrambled for answers—a trick, a film set, a dream? But the ringing in his ears felt too real for fantasy.

A soft touch on his shoulder interrupted him. "Thomas, what's wrong? You're acting so strangely," Margaret asked.

He faced her, struggling to explain. "I feel… lost. Like I'm somewhere I don't recognize, though I should. Perhaps it's amnesia. I wish I could tell you more."

Distant sounds of bombing seeped into the shelter. Children ran about, playing with the joy of being up past bedtime. He looked back at her. "Margaret," he asked slowly, "is that your name?"

"What?" she replied, stepping back.

"I'm sorry," he said, confused. "I don't mean to be rude, but I don't know where I am—or who I am. And it's not because of the blast."

She hugged him tightly. "Thomas, love, you're scaring me. Please, this isn't funny." Her fear was obvious, and hard not to feel.

"This has never happened before… at least, I don't think it has," he said, pausing. "I just need some time to figure out who I am—and why I'm here."

"Why you're here?" Her voice held a mix of worry and frustration. "You don't know who you are, but why you're here?"

"Forgive me," he said gently. "I need to think. A little walk. None of this makes sense. I'll be right back, all right?"

Margaret nodded, reluctantly letting him go, and sat beside Mrs. Somerville.

"Where's he off to?" Mrs. Somerville asked.

"I don't know. Thomas is acting very strange. Says he doesn't know who he is or why he's here." She sighed. "He looks like my Thomas, but he's not acting like him."

Mrs. Somerville patted her hand reassuringly on Margaret's shoulder. "Of course, he looks like your Thomas. And those are curious questions he's asking, don't you think? Still, he won't wander far down here—none of us will."

Chapter Five

The Secret Cabinet War Rooms
Whitehall, London

John "Jock" Colville, private secretary to the Prime Minister, paced back and forth outside the Telephone Room, glancing at his watch. It was well past midnight, nearly thirty minutes since he'd received the urgent message. He knew better than to interrupt Mr. Churchill when he was on a call with the Americans, but this message weighed heavily.

Given Churchill's robust presence, the Transatlantic Telephone Room was a tight fit—no more than six feet by seven. Behind a plain wooden door, two shelves painted an unremarkable industrial green lined the left wall, mounted above an old two-drawer table barely stretching across the cramped width of the space. Before the table, an oak chair sat sturdily, bearing marks that spoke of the last war.

A single brass lamp with a green glass shade cast light over the table, illuminating the sole object of importance: a black telephone of humble origin, plucked from some office upstairs. Little could the installer have imagined that this phone, once set down, would stay precisely there for decades to come. Save for these items, the room looked as it had in its previous role, as a storeroom for brooms and domestic cleaning items.

This plain black telephone was the only means by which Sir Winston Churchill, the Prime Minister of Britain, and Franklin D. Roosevelt, the President of the neutral United States, could confer on matters of utmost secrecy. Some of the war's most pivotal decisions traveled through this unimposing device.

From this small room, their conversations journeyed by cable to a secure London terminal hidden beneath Selfridges on Oxford Street—a place assigned the code "X System." There, Sigsaly, a hulking American invention by Bell Labs, scrambled their words, transmitting them first to Scotland, then across the Atlantic to Washington, D.C.

The Telephone Room was but a piece of the Cabinet War Rooms—a hidden warren of offices deep beneath Whitehall. Initially built in

Edwardian times to manage the Commonwealth, Whitehall's public buildings, including the Law Courts and the British Museum, held secrets of wartime operations in their depths. After Britain declared war, the Whitehall basements were reinforced as the headquarters for the nation's war effort, and the Office of Works was positioned between St. James's Park and Great George Street. This building, the first in Whitehall constructed with steel-reinforced concrete, was given the codename "No. 1 Storey's Gate"—an address so blatant they thought no one would believe it true.

Conveniently close to both Parliament and No. 10 Downing Street, the Cabinet War Rooms were linked by underground tunnels. These rooms housed Churchill's office bedroom, a Map Room, the Cabinet Room, and basic sleeping quarters for staff. Initially designed for just a few months, the rooms would shelter the government and military strategists for five long years. When peace came, Churchill had the lights turned off and the doors locked. He wanted the site ready for a future war with Russia that he felt loomed on the horizon.

At last, Colville heard the scrape of Churchill's chair inside. The door opened abruptly, catching Colville in the back while he checked his watch.

"Mr. Colville!" Churchill's voice came gruff and loud.

"Yes, Prime Minister?"

"Of all the space allocated to wage a war, why would you choose to stand where a door might cause you harm?"

"My apologies, sir," Colville replied, regaining his poise. "You, er… caught me off guard."

"Tell me, Colville, who assigned you this new duty?"

"Sir? Which duty?"

"Guarding, Colville, guarding. You said I caught you off guard.'"

"Oh! No, sir, I… er…"

"Let it pass, let it pass," Churchill sighed, faintly amused. "Merely a bit of levity—though it seems I've missed my mark. Distracted, I daresay?"

"Yes, sir. I've just received this from Avery Doyle at the Home Guard." Colville handed over the message and a pen.

Churchill signed the transfer slip and read the note, his face darkening. After a pause, he adjusted his spectacles, shifted, and reread it.

"It's a somber thing, Mr. Colville, that such a grave warning could arrive on a single slip of paper."

"Sir?"

"Hitler, Colville, in a fit of folly, has changed the rules. Amersham was bombed tonight, but we shan't be deterred. Summon Air Vice Marshal Portal—he's in town, I believe—and Major-General Ismay. Have them meet me in the Map Room at once. I'll be in my office."

Churchill turned to leave, then paused. "Ah… and Mr. Colville, no need to disturb Lord Halifax. We can manage without his usual objections."

"Yes, sir."

Chapter Six

London Suburbs
Amersham Tube Shelter

Sometime later, a contemplative Thomas Watson ambled back toward where the women sat. The "all clear" siren rang out as his gaze met Margaret's. There was a stir among the others as they gathered their belongings, save for those intending to stay the night on cots. Margaret looked at him expectantly as though he might say everything had returned to the ordinary. He offered no such words, instead helping Margaret and Mrs. Somerville to rise. Margaret made her way toward the stairs leading them out of the station and into the night beyond. Thomas followed a close behind, silent as a shadow.

Thomas glanced down a neighboring street toward the scene of the blast. A fire brigade worked tirelessly, and engines and rescue crews were in urgent motion. Flames leaped from what seemed to be three homes in a row, though smoke and flames muddled much of the view. He could feel the fierce heat from where he stood.

"Ah, the National Fire Service," he thought, recalling the blend of volunteers and professionals donned in their stately uniforms. Their legacy in the history of the war would be saving hundreds of lives from burning buildings. Even after the war, folks would remember the sight of them racing down the lanes as a morale-boosting beacon during the Blitz.

"The Blitz? In history? Where's that thought come from?" he mused, his mind spinning.

Before he could fully gather his thoughts, Margaret's voice cut through, "Are you coming, or have you forgotten where you were before the shelter?"

Thomas nodded, trailing her as they walked back in silence to her home. Margaret unlocked the door, casting her coat onto the couch in the dimly lit sitting room. He heard her voice murmur through the darkness, "The power's out again. We'll have to make do with the lamps." She guided him gently toward a divan, cautioning him about the throw rug underfoot.

She moved to a drawer in a pale-colored chest and, with practiced hands, retrieved matches and a candle. With swift precision, she lit three lamps, placing each carefully about the room, which now glowed with a warmth only lamplight could bring.

Thomas glanced around, noting details he'd overlooked earlier in their rush to the shelter. It was a modest, well-kept room, each item neatly arranged, save for a singular, striking painting—Henri Matisse's "*Femme au manteau violet*." The oversized piece felt almost too grand for such a simple space, and he recognized it instantly. Matisse's style was unconventional for the era, typically appreciated only by those who defied social norms. The painting spoke volumes about its owner.

As the last lamp's light bathed her face, he observed Margaret more closely. She moved about the room with a natural elegance, and he'd noticed earlier how her hands became animated whenever she grew excited or impatient. He couldn't quite discern the color of her eyes in the dim light, but her complexion hinted at Irish roots. Yet more than anything, it was her quiet beauty that struck him. Despite his disorientation, his first impression of meeting her in that first strange moment was her beauty.

She absently refolded her coat, placing it neatly on an empty chair. She settled on the other end of the divan, arms, and legs crossed, and said, "All right then, where do we begin? Do you even know who I am?"

Thomas struggled, unsure how to make things right. What was right, anyhow? His mind raced as he thought, "It's the middle of the Second World War," he thought, adjusting the notion, "more like the beginning since it won't end till '45. But how do I know that, yet not know myself?"

"It's more than just amnesia," he pondered. "I feel like I don't belong here, like an outsider looking in. Life usually makes sense, but this is utterly strange."

Margaret's voice interrupted his thoughts, "Thomas, are you going to participate in this, or must I go it alone?"

"Margaret," he replied, "that's your name, isn't it? I believe you care for me. I heard the concern in your voice when that blast knocked me down, and," he glanced at her legs, where one nylon was still absent, "there's..."

Following his gaze, she saw the same and, with fists on hips, shot back, "We're married, you daft man! That's the first thing you'd better remember. I'm your wife," pointing between herself and him with exaggerated precision.

"Got it," he replied.

"Margaret?"

"What now?" she retorted, becoming frustrated, arms crossing once again in an exaggerated motion.

"I didn't intend for any of this. I'm lost—not just memory-wise, but there's a fog about what I know and don't."

"Like what?"

"Like... well, I don't know who I am."

Margaret, showing her best effort at patience, just looked at him.

"But then there's the knowledge I shouldn't have," he gestured toward the outside world. "Like the art world will come to admire Matisse, your radio will become something akin to a cinema screen, and... we shall win this war."

"This war?" Her brows rose in disbelief. "The one we're fighting?"

He nodded.

"How on earth would you know that?"

"That's the puzzle, Margaret. I'm not guessing—I know. Somehow, history is part of me."

"Thomas, my dear, this war is far from being a thing of the past. The last war is history, but this one's outcome remains uncertain. There's talk of an invasion, the Home Guard is being reinforced, the bombings grow heavier each night, and tonight, civilians were hit. We are nowhere near victory."

She stood up as if ending the current discussion and approached a small cabinet, pulling out a bottle of Advocaat liqueur. With a soft smile, she said, "Fancy a drink, love? Here's to winning the war and a fresh start to this discussion."

Thomas looked at her with the bottle in hand. Smiling, he said, "I'm not so awful, Margaret."

She chuckled. A flicker of warmth broke through the air. "Oh? And given this conversation, how would you know that?" she teased, waving the bottle. "Yes or no?"

"Absolutely," he said. "But, Margaret, there will be no invasion. Hitler turns his sights on Russia instead, chasing Napoleon's folly and freezing for his efforts. But promise me, don't tell a soul. They wouldn't believe you anyway."

"Thomas?" she whispered, bringing two small glasses filled to the rim. She perched on his lap, extending her arm around him. They clinked glasses, and she said, "Cheers."

The liqueur tasted of sweet brandy, a pleasant surprise. After a sip, Margaret peered at him over her glass, hesitating. Then, out of nowhere, she said, "Do you love me?"

"I… don't know, Margaret. I want to, but it's been mere hours."

She held his gaze, a silence heavy between them. "Life seldom hands us second chances, Thomas. So, we'll have to begin anew," she whispered, almost to herself.

Thomas thought it was a strange comment, even if he was in the right state of mind.

Then, realizing she was no longer at ease, she slipped from his lap, put the drink down, and checked the blackout shade. "Must keep the light in," she muttered to someone; it wasn't him.

Overcome by all that had happened, she sighed, "Between the train and the bombing… I could do with a bit of rest. Sleep sounds perfect." She paused, catching herself. Thomas likely hadn't recalled their earlier train journey to see her mother. "Perhaps if we hadn't gone, none of this would've happened," she added quietly.

Thomas remained silent, unable to follow her reasoning.

Without further words, she took a lamp and extinguished the others. Thomas followed her into the bedroom, noting her gestures as she showed him where his things were kept. She disappeared to ready herself for bed. Returning, she was dressed head to toe, almost wearing more than she'd previously had on. He remembered the full slip he'd seen earlier and her great modesty. He stood up. She passed him, saying something about being done and that it was his turn.

He hesitated and hoped his uneasiness wasn't apparent as he stepped into the bathroom and slowly closed the door behind him. Looking around the room, he noticed that faint light filtered in from the bedroom through the glass in the door. He couldn't help but lean over the counter toward the mirror and look into his eyes. He closed them for a second, receptive to even the slightest explanation his mind might provide; he opened his eyes. He was still here—or there. Somewhere.

Returning, he lifted the blanket on his side of the bed. It was peculiar, not knowing quite how to act. Margaret leaned close, head on his shoulder.

"It will be all right, Thomas," she said softly. "We'll face it together. This… is just another thing to work through."

She blew out the lamp, casting the room into darkness.

"What's tomorrow?" he asked.

"Monday," she replied, "though school's out. Why?"

"Then it will give us time to talk? I have lots of questions."

"Yes, it will," she said. "And so do I."

Chapter Seven

London, Whitehall
Secret Cabinet War Rooms

Air Marshal Charles Portal, Commander-in-Chief of Bomber Command, [1]arrived first, none too thrilled by the late hour. He'd insisted on being present at the debrief of the last Wellington flight from France, which returned at 23:30, so he'd barely had a chance to settle into bed before Colville's call summoned him. Portal knew the Prime Minister was a night owl, but such a late gathering was unusual. Portal, too, wondered if Halifax would attend—his absence would mean a meeting without the endless, tense debates that stemmed from Halifax's long-standing rivalry with Churchill, ever a reminder of the Prime Ministerial role he'd nearly claimed.

"The Map Room, is it?" Portal remarked to Colville, who stood at attention, restraining a salute. Churchill insisted that the War Rooms retain a relaxed formality.

"Yes, indeed," Colville replied. "Given the hour, I presume some tea is also included in the meeting. Elizabeth can prepare it straightaway."

"Mrs. Nel? Does the woman ever sleep?"

"She's finishing her late shift this week. With Mr. Churchill's night schedule, he has three rotating shifts of secretaries to keep up." Colville nodded toward the Map Room. "Go on in. I'll see to the tea."

---

[1] Air Marshal **Charles Portal** was Commander-in-Chief of Bomber Command from April 1940 to October 1940, when he was promoted to Chief of the Air Staff. During his brief tenure, he ordered the first bombing raid on Berlin on August 25, 1940. **Arthur Harris** succeeded as Commander-in-Chief of Bomber Command on February 22, 1942.

Meanwhile, Sir Hastings Ismay had just crossed Great George Street, noticing the new wall of sandbags that lent extra fortification to the underground war rooms' entrance. The chilly air hastened his steps from the Home Secretary's office. He took one last look at the now-quiet sky before ducking into the complex's entrance. He had managed the construction of the network of rooms that was his destination. He produced his military ID for the guards before heading down three flights of stairs toward the awaiting Prime Minister.

Ismay, a dedicated Army man schooled at Charterhouse and Sandhurst, bore the hard-earned wisdom of an officer with a career of trials—from the bruising campaigns with the 21st Cavalry Frontier Force in India to wounds endured in Somaliland. He rose steadily through the ranks of the British Army, with numerous political victories and a heart-breaking marital defeat. The latter had been almost five years ago, but it was like yesterday. Though the personal loss lingered, he chalked it up to the price one paid for his unwavering loyalty to Churchill, resulting in his being named Chief of Staff. He suspected the message's urgency: the news he'd just received from Avery Doyle signified a sharp turn in the entire tenor of the war.

As he descended the final step into the main hall, he found himself directly in the path of Elizabeth Nel, Churchill's trusted secretary, carefully balancing a full tea tray. Acting quickly, Ismay steadied the tray and caught her eye.

Elizabeth Nel was a soft, patient soul whose demeanor effectively concealed an extremely disciplined administrator at the rock center of Churchill's staff and secretaries. She was in her late forties, the mother of three, and the only person who could eloquently tell the prime minister to settle down and stop scaring the clerks without being shot at sunrise.

"Major, what a startle!" she chuckled warmly, unperturbed.

"My apologies, Elizabeth—I seem to be wandering mentally this evening."

"No harm to the tea, and that's what's important," she said. "Vice Air Marshal Portal is waiting in the Map Room, and I understand Mr. Colville has the PM on his way."

"Yes, thank you. May I take that in for you?"

She waited momentarily and said, "That would be very kind of you, as I must finish preparing a paper for Mr. Churchill." She revealed a knowing smile. "Right away, if you know what I mean?"

Knowing the PM's notorious impatience, Ismay laughed and reached for the tray. "In that case, I believe I'm obligated, don't you think?"

"In that case, Major, off you go."

As Ismay carried the tea into the Map Room, its walls crowded with maps of Europe, the Atlantic, and beyond, he found Air Marshal Charles Portal intently examining southern England's defenses.

"Keeping the same late hours as our Prime Minister, Charles?" Ismay greeted.

"Hardly by choice, my friend. I see you're Mrs. Nel's new tea bearer," Portal quipped, pointing his pipe at the tray.

"Well, Charles, we all qualify for something now, don't we?" Ismay said, putting down the tray and extending a hand.

"How have you been, my friend?" Ismay asked.

"Well, now, let's see, other than I can't replace bomber pilots and planes as quickly as I'm losing them, it could be worse. In addition, we get intelligence about the same time it's being played out across the sky. Can't those chaps at Bletchley press on through a tea break and get us something a bit more timely?"

"It's coming, Charles. It's a tough project. We need a breakthrough, as well as a little luck. I know it's on the prime minister's mind; he thinks the information is essential to winning the war. I also know that additional funding and everything Bletchley had requested is being approved this week."

"I know, Hastings, but things are getting a bit tight. My young boys give more than they have and then give it again. When this is over, we should knight them all."

Churchill entered briskly. "Gentlemen, I appreciate the interruption of your schedules. Charles, I hear you were booked through the night," he grinned.

"Accurate, sir, though here by your command," Portal replied, chuckling.

"We face a pressing issue," Churchill declared, putting down a folder. "Avery Doyle at the Home Office reports deliberate German bombing of residential homes near Amersham."

"An aerial bombing? I should ruddy well think not. That's almost London proper," Portal said. "I've seen the reports of a stray hit now and then, mostly scaring cattle and strafing inland trees. Moreover, if true, this is an attack directly on London or at least on the outskirts. Why would he do that?" Portal started pacing with his pipe, looking at the floor.

"I'm afraid it's all too true," Ismay said. "I've just come from Avery's office, and he confirmed the information. Thankfully, there were no injuries, as the Home Guard sector had most people in the shelters.

It'll be the last time they moan about the drills. First reports say it took out about a half block."

"But what does it mean?" Portal said. "Is he sending a signal? I thought we'd intercepted traffic that established Hitler's orders to the contrary. To not attack civilian targets." He was in disbelief and becoming agitated. "It wouldn't surprise me that intercepted messages ordering this raid are still in a cavern at Bletchley."

There's no military target within miles of Amersham besides a few broom factories and 14th-century buildings lacking the proper plumbing. It means he has directed attacks against civilian targets, and we cannot be the lamb on this," Churchill said as he pulled out a cigar, yanked the wrapper off, and put it on the table.

Portal stood up and leaned over the table toward the tray. "I think I'm in need of some of that tea."

"I as well," said Ismay.

There was silence for a moment as Portal filled the second cup. Without finishing, he put the cup and teapot down, looked across the table, and said, "We've no choice but to strike back."

"Bloody hell, we ought to level Berlin," Churchill almost yelled as he hit the table with his fist, causing the tea cups on the tray to collide. "That bastard Hitler or Göring or whoever ordered this will pay, and quickly."

The outburst startled Ismay. He'd seen the PM irritated but hadn't seen him use more than his sharp tongue to express it. Colville rushed into the room at the noise, not knowing what to do. He found all three men staring at him.

Standing at attention, Colville said, "P…Prime Minister, is there anything I can do?"

"Yes, Mr. Colville, you can tell Mrs. Nel that this is no time for a holiday, and if she would find her typewriter, we all will be in her debt."

"Yes, sir," he said, leaving as quickly as he'd entered.

"Indeed," Churchill said with vehemence. "I propose a bombing raid targeting a military site near Berlin, a clear message that we will not yield." He leaned forward. "Charles, it's to be done tomorrow night, no delays."

"Sir," Portal began cautiously, "might we consult a broader consensus before so bold an escalation?"

"I'll manage the political repercussions," Churchill cut in. "You handle the Germans."

Porter nodded and said, "Very well, but I anticipate high costs. Our Hurricanes and Spitfires aren't equipped for night operations nor have the range to escort bombers deep into enemy territory. The resistance will be intense. This mission is going to be extremely challenging."

Churchill's tone softened. "I know the costs, Charles, but we cannot be the lamb on this. A tepid response could affect their future decisions and opinions regarding our resolve. Obviously, the rough ride that awaits these boys shall be shared in whole and not in part by their country." Churchill turned to Ismay.

Ismay knew he was looking for his consensus. There was no doubt that these were tense days—dark days. England faced invasion for the first time since 1066 with the Norman incursion onto British soil by William the Conqueror. This war, barely a year old, had been going Hitler's way. The German army had rolled up a series of very successful campaigns, having conquered France and come very close to defeating the only other significant power in the world. Ismay thought of their responsibility to future generations of Europeans, who would face learning the dark art of living in a totalitarian state. These were dismal days indeed.

Ismay reached for his cup on the tray. "Prime Minister, even though I have no choice, as you've made up your mind, I fully support your position as though you hadn't. The long-term strategic cost could be higher. If we were to let it pass without a response, it might lead to the bombing of London. However, I'm most perplexed by the strategic issues. What does he have to gain by changing the front to civilians?" Ismay got up and walked over to the map of southern England and the Channel. "Their targeting of the southern airbases has put us in a perilous situation."

"To say the least," Portal followed. "The southern shore attacks on 15 August between London and Croydon stopped production in four aircraft factories. In addition, they damaged five of my airfields. My boys are scrambling to repair several runways and three aircraft maintenance facilities. The attack on the 12th knocked one radar station out completely, and five are under repair. We should have four of them fully functional by tomorrow afternoon. Perhaps I should say this afternoon. It's an unpleasant situation as we're not keeping pace with the losses."

"That about puts it in perspective," Ismay added. "All he needs to do is to keep to his original plan of attacking the airbases. It's why this doesn't make sense. Has the Ultra team picked anything up at Bletchley?"

Churchill looked uneasy. "I'm afraid that they're woefully behind in deciphering messages. It's a truly complicated affair requiring an untold effort. They're working on a new machine to aid in the deciphering that utilizes quite sophisticated electrical works. I've been led to believe it's faster, but we shall see."

Colville entered the room with a folder and placed it before the prime minister, who quickly glanced at the one-page document. Then, with a fountain pen from his pocket, he scrawled at the bottom, blotted the signature, and handed it to the air marshal.

"Charles, these are your orders. Take all the aircraft you can muster. You're with me on this?"

"Yes, without reservation," Portal replied firmly.

"Again, I agree," said Ismay. "Reluctantly, but I agree. We've no alternative, but I would like to be in Göring's pocket when he must explain away his broken promise to the people of Berlin. It looks like his impenetrable defense, provided by his beloved Luftwaffe, will have a big hole punched right through it. He'll have an angry, stunned population, will have soiled his family's name, and he'll be more than angry," he said, smiling.

"War, Mr. Ismay," Churchill added, addressing the end of his unlit cigar, "is a burden to the souls of all that partake. To it then, shall we?"

The three departed, resolute and burdened, each with a part to play in the night ahead.

Chapter Eight

Amersham
Mrs. Somerville's Home

In the early morning light, Mrs. Somerville gazed intently at the faded photograph, its edges nestled in the black corner tabs of an album she'd retrieved from the top drawer of the dining room credenza. Steam from the train swirled about in the image, partially veiling the gleam of his polished boots but not enough to obscure the tall, lean figure and the sharp lines of his uniform. It was the day he shipped out and the start of the rest of her life. Since their marriage in 1910, she and Charles had lived seven years of unbridled joy, their days passing like a taximeter spinning wildly, charged with his boundless energy. He had stormed into the life of—Bethany Leeds, then twenty-five—like a whirlwind, transforming her every moment into a kaleidoscope of surprises. Then, just as swiftly, he had gone, joining the Canadian troops and meeting his fate at Vimy Ridge on that fateful day, 9 April 1917. The joy he brought had drained from her life as thoroughly as the breath had left his body. Leaving every aspect of her empty

Like this one, that conflict had begun with promises of an easy war, only to demand everything from those it touched. Though Charles was initially assigned to civil duties due to his age, the tides of war soon swept him to the front. Before he left, they made a solemn vow: if he didn't return, she would carry their shared spirit, ensuring it endured in her life. Like so many wives, she had believed, deep down, that it would be someone else's husband who failed to return.

She reached for the loose edge of a photograph and pressed it firmly back into place, smoothing it beneath her hand before closing the album's velvet cover. Her palm lingered on the surface as though the images inside still pulsed with life, their essence radiating into her touch. In quiet moments like this, she could almost feel Charles—not as a ghost in the room— but as a steadying presence. He had found her among countless others who had given her those happy years now confined to the album. A pang of bitterness swept over her. Two wars in one lifetime and the first was supposed to end all wars.

She sighed, berating herself for the self-pity that crept in, though it was rare. She couldn't recall the last time she'd taken the album from its drawer. True to their pact, she had lived a bright and optimistic life. Yet now, as she sat, she wondered what had led her to revisit a time so given to affection and devotion, and the image of Margaret's professor drifted into her thoughts.

Why had he unexpectedly noticed she was there, let alone offered the slightest hint of kindness? Last night, something different about him had touched something sleeping within her, bringing it into daylight. Something other than his story of not knowing where or who he was.

His eyes, she realized, had changed. It was the same look Charles had given her that day on the platform, waving her handkerchief as the train pulled away. Amidst the whistle's shriek, the clatter of wheels, the shouting crowd, and the brass band's fanfare, she saw him say, *"I love you… I won't be back."* She hadn't heard them, only seen their shape on his lips. Her arm froze mid-wave, her breath caught, and the crowd hemmed her in before she could react, and Charles vanished into the distance. That was the last time they'd had any contact, his path leading directly into battle to liberate a patch of earth now turned to farmland.

Last night, the professor helped her to the floor—a small act that seemed to mark a shift. Before then, he might have moved a piece of furniture if asked, but he'd never honestly noticed her. Nor, truthfully, had she given him much thought, though his wife, Margaret, was another matter entirely.

"Margaret, my dear Margaret," she said aloud, picturing the beautiful, headstrong young woman who had thrown away her privileged life to defy her domineering mother. Margaret had chosen a man wholly unlike Charles, a man entirely unsuited to her spirited nature. She vividly remembered the day Margaret arrived, clutching the newspaper advert. She was inquiring about the house she and Charles owned next door. She had already turned down several others, but Margaret's determination had won her over.

Since then, she had grown fond of Margaret, though her feelings about Thomas were less charitable. He was inconsistent, cheerful, and buoyant one moment, sullen and withdrawn the next, mainly when Margaret was absent. In her rebellion, it seemed as though Margaret had rushed into a choice she now quietly regretted, surprised by the reality of the man she'd married.

Thomas was charming when he needed to be, but it always seemed more a performance than a natural quality, a mask donned for effect. Yet, although he looked the same last night, she knew there was something different about him. He had moved with purpose, spoken with conviction, even if his words betrayed confusion. Something in him had shifted, and Mrs. Somerville, despite herself, could not help but notice.

Chapter Nine

Amersham - Margaret's Home

The morning sun poured through the windows, casting a golden light over what should have been a typical day. Thomas had risen early, leaving Margaret in bed, seemingly fast asleep. Perhaps she was mulling over the tumult of yesterday's events and didn't wish to be disturbed. Equally possible was that she preferred not to rise while he remained in the room. Margaret, it was clear, was not yet at ease with certain aspects of her new life, and who could blame her?

As Thomas made his way to the kitchen, he passed a narrow hall table beneath a wooden-framed mirror. At its center sat a Chinese porcelain bowl filled with potpourri, surrounded by photographs of himself and Margaret. The photos were arranged in silver and brass frames, their polished surfaces glinting in the morning light. He paused, picking one up to study it more closely, then glanced at his reflection in the mirror. There was no doubt—he looked just like the man in the picture.

Three steps later, he entered the small kitchen he had seen the previous night. At first glance, it seemed cluttered, but upon closer inspection, it was a purposeful sort of disorder, the kind created by someone who loved to cook and took pride in their culinary tools. Behind the glass cupboard doors, he saw neat stacks of Rockingham China, Lalique crystal glassware, and an ornate silver tea set. He noticed a strikingly large Philco wireless sat on the small table, its single round speaker resting above three polished dials.

In deep contrast to this array of items that appeared to exceed one's station were the cooking pans that hung from a small wooden ceiling rack. In short, they looked like the invasion had already occurred, and Margaret had single-handedly fought off a mechanized Panzer division, with heaving swings of her sauté pans and boiling pots.

Then, in a strange way, he didn't understand, but he remembered that people donated every available aluminum pot and pan. After melting and manufacturing, the pots reappeared as diving Spitfires or Hurricanes flying high in the sky. Consequently, the owner had to settle for decidedly inferior enameled substitutes that tended to chip and apparently came in fascinating colors.

From somewhere in the back of the house, he heard movement. Searching the kitchen, he realized he couldn't find what he was looking for. He wanted to surprise Margaret with a small, thoughtful gesture, but he seemed to need her help. Opening the last cabinet door, he called, "Margaret, where's the coffee pot?"

She appeared almost instantly in the doorway, cinching the belt of yet another dressing robe. "Coffee? You want coffee? Who drinks coffee? Certainly not you. If you're going to start drinking that stuff, we've some serious talking to do. You'll drink tea if you want my support through whatever this… situation… is. Unless, of course, you plan on turning into one of those precocious Americans," she said with a laugh.

Then, pointing firmly toward the hallway, she added, "Now, if you'd be so kind, please remove yourself from my kitchen."

Thomas smiled, feeling the tension of the previous evening began to dissolve. "Good morning, Margaret," he replied lightly. "I'm just trying to lend a hand with the chores, so you'll think I'm a decent sort." After the silent, uneasy night, he appreciated the lightheartedness of their exchange.

"Lending a hand or just drinking coffee?" she quipped with a playful smirk. You're not making me like you—you're scaring me half to death. When was the last time you helped around the house? The answer to that is never. In fact, when was the last time *any* man helped around the house? I think we're dealing with more than just a memory lapse here.

"If you're keen on doing something nice for me, I'd love cream cheese turnovers with fresh strawberries. Or, better yet, a million pounds sterling," she added with a wry grin, bending to open a lower cupboard. Straightening, she turned toward the teakettle and said briskly, "Now put your trousers on. I'll bring our tea out to the garden."

Thomas glanced down in amusement; he was already wearing his pants, though Margaret clearly hadn't noticed. Wandering toward the back of the house, his eyes fell on an odd structure in one of the rooms. It was a large metal cage about the size of a kitchen table, with wire mesh sides and metal tubing. A riveted tag on the top read *Morrison*. Books and papers were haphazardly stacked on its flat surface.

After a moment, realization dawned—it was a Morrison shelter designed to protect families from falling debris during bombing raids. While it wouldn't prevent injury, it was sturdy enough to save lives by supporting the weight of some collapsed walls and ceilings. Churchill had ordered their production and distribution, knowing they offered little practical defense but a great deal in bolstering morale.

"Thomas would know this," he thought suddenly. "But how do *I* know it?" A strange certainty crept over him, unbidden and unsettling. Perhaps, after all, he really was Thomas.

Chapter Ten

The Embassy of the Union of Soviet Socialist Republics
5 Kensington Palace Gardens, London

At the crack of dawn, Yuri Stakova stepped briskly through the front gate of the Russian Embassy, the morning air sharp with the chill of early day. Passing the British guards stationed outside, he offered them a subtle nod, paired with the faintest lift of his hand—an acknowledgment more perfunctory than cordial. The hour itself was peculiar, and the summons from the ambassador even more so. As he moved through the dim light, Yuri's mind churned over the layers of meaning buried within the situation, for in Soviet diplomacy, the spoken word often concealed more than it revealed. He had long since mastered the delicate art of navigating the gaps between what was said and left unsaid, where every shred of information bore a multitude of interpretations. Such a skill was essential, though it rendered righteous action a perilous and slippery undertaking. Yet, Yuri was no naïf; he understood all too well that the system was designed as much to protect as to entrap, and he knew how to play the game.

Years earlier, Yuri had bonded with the ambassador during their shared posting at the Italian Embassy. Though time and fate had pulled them along separate routes through the labyrinth of power, they now found themselves reunited in London, that crown jewel of Foreign Service appointments. As the head of embassy security, Yuri entered the ambassador's office to see the chief legal counselor, who was already present. The man was an uninspiring figure of relentless precision, perched stiffly in his chair with a notebook balanced on his knee, his entire demeanor that of a clerk cast from stone. Saying nothing, Yuri seated himself without ceremony.

The ambassador, seated rigidly behind his desk, began speaking in tones of rehearsed formality. With deliberate monotony, he invoked directive SVD435.9, reminding Yuri of the embassy's strict policy to steer clear of NKVD entanglements. The words were intended less for Yuri than for the counselor, who dutifully scribbled every syllable into his notebook. For now, Yuri listened, choosing to bide his time.

After a pause, the ambassador's tone shifted, though it remained clipped. "I am to inform you," he said, glancing at the paper in his hand, "that a courier—or perhaps an officer; it isn't entirely clear—is en route from Moscow Center. He carries a message about the security of this embassy, which falls under your purview. The orders stipulate your immediate return to Moscow and reassignment to duties there. In light of this, I have arranged for the courier to meet you at your flat, which is not on embassy grounds. Do you understand?"

Yuri inclined his head. "Of course, Comrade Ambassador."

The ambassador hesitated briefly, his eyes darting toward the counselor before continuing. "You will report the results of this meeting directly to me. Is that clear, Comrade Stakova?"

Yuri held the man's gaze, his expression measured. "Yes, I understand."

With an air of finality, the ambassador rose. "That will be all for now. You're dismissed."

Yuri stood, the legal counselor following close behind with his notebook tucked under his arm. They had nearly reached the door when the ambassador's voice halted them. "Comrade Stakova, one moment." The counselor was promptly dismissed, and as the door closed behind him, the ambassador's posture softened. Unbuttoning his jacket, he gestured for Yuri to sit once more.

"Yuri," he began, his voice quieter now, more familiar, "we've known each other too long for pretenses. I'll speak plainly. Something is stirring, and it's not the Germans. The winds in Moscow are shifting."

Leaning in slightly, the ambassador dropped his voice further. "Unofficially, I've been told you're being replaced as station chief. The name Joseph Alexikov has surfaced—a man I know nothing about. Tell me, Yuri, is there something I should know?"

Yuri shook his head, his expression calm. "Not to my knowledge, though I see no obvious reason for such a move. Could this Alexikov be the courier?"

The ambassador sighed, lighting a cigarette and exhaling slowly. "It's possible, though I can't say for certain. That's why the counselor was here, to ensure every step of mine is recorded. Ivan sent me a coded note. His NKVD contacts know little of Alexikov except that he's ambitious and ruthless. This chaos at home gives every opportunist a moment to climb. Be careful, Yuri."

Yuri gave a measured nod. "Always, Comrade Ambassador. Thank you."

The ambassador stood, extending his hand. "Good luck, my friend. I fear my ability to help may soon be limited."

Yuri shook his hand firmly and turned to leave. He paused as he reached the open door, glancing back with the faintest smile, a picture of composure. "As you wish, Comrade Ambassador. I'll see to it immediately." And with that, he disappeared into the corridor, his steps steady, his resolve unwavering.

Chapter Eleven

Amersham - Margaret's Home

Leaving Margaret in the kitchen, Thomas returned down the corridor until he reached the door leading into the small glassed conservatory at the rear of the house. From within, he could see a small garden plot outside, where every inch of earth had been meticulously cultivated into tidy rows of plants and vegetables. It was a picture of order and purpose, a reflection of the woman who had created it.

"So," Thomas thought, "she cooks, she gardens, she's beautiful, and she's got a cracking sense of humor. Things could certainly be worse." Yet, the weight of his situation pressed heavily upon him. It wasn't fair to her—not fair to thrust her into this uncertainty, nor was it fair to himself to endure it without answers. He stepped outside, crouched low to the earth, and idly drew a twig through the loose soil, his breath misting faintly in the chill air. The question hung in his mind, nebulous and unanswered: *What is 'it'?*

The faint clatter of china pulled him from his thoughts. Turning, he saw Margaret placing a tray on the table inside the conservatory. Rising, he brushed off his hands and stepped back indoors, shoving them into his pockets to appear casual.

"Cold out there," he remarked, trying to mask his unease with an air of normalcy. He hoped she might still be in the playful mood that had sent him retreating from the kitchen earlier. Margaret, now pouring tea, made no reply. Her focus was elsewhere. She finished the task, then turned and disappeared back into the house, leaving Thomas with his thoughts again.

"This isn't going to be easy," he admitted. How could he possibly explain this? Walking into her life, uninvited, unremembered, and apologizing for it all? Her first husband was gone, and now, here he was—an inexplicable replacement that looked the same but wasn't. He'd spent the long, sleepless hours of the night trying to piece together an explanation that even remotely made sense. Even a visit to the mirror in the bathroom had offered no revelations and only deepened his frustration.

Margaret soon returned, carrying a small bowl. "I brought sugar," she said, setting it on the table. "I'm not sure how you take yours—or if you even know how you take it." Then her tone shifted, sharper and laden with strain. "Thomas, I'm having a devil of a time with this. How does a person forget who they are? We had a wonderful day yesterday—besides the bit with Mother. We came home, you went into the bathroom, and then—bang—you were gone. You were still here, but not really. I don't know what's happening." She threw up her hands in exasperation, her voice cracking under the weight of her emotions.

Thomas looked at her carefully, noting the redness of her eyes and the gloss of unshed tears. Reality, it seemed, was settling in, harsh and unrelenting. She snatched a napkin from the tray and turned away as though wiping her tears was a private matter. He wanted to comfort her, to hold her, to bridge the gulf he'd unintentionally created, but something held him back. He hesitated, and regret had already taken root in that brief moment.

"I'm usually stronger than this," she said over her shoulder, her voice faltering.

"That was my chance," he thought, and then, "Yes, she'll let me."

Gently, he reached out, turning her toward him as he wrapped his arms around her. She looked up at him, surprise flickering in her expression. "Thomas?" she asked softly.

He held her gaze. "Yes."

"...Nothing," she replied after a beat, her voice barely a whisper.

Margaret rested her head against his chest, folding herself into his embrace like a child seeking solace. "Thanks," she said. Then, after a pause, she added with a faint, rueful laugh, "Whoever you are."

Thomas held her close, a strange but marvelous warmth filling him. He tightened his arms around her protectively. "I don't know who I am, Margaret. Are you all right?"

Her head nestled against his cheek, and he felt the silky smoothness of her hair against his skin. "Sure," she said, though her tone suggested otherwise. "Wouldn't you be? Just tell me this is going to be all right. Lie if you have to."

Still holding her, he said softly, "Margaret, I don't think this is something easily explained. It's not just amnesia—though it feels like my memory starts and stops with that moment in the bathroom. The thoughts in my head don't add up to a whole picture."

Margaret pulled away slightly, retrieving her teacup and moving to the window. She traced a finger along the cold glass, her thoughts clearly elsewhere. Her gaze fell on the garden beyond, and Thomas suspected she was thinking not just of him but of the man she'd lost before him.

He tried again. "It's not just about memories, Margaret. There's a part of this that's harder to explain. Some of my yesterdays haven't even happened yet."

She turned to face him, her brows furrowed. "That's as clear as mud," she said flatly. "What's next? Some nonsense about being found in an Egyptian basket at Stonehenge? If you're trying to confuse me, Thomas, you're doing an excellent job."

"Margaret, please," he pleaded. "Be patient with me. I'm trying to make sense of it myself."

She sighed, then managed a faint, weary smile. "All right. You've got until lunch." Crossing her legs, she rested her chin in her palm, a picture of reluctant curiosity.

Thomas hesitated, then began again. "It's as though I know things—not just the past, but what's to come. Margaret, something happened last night. It wasn't an ordinary air raid. A German bomber dropped its payload by mistake on Amersham, close enough to London, creating a great deal of concern in the government. Up to now, the Germans bombed military targets. And now, Churchill's going to retaliate."

Margaret stared at him, incredulous. "How can you possibly know that?"

"That's the question, isn't it?" he said. "I don't know how I know. I just… do."

Her expression wavered between disbelief and something else—hope, perhaps? "Well, I suppose we'll find out tomorrow," she said quietly, though she didn't believe him.

She turned back to the window, cradling her teacup. "Where's my Thomas?" she whispered.

"I wish I knew," he replied, his voice heavy with regret. "I wish I knew where the other *me* was, too."

Chapter Twelve

London, Silvertown

London Docks

Yuri stepped out of the underground transit car and looked in wonder at all the people coming and going to work. He wasn't sure how the British people maintained an everyday life under these circumstances, but to their credit, they kept on with the day-to-day. Toward the far end of the station area stood rows of cots used during air raids, which just re-asked the question.

With a minor limp, the result of a fall as a young man, Yuri trudged up the tube station's tile steps and out the entrance of the Silvertown Station into the sunlight. Yuri was a burley fifty-five and saw those steps as a challenge he conquered daily. He stopped by the newsstand, read the headlines, "Bismarck Enters Service," and purchased a Times newspaper. He folded the paper, placed it under his arm, and turned toward the outlines of multiple gigantic ships drawn up along the quayside.

He was heading home to a lovely flat by the docks and wharves in London's East End. The flat was larger than usual for a single person because it also served as a place for Russian 'visitors' to stay when they came into town. The flat was in the poorest section of the largest city in the world. Being this close to the docks allowed Yuri to observe shipping traffic. The Victoria and Albert Royal Docks, with their towering cranes and grain elevators, were the commercial center of the most significant trading empire the world had ever seen. The flat was also removed from any military bases, which were the targets of the nightly bombing raids. At least the targets were military until last night.

Yuri's official job at the embassy was military liaison to the British First Sea Lord. The First Sea Lord was the highest military position in the British armed forces and was held by Winston Churchill until last May. During that time, Yuri got to know the man leading his nation to war well. However, Yuri was the London station chief for the NKGB, the People's Commissariat for State Security, the Soviet intelligence service. Yuri Ivanovich Stakova was a spy.

For seven years in London and twelve years in various countries, he'd lived in the shadow world of intelligence, counter-intelligence, and double counterintelligence. It was an insane job, requiring complete concentration as he tried to sort out the real from the surreal. The gathering years of constantly remaining one step ahead had taken its toll, but he was still one of the best.

Being a spy meant his actual function was to complete anything the higher-ups in Moscow felt was necessary. As a spy, he was sentenced to endure Moscow bureaucrats who had never left the home country, telling him precisely what needed to be done and how to do it. They were always wrong—always. He'd survived these many years by learning the art of balancing the literal directive with what he knew to be the operation's actual requirements for success and then delivering that in a manner that made the dim minds in Red Square look like bright, shining lights. Quickly and without warning, this morning's meeting had set up his retirement from the field with a desk job at home.

By this time, Yuri wasn't sure where home was, as his years in the field had made him a man of the world. He admired the British for their tenacious resolve, the Germans for their machine mentality, the Italians for their women and food, and the arrogant Americans. Well, what can you say? They're Americans.

He enjoyed his freedom and wasn't looking forward to returning home. Enduring the secretive games was an integral part of his beautiful homeland. He struggled to understand how a government full of bureaucrats, all half as brilliant as a bottle of vodka, could have all the answers for all the people. The system appeared to work from the outside. However, inside, Stalin brutally crushed an entire nation's will.

Today, he was to meet his replacement, Joseph Alexikov, a young rising star in the company. It had shocked Yuri that someone from the home office was already in town, and he hadn't known. Yuri usually knew everything. The official reason for the change was to have a new man in place for the coming German invasion. There had been no previous sign that Moscow was thinking in that direction.

Yuri, a big man, was walking very lightly now through things he couldn't see.

Chapter Thirteen

Margaret's House
Amersham

The next few hours were challenging for Thomas as he tried to unravel the story and learn about his life with Margaret. They started to establish an understanding. She wasn't hard to like; it wasn't hard at all. One of the strangest things about all of this was that he felt attracted to her immediately when she stood in front of him in the bathroom.

It was easy to see what appealed to Thomas. Her humor, intelligence, and self-confidence were out of place for a woman of this time. She was a professor in the English department at the local college. He held some research positions at Cambridge and did most of his work at home. They were both off for the summer. Her father died about five years ago, and her mother lived in the family mansion in the exclusive Fernhurst area outside London.

During the day's conversation, it became apparent they enjoyed each other's company. Everything would go along splendidly, then one would remember their predicament—and silence would follow. She listened to his assertions regarding what was to come of this or that. However, Thomas thought she was reserving judgment until tomorrow morning.

Fixing dinner, she turned on the oven and said it would take time to heat, so he had to be patient. Thomas indicated there would eventually be ovens that would heat food in minutes using radar waves. "It's the same basic electrical technology used by the RAF to track German planes coming over the Channel," he explained. He talked of things he could remember from the future that might interest her, like the tunnels under the English Channel, and she wouldn't believe it.

"Why not?" he asked.

"It's simple—the French wouldn't allow it. Their poodles might breed with our beagles."

"How about the British?" he asked. "Would they allow it?"

"Of course," she said. "We don't have a distorted view of ourselves and haven't favorably rewritten the world's history to revolve around ourselves like Frawnce!" She drawled out the final word with her chin up, hand extended, and a pinkie in the air.

Thomas wanted to return to learning about this person, a charming woman who was bringing him slowly into her world. Trying to move to a subject that hopefully would result in her revealing more about herself, he remembered the oversized painting by Matisse in the living room. "I'm fascinated by the painting in the front room.

"When did you get it?"

"Oh, that's quite a story, that one," she said. "Well, I would very much like to hear it."

"I keep the painting as a reminder of how much I have to learn about myself and the world."

She told him about being at a private showing at the Mersinet Galleries when she was about nineteen. Her father allowed her to have run of the place while she was still living at home. She'd left in a huff after some silly argument with her mother and wanted to stay away long enough to make her worry. Margaret could have easily asked the chauffeur to take her anywhere, as she'd known all the drivers since childhood. Instead, she opted to catch a ride to the nearest station for a bus into the city. During the ride, Margaret enjoyed looking out the window and being free.

Closer to London, she passed the gallery. It was pretty busy, with people queued outside, all waiting to get in, and others milling about. They were all very formal, as was she, having previously dressed to go to a party with a group that didn't meet with her mother's approval. That was the basis of their argument. Margaret decided the gallery was the perfect place to spend some time. Running to the front of the bus, she asked to get off at the next stand, and the driver smiled and pulled over at an unscheduled stop right then and there.

She thanked him through the glass, giggled, and turned back to address everyone else on the bus, saying, "Thank you. Sorry for the delay." A scruffy man in the back said, "Oh, it's all right, miss. If I looked like you, he'd be stoppin' for me too, but then I don't, do I?"

Everyone laughed, and she bounced down the steps, waving vigorously at everyone through the windows as the bus drove off.

Once inside the gallery, she wandered about, not interested in anything and aware that everyone was much older. Margaret liked art and enjoyed reading about the artists and listening to the comments people offered and the opinions they argued.

Eventually, one piece took her fancy. The Mersinet was three stories, and she found a painting in a corner on the third floor that spoke to her. She stood for a long while looking at the only Matisse on display and found herself alone almost the entire time.

She knew of Henri Matisse from conversations among Mother's guests during the afternoon teas Mother insisted she attend. Mother said the teas were training so she could observe firsthand how proper women spent the afternoon. The women never spoke of Matisse in a tone that would have been reassuring to a developing artist's career. This small talk had far-reaching effects, as polite society tended to move, as a whole, with little tolerance for the freethinker. Person after person at her tea gatherings ridiculed Matisse's painting and his approach to life. The subject of his painting wasn't what captured Margaret. Instead, it was the spirit the artist put into the color and his application method. Behind every stroke was a stout heart that persistently presented his vision of the world in his unique style against a chorus of lesser minds who didn't consider Matisse's efforts actual painting but a faint attempt at real art by an untalented ruse.

At the gallery, Margaret had tried to explain to people walking by that the artist presented the observer with an impression, intending for the viewer to participate in the ultimate image. It was to no avail; she talked until she was blue, and London's proper Society would have none of it.

From behind her in the gallery came a voice. "Get the man a proper brush and let the starving sod try again," said a man with pipe and bowler, tapping his umbrella on the hardwood floor to emphasize each of the last three syllables.

Later, arm in arm, a grand old couple was walking by the spot that Margaret was starting to defend. He was a perfect portrait of old money, with a bright white beard and hair, in a summer gray pinstripe suit and a dark wool derby with a gray faille band. A substantial gold pocket watch chain curved under his sizable girth to a ticking bulge in his silk waistcoat. With an apparent engagement later in the evening, the woman wore a cream-colored taffeta ball gown that glistened. Her matching round profile-style hat and veil presented the perfect semblance of the opera-gloved elite. She was much younger than her husband, although she appeared over sixty. They paused behind Margaret, observing the painting, and then her husband, resetting his pince-nez, said with unfiltered disdain, "It would appear my spectacles require adjustment."

"I rather like it," the wife said. "Besides, one can't appreciate art with a simple observation. One must appreciate an artistic piece through one's heart. If you stand back, Charles, the whole becomes known; his style requires participation," the woman elegantly said.

"I'll stand back, all right. It shouldn't be in the building. If it's your fancy, you had better inquire now. At the rate his paintings sell, he'll be the ghost of a starving artist," he said.

At that exact moment, Margaret decided to buy the painting and, with a gallant tilt of her head, called the owner over in a loud voice that everyone in the building heard.

"Good for you, young lady," the wife said with a knowing smile derived from her years. The husband moved on, but she asked him to wait. She dropped his arm and walked back over to Margaret. She looked at young Margaret standing there, with her chin up a little too high, then at the painting, and then at Margaret. Moving forward a step, she placed a soft hand on Margaret's arm and, in the tone of a caring mother and with courteous deference, said, "It's admirable to meld your independent thinking to action. However, considering life's larger decisions, I would mind your true reaction to this purchase. You must not be swayed solely to embrace the contrary over what could be the superior path." She smiled. "If I may offer advice, of course, to someone so young and noble."

"Yes, Mum. Thank you, Mum," Margaret said with a quick curtsey. The well-meaning, experienced advice fell on young, obstinate ears.

Listening to the story, Thomas became more engaged by the minute and concentrated on her every word. Time took flight as conversations continued over drinks into the night.

"Tell me about your mother," Thomas said.

"What's to tell?" Margaret said, lifting her voice at the end of the sentence. "She doesn't like you."

"Well, that's to the point. Would you be so kind as to elaborate on that, Miss?"

"I told you, Thomas Watson, we're married. I'm a Mrs. Your Mrs."

"Okay, sorry. You're my Mrs.," he said with equal emphasis.

"On second thought, I'm not your woman—I'm my own woman!"

They both fell into much-needed laughter.

The story of her mother started with her father. Margaret had decided at a very young age that her father was unique, and she related to his no-nonsense approach to life. He taught her that her mind, not her lineage, would determine her station in life. As a direct reflection of his family's exemplary record of service to the Royal Court and his business success, Sir Ian Everett Hatcher II had entered peerage as a knight. Sir Winston Churchill had placed him on the 'watch list' for noble acts of skill and courage. This vague honor referred to a mysterious business agreement between the government and his company. There was quite the pomp and circumstance, with no one ever knowing exactly why he received the honor. However, she knew it was important and wouldn't be the last time.

Sir Hatcher's close ties extended into the inner circles of the English government. He produced many fabrics and materials in several stone-walled Northern England and Scotland textile factories. Since the war, the bulk of the company's sales came from custom bolts of cloth used by the military for their uniforms. He would always revel in doing his bit to promote inter-service rivalry, keeping each department insisting on a unique texture and weave. Custom fabrics required unique designs, requiring each bureau to place orders separately.

Margaret recalled how her father had said late one evening, "It's in the tank, my dear, if those blokes ever sober up and order the same lot across the board." He then spun his finger in a corkscrew from above his head to the floor while making obnoxious airplane sounds, laughing, and spilling his brandy on his shoes.

His most significant contract was with the Royal Navy, and during his best years, Sir Winston Churchill was First Sea Lord. Being an island nation, England rightfully regarded its Navy with almost religious reverence. The men's relationship started with Margaret's father and Mr. Churchill, discovering a mutual lack of patience for the obliqueness and lack of transparency of high society and an affection for the same brandy. It turned into a full-blown friendship when they quickly discovered they also liked their brandy in the same quantities.

With these common bonds, they spent years spoiling scores of fancy dinner parties, with footmen in livery behind each guest, telling ribald stories more appropriate for paneled rooms where only the men would retire for liqueurs and cigars. Many times, bored with the boorish attempts by guests to curry favor, and before the main course, Mr. Churchill would crow above the dinner conversation: "Why, Mr. Hatcher, brandy and cigars appear to be missing from the menu."

Looking at the card next to his place, Mr. Hatcher would reply, "My Gawd, Mr. Churchill, an observation with chilling consequences."

They'd then excuse themselves for an excursion to locate the missing ingredients essential to a civilized evening. Their actions were, of course, to the ashen shock of the hostess, who invariably had worked years to get Mr. Churchill to her much-publicized dinner.

Young Margaret Hatcher loved her father. He taught her to be independent and follow her feelings when "girls" were still supposed to retire to the parlor. Her father would say, "Don't ever let a man see you gossiping in a parlor, my dear, or in his mind, he'll never see you out of it." Mr. Hatcher had died in a plane crash on a trip to a factory about five years before.

She didn't know what to do with her life. Instead of becoming closer, his death caused her and her mother to grow apart. Her mother wanted Margaret to finish college and marry any of the six young men she'd picked. Her comment, "Should I try them all, Mother, or do you have a favorite in mind?" added fuel to the fire.

In frustration, Margaret moved out of the family mansion, taking only a few special things, like the Matisse. She also left behind the monthly allotment, which created immediate problems, like finding work and a place to live. Alastair, her father's manservant and head of household, just happened to know of a small house up for let at week's end. It saved her the embarrassment of having to put up at a hotel. Shortly thereafter, she applied for a position as a teacher's assistant at a local middle school. It wasn't easy, as Margaret refused to produce any letters of recommendation and wouldn't divulge her previous address. The headmaster took a chance on something he saw in the young woman, and the decision bore fruit for the school and the students.

It was unnecessary to say that her mother didn't approve of these actions. Upon discovering that Margaret was seeing someone, she insisted on meeting him, which created more strife, as she dismissed him as an opportunistic nobody unworthy of their time.

She disapproved and was more than a bit out of sorts when, days later, on a Saturday afternoon, Margaret announced she'd gotten married to one Thomas J. Watson, an aspiring educator at the university. It was the great war all over again, but it was particularly wretched this time. They didn't speak for months as Mother had insisted that their kind arranged marriages with proper regard to position, fortune, and community of circumstances. Margaret believed that the underlying cause of her mother's extreme anger was her presiding at center stage in a Chanel gown at a glittering high-society wedding. Indeed, the pinnacle event in the life of a mother who was first a socialite and, therefore, saw it as an obligation. In that regard, Margaret was definitely her father's daughter.

Eventually, mother and daughter connected on this and that; conversations turned into overnight stays, and things smoothed into an all-new relationship. Nevertheless, her mother's contempt for Thomas was hard to ignore. She perceived him as a man entering into a world far above his station and using Margaret to enable his advances toward the family estate. Margaret conceded her husband was mysterious at times but, with her head held high, quickly added that they were working on it and making significant progress.

Margaret recounted how Mother had never made a slight or even a 'polite' effort to inquire about Thomas's work at yesterday's visit. She always believed real men run businesses and don't spend time researching historical minutia.

She once said, "It's a useless endeavor. The past cannot change, and documenting it won't increase its chances." Shortly after that, Margaret started postgraduate work in history.

Thomas looked across the table, completely taken by this Margaret, having no desire for the day to end. He suggested a walk, and the conversation continued uninterrupted through tea at a café. They then sat on a bench surrounded by a green and took a long way home. However, it was getting late, and after tidying things up, they went into the bedroom. Then, the free flow of the evening came to a halt as a certain tenseness entered into what had been two people enjoying each other's company.

Margaret went to the bathroom to change. When she emerged, she wore an assemblage of clothing good to minus 20 degrees centigrade. Thomas looked at the layers of flannel. Moving toward her armoire he said, "Surely you've something that doesn't double as medieval armor."

Margaret said, "I'd leave it be if you were a bright man, mister. You've spent the better part of a fine afternoon with your stories of being uncomfortable with your situation. Well, it may surprise you, I'm not quite comfortable with this either and feel like a little tart cheating on her husband."

"Are you going to cheat?" he asked with an irrepressible smile.

"I AM NOT! Moreover, you'd better find another way to be funny if you want to live. Get the lamp, be quick about it, and stop staring at me."

For the second night, they were in a new world neither understood. He was exhausted from lack of sleep the night before. So was she, for there was telltale deep breathing as soon as her head found the pillow. After an extended period spent trying to quiet the thoughts racing through his head, he slowly reached over and quietly turned on the light. She didn't move. He rose on an elbow, leaned over, and looked at her sleeping face. Observing someone as they're sleeping reveals much to the observer, and he deeply admired everything he saw in Miss Margaret.

Chapter Fourteen

London

Whitehall, Air Ministry

Upon arriving at his office that morning, Air Marshal Charles Portal settled into the routine of intelligence briefings, damage assessments, and combat readiness reports. However, this day would be marked by a singular focus—Bomber Command's mission to strike deeper into Nazi Germany than ever before, at the Prime Minister's directive. Throughout the day, Portal kept a closer watch than usual on preparations, ensuring every detail was in place before he made his way to the airfield.

The target lay deep inland, near a civilian zone outside Berlin. Though the Germans had bombed Amersham in The Chilterns, this mission was not meant to create civilian casualties but to send a message: if the war were to escalate, Britain would bring the fight to the very heart of Germany. This would be the first attempt to bomb Berlin. The pilots understood the gravity of their task—they would be flying over the most heavily defended city on Earth without fighter support and with a slim chance of returning.

As names appeared on the alert board, a quiet tension settled over the squadron. The briefing officer knew what was on their minds. They left letters to their families with comrades not scheduled for the mission, a somber ritual they had all grown too accustomed to. The air was thick with apprehension.

The officer concluded the preflight briefing with a grim resolve. "Gentlemen, we didn't start this war, and I, for one, don't give a bloody damn if we flatten that city tonight. Last night, they bombed Amersham—families like your own lost their homes. Let's return the favor. Let's show the Jerries what it means to wake up to the sound of bombs in their backyards. Tally ho, lads!"

A cheer rang out, more an attempt to push back the fear than genuine enthusiasm. As the men filed out to their planes, two ducked into the lavatory, their nerves betraying them. Yet, as always, they steadied themselves. Fear and courage lived side by side.

Portal stepped out of his office and into his staff car, the corporal holding the door. The 1938 Ford, painted dull British green, bore the scars of two years' hard service but was still roadworthy. Seated in the back, Portal's thoughts drifted less on the night's mission than on the broader war effort. He knew the Prime Minister was well aware of the precarious state of Fighter Command. Britain was losing the battle of production. The steady loss of pilots and aircraft was unsustainable. Even with Canadian, Polish, and a few American pilots bolstering their ranks, too many planes were left grounded due to shortages. More often, radar stations detected incoming attacks, but the RAF lacked the squadrons to counter them. How long before the Germans grasped the actual state of Britain's airpower?

Yet Portal refused to believe it was hopeless. The RAF needed time to transport fighters from the factories to the front lines, repair battered airfields, and, above all, time for pilots to recover from the relentless strain of war. They could not fight on forever without respite.

"To the officers' quarters, sir?" the driver asked.

"No, son," Portal replied, uncharacteristically informal. "Take me to the field control tower."

"Right away, sir."

The driver shifted gears, and they were off.

"Where are you from, soldier?"

"Pennington, sir. Still, live with me, Mum and sister."

"Your father?"

"Lost him in the last war, sir. But we're getting on. Me sister works, looks after Mum."

A silence settled over the car. Everyone had a story, each reflecting the quiet sacrifices of ordinary people navigating extraordinary times.

By 2210 hours, Portal was at 11 Group's Uxbridge Flight Control Center. He had come to watch the Group take to the skies, to witness the moment they stepped into uncertainty. He had asked them to do this—he owed it to them to see them off. He took a deep breath, aware of the immense responsibility resting on his shoulders. A young orderly appeared before him, offering a cup of tea.

"A minute for tea, sir?"

"Just the thing, lad," Portal said, wrapping his hands around the warm cup as he watched plane after plane ascend into the night sky. The Bristol Blenheim IV bombers—once formidable, now aging—were all they had. "If America enters the war," he thought, "perhaps we'll get a new fleet. For now, we fight with what we have."

"Message, sir."

Portal set down his cup and signed the acknowledgment from the young flight lieutenant, who saluted smartly before returning to duty. "These boys should be in classrooms, not cockpits," Portal thought bitterly.

In repairs, Melville reported that seventy-eight aircraft were taking to the skies—fifty-seven fit for combat, nineteen recently repaired, and two fresh deliveries. That was all they could muster. The rest were undergoing maintenance or reserved for pilot training. Only twenty-eight Spitfires from 11 Group could escort the bombers to their maximum range. He had twenty-nine aircraft, but only twenty-eight pilots were fit to fly. It was another remarkable effort by the ground crews, considering Northolt's repair facility had been bombed that very day. They had only just patched up the runway before takeoff.

"Where are the medals for those boys on the tractors?" Portal thought. In the last raid, three heavy repair vehicles had been lost, making it harder to restore the airstrips in time. They would repaint the camouflage along the runways at dawn, hoping to deceive German bombers a little longer.

His preflight report had carried grim news—Squadron Leader Paddy Hemingway had been forced to bail over the Channel that morning. An RAF rescue boat had plucked him from the sea, but Dickey Lee's wingman had gone down with no chute spotted. Dickey, with his irreverent humor, would be missed in the officers' mess.

"They'll raise a pint for him tonight," Portal thought. "Another of their own, gone."

Paddy refused to let anyone touch Dickey's things. He would be the one to send the package home, the letter to his parents.

Portal left the warmth of the control tower and stepped onto the observation deck. He gazed skyward as the last bombers disappeared into the dark, their engine roars echoing in the distance.

"These are my boys," he thought. "Not just England's. Mine."

The Prime Minister may have given the order, but Portal had decided who would ride into the unknown. Boys are forced into manhood too soon, fighting not for abstract ideals but for their families and their homes.

They had fought 'the war to end all wars,' yet here they were again. He pulled out a worn, folded page from his wallet—his mother's keepsake, a poem he had promised to carry as long as he wore the uniform. He read it once more as the final aircraft faded into the horizon:

You smug-faced crowds with kindling eye,
Who cheer when soldier lads march by,
Sneak home and pray you'll never know,
The hell where youth and laughter go.
— Siegfried Sassoon

Chapter Fifteen

Margaret's House

Amersham

Thomas awoke, lying on his back, staring up at the ceiling. It was blank, like his memory—a nothingness that did not explain his odd situation. Still, the ceiling was familiar, a steady presence he recognized from the day before. His mind clung to the familiar without any clear understanding, and the bare ceiling became the one small sign of normalcy. He could feel the weight of the covers at his feet and near his neck.

"This is supposed to be my bed," he thought, "but there's none of the usual bond between a person and their surroundings." The bed felt alien, untouched by the imprint of his daily routine. But the ceiling, at least, offered something—a fresh memory to cling to.

A faint shadow crept across the cabinets and the wall as he lay there, and his mind wandered to more comforting things. The laughter and conversation from yesterday returned to him, vivid and warm. He could almost hear Margaret's voice, racing through topics faster than he could keep up. And there she was, spinning about in playful joy, mimicking her father's grand gestures, holding her hand high and then bringing it down to knee level. Setting aside the darker bits of the day, yesterday had been a perfect start to something new—a first date like no other. Deep within, he felt it: Margaret was becoming a significant part of his life faster than he could have imagined.

A smile tugged at his lips as he turned toward her, hoping she was awake. Instead, he found only the empty space where she had been. A strange sound drifted in from beyond the bedroom, unsettling and foreign. His heart skipped a beat. He quickly leaped from the bed and grabbed his robe from the armoire. He slipped his arms into it as he hurried toward the noise.

As he rounded the corner into the living room, he saw Margaret sitting on the couch, her face hidden behind her hands, her elbows resting on her knees. She was crying. The sight of her grief hit him hard, deep in his chest. He wanted nothing more than to see her happy, never to be the source of her sorrow.

Without hesitation, he walked over and knelt before her, but she didn't look up.

"Margaret, what's wrong? Are you all right?" he asked softly.

She didn't answer. Acting impulsively, Thomas moved beside her and gently draped his arm around her shoulders. She flinched ever so slightly, and he pulled back.

"Thomas," she said in a low, trembling voice. "I just want things to be as they were. But everything feels so wrong." She lifted her head and met his gaze, her eyes heavy with sadness. "I'm scared," she added, standing up and tossing the morning paper onto the couch. "Where's all this leading? It doesn't belong in this world. It's unnatural. How can you know about the war... about the future?"

Thomas turned his eyes to the paper, and the headline struck him like a slap. "RAF Bombs Berlin—Munitions factory targeted near civilians." It was a moment of clarity for them both, though for vastly different reasons. Across the country, newsagents' placards would be black with the same alarming news. And here, on the front page, was proof that he knew what would come—at least, the parts he could remember. It was also a reminder that the future would not offer the simple, ordinary life Margaret seemed to long for. This was not a world of everyday life but one of turmoil, where good and evil coexist in a strange, perilous dance.

In no uncertain terms, it confirmed that he possessed some foreknowledge of future events. And while this knowledge could be invaluable to those fighting the war, it came with heavy burdens. His first instinct was to offer whatever help he could, but a more reasoned voice in his mind cautioned him. To act carelessly would risk drawing unwanted attention to both him and Margaret. It would be wise to proceed with great caution. The question loomed large—how could he share what he knew without causing fear or hostility? Or perhaps the real question was whether he should share it at all.

He thought of the witch's tales from Salem, where people who dared to speak of the future were condemned, unable to fit their truth into the accepted order of the world. The desire for comfort and stability in life was a universal thing. Wise counsel would say to avoid any situation that could expose them to forces beyond his control. But the thought of doing nothing, of staying silent while the world burned, was equally unbearable. Hitler and his inner circle were marching toward domination, their power growing daily.

With a heavy heart, Thomas knew that silence was not an option. The moral obligation to those fighting and dying in the war demanded action, however difficult. His knowledge, though unclear, had committed him to share it regardless of the consequences.

Embracing his strange gift—or curse—meant accepting a world without clear rules or predictable outcomes. The universe, it seemed, had decided to throw caution to the wind.

Thomas felt a bitter anger rise as he pondered the forces that had chosen him to carry this burden. "What forces or people are aware of this gift I never asked for? And what part will they play in all this?" His mind searched for the familiar thoughts that once gave him comfort and clarity. But they were gone, lost somewhere, suspended in a place he couldn’t reach.

Chapter Sixteen

Croydon Satellite Airbase
11 Group Kenley Sector

The morning sun, like from a master painter, rose from the horizon, casting its warm light through scattered clouds to greet the new day. It was a stark contrast—the beauty of the dawn clashing with the violence that still lurked in the sky above. But such thoughts were far from Flight Lt. Paddy Hemingway's tired mind as he thought of never seeing his friend Dickey again. They had scrambled at first light to provide cover for the bombers returning from their Berlin run, but the Germans had not followed them past the French coast.

Paddy adjusted the flight stick slightly to the left, and the plane responded with a smooth bank, lining up with the runway still miles ahead. His squadron was heading for Croydon, their alternate field. Kenley, their home base, had taken a severe pounding from a German bomber attack during their absence. Crews were still working on the runways, and it would be at least four hours before they could return. Croydon had been lucky, though; the bomb drop had missed by a good margin, with only the tail end of the bomb pattern hitting. Even so, Paddy could see smoke rising from the enormous craters scattered across the fields and from a dispatch hut near the woods.

The rest of his squadron had already landed. He was the last to touch down. He felt the cold in his bones, his mind muddled. His vision blurred, the exhaustion from two sleepless nights catching up with him. He should have taken a shift off, rested—but he hadn't. Now, he was using every ounce of energy he could muster to focus on the task at hand: landing.

Yesterday, as the sun sank, the escort force had turned back, their job done. The bomber pilots knew what was coming—German Me 109s within minutes. The Supermarine Spitfire Mk IIA, with a range of 497 miles, could not provide cover after that. The Germans knew precisely when the Spitfires would have to turn back. It was a bitter feeling for a fighter pilot—knowing they couldn't protect the Blenheim IV bombers beyond that range—but it was worse still knowing the bombers couldn't defend themselves. The bombers were flying coffins, barely able to hit 260 mph, with only rear-facing 7.6mm tailguns for protection and no fighter cover. They stood no chance against the 347-mph Messerschmitt.

It was one thing to risk your life, but another altogether when courage had no hope of saving it.

Paddy thought of the bravery it took to keep flying, day after day, knowing you were fighting for something—your family, your friends, or someone you loved. For Paddy, that someone was Edith Bristo. A girl he'd known for a while now, or at least what seemed like a while in his book. Lately, he'd realized just how serious he was about her. She was perfect in every way. They spent every moment they could together, and when he was with her, he felt a warmth and happiness deep inside him. He wanted that feeling to last forever. He'd often been invited to her family home and had gotten on well with them. Edith understood his need to fly and always encouraged him to pursue what made him happy.

He glanced down at his stiff, frozen fingers. They felt like they were shaped to the stick itself. His feet, too, were numb as they worked the trim pedals. He needed every bit of focus now; things were getting tight. Last night, they had pushed their planes to the limit, flying out as far as they dared, and returning to the English coast meant dumping all the ammunition into the channel to lighten the load. But just ten minutes ago, the needle on his fuel gauge had been sitting firmly on empty. If he was going to get this plane down, it was all down to his instincts—he'd have to fly it as one of the best pilots in the squadron.

He eased the stick back, leveling the plane out. Reaching down, he placed his frozen left hand on the throttle.

"Slow it down just a touch," he muttered to himself. "Keep the nose up... that's right."

The cockpit was tight, his breath fogging the canopy when he glanced down. Churchill had been going on about how vital it was for America to join the war. The trouble was that the Americans didn't want to get involved. They saw Britain as little more than an imperial power trying to hold onto a crumbling empire. Let them have the world, the isolationists said. But there had been a shift once the battle above Britain started to make headlines. Ed Murrow, covering the war for CBS, had broadcast a report from No. 14 Squadron weeks ago. In the middle of it, the Germans had made a move, opening their bomb bay doors live on air. It was broadcast directly into American homes, causing quite a stir. Paddy hoped it was enough to get America involved. The Americans were already part of the war, whether they liked it or not.

Suddenly, a voice crackled over the radio, "R23, what in bloody hell are you doing? You're too low. Pull up, now!"

Paddy snapped his head forward, looking through the windscreen. He saw the sunlight breaking over a massive shadow ahead. Instinct kicked in, and he pushed forward on the throttle, pulling back on the stick. The plane responded, climbing just in time to clear the trees.

He'd drifted badly off course, and the scare was enough to make him shiver. He brought the plane back on track, heart hammering in his chest. The voice in his ear came again: "R23, lower your undercarriage. Do you hear me?"

Paddy fumbled with the lever on his right, pushing it forward. The gear dropped with a heavy thump, one wheel at a time. As the gears descended, the plane yawed left and right, but he kept it steady.

"Undercarriage confirmed down. Paddy, can you hear me? Talk to me."

"R23 here. Sorry, chaps. I must've nodded off for a second there. Am I clear to land?"

"You're clear. Get her down, man."

Paddy eased back on the throttle, keeping the nose up as best he could. He was high, far too high for a smooth landing. He thought grimly, "If you know how to fly this thing, mate, now's the time to show it. There's no fuel for another go."

He turned the wheel to deploy full flaps, cutting his stall speed.

"That'll have to do," he muttered.

The runway was coming up fast. He needed to lose altitude and be quick. He pushed the stick forward sharply, bringing the nose down. The leading edge of the runway was now in his sights, and he knew this was it—one way or another. At the last moment, he slammed the throttle forward, past its usual stop, and yanked the nose up just enough to keep it from stalling, using the heavy morning air to cushion his descent. He managed to lose the altitude, but his airspeed was dangerously high.

Seconds later, the wheels hit with a bone-jarring thud, and Paddy felt the impact shoot up his spine. The plane bounced its wheels, lifting off the runway, delaying his chance to brake. As he came down again, he cut the power. But braking too hard could flip the plane over. With careful hands, he gently lifted the nose until he felt the wheels hit. Then, he pressed down hard, willing the brakes to hold.

Smoke from the burning tires and the acrid smell of hot brake pads filled the cockpit. Paddy killed the engine entirely, feathering the prop as an air brake. The smoke was thick now, so he flipped the canopy release lever, which only opened an inch. He fumbled for the oxygen mask and held it to his face while twisting the valve beside the throttle. The fumes were choking, but at least he could breathe.

He couldn't see anything now, but he knew the buildings were near, and he was losing his sense of direction. The plane had become wild as he fought to keep it straight, hoping he was still on the runway.

Just as he thought he might be in the clear, the plane veered off the runway with a violent thump. Paddy felt the rough, uneven grass beneath the wheels, knowing it wasn't good news. But at least it meant he was away from the hangars.

He was moving swiftly as the plane hit a bomb crater, and the left gear collapsed with a violent snap. The forward momentum spun the aircraft around, and Paddy's head slammed sideways into the glass. He lost consciousness as the plane spun, smoke and dust filling the air. It came to a halt a thousand feet from the runway, its nose in the dirt, the tail tipped up, and one wing pressed flat against the ground.

The ground crew's truck skidded to a stop beside the plane. Someone shouted about unexploded bombs as fire extinguishers sprayed the burning wheels.

Denis Legget, Paddy's commanding officer, climbed onto the wing while Diggins, the best mechanic in the squadron, worked on the canopy. After a few hard shoves, the canopy slid back to the stops. Inside, they found Paddy slumped over, still strapped in, oxygen mask in place. Diggins yanked the hatch fully open, pulling at the harness. Paddy stirred, groaning softly.

"Don't move," Diggins said.

Paddy lifted his hand to his head and grinned through the pain. "I think I'm all right."

"You don't sound it," Legget replied. "You were out cold, mate. How would you know?"

"Because I know I'm about to catch hell for wrecking this plane," Paddy said, wincing.

"You're right there," Diggins said with a half-smile. "Not touching one of mine till you learn to fly."

Legget turned to the crew. "Get him out of here before this thing blows."

Paddy winced, but with a slow smile, he said, "Not a drop of petrol left, mate. We're safe."

He was helped out of the cockpit and onto the ground, where the medics waited.

"Sorry, lads," Paddy said, "but I'm walking away from this one. Every pilot in the county is watchin'."

He put his arm around Legget's shoulders and headed toward the truck. He pulled off his leather flight cap and turned to Legget, still a little slow in speech.

"I need a favor, mate. I've got to see Edith—soon, today or tomorrow. Can you swing me an evening pass?"

Legget paused, then nodded. "I can do that. If you hit the infirmary, I'll make it a forty-eight-hour leave. But," he wagged his finger, "you've got to promise me you'll sleep at least part of it."

"Not a minute of it," Paddy replied with a laugh. "I've got a chance to see Edith, and I reckon some others won't be so lucky."

Legget glanced down at the ground as they walked, thinking of the close calls and the narrow escapes. There was a quiet understanding between them, a bond forged in the sky, and no more needed to be said.

Chapter Seventeen

Margaret's House

Amersham

Margaret's eyes were still red as she moved from the divan and into the kitchen. She was folding a towel when Thomas followed her in, his voice soft but urgent.

"Margaret, look, I'm sorry. I'm sorry that the news upset you. But if you're up for it, I think we need to have a serious discussion."

"And what would you call that out in the garden?" she asked, not looking up from her task.

"I mean a conversation that's not about me or us, love. In fact, it's far bigger than England. It's about… humanity. Mankind."

"If you ask me," Margaret said, tossing the towel aside with a flick of her wrist, "and you haven't, they should change the term to 'womankind.' It's plain to me that the men have had their go and failed miserably. Thomas, you don't need to tell me this is an important time. I'm not walking around with my head stuck in the sand, though I must say, it looks mighty inviting just now."

"That's not what I'm saying," he replied. "No one quite realizes what's coming, not in the way I do. It's a turning point in a global struggle. The only country capable of turning the tide against the Germans is the United States. It doesn't take a Sandhurst education to know it's impossible to invade Europe from New York. The invasion has to come from England."

"The Americans won't even consider helping us," she said, her voice tinged with disbelief.

"Maybe you're right. But regardless of what the Yanks think, if England falls, Europe's fate is sealed for the next fifty years. Let me remind you, it's the same planet they call home."

Margaret's lips tightened. "Americans. There must be other ways. Someone else will take up the fight. I believe that."

"Despite your attitude toward the Yanks, it will be the United States. They'll join in, but not until they declare war on Japan."

"Japan?" she asked, her brow furrowing in confusion.

"Right. That's another story altogether. Japan attacks the U.S., and two days later, for reasons only a fool could explain, Hitler—yes, Hitler—declares war on the United States."

"That doesn't make sense. Are you sure? Even a girl knows you deal with the first bully before you pick a fight with the next one. Especially when the next one's bigger than you."

Thomas threw his arms wide, laughing. "I knew it. Under that little girl charm of yours lies a true military strategist."

"Don't mock me," Margaret snapped. "I had it right, didn't I? Besides, you're not the only genius in the room."

"Ah, my dear," Thomas said, his tone light but serious, "there's only one genius in this room, and it's not me. You're right; someone will take up the fight. But there's an enormous problem that has to be addressed first. And it's about us."

Margaret's head snapped up, eyes flashing with frustration. "Us? Us? We can't even decide who we are, let alone take on saving an entire continent. And don't call me 'dear' unless you fancy a lot of pain," she said, her voice low and dangerous.

"Margaret, please. If I show you how, will you help me?"

"No!" she barked.

"Good then."

"No," she repeated more firmly.

Thomas sighed and sat down, pulling a chair out with a loud scrape. "I'm not sure how, but we must ensure England's leaders don't surrender in what will seem like a hopeless situation."

Margaret threw her arms up in frustration. "Oh, is that all? But you said the Germans didn't win the war. Do you see how daft that sounds? How can they 'didn't' win the war?"

"They won't. And they didn't. That part's straightforward enough. The problem is, I don't know why I'm here in your life, and with a few things still shrouded in mystery, I'm not sure about anything."

"Thomas, I strongly suggest you start making sense quickly. Otherwise, this serious discussion will be a very lonely one. And it wouldn't be any more absurd than some of the things you've been saying."

"I'm trying to make it simple, but I don't have all the answers either," Thomas said, running a hand through his hair in frustration.

"Simple? Nothing that's come out of your mouth is simple, let alone logical! And by the way, did you hear me say no?"

"Margaret, take a deep breath." He raised his hands in a calming gesture.

"This is scaring me. Tell me again how England wins this war."

"Eventually, England does. But it all hinges on one meeting of the War Cabinet. In that moment, history, balanced on the head of a pin, rests in the hands of one man—Churchill."

Thomas stood up, pacing a little, the tension in his shoulders telling Margaret they were approaching something serious.

"Look," Margaret said, her voice cutting through his thoughts, "it's a lovely story, but am I missing something here? According to your version, they make the right decision, right? So why must we come to the rescue? Leave it be."

Thomas sighed and shoved his hands into his pockets, knowing this wouldn't sit well. "Because that history hasn't been written yet."

Margaret's body went limp, her expression falling. Silence settled in the room, a weight Thomas had not expected. She hadn't spoken yet, so he pressed on.

"Margaret, the events leading to that moment are based on a razor-thin margin of error. If they aren't repeated exactly, the history I know—the one where England wins—may not unfold at all. Churchill barely won the argument. In fact, with the information they had at the time, most would argue he shouldn't have. Honest men might come to different conclusions, with equally valid but differing outcomes." His voice had risen with his hands as he spoke, the words tumbling out.

He slowed, lowered his hands, and took a breath. "You're right. If history repeats itself exactly, there's little cause for concern. But the real question is, does it? If it does, then what am I doing here? Was I here before? Does anyone else know this? And if I was here before, did I use my knowledge to ensure things went as we know, or did it happen without me?"

"Thomas, I think you're losing sight of your position." She leaned forward, her face a mixture of exasperation and concern. "First, you say one thing, then you say another. What do you mean 'in the future'?"

"When we look back, history is set. But in the past, it's still being made every day," he replied, his voice quiet but resolute.

"Oh, no," Margaret muttered. "Please tell me you've got something in that mind that actually makes sense. Thomas Watson, I'm getting worried about you—more than I am about England."

Thomas chuckled softly. "Margaret, I'm sorry. I know it's all a bit much."

She pressed her palms together, resting them against her lips like praying. "What happens now?"

Thomas paused, his gaze lingering on her before he answered. "Actually, I'm not sure. I know what should happen, but I wasn't exactly handed a plan of action."

He could see she'd reached her limit. He sat back down and reached for her hands.

"We need to change the mood from dire to something a little more... manageable."

"Agreed," she said, the hint of a grin tugging at her lips.

Without warning, she sauntered around the table, plopped herself down on his lap, and wrapped her arm around his neck with a grin that was pure Margaret. Thomas blinked, captivated, as always, by her ability to stop him dead in his tracks.

"Thomas, why would you know *what* but not *why* you know it?" she asked, her voice mischievous.

"I thought we stopped talking about that. And that sounds like it came right out of my book, not yours."

"I don't recall anyone saying I can't talk like that. Why should you be the only one acting completely mad?" she teased.

"There should be a law," he said, half-seriously, "that says you can't wear that mischievous grin without explaining it to the person most likely to be affected."

"That's rubbish," she said, laughing. "It'd ruin all the fun of a good conversation. Besides, every woman deserves her secrets."

Thomas glanced around at the kitchen, noticing how she'd rearranged the pots. He gestured to them. "Do you know how to use any of these toys? I'm not changing the subject or anything, but I'm getting hungry."

"There! See? You're not changing the subject at all. I think you owe me a nice lunch. We're certainly on the same wavelength, wouldn't you say?" she said, tightening her arm around his neck, threatening to choke him.

Thomas made a strangled sound as she grinned through her clenched teeth, still half-laughing.

"Say yes, and I'll let you breathe," she said, barely able to keep a straight face.

Thomas made a noise of mock desperation, clutching his throat. She leapt up, frantic.

"Oh God, Thomas! Are you all right?"

He straightened up, adjusting his collar, his tone completely unaffected. "Of course. We men have our ways and our secrets."

With that, he darted toward the door as she shouted after him, "Mutant sod!" A potholder whizzed past him as he left the room.

Later, as they readied themselves for lunch, Margaret suggested a place that sounded a bit too stiff for Thomas's taste. "Anything a bit less formal?" he asked.

Margaret shot him a teasing look. "Mr. Watson, when a man takes a lady out, it's not to a café."

Knowing he had no chance in this battle, Thomas tactfully let her win. They'd had enough war talk for one day.

Chapter Eighteen

Kenley Airfield
11 Group Kenley Sector

Kenley wasn't much of an airfield. You'd find it was merely a neat strip of tarmac flanked by vast, flat grass fields. Opposite the still-standing maintenance depot lay the machinists' shop, utterly wrecked in a raid but a fortnight past. By some stroke of luck, the red telephone box—complete with its gleaming crown—remained, though every window opening was bereft of glass. Paddy waited for the chap inside to finish his call. Only uniformed personnel were allowed non-military phone use, and the ever-impatient Paddy found himself third in line, marking time. He had already endured his debriefing and medical check and even managed a bit of sleep. Now, his thoughts turned to Edith—he needed to see if she could secure some leave for the evening. For one never knew from one minute to the next whether they'd be allowed to see each other; indeed, he scarcely knew what her role in the war entailed. She'd made it abundantly clear that the subject was strictly off-limits in their conversations.

Paddy ambled back and forth, hands deep in his pockets, mulling over exactly what he would say when, from behind, he heard a clear voice: "Well, Paddy Hemmingway, what're you doing here?" Turning, he spotted Lonnie Garrah approaching. Lonnie, a Squadron Officer of the WAAF at Croydon Airfield, was no stranger to him. Their history, though a thing of the past, had ended with them parting as dear friends rather than lovers. She'd always believed he would never take their relationship further, though she still harbored affection for him; sometimes, life was maddening. Lonnie had come to see ending their liaison as the proper course—while Paddy remained less certain. She would regret her decision in time, but that time had long since passed. The gold braiding on her cap gleamed in the sunlight as she advanced. Her fair complexion contrasted sharply with her styled, sandy-brown hair and the crisp, dark blue of her uniform. Lonnie was never the type to attract racy whistles from the other side of the street; her unique sparkle and deep humanity were evident to those who looked beyond the surface.

Paddy's eyes widened ever so slightly—it had been months since he last saw her at a party in Brighton, where they'd been having a jolly good time until, rather curiously, she'd excused herself abruptly. Upon seeing her again, he smiled broadly, straightened his stance, and even saluted—though, as an officer pilot, he technically outranked her.

With a brisk wave toward her cap, she said, "Oh, put your eyes back in your head and hug me." A young mechanic loitering by the phone pretended not to notice, casually lighting a cigarette. Paddy stepped away from the phone area and moved closer, gently taking Lonnie by the shoulders and appraising her. She had lost a fair bit of weight—transforming from a charmingly plump figure to one defined by three distinct curves.

"Will you stop it?" she chided, feeling a blush rise as she drew a deep breath.

"Stop what?" Paddy replied, his tone teasingly defensive—as if accused of nicking the last biscuit.

"Stop looking at me as if it were 0200 in a pub. It's not going to get you anywhere."

"Lonnie, you look absolutely fabulous—and, honestly, I wasn't thinking that sort of thing at all," he said, flashing a roguish smile.

"Yeah, and planes don't fly—well, they do, but some pilots can't keep them in the air," she laughed. "I heard about your landing. Are you all right? That bandage on your head looks grim."

He reached up to feel the bandage. "Well, the canopy sort of up and smacked me, but the doc gave me the all-clear—save for a dire need for sleep. Thirty minutes worked wonders, though it's a pity I picked it up during debriefing."

Lonnie shook her head, aware that his tale was likely the truth. "How does a perfectly competent pilot find himself in such a scrape? Aren't there limits to how many hours one can fly?"

"Normally, there are, but things have grown rather frantic—there aren't enough pilots or aircraft to fly escort. A few of the bomber lads I know were dispatched on an almost impossible mission, and I felt compelled to support them. Regrettably, it was after two scrambles earlier in the day. I had to ditch on the first, though the Navy chaps did treat me to a hot dinner when they brought me back. That's the good news; the bad is we lost Dickey Lee."

"Paddy, I'm so sorry," Lonnie said, noting the strain etched on his face and the tight set of his lips as he held back his feelings. "Why do men behave like that?" she silently wondered. Then, opening her arms, she hugged him. He clutched her tightly, and Lonnie felt her old emotions welling up anew in the embrace.

Paddy held her silently for a time, and Lonnie allowed him all the space he needed. He had always been there for her, and now she was grateful for the chance to be there for him. When his grip finally loosened and he paused in thought, she chose not to disturb him.

After a moment, he finally said, "Actually, I'm not entirely all right. It was a bit of a scare, but it cleared my head and redefined my priorities."

They were no longer locked in an embrace but stood quite near. "Paddy, my dear, this doesn't sound like you," she remarked. "What do you mean by priorities? What has changed?"

Gently, he placed his hand on her elbow and led her away from the wreckage of the building. "As I was battling that plane and fighting for sleep and knowing I was coming off the runway, a thought struck me with absolute clarity. You can't wait until tomorrow to live your life—there are no guarantees of a tomorrow, especially in the middle of this bloody war. I lost a dear friend; one moment, he was there, and the next, he'd vanished from my sight. As I found myself alive and being helped from the wreckage this morning, I made a commitment."

Something stirred within Lonnie. "What sort of commitment?"

"I'm going to ask Edith to marry me—hopefully tonight. Denis has granted me a few days' leave, though the trouble lies in getting her away from her mysterious job. In any event, I must act now—I won't delay any longer. I haven't any grand plans, so it might be in a pub rather than the Savoy, as tradition would demand. Truth be told, I don't even have a proper ring—perhaps I'll fashion a makeshift one of string and kiss it onto her finger. I'm not entirely certain, but such details pale in importance right now. Lonnie, I truly love her, and I want to show her that now, not later."

A surge of emotion welled up in Lonnie, catching her by surprise; only moments before, her feelings had been entirely different. Now, she found herself riding an emotional carousel. Though she had never met Edith, she was well acquainted with their relationship—after many nights spent discussing Edith over drinks, it was a familiar subject. It was a peculiar predicament, assisting Paddy as he unraveled the very frustrations with commitment that had once marred their relationship. His earnest expression and measured tone brooked no doubt—he meant every word.

Lonnie was at a loss for words, caught in a quandary reminiscent of a schoolgirl caught between a new beau and a former flame. What makes one glance back after resolving to move forward? Was it pride, selfishness, or merely ego? She wasn't sure, but the feeling was undeniable. Realizing that they had chosen permanently divergent paths, she felt the emotions surge uncontrollably; her face flushed, and a single tear slowly descended before she could catch it.

Paddy was abruptly drawn back to his own words. "Lonnie, that wasn't fair. I shouldn't have—"

"Oh, hush it, Paddy. I'm truly happy for you," she replied, brushing away another tear with a gentle chuckle. "Can't you see I'm delighted for you?"

Paddy fell silent, mulling over the tangled emotions of life—where nothing was ever quite as it appeared. He knew he'd hurt her, and that was the very last thing he desired. "God, I'm so stupid," he thought.

"Lonnie?" he ventured hesitantly.

"Paddy Hemmingway, you old sod—you can't propose to a woman without a proper ring."

"Isn't the act of proposing far more significant than a mere piece of metal?"

"No, certain things matter to a woman—war or no war. They seek a dependable man, they desire security, and above all, they crave romance."

"Romance? Come on, Lonnie, a mere twenty minutes after I ask her, the Germans might be on the beaches. Certain things aren't so easily procured. Wedding dresses aren't exactly springing forth from Paris these days. I'm not even sure I'll see her tonight, let alone arrange a proper dinner in London at a decent hotel."

"Some things are more important than others." With a deft movement, Lonnie brought her hands together and slipped a ring from her right hand—a simple band set with three petite sapphires, the first indulgence she'd purchased after leaving home, something she desired though hardly necessary. She took Paddy's hand, placed it in his palm, and closed her fingers around his hand.

"Lonnie, you can't do this…" he began.

She pressed a finger to his lips. "You're not a woman—I wouldn't expect you to understand. It may be too large, but it will see you through the moment. Promise me you'll never mention it to her nor attempt to return it. You can always get her a proper wedding ring later."

He opened his mouth to protest, and she interjected sharply, "Do I have your promise?"

"Yeah, but…"

"Paddy, I mean it. Never tell her." He looked from the ring in his hand back to Lonnie. "And there's one more thing you must promise me.

If there are any more like you, Paddy Hemmingway, you must send them my way." She glanced over his shoulder and added, "The line's clear; you'd best make your call."

Releasing his hand, she turned briskly. "I'm off to Birmingham, but I'll be back on Thursday. Let me know how it goes—you can reach me at the base."

With that, she strode away, her pent-up emotions finally breaking free as tears streamed down her face.

"Lonnie, I didn't know," he called after her. "I really didn't."

"I know, Paddy," she replied, her gaze straight ahead. "I know." And just like that, she was gone.

Chapter Nineteen

London

Embassy's Flat—Silvertown, East End

Night fell over the East End of London. Yuri sat at the small table, writing his rent payment for his modest flat supplied by the embassy. The wireless crackled softly, pouring out an aria from an Italian opera. Emotional, those Italians. Brilliant on the stage, hopeless on the battlefield. He had to chuckle at their peculiar way—designing magnificent helmets adorned with plumed feathers yet incapable of firing a rifle properly. What good was all the flair if one couldn't shoot straight? The absurdity of Hitler's pact with Mussolini never failed to amuse him. It was like a machinist striking a business deal with Prada—wholly impractical. The Italians had one task: hold a portion of Africa, their so-called colonial backyard. It had taken no time at all for them to be routed. Now, the Germans were left to clean up their mess, expending resources on another front. It was not sound business, making him wonder—was Hitler as clever as everyone thought?

A sharp rap-rap at the door. About time. He'd been expecting it since his morning meeting with the ambassador. Without haste, Yuri reached over, twisted the dial on the wireless, and turned it off. Rising, he moved to the entry hall, where his long coat hung neatly on the tree. He pulled it open, slipped the rent envelope into the hidden pocket inside the lining, and straightened the fabric with practiced ease. A last glance around the flat—nothing out of place—before he moved to the door and opened it.

A stout young man stood in the doorway, round-faced and ill-fitted in a brown business suit two sizes too large.

"Welcome, Comrade Stakova!" the man declared loudly in English.

Yuri leaned forward, peering down the corridor, scanning the dimly lit stairwell that led to the first floor and the building's entrance. It was why he'd chosen this flat—the entry foyer was visible from just outside his door. He saw no one. Without acknowledging the greeting, he grabbed the man's arm and pulled him inside before shutting the door firmly.

"And you would be…?" Yuri asked in English, testing him.

The man straightened, smoothing his lapels. "Comrade Joseph Surkovich Alexikov," he replied in the same language. "It is an honor to meet such a distinguished comrade whose service to the Motherland is greatly admired in Moscow. I can only hope to achieve such distinction myself one day."

"Comrade Joseph, if I may call you that?" The man nodded. "How long do you anticipate holding the post of London station chief?"

Joseph hesitated just a fraction too long. "Well… as long as I am required, of course. A curious question." He removed his hat, tucking it under his arm.

"If you wish to remain here for any length of time, I would strongly suggest you refrain from announcing yourself as a spy to the entire building outside my door. You've already made me an accomplice."

The man stiffened. "I—of course—ensured no one was nearby. I checked. There was no one there." He folded his arms. "Naturally."

"Naturally," Yuri echoed, taking the man's gas mask and hat and placing them on the small entry rack beside the umbrella. He moved into the center of the room, slipping his hands into the pockets of his neatly tailored trousers—the work of Mr. Stevens, the discreet purveyor of suits on Savile Row. Of course, Mr. Stevens was no such man. His real name was Isaac Sharfberg, and his establishment would be one of Joseph's first necessary visits.

"Comrade Alexikov?" Yuri prompted.

"Yes?"

"The regulations," Yuri said in Russian, "which I am certain you have committed to memory, dictate that we must speak English at all times, even in private, to eliminate the slightest risk of exposure. How is your English?"

Joseph straightened his shoulders. "It is very worthy. I studied and accepted top passing in my section."

"Grade," Yuri corrected.

"Grade?" Joseph frowned.

"Yes. You received a top grade."

"Of course. Grade," Joseph said, arms folding once more.

"What are your plans, Joseph?"

"I am requesting we…" He paused, searching for the word. "Proceeding… the last case that must conclude before your leaving. I have information on entire local assets and…" another pause, "…

ongoing operations. I have exact directives carrying out in short time but cannot… proceed until this final issue is come to a… halt."

Joseph reached into his breast pocket, withdrew a sealed envelope, and handed it to Yuri. "I have carried this perso—myself—from Moscow. The director of Mission Central pressures you complete very quickly these instructions and be home back with these directives… ah… directions."

Yuri read the letter.

> People's Commissariat for Internal Affairs (NKVD)
> Comrade Yuri Ivanovich Stakova
> August 15, 1940
>
> You are instructed to retire the officer Thomas Watson for failure to provide the promised information for which we paid handsomely. With recent developments, this officer is now considered outside our charge and cannot be allowed to act beyond our control. Such activity poses an unacceptable risk to other regional assets, particularly with the invasion mere days or weeks away.
>
> This issue is your responsibility. Completion is mandatory, with updates to Moscow Center regarding your success.
>
> Upon completion, proceed to the Hartford Street location in the port city of Glasgow and await further instructions regarding your transportation back to Moscow.
>
> Comrade Andri Ganova Schikova
> Director, Foreign Operations, Western Sector

Yuri folded the letter and looked up. "Recent developments?"

"Yes, he…" Joseph began, slipping into Russian.

"English, please," Yuri said sharply.

Joseph narrowed his eyes at the rebuke. "Yes. It is the point you reported—about more money."

Yuri stiffened. Watson had demanded more money. He had been displeased but not so displeased as to warrant an execution order. "And yet I was not informed the Center considered it this serious?"

"You have been substituted on another, more meaningful directive. Watson matter is considered… abolished… ah… over. This case file is a single one I not receive… did not receive. Moscow wishes you completed this case file. How into this… mess did you arrive?"

Yuri's gaze hardened. The young man's tone was borderline insulting, as if he had botched an operation.

"It is not a mess," Yuri said evenly. "It is a situation I do not yet have complete information on."

"Well, Comrade," Joseph replied, "the Bureau… deathly avoids with anybody, as in English say it, 'put out to farm.'"

Yuri exhaled. "It's out to pasture," he corrected.

"Pasture?"

"Yes. The phrase is out to pasture. I suggest you stick with the basics until your English improves."

Yuri walked over to a low cabinet, retrieved a bottle of vodka, and set two glasses on the table before the divan, where Joseph had seated himself.

Joseph grinned. "Comrade Stakova, a most generous host indeed. Is vodka accessible here?"

"Yes, but I never drink it in public."

"Why not?"

"Caution. I always drink the local beer."

"Ah, yes. The famous English beer. What is taste like?"

"Warm."

"No, not true. You are making fun with me."

"I assure you, it's warm," Yuri said dryly.

Joseph scoffed but let the matter drop. Yuri studied him carefully.

"Tell me, Joseph—have you ever traveled outside the Soviet Union?"

"No. This is also interesting question."

The war had forced an expedited approach to intelligence work—there was no time for the usual in-country training, language refinement, or cultural immersion. The result? Officers deployed too soon, too raw, lacking the instinct to blend in.

And Moscow had sent one of them to replace him.

That explained much. Yuri looked at him intently. Joseph wasn't as slow as his English made him sound, but his job would require fluency in the local language. His lack of in-country training was just too obvious. Joseph wasn't of the caliber to be 'rising fast' in the Bureau and cutthroat in the process, as the ambassador indicated. He wasn't the new station chief. That meant someone else was out there—someone who met those qualifications.

Yuri hadn't told Joseph everything and perhaps had told him too much. Several things weren't adding up. There are too many holes. This wasn't being handled according to the rules, and field operations were always executed by the book. Yuri had Watson under surveillance, and there had been no change to his situation since the last report: he was at home with his wife. Watson wouldn't do something as stupid as cutting a separate deal unless he really *was* stupid. If he was about to go turncoat, a low profile was a very healthy thing, and the last few days, Watson had done precisely that. So far, the only unusual thing was the Moscow directive. Tomorrow, he needed to get more information.

Chapter Twenty

London

No. 10 Downing Street

It was early, but Churchill was already in his nightclothes. He often conducted affairs from his bed, whether in the morning's first light or deep into the night's stillness. With a weary sigh, he set the papers on his lap table and slipped off his spectacles. The manufacturing reports were as bleak as ever. Truthfully, very little of late had offered any cause for cheer.

His gaze drifted to the wall, his mind impatiently awaiting the secretary's arrival with the most recent inventory of raw materials up to the last convoy. Everything took too damnably long. Strategy, progress, victory—they were all mired in delay. Setback followed defeat, yet still, they pressed on. He had barely crossed the threshold of Number Ten before history had thrown the calamity of Dunkirk at his feet. And yet, by the sheer mettle of those brave lads, what ought to have been a rout had been turned into something of a triumph—one wrenched from the jaws of catastrophe. He had insisted, against doubters and naysayers, that the nation's future hung upon holding that narrow stretch of land. The moment had been fleeting, the peril immense—but it had been done.

Yet any stumble under his watch and the papers would soon enough dredge up the old specter of the Dardanelles. It was his shadow, his albatross—the charge laid at his door since his days as First Lord of the Admiralty. A commission had ruled the failure lay in the field, in the execution of orders rather than in their conception, but no matter. Its stain clung to him like chewing gum to a boot sole, refusing to be scraped away. He could feel it even now, in the walls of the Prime Minister's office—the whispers, the doubt. But it would not sway him. He had not clawed his way back to power to pander or prevaricate. He would lead with truth, with conviction, and let the chips fall where they may.

There was only so much one man could do to save an island. He knew in his bones that his "senseless stubbornness" was right, yet he could feel the tide turning—weariness creeping into the national spirit, a whisper of surrender in some quarters. He let his mind wander back to his youth in South Africa and the days when he was a soldier-correspondent fleeing for his life from the Boers, only to return home a national hero. The world had been simpler then. Right and wrong, black and white, honor upheld. Now? Now, the old standards were trampled beneath the march of expediency. Even the bombing of civilians had become an acceptable footnote of war.

Chapter Twenty-One

Margaret's Home

Amersham

Thomas awoke early, staring at the ceiling, caught in that strange, muddled space between certainty and doubt. Why was it that his thoughts seemed to exist in this perpetual grayness? "We're given control over only so much," he mused. And at present, his own life did not appear to be among those things.

Still, he resolved that matters could only improve. There was Margaret, after all—the silver lining in any cloud that might darken his horizon. Since their talk about his knowledge, the days had been grand, much like the one before. He could sit for hours, utterly captivated, as she spoke with that high-speed animation, veering from politics to history, art, family, and even to the precise contents of her kitchen cupboards. By nightfall, they were exhausted, tumbling into bed and deliberately steering clear of any lurking uncertainties.

Margaret had awoken brimming with energy. She declared, in no uncertain terms, that she would dearly love to sock that Hitler fellow right in the nose. With war raging, invasion looming, and grim faces on every street, Margaret maintained that the best way to defy the Reich was to carry on precisely as though it didn't exist. She had, she insisted, a secret weapon—a covert act of resistance. And at last, she revealed it: a picnic in the countryside.

Determined to see her plan through, she marched next door to persuade Mrs. Somerville to loan them her old Austin for the excursion. As the landlady fussed about the counter, Margaret caught the unmistakable glint of mischief in her eyes—an expression she had come to recognize well in the woman who had, quite unexpectedly, become a dear friend.

"Well, now," Mrs. Somerville said, setting down a dish with a decisive clatter. "You can borrow the Austin on two conditions. First, it still has to run—which, in all honesty, may sink your grand plans from the outset. Second, you must grant me a promise."

Margaret, toweling off a heavy blue enameled pot, raised an eyebrow. "And may I ask what this promise entails?"

Mrs. Somerville leaned against the counter with a knowing smile. "Oh, Kitten, of course, you may. It's nothing much—just a trifle. Knowing how much you enjoyed your day so I might live it vicariously through you would bring me great pleasure. Much more entertaining than rummaging about in *my* old memories, don't you think?" She tucked another dish into the cupboard and shrugged. "I'm an old lady with simple needs."

Margaret narrowed her eyes, setting the last dish aside. "You're not an old lady at all. I see a very clever woman with far too much twinkle in her eye. That, madam, is what I think."

Mrs. Somerville let out a deep, rich laugh. "Yes, well, we all have our opinions, don't we, young lady?"

She wandered into the dining room, disappearing briefly behind the louvered doors of a large storage cupboard beneath the stairs. There, among a modest collection of bottles, she made her selection, carefully inspecting one, then another, before settling on a choice. Dusting it off with the towel slung over her shoulder, she handed it to Margaret.

Margaret stared at the bottle in astonishment. "Do you know how difficult it is to come by a decent wine these days?"

"Of course, young lady. That's precisely why I'm giving it to you." Mrs. Somerville gave her a pointed look. "A picnic deserves the scent of a fine Bordeaux. And more than that—it deserves its effect." She arched a brow. "If you're going to do this, you may as well do it properly."

Margaret cradled the bottle, shaking her head with a smile. "There it is again—that grin. This wouldn't have anything to do with the resulting story, would it?"

Mrs. Somerville feigned innocence. "Honestly, you're so young. More like a daughter, really." She turned to her credenza, slid open the top drawer, and rummaged through its contents before pressing two petrol ration cards into Margaret's hand.

"I'll never use these," she said. "And even if that old Austin does start, you won't get far without them. If you ever need more, you know where to find them."

Margaret hesitated. "You should keep them."

"My dear girl, I can't drive. What on living earth would I do with petrol ration cards—except perhaps trade them for butter, which, as you may observe, I do not need."

Margaret's eyes drifted to something else in the drawer—an ornate, velvet-covered book. "Mrs. Somerville, what's that? It's beautiful."

The older woman hesitated. "That," she said slowly, "is where I keep Charles. Photographs of the life we shared." She exhaled, closing the drawer gently. "One day, we'll sit down, and I'll tell you about them. But not today."

Margaret smiled warmly. "I'd like that. I have a feeling you have got a few stories to share."

Mrs. Somerville shook her head, chuckling. "Daughters," she muttered again. "Off with you now. And don't forget the wine glasses."

It took some coaxing, but the Austin eventually sputtered to life, though not without protest. Margaret and Thomas loaded the picnic provisions into the boot, climbed in, and set off.

Well—Margaret did.

Thomas had taken the wheel at first, but something felt amiss. When he attempted to downshift on a slight incline, an ungodly shriek erupted from the engine—a noise that suggested he had, somehow, reversed the gearbox's entire natural order. Margaret, between fits of laughter, graciously took over driving.

Relieved of the task, Thomas found himself pondering something peculiar. "How do they deliver the post with no street names?"

"Oh, the postmen know them well enough," Margaret said breezily. "They took down all the signposts, you see—to confuse the invading hordes. Or should I say, the Huns?"

She led them to a place she had loved since childhood—an old farm where she and her father had spent long afternoons walking, talking, and debating. After he passed, she stopped coming. The place, once full of warmth, had turned hollow. Life had changed. Her mother, once engaged, had retreated into the comforts of Harrods and high tea, where gossip and cucumber sandwiches replaced meaningful conversation.

Now, as they wandered into the meadow, a great maple standing sentinel over wild grasses and poplar trees, she allowed the past to settle. Thomas, watching her, realized something was intoxicating about her presence—not just her wit, nor her beauty, but the sheer energy of her. She was a woman who carried light, even in wartime.

As they unpacked, Margaret produced the bottle of wine with a flourish. "A gift from your dear friend, Mrs. Somerville."

"My friend?" Thomas blinked.

"Yes, to my surprise, she's taken quite the liking to you," Margaret smirked. "Before, she hardly noticed your existence. Now she gets that twinkle whenever you're around."

Thomas grinned. "Ah, well. I do have a certain intrinsic charm. Must be genetic."

Margaret shot him a look before sending a napkin holder sailing past his ear. "No nonsense. This meadow is sacred ground."

"As is anywhere you walk," he said, blowing her an exaggerated kiss.

They talked, they laughed, they drank. And as the sun began its slow descent, Thomas realized something: he didn't want this day to end. He had spent so much time trying to make sense of his past—his knowledge, his memories—but now, with Margaret, he was beginning to wonder if the present wasn't far more important.

The war, his strange predicament, even the looming question of his own identity—those would wait. For today, at least, there was only this.

Chapter Twenty-Two

Outside Amersham

Pavel, an officer at the Russian Embassy who reported directly to Yuri, was neither comfortable nor particularly pleased. His legs ached from standing too long, pressed against the rough bark of a tree, and his patience had worn thin. The Watsons had been under that damned tree for what felt like an eternity. He had edged closer, hoping to catch more of their conversation, but this was as near as he dared get while remaining unseen.

He badly needed a cigarette. He was hungry. And he certainly did not appreciate trudging through damp undergrowth in his best dress shoes. The whole operation had been a wretched nuisance. He hadn't known where they'd spend the day, so he'd hardly been prepared for this endurance test. "Good thing they didn't decide to go mountain climbing," he thought sourly.

Even at this distance, listening was a challenge. He caught only snatches of conversation, not enough for a complete picture. But then—had Watson just mentioned Bletchley? Pavel knew of Bletchley, as did anyone with an ear for rumors. It was widely believed to house a secret machine, something the British guarded with almost religious zeal. If Watson was heading there, it wasn't to confess to being a Russian spy. No, this man was too clever for that. More likely, he was sniffing around for information. He had the mind that could turn a potential execution into an opportunity—for money, for survival, for something.

Pavel hadn't learned everything today, but he had learned enough. This was a valuable piece of intelligence, the sort of lucky break that could get him out of fieldwork and into the far more comfortable world of political maneuvering at the embassy. Yuri would be pleased.

He watched the couple packed up, stowing their things in the car. They were too far now for him to hear their parting words, and there was no more cover between him and the vehicle. Moving closer was out of the question. Besides, he had already given enough for Mother Russia today.

Amusement flickered across his face as the woman took the driver's seat. He had been watching her long enough to know she was no ordinary woman.

Following from a safe distance, he nearly caught up with them when they suddenly stopped and switched drivers. First, he heard her laughter—clear, unrestrained—then the car pulled away again.

Still hidden, he listened as the sound of their engine faded into the distance, the gearbox shifting quickly as they gained speed. Only then did he allow himself to reach into his pocket and strike a match. The cigarette flared to life, and he inhaled deeply, the smoke settling his nerves. He decided against following them back. There was no need. He would return to the embassy, write his report, and, most importantly, find a private place to telephone Yuri.

The first few draws of the cigarette were satisfying, but soon the craving passed. He wandered over to the tree where they had spent the day, scanning the ground out of habit. It was standard tradecraft to check if anything had been left behind. It was mostly an excuse to stretch his legs before returning to the car.

Bending down, he picked up a small polished wooden ring, oddly out of place in the wild grass. He turned it over in his fingers, smirking. "Perhaps it's a tiny bomb," he muttered to himself. How had he ended up in this business, anyway?

He took another slow drag, holding the smoke in his lungs for a moment before exhaling into the cool air. In truth, he had always disliked cigarettes. Messy is inconvenient and an absolute liability in his line of work. It was difficult to remain unnoticed when clouds of smoke betrayed your position.

Following the path the couple had taken back to their car, he glanced around one last time—nothing else of interest.

The sky had darkened. He sighed. He hated driving at night.

What had brought them out here? He thought momentarily, then smiled faintly, grinding the cigarette into the damp earth beneath his heel.

Love.

It explained a great many foolish things.

Chapter Twenty-Three

After the Picnic

Margaret handled the shifting and steering with practiced ease, her mind barely tethered to the road ahead. The low sun flickered through gaps in the trees and barns, sending bright, rhythmic bursts into the car as they wound through the rolling pastures.

Returning to the farm felt like stepping into another world where time slows, and troubles hold no dominion. But now, on the journey home, each flash of sunlight dragged her steadily back to reality.

Two days ago, she had been in control of her life—or at least she had believed so. Now, that certainty had been shaken to its foundations. She had thought herself in control of her emotions, but they had betrayed her, slipping through her fingers like sand. What overpowering force was rising within her, this deep, unshakable pull toward the man beside her? How could he so wholly and effortlessly erase any attraction she had once felt for the same man two days prior?

Marrying the old Thomas had been a mistake. She did not hate him—he had been an amusing curiosity, a diversion. A fling without the fling. He had swept into her life with a reckless charm, spontaneous and daring, offering a brief respite from the suffocating dictates of her mother, who seemed determined to enforce the rigid codes of a bygone century.

She had entered the marriage on her terms, fully aware of the risks, but it had not taken long to sense something was amiss. A part of him remained hidden, an intrigue she could never quite grasp. Before their wedding, his fascination with her family had outstripped his interest in her—a warning sign if ever there was one. He had pursued her, yes, but with a peculiar restraint, his attentions more fixated on her lineage than on winning her affection. She had held him at bay with the old, reliable line: I'm not that kind of girl. It was a lie, of course. Every woman was that kind of girl when she was with the right man. And Thomas—the old Thomas—had never been the one.

She had known it would be an issue after the wedding. To preempt it, she had made her position clear just minutes before the ceremony. With a steady voice, she had informed her soon-to-be husband that she wished to focus on the *important* aspects of their relationship before they embarked upon a *full* marriage. He could take it or leave it. If he agreed, she thought, it might prove he was capable of honesty—that she could work through his more dubious qualities.

Yet his relentless interest in her family had only deepened. Her mother had taken an instant dislike to him, and despite repeated rebuffs, he had persisted in trying to win her over. The inevitable confrontation had come to a head one afternoon in the library, where her mother had ordered her—*ordered* her—to end things with Thomas at once.

That had been the breaking point. Every buried frustration, every unspoken resentment, had erupted in that moment. Their battle of wills had been years in the making, fueled by everything from Margaret's refusal to conform to her mother's expectations to the undeniable truth that she had always captured more than her fair share of her father's affection. And then—silence. A final, immovable wall between them. Without another word, Margaret stormed out of the house, only later realizing that she had left Thomas inside.

She thought now of that word: *ordered.* The moment it had been spoken, all other logic had fled. If her mother had chosen any other approach, Margaret was sure she wouldn't be married today. But the need to prove her independence, to assert herself in the face of command, had driven her forward, blind to the consequences.

And then there had been the woman in the gallery—that wise, nameless stranger who had warned her of this with quiet certainty. That one day, she would find herself doing precisely what she had sworn she never would.

And here she was.

The part that defied all reason that shook her foundation was how completely and utterly she had fallen for the new Thomas. It was a runaway train, unstoppable and terrifying. This wasn't something she could control, and that made her uneasy. She had known romance before, but never like this. Never had she been swept off her feet—not like this. The men in her past had been diversions, passing amusements, their affections met with detached amusement. But this—*was this it? Was he it?*

Unlike the man before him, this Thomas was utterly transparent, yet he carried with him the burden of memory and impossible foresight. She gripped the wheel tighter.

What in the bloody hell had happened in that bathroom? How could the great love of her life have arrived in the same man she had regretted marrying? She didn't know how to handle it.

She violently downshifted, pressed the accelerator, and hurled herself into the next bend. No more thinking. It was done. Her heart had already decided. This man—this new Thomas—was the love of her life. And she had known it that very first morning.

She abandoned all unanswered reasoning and surrendered completely at some bend in the road she would never recall. A strange, tangible calm settled over her.

Thomas, painfully aware of imminent danger, braced himself against the dashboard. "We could arrange for you to have flying lessons in a Spitfire," he said. "On second thought, perhaps that's not fast enough?"

"Are you trying to make me laugh?" she asked, her eyes fixed on the road.

Thomas observed her—hair flying, jaw set, foot firm. "Make you laugh? No, I wouldn't dream of it. In a moment of pure selfishness, I would settle for you returning to Earth before we both meet our end—preferably taking a few Germans with us."

She said nothing.

Margaret may have been lost in thought, but Thomas was also thinking. He had always known that a woman was meant just for him somewhere in the world. He had never expected her to appear under such peculiar circumstances.

Strange or not, it changed nothing. She was *the one*.

Margaret, likely breaking every speed record she had set that morning, returned them to the house in one piece. They unloaded the Austin and went inside, Margaret immediately setting to work tidying up. She busied herself unpacking the basket, rattling dishes, and shifting things about when suddenly she stopped.

"We're missing one of Mrs. Somerville's napkin holders," she said, holding the empty wine bottle.

Thomas leaned against the doorway, arms folded. Watching her, he asked, "Margaret, do you believe in love at first sight?"

She froze. Her head snapped around. "What?"

"I said—do you believe in love at first sight?"

She scoffed. "Oh, absolutely. Preferably, the gentleman in question is impossibly handsome, atop a white horse and towing a wagon full of picket fences. Did I mention *gobs* of money?"

"Margaret, I'm being serious."

"So am I," she said, eyes twinkling. "Can you ride?"

"No, but I can horse around."

She laughed, rolling her eyes. "Thomas Watson, must I remind you that we are already married? And only to me, I might add—though you're not quite sure about that. Bridesmaids, bills, dishes—the whole tedious business. A bit late to be pondering love at first sight, don't you think?"

Thomas smiled and then disappeared, heading to the bedroom.

"Where are you going? You just asked me a question."

Following, she appeared at the bedroom doorway. She placed one hand against the door to steady herself while removing one shoe and the other.

"As I said, I'm your wife, which should put that question to rest."

With a mischievous look, Thomas said, "Margaret, you didn't marry me. You married that other guy."

She glanced up, and the smile on her face turned into a curious look. "Thomas, I get the feeling that you're actually trying to be serious here. Could this be true?"

"Yes, I'm trying to reach a point," he blurted.

"About us?"

"Yes," he said, "about us, you and me. Although I might wander off to the occasional errant concept, there's something I know for certain."

"That's refreshing." She said.

"Margaret, I truly believe I fell in love with you at first sight. I want to spend the rest of my life with you and …"

"Well—it's—about—time," she said, emphasizing every word. Filled with the emotions of her recent realization, she thought, "This was the man, the right man, and he just proved it."

"Oh, brother," she whispered, almost to herself, "Mrs. Somerville is going to love this part."

"What does that mean?" Thomas said as he stood next to the bed.

"Never mind." Still standing in the doorway, Margaret had placed one hand on her hip while the other held an invisible cigarette with a limp wrist. She said, "Hey, sailor, got a light?"

Nothing hid the confused look on Thomas's face.

Standing before him, she sauntered over and looked up with a very impish and determined smile. Holding his gaze, she tucked her hair behind her right ear and proceeded to undo the top button of her blouse.

"Oh!" he said, realizing her intent. "Where did that phrase come from?"

"I heard it in a Hollywood movie once. I've always had a soft spot in my heart for a guy in a uniform. It was Daddy's business, you know. Anyway, it's a lot more ladylike than shouting, 'I'm available!' across a crowded pub. So, Mr. Thomas Watson," she said, now on her fourth button, "If you're so damn good at predicting the future, try predicting what's going to happen now."

"That's easy. You're going to change blouses," he said with a mischievous smile.

"You *sod*!" she said, taking a playful swing at him, missing and spinning in the process. He ducked and grabbed her around the waist, pulling her toward the bed. He put his hand out to break their fall, landing on her. She immediately started to push him off and get up.

"Oh, no, you don't," he said as his weight held her down. "You, my lovely, aren't going anywhere, as I'm pretty convinced this was your idea."

"I'm not that kind of girl, Mr. Watson," she said as she stopped resisting. Her head fell back onto the bedspread as she said, "Okay, maybe I am with you, but who said I wanted to get up?"

"Well, what is it then?"

"I want to be on top."

"What!"

"You heard me. This was *my* idea; now move over!" Margaret said with a shove.

He felt the pressure on his shoulder but didn't move. They remained face to face; a full twenty seconds passed. Before him was the complement to an inner part of his heart that had been missing for a long time. Thomas was immersed in a sensation transcending all that had come before and any that would succeed. His senses were aware of everything. He knew this was right with a certainty that he couldn't fathom, let alone explain. He didn't want to explain. If there was sand in the hourglass of time, he would will it to stop. Each grain would stay in place at this exact moment, proving that raptured adoration defies the universe's physical laws. Then, with glistening eyes and emotion in his voice, he managed to whisper, "Margaret, I love you."

They looked at each other, and she placed her hand gently on the side of his face. She pulled his head down and slowly and deliberately kissed him, touching every part of his mind and body. He felt a soft, powerful energy and a feeling of invincibility that only the love of your life could give you. They were one in soul, with Margaret first among equals.

"I know," she said after the kiss. "I'm a little overwhelmed with where my feelings have gone. I know I do love you, the you here today. Just promise me you won't go away as mysteriously as you arrived."

"I promise," he said.

Then, still face to face, she took her index finger gently but directly, placing it right on the end of his nose, saying, "Now move over."

Chapter Twenty-Four

Russian Embassy

Viktor Grigoryevich Krivitsky moved through the darkened halls of the Russian Embassy with the quiet assurance of a man who belonged. He was among the elite of his country, a nephew of a member of the Communist Central Committee, placing him far above the ordinary ranks. He arrived on a diplomatic charter with three other embassy personnel earlier that afternoon. He had no interest in them and had spent the flight silently contemplating what lay ahead.

A rising star in the NKVD—the Company, as it was known—Viktor had little regard for his so-called peers. To excel among such feeble competition tainted the honor. He knew precisely what he wanted in a sea of men content merely to hold a position.

Night had long since fallen as he surveyed the embassy. His credentials had granted him access to the files he sought—those concerning one Yuri Ivanovich Stakova, the embassy's chief of security. Now, with a master key, he had access to the entire Security Department.

He read through the reports until his eyes burned. The long journey had taken its toll, and the grueling flight aboard a Soviet transport made him long for the bed in the flat he had secured. It was time to call it a night.

As he made his way down the hall, he caught sight of a man emerging swiftly from the stairwell and slipping into the room Viktor had just vacated. The quickened pace set off a warning in Viktor's trained mind. Diplomats never moved with such urgency—by nature, theirs was a profession of slow, deliberate steps toward pointless non-agreements. This man, whoever he was, did not belong to that world.

Inside the Security Department, Pavel moved toward his desk, one of many identical workstations in the large office. Each bore its brand of disorder, reflecting its owner's approach to organization—or lack thereof. Pavel's, however, was an unholy wreck, resembling a filing cabinet that had tipped over and spilled its contents. Amid the chaos, a small mountain of restaurant menus sat by the telephone.

He pulled the chain on the desk lamp, casting a dim glow over the disarray. He needed to make a call. Yuri would want to hear this immediately.

Viktor followed him in, silent as a shadow.

Pavel, oblivious, was flipping through the small notebook he had retrieved from his breast pocket. His finger paused at a name—*Stags Pit*—a local tavern known for keeping a portion of the embassy's vodka and smuggled Johnny Walker behind the bar. Next to it was Yuri's home number.

The sudden movement of a hand offering him a cigarette startled Pavel.

"Papirossa?" Viktor said in Russian, holding out a fresh pack of cigarettes.

Pavel looked up at the unfamiliar face, taking in the professional smile, the calm confidence. He recognized the cigarettes instantly—Belomor Kanal's. These were no ordinary cigarettes; they were a rare luxury produced only at the Uritsky tobacco factory in Leningrad since 1932. Belomor Kanal was known for delivering a unique and harsh experience and was reserved for party favorites. This man was someone important.

Pavel nodded and reached for one.

Viktor produced a lighter from his coat pocket. "*Zippo*," he said, tossing it in his palm. "Built like a Russian tank, but American."

Yet, instead of using it, he struck a match and held it out, forcing Pavel to lean in for the flame. The flicker cast sharp shadows across Viktor's angular face, illuminating the cold intelligence in his eyes.

"Class games," Pavel thought. "Always cause for caution."

Then, with an air of nonchalance, the man tossed the book of matches toward Pavel as if they were beneath him.

Pavel caught them reflexively against his chest. He nodded his thanks but remained cautious. Overconfidence was often the mark of a fool—but sometimes, it belonged to a man who knew precisely what he was doing.

He took a slow drag, the sharp bite of the tobacco pulling him back to memories of long nights in a dim tavern cellar, vodka warming his throat, laughter echoing in the smoky air from black market Belomor Kanal's.'

"My name is Viktor," the man said in Russian. "I arrived today. And you are?"

"Pavel Nikitin," he replied, inhaling again. "Welcome to London, Comrade Viktor. The Luftwaffe's favorite target."

"How often do they bomb?"

"Nightly," Pavel said, exhaling. "Factories, mostly or until two nights ago. Moscow has provided our location to avoid being a target.

Viktor smiled. "And what is it you do at the embassy, Pavel, that keeps you here at this hour when you might be home enjoying a dull Moscow report and a glass of something stronger?"

Viktor reached into his coat. Pavel tensed slightly.

Viktor cut off Pavel's answer by flipping open a small leather wallet and holding it up for effect. The bright red and gold emblem of the NKVD glinted from the lamplight. Three stars.

Pavel read the name beneath it: Colonel Viktor Grigoryevich Krivitsky.

Immediately, he straightened, moving off the edge of his desk to stand at attention.

Viktor smirked. "Please," he said, gesturing to the chair. "It's late. I've always believed that formality should retire with the sun." He took the visitor's seat himself. "Now, tell me—what exactly are your duties at the London bureau?"

"I'm a security officer."

"And you report to?"

"Comrade Yuri Ivanovich Stakova. Officially, he's the military liaison to the British. Unofficially, he's station chief."

"Was today part of an assignment?"

Pavel hesitated. The man was pressing too hard.

"Yes, a routine matter," he answered cautiously. "I monitor one of our resident officers. I doubt it would be of any interest to you."

Victor said, "I understand Watson is working on obtaining information on the cipher machine that the British may use to decode German messages. This program is a big issue in Moscow Center, so it's not a bother. Is there such a machine?" Viktor asked.

Pavel again became very cautious. "Enough information exists from several sources to believe the Hatcher family might be assisting somehow. However, we've never obtained any solid evidence. Watson has managed to marry the Hatcher daughter but has produced nothing of value other than stories of his previous female conquests while being paid to sleep with a beautiful woman. Thomas Watson is completely unreliable and a pain to everyone. He lives his life like a circus in which he substitutes sleight of hand and illusion for reality."

Viktor exhaled, looking past Pavel in thought, "Why has Yuri not been able to run the operation with better results? He's supposed to be a pro, but it makes me ask: Does he know what he's doing?"

"Comrade Stakova is excellent at his job. Obtaining results has been difficult because Watson is only interested in games and money. There's also the real possibility that this machine doesn't exist."

"Well, my friend, unfortunately for Comrade Stakova, he should have answered at least that question by now. Anyway, priorities have changed with the invasion eminent, and with that comes reorganization."

"What kind of reorganization?"

"You'll know soon enough and in good order. You were in a hurry to make a call. May I know what it was about?"

Pavel, now sitting, tapped the end of his cigarette on the ashtray, taking measure of his following words. "Yes, I was reporting some observations to Comrade Stakova that I felt couldn't wait until morning."

"Then it must be of interest and…," Viktor paused for an uncomfortable length of time.

Pavel felt the pressure of silence and shifted nervously in his chair. The man clearly outranked him, and rank was everything in the Russian Republic. Yuri wouldn't be happy at the intrusion, and Pavel knew either way, he held a losing hand.

Viktor, schooled in the game of intimidation, knew it was working. He said, "I'll meet with Comrade Stakova shortly and could carry your message in person. I would prefer it that way. I would be your personal envoy," he added, smiling.

Again, Pavel felt the noose tighten. "Well, the current arrangement has me reporting…"

"*Pavel*," Viktor spat out.

His voice startled Pavel.

Viktor said, "The current arrangement is exactly why I'm here. It is part of the problem and not the solution."

The man's credentials, coupled with the curt manner and energy in this statement, left no doubt Pavel was in over his head. The Byzantine methods of Soviet security services were, by design, beyond understanding, and his best response was precisely the one he gave.

"Yes, Comrade Colonel."

Calm returned to Viktor's voice, "So, now that we're of one mind, what was this news that couldn't wait?"

"Last week, Watson asked Comrade Stakova for more money. Yuri refused to consider it and pushed Watson to get results. Since then, we've increased surveillance on both Watson and his wife. The original agreement was extremely generous, so we viewed additional requests skeptically. Watson wasn't happy, very unhappy, you might say. Today, I followed them from their house in Amersham into the countryside, where they had a picnic somewhere off the road. I tried to get as close as possible, but it wasn't easy. I managed to hear Watson say he was going to Bletchley Park tomorrow, but I didn't get the entire conversation."

Pavel continued, "Watson is very independent and clever, and being unhappy could be contacting the British to tell them what he knows, if anything, about the decoder. He's unstable enough to blackmail the British and resourceful enough to make it sound like he's a patriot. However, a catastrophic alternative would be that he tells the British he's spying for us, thus putting the entire Soviet presence in the country at risk just before the invasion. The British could very well throw us out or severely restrict our operations. Even if I'm wrong, this is something Yuri should know."

Viktor's political senses came to the forefront in a rush, and he could feel his eyes grow large. This officer had just presented a once-in-a-career opportunity to provide heroic service to his country and, more importantly, reap the rewards. This was precisely the type of situation Moscow Center had feared when they ordered Yuri to eliminate Watson and return home. Viktor knew the instructions in the directive presented by Joseph. Moscow thought Stakova had spent too much time in the field and could no longer count on his complete allegiance to the State. They were calling him back to a desk job or worse.

Viktor knew his uncle's position within the Central Committee would insist he carry out his orders without interpretation. Nevertheless, before him was a potentially grave situation. Watson was obviously dangerous and needed to be stopped quickly. There was no doubt. Knowing Watson had definite plans, Viktor had reason to act independently, and only one other person knew anything. If he worked quickly, he could eliminate Watson before his predecessor had the chance, making Yuri appear slow in reacting and Viktor taking the initiative in a dangerous situation. Moscow would view this decisive action as having averted a very public foreign policy embarrassment that could damage its espionage capability for years.

These weren't exactly his orders, so there was an element of risk and failure, but it was worth taking. A lesser bureaucrat would leave well enough alone, but Viktor was an experienced field operative. He could feel the rush.

"Surely," Viktor thought, "Watson, out of caution and feeling the increased pressure for results, wouldn't be stupid enough to return to his house." He decided that any attempt to eliminate Watson had to occur at Bletchley. It was the only place he could count on Watson being at a specific place and time. Viktor considered contacting the Center but knew a decision would never arrive in time. Everything from the Center came after the nightly shots of vodka and 'entertainment' provided by the State, so accurate decisions never emerged until late morning. Bletchley wouldn't be easy, but reports were that security was intentionally light to avoid scrutiny. Anyway, he'd completed field tasks of greater difficulty before. "No risk, no gain," he thought. Besides, three of the officers he'd previously sent into the country were without identification and were expendable. The other two were to fill out his new staff. It was a decision a man in his position must make for the greater good.

He emerged from thought and turned to the officer sitting across from him. "Pavel, for a field officer, your instincts are excellent. I believe your thoughts about Watson are correct. However, there are issues in motion that prevent any obvious solution. For this admittedly vague reason, I want this information kept secret and only acted upon by Yuri and myself.

"Now listen carefully. Before formal notification, I'm informing you that I'm the new station chief replacing Yuri, and you are now reporting to me. I must repeat: Your observations today must remain confidential, and I'll present them to Yuri for our evaluation. Do you understand, Comrade Pavel?"

Saying nothing, Pavel picked up some papers from the pile on his desk while looking at the Colonel.

Viktor said, "Now, as your new superior, I'm reassigning you. You're no longer to be involved in the Watson case."

It surprised Pavel, who said, "But shouldn't we tell Comrade Stakova about the change now, tonight?"

"I said Yuri and I would take care of it. Officer Pavel, your service to your country has been invaluable, and that will certainly make it into my report, but the reassignment is an order. Do nothing to change my mind as to your continued usefulness. You're to take a few days off until I contact you. Leave me your private number, and I'll call you directly with details on your new duties." Viktor added, "Being the excellent officer you are, I'm sure you have surveillance pictures of Watson. I want them and the file."

Pavel quickly saw through the charade but wasn't in a position to control anything. He could disappear into the frozen oblivion if he disobeyed the order and contacted Yuri. A few hundred top generals and State officials disappeared whenever a paranoid Stalin judged them a threat. He knew there was no one to witness the direct order, and if Viktor disappeared tomorrow, Pavel had no evidence to prove his side of the story. It was hopeless.

He jotted down his number on a sheet of paper, reached into his desk's middle drawer, shoved the packet of photos into the case file, and handed them all to the man.

Viktor smiled and light-heartedly said, "Pavel, you must look at this as an opportunity. Take the time to catch up on some personal things because events will soon become frantic, and you'll be happy to have gotten this break in the routine. Now, off to your flat and a good book. We will take care of this, and Watson will no longer be a threat to our operation."

Viktor watched the officer leave the room and wondered if he would follow orders. He had to keep him out of the way but alive to provide the reason for his actions. It was a thin thread from which Pavel hung. Viktor thought, "The officer knows I have him in a box and better be smart enough to follow orders." He would assign an officer to watch Pavel's house in the morning.

Viktor pushed his foot against the desk before him and rocked back in his chair. Things were falling into place as if emanating from a grand design. Viktor was glad that at the last minute, he'd sent his assistant Joseph to the meeting with Yuri, as Viktor wasn't yet ready for Yuri to know who he was. Viktor knew that sending Joseph would make Yuri think he was dealing with a lower-level bureaucrat, not a gifted professional. Things would need to come together quickly for this to work, but he had the assets and was in charge.

Viktor smiled, reached down to the desk for the Belomor Kanals, and pondered his next move.

Chapter Twenty-Five

Uxbridge Operations Building

Two workmen strained above the bunker as they drew the last of the support wires tight, fastening them to one of the many aerials atop the Uxbridge Operations building. A nearby bomb blast had played merry hell with the equipment, throwing the whole lot into disarray for the RAF lads below. The top of the bunder had been planted to look like a park to disguise its real purpose. Thanks to a full moon, they'd worked through the night without lights, mending what they could. Still, whatever their task, it never seemed to be finished fast enough or in the correct order.

Straightening up with a groan, one of the men rolled his shoulders. "That ought to do it, then."

"Aye, just a week behind," the other replied with a smirk.

"Those boys down below seem on edge, don't you reckon?" the first muttered.

"Too right, mate. And that's not good news," the other said, shooting a glance toward the bunker's entrance. "Whatever they do down there, I doubt it helps us if they're feelin' the squeeze."

Martin snorted. "And what the bloody hell do you know about it?"

"I've got me sources, you wazzock," the other said with a knowing grin. "Come on, let's grab a fag and a sit-down before we head in. No one'll be the wiser."

The operations building beneath their boots had changed since the war began. Bulldozers had banked the earth high against its walls, forming steep slopes from ground to roof. They'd laid two feet of reinforced concrete on top, then sandbagged it twice over. Below, sixty feet down a pair of narrow stairwells, lay the operations bunker—a world apart, sealed off from daylight and the passing weeks, where ordinary souls toiled ceaselessly for those they'd never meet and those they cherished beyond measure.

Inside, Edith Bristo, at end of shift, strode towards the watch guard, waiting as he placed a fresh sheet on the clipboard for her to sign off.

Well into his sixties, George still had an eye for what put a little spring in his step. His war work suited him well enough, though his post had dull stretches. But the shift change—ah, that was the best part of his day. Some girls barely noticed him, and some were all chatter, but Miss Bristo always had a word and treated him with uncommon courtesy.

He handed her the clipboard with a smile. "How was today for ya, Miss Bristo?"

"George, you know how I adore it here," she quipped with a wry grin. Then, softening, she sighed. "I'm sorry, that was unkind. It's been tense—worse than usual. Poor communication led to a muddle, and a few German bombers slipped through unchallenged. We'd normally have had our boys on them, but the next shift'll sort it. Well, there you have it, and I've already told you too much." She gave him a playful look. "You might be one of those dashing undercover spies—harmless on the outside but lethal in six ways. Besides George, Mr. Undercover Spy, didn't we discuss you calling me Edith?"

George chuckled. "So we did. Edith, it is."

She eyed him slyly. "Any fish left in that river of yours, George?"

His eyes widened before narrowing in a grin. "If there's a single one left, I'll have it for me own, make no mistake. Got me a secret spot I've kept for forty years. Could bring you one—beauty of a catch," he said, stretching his hands far apart and beaming.

Edith said, "I daresay the fish, and I would be happier if it stayed with its family. But thank you all the same. See you tomorrow."

"A good evenin' to you, Miss B—Edith," he called after her, touching the brim of his cap. Turning he took in the rhythmic manner of her walk as she transformed something very ordinary into something exceptional.

"She looked a little tired today," he mused.

Edith pushed up the sleeves of her blue sweater as she made her way down the corridor, casting a skeptical glance at the tangled mess of cables, tubes, and wires threading along every wall. Lord only knew if half of them led anywhere useful. She was sure only of the pneumatic Lamson tubes—those, at least, she relied on daily.

Crossing the ring corridor, she stepped into the women's cloakroom. Before the war, the girls swore the place had been a museum for pipes. Every variety ran across the ceiling, down the walls, and around the baseboards. At the center stood a battered set of old school lockers, grey as a stormy sea. They were relics of another age, built small long before students had large textbooks to store. But they served well enough for a handbag, a purse, or a pack of cigarettes—just never all three at once.

Edith fished out her bag, locked the door, and tucked the key into her handbag for tomorrow. There are not enough lockers for all four shifts, so access is available on a first-come, first-served basis.

Life had changed for Edith in ways she'd never foreseen, especially these last six months. Once quiet and uncertain of herself, she now found people took to her quickly. She had a knack for conversation, a way of putting others at ease. She counted many as friends—men, too, who often struggled to strike up a word with someone as well-liked as she.

She'd grown up in the East End, the youngest of three, listening while her brothers did the talking. They had her convinced she was nothing special, though, in truth, they were just being brothers. Now, at twenty-three, she'd come into her own. Confidence had replaced self-doubt, and she'd blossomed into a statuesque beauty, a fact not lost on those around her. She carried herself in a way that masked her humble roots, wore her hair to soften her father's full-cheeked inheritance, and wore every dress as though it had been stitched just for her.

Being posted to Uxbridge had been a twist of fate. Her job? Compiling readiness reports for every squadron in the sector. These reports, in turn, determined the day's battle plan and were used by the Air Marshal Portal, who issued commands based on available assets. The trouble was that maintenance crews loathed committing to figures before their repairs were done—especially if the damage ran deep. Over time, Edith won their trust. Her proposal was simple: give their best estimate, and if the plane wasn't ready, she'd strike it from the list at the last moment. No one would be the wiser. It was not strictly by the book, but it worked.

Then came the offer—volunteer for a secret project, sign the Official Secrets Act, which carried rather severe penalties if breached, and take on a role of critical importance. There was no description of the task offered other than the title of a plotter. The work was intense, but women were preferred for their ability to keep calm under pressure. She jumped at the chance. The extra pay meant she could finally move out, sharing a flat with a new friend. The new job, independence, and social life were a world apart from the drudgery her parents had mapped out for her.

According to her family, her future was preordained; she was to become a clerk at a department store, making three pounds a week, which she'd done before the war. She was to continue doing this while waiting for someone to marry her so she could have kids. Somehow, society had decided that most women came up short in the workplace. The male clerks were the only employees allowed to ring up a customer's purchase at the department store because "women were not good at figures."

And then, there was Paddy—a cocky fighter pilot who'd tried his luck at Battley's Pub. Again and again, he plied her with charm, but she refused to give in. Until Janet, her flatmate, had enough. "If you don't say yes," she warned, "I'll ask him myself. Either way, we shouldn't lose him to some loose Piccadilly harlot."

And so, Edith had relented. And from that moment on, her life was never quite the same, as Edith Bristo was in love. However, the guy was much less committed to discussing something as touchy as being "tied to the ground," as the pilots would say. Still, Paddy was kind and considerate, and she knew he had feelings for her, so she'd decided to ride it out and see what might lie ahead.

Chapter Twenty-Six

Uxbridge Operations Building

Edith approached the final security checkpoint on her way home, her coat draped over her arm. Duncan was at the desk, while George was nowhere in sight. Duncan, a perimeter guard, stood in full uniform, pistol holstered at his side—handsome but very much married. Flirting with him was a harmless bit of fun, especially since she wasn't the only girl who did it. Besides, he was all business, the exact opposite of George downstairs, which made him an easy target.

She placed her things on the table without a word. Keeping up his solemn act, Duncan peered into her handbag, gave her coat pockets a cursory pat, and handed them back.

"Find anything of interest, Corporal, sir?" Edith asked with a smirk.

In his best imitation of an authoritative tone, he looked up and said, "Not this time, Edith, but I know you're smuggling something." They both laughed.

She chuckled, pleased to have cracked his stern façade. "Course I am, you silly bloke. I'm smuggling coats." She barely got the words out, pressing a hand over her lips to stifle her laughter.

"Best be careful, Edith. This building isn't the place for joking. People tend to lose their humor once they step inside," he said, nodding toward the exit.

"Oh, come now, Duncan. What else do we have left? We can't let the Jerries take it all." She hesitated before adding, "I know I asked yesterday, but…"

"Yes, I'm still married," he interrupted, grinning. "And you're not serious anyway. Your lot can't stand that I love my wife."

Edith handed back the clipboard with a knowing smile. "That obvious, is it?"

They were still grinning as he opened the steel-reinforced blast door, and she stepped out into the cool evening air.

Edith worked the D shift, and today was supposed to be a special day—her brief respite after four grueling days of six-hour shifts, on and off. Twenty-four hours of freedom. She'd planned to sleep most of it away. But her supervisor had other ideas. Lucy hadn't shown up, and with the increased activity, they needed a full crew.

He had made some calls, only to learn Lucy's street had been hit in last night's bombing. The Home Guard was searching, but the fires were still raging, so the report had been given defense priority. Everyone loved Lucy. His concern was more than professional—it was deeply personal.

Sandbags lined either side of the path leading to the entrance. Edith fished the keys to her well-worn MG out of her handbag, still walking when she heard her name called. Turning, she saw George's stout figure emerge from the gloom, practically bouncing toward her.

"Miss Bristo, there's been a call, and I reckon it's tha' gentleman who rang last week. He's in quite the rush—sayin' it's very important that I bring ya to the phone."

George stopped a few steps short of her, hands on his knees, red-faced and panting as if he'd been running and delivered the entire message in one breath.

"Oh, George, you didn't have to run," Edith said.

George took a wheezing gulp of air. "He sounded serious, so I thought it best." They walked together back inside.

Edith knew Paddy was the only man likely to call. But why? Perhaps to make up for standing her up on one of their rare shared evenings. He'd given a perfectly reasonable excuse, but every woman knew to leave a bit of space around a man's explanations. And yet, most broke that rule more often than they'd admit. She hoped they were building something real, though deep down, she wondered. Was this *that* call? The *I'm going to be busy for a while* call every woman dreaded?

At the security desk, George said, "You can take it on Duncan's phone, that ways you won't have ta sign back in."

"You're a dear, George. Thank you."

"Hay, what about me?" Duncan piped up. "It's my phone, after all."

Edith cast him a teasing look. "We can still share phones, Duncan. After all, we're just dating."

Duncan held up his left hand, waggling his wedding ring in her face.

She waved him off. "Means nothing to homewreckers like me. Besides, I've already pledged my heart to George."

George puffed up with exaggerated pride. "That's right, Duncan. Best give her some privacy."

Meanwhile, Paddy leaned against the phone booth, waiting. The man on the other end had told him to hold, so he figured Edith was still on her way. He exhaled, rubbing a hand over his jaw. The morning's events replayed in his head. Something was wrong; it was taking too long. Maybe this wasn't meant to be. Maybe…

"Hello?"

"Edith, it's Paddy."

She detected something—an edge to his voice, an urgency. Trying to lift the mood, she quipped, "Well, flyboy, couldn't you find another date?"

"No, no, it's not that." He hesitated. "How are you? Can you have dinner tonight? I really mean—can I see you?"

Edith frowned slightly. Paddy was never at a loss for words. "Of course, you can see me. But not tonight—I have to be a little hard to get, you know. Any decent girl would make you jump through a few hoops first."

A few beats of silence. Then, softer, she asked, "Paddy, are you all right?"

"It's been a hell of a day."

"I'm sorry, Paddy. I was only joking." She sighed. "I've got to pull Lucy's shift. No one else can. And by the time you get here…"

Paddy's frustration flared. "My God, Edith, are *you* running the bloody war now? What could possibly be so important? I can't stand this war. What happened to personal lives?"

"Paddy, we've had this discussion. By tomorrow morning, I'll be desperate for sleep. Can we make it a late lunch? I've got twenty-four hours off."

He let out a long, audible breath. "I'm being sent to Castle Bromwich to pick up a new plane. Won't be back till after seven."

"What happened to your plane? Why do you need another?"

"That's part of the story, I suppose. So, tomorrow night, then?"

"Yes, of course. I can meet you halfway—the MG's running fine, and Janet and I have enough petrol coupons. It'll give us more time together. Do you know a place?"

"How about the Fox? It's known for surprises on the menu."

"That sounds wonderful. I can't wait."

"No, Edith. *Seeing you* will be wonderful."

She softened. "I miss you, Paddy. I'm not trying to make things difficult. It's just…"

"I don't know, Edith. Not knowing makes it hard. But tomorrow night will erase all that. Edith…" He trailed off, then took a deep breath. "I want to tell you something—"

But his voice faltered. He took another breath, barely managing, "I'll see you," before hanging up.

Seeing Edith staring at the phone, George wandered back to the desk. "Everythin' all right, Miss?"

She hesitated, then nodded. "Yes, thank you both. That was a very important call."

Duncan tried not to look concerned. "Your friend—he's all right?"

"Yes," she said, smiling, though it didn't quite reach her eyes. The guards let it go.

She stepped outside, drawing in the cool air. "Good night, boys. And thanks again."

Chapter Twenty-Seven

Whitehall
War Rooms

Colville pushed open the door and announced that General Ismay had scheduled a time for a requested report.

"Yes, bring him in," Churchill said.

Ismay entered, took his seat before the Prime Minister's desk, and, with practiced efficiency, unclasped his briefcase, withdrawing a single sheet of paper.

Winston, watching him keenly, remarked, "I once held the firm belief that any report confined to a single page could contain nothing of great fortune nor dire calamity. On that, I have, of course, been proven wrong time and again."

Ismay did not smile. His talent for managing great organizations had never extended to humor, nor did he see much use for it in such matters.

"Prime Minister," he began, his tone formally measured, "the people wish to express their deepest gratitude for your unwavering vigilance in these trying times."

"Ah, that is most kind," Churchill replied. "A pity they do not all work in this building, for it would lighten the burden considerably. It reminds me somewhat of the French nobility, applauded for their generosity in donating their estates to the people—just before the guillotine took its inevitable drop."

Ismay's expression tightened at the imagery but pressed on.

"Per your instructions, I have personally inspected the locations in this Readiness Report. I have spoken with the station commanders, officers, and pilots—save for the Czechs, whose English is scarce but whose appetite for staying in the sky and killing Germans more than compensates.

"You are well aware, sir, that the enemy remains steadfast in their efforts to obliterate our airfields and factories. Of late, their focus has been Biggin Hill. As of this morning, it is barely operational. The toll from yesterday and last night is—thirty-nine RAF aircraft lost in combat, with further losses on the ground. The Luftwaffe, for their part, lost forty-one. But of course, we cannot afford to trade them one for one, for they would win by sheer attrition. The Southeastern airfields—RAF Biggin Hill, Manston, West Malling, Lympne, and Hawkinge—are all undergoing repairs, most expected to be serviceable within twenty-four hours. However, south of the Thames, only two RAF Sector Stations remain operational; the rest are under repair, though they will be restored soon enough."

Churchill cut in, "That puts the Luftwaffe perilously close to their objective. But whether they realize it is another matter entirely."

"Precisely, sir," Ismay nodded. "But it also means we are in no position to take the fight to them. Our fortunes now rest upon the determination of our ground crews to return every salvageable aircraft to the sky.

"As for radar, all stations save the fifth are operational. That one will require seven to ten days for restoration—an unavoidable delay, I'm afraid, given that the A1 radar was hand-built and spare parts are not exactly waiting on shelves.

"Across all quarters, I found an unshaken commitment to duty. The men are acutely aware of what is at stake, yet their resolve is uniform, undaunted despite the circumstances. In sum, sir, your assessment is correct—Göring is nearer than ever to seizing air superiority and securing his place in Hitler's favor."

Prior to this report, Churchill had already taken measures—moving RAF reserve fighters southward from other sectors, though each day, they found fewer airfields to land upon. The shift also left the north vulnerable to an attack from Norway. Meanwhile, the Royal Navy had repositioned reserve units from Scapa Flow, establishing a defensive line off the northern shores. Inland, the Prime Minister had ordered regular Army divisions southward, ready to counter any invasion. Further inland still, defensive lines crisscrossed the countryside—pre-positioned and fully stocked with supplies and ammunition. The one glaring deficiency remained the absence of heavy artillery and tanks, most of which lay rusting on the beaches of Dunkirk. There had been no time to recover from losing an entire expeditionary force's equipment.

Ismay closed his briefcase, resting both hands atop it. "In all of this, sir, I must say—what the men need most is time. Each blow they suffer puts them farther behind, yet they persist. God alone knows that if this war is to be won, it shall be won by ordinary men doing extraordinary things."

Churchill leaned back, fixing him with an appraising eye. "General, as senior statesmen for this beleaguered isle, I would ask that you keep such eloquence confined to this room. Were your words to reach the public ear, I should be relegated to a junior statesman in short order."

Ismay allowed himself a faint grin for the first time but said nothing.

Churchill had finally drawn a lighthearted response from his old friend.

"Let me thank you," he continued, "for your efforts on such short notice. Formal reports, as you know, tend to varnish even the sourest of apples. I required an unvarnished account of our position—and that is precisely what you have given me."

Chapter Twenty-Eight

Margaret's House
Amersham

In the early morning hours, Thomas and Margaret strolled down the quiet street, arm in arm, in relative silence. Margaret had set her mind on breakfast at the pastry shop and was quite pleased that Thomas had agreed to accompany her.

Ahead, a milkman's horse-drawn carriage clattered along, pulling away from a small shop as they passed. He was making his rounds, keeping to the same strict schedule as every other soul in the country. In the countryside, such sights were still commonplace—most available motorized vehicles had long since been pressed into the war effort.

As they neared the bakery, Thomas caught sight of a sign in the window: "More Open Than Usual." It was a wry acknowledgment, both to customers and the world at large, of the indomitable spirit of a people sorely tested.

The Saxby Bakery was familiar to Thomas—he recognized it at once as the very place where, on that first night, he had seen an elderly couple locking up just before Margaret had dragged him to the shelter. That night felt far further in the past than it truly was.

Stewart and Emma Saxby bought the shop years ago to supplement their modest pension, which was never enough to see them through. They had lived in the area for as long as anyone could recall. When stopping by after school, local children called Emma "Mum," proudly presenting bits of anti-aircraft shrapnel scavenged from the streets after the latest raids. Whoever brought in the largest piece won one of Emma's biscuits, leaving the others pouting in disappointment. The children created games from whatever lay at hand—stacking bricks and holding secret club meetings in bombed-out buildings. The bakery was part of their world, a warm and familiar corner of England's daily life.

Thomas immediately took in the display case, and the extensive menu scrawled across the back wall above a small work counter. The usual toasters and mixers lined the space, and in the far-right corner sat an icebox stocked with chilled drinks. Margaret had already mentioned wanting to sit outside, but Thomas wondered what the alternative was, given the shop's modest size. The temperature was hardly a concern; even with the morning chill, August seldom dipped below eleven degrees, and it was generally the finest month of the year.

"Emma, I don't believe you've met my husband, Thomas," Margaret announced. "He never got the chance to stop in before, which is why I always took my things bagged."

"Well now, Mr. Watson," Stewart Saxby said, wiping his hands on his apron, "it's fine to meet you at last. We know almost everyone in Amersham, and now we can count you among 'em."

Thomas nodded, and Mr. Saxby, stepping out from behind the counter, apologetically raised a pair of damp hands. "Just a tick," he said, reaching for a towel and rubbing it before extending a hand toward Thomas.

"Stewart Saxby, sir. A pleasure, truly. 'Bout time, after all this while. I've seen ya in the shelter, but ya never looked much fer conversation."

At this, Mrs. Saxby shot her husband a glance cold enough to curdle milk.

"Well, what d'ya want me to say?" he muttered, unrepentant. Turning back to Thomas, he added, "Weren't ya the one got knocked about when that blast went off?"

"Yes," Thomas admitted. "Though the Service Guard took the worst of it, I think."

"Oh, that'd be Bernie Sheldon," Stewart said, nodding sagely. "Bernie's righ' as rain. Built like a brick wall, tha' one. Enough o' Mum's pastry in 'im ta blunt a tank shell."

He jerked his chin toward his wife in mock deference.

Emma's hand went up in a warning gesture. "That will be quite enough outta you, Mr. Saxby. Mind your manners, if nothing else." She turned to Margaret. "Sorry, love."

Stewart, utterly unbothered, merely shrugged and wore a sheepish grin as though he had no notion what he'd done wrong.

"Mrs. Somerville was in earlier," Emma continued, "said you might be by. That woman's up before the birds, I swear. Now then, what can we do to brighten your morning?"

Thomas, realizing just how hungry he was, rubbed his hands together.

"You've a grand little place here," he said, glancing up at the menu. It boasted an impressive list—Traditional Welsh Cakes from an "Old Saxby Family Recipe," Queen Cakes, Crumpets, and Hot Cross Buns.

Then his eyes landed on Scotch Shortbread Biscuits. The name alone sounded delightful.

"I think I'll have one of those," he said, pointing. "The shortbread biscuits."

He glanced down at the case as Mrs. Saxby retrieved a tray and placed a biscuit on a delicate china plate.

Margaret, meanwhile, had gone up on her toes, craning her neck to peer toward the back of the bakery.

Emma caught the movement at once. "Margaret, and just what is it you're lookin' for? As if I don't know."

"Oh, I just wondered if you had any strawberry turnovers—perhaps they're just not out yet? They don't have to be fresh, mind you, but—"

Emma cast a glance at her husband, the expression of a mother humoring a child's breakfast request. Seeing Stewart nodding proudly, she said, "Well, as it happens, Daddy made a few for us this morning, with berries right out of his Victory Garden."

"Made 'em meself," Stewart added, stepping up to the counter with evident satisfaction.

"Oh, in a few more years, you'll be a full partner in the business," Emma remarked dryly.

Margaret hesitated. "Oh, I wouldn't want to take yours. That wouldn't be right."

"Oh, don't you fret," Emma said, waving her off. "We're done eatin', and they won't last unless we put 'em in the icebox. And then they wouldn't be fresh, now would they?"

Margaret, beaming, clasped her hands together and bounced on her toes.

"Splendid, Mum—just splendid. It's going to be a good day."

Chapter Twenty-Nine

An Unexpected Visitor

Outside, Thomas and Margaret arranged their teacups and the steaming pot on a small round table. They sat, ate, and talked—talking had never been an issue between them. A topic of interest was always within arm's reach, something to seize and dissect fervently. Each exchange revealed more of this captivating woman, and with every revelation, Thomas still wanted more.

"What's that mind of yours up to?" Margaret inquired, tilting her head. "You've drifted off."

He set his teacup down, his gaze steady upon her. "Have I told you I love you today?"

Margaret leaned back, smoothing her hair behind her ear as she considered, then rested a thoughtful finger upon her chin. "Well, given that we finally got to sleep well after midnight, I'd say yes, Thomas, you've quite covered that for the day. However, if you truly loved me, you'd abandon this ridiculous notion of Bletchley today."

He gave the slightest shake of his head in response, and Margaret, pouting, propped her chin on one hand, her elbow resting heavily upon the table. Without a word, Thomas reached across and found her other hand, giving it a quiet, reassuring squeeze. He was just about to speak when a looming presence interrupted them. A man had appeared at their table, materializing from nowhere, standing uncomfortably close.

In his mid-fifties, the figure bore a strong face, broad and fleshy, with a build that suggested years of indulgence rather than labor. He was clad in a London Fog overcoat, shoes so impeccably polished they mirrored the pavement, and a fedora tipped just enough to make a statement. Beyond his attire, he carried himself with an air of authority, his stance far too intrusive for casual conversation.

"Well, well," the man declared, his voice too loud. "And who do we have here?"

Margaret tensed; the spell of their morning shattered. Thomas noted the discomfort in her face at once. The man's accent—something off about it. It's not quite British. As Thomas stood, his metal chair scraped and then toppled backward, the clatter jarring in the morning air.

"Now, now," the man said smoothly. "No need to go anywhere just yet, and you're certainly not about to do anything foolish."

His hands were buried in the pockets of his overcoat. Slowly, deliberately, he withdrew one hand—the left—while the right remained concealed, the implication unmistakable.

Margaret glanced anxiously at the pastry shop, but Mr. and Mrs. Saxby had disappeared into the back, unaware or unwilling to be drawn into whatever was unfolding.

"We need to have a word," the man stated evenly, his eyes fixed upon Thomas.

A thief? No, not a common one, at least. The cut of his suit and calculated confidence didn't match.

Thomas exhaled. "Look, if this is a robbery, we've little to offer. You can take what we have."

The man scoffed. "Oh, I beg to differ. You've rather a lot to offer."

"You're mistaken," Thomas replied coolly.

"That's quite enough for now," the stranger said, dismissing further protest. He jerked his head toward the Stag Pit with an oversized door and an air of secrecy. "Come along. Let's continue this discussion somewhere more... private."

Thomas exchanged a glance with Margaret, then gestured subtly toward the man. Together, they rose and followed.

As they crossed the street, Thomas noticed the man had a slight limp. It didn't seem to hinder him, but something else nagged at Thomas. Why was the man leading the way if this were a simple robbery?

"Why a pub?" he asked the man.

"The back room," came the curt reply. "Memory slipping, is it? Explains a lot."

Thomas let that pass.

A weathered sign dangled from the pub's door—*Closed*—with a shade drawn inside. Their escort knocked sharply. "Come on, Evan, open up. Need the card room for a bit."

He rattled the knob for effect, more show than expectation, then knocked again. The shade twitched aside, and a suspicious eye peered out before the door eased open.

The barman squinted. "Yuri, Thomas—what in bloody 'ell are you doin' 'ere at this hour?"

"A favor, Evan. Just a favor," Yuri answered smoothly.

Thomas took that in. *Yuri*. The name settled uneasily in his mind.

Thomas concluded the big man must be someone out of Margaret's past, and it was apparent the visit wasn't social. Thomas looked at Margaret, trying to glean some message, and got nothing.

Evan hesitated.

Yuri leaned in slightly. "Come now; you do recall that shipment of Johnnie Walker I so graciously navigated past customs?"

Evan exhaled through his nose, then opened the door fully, stepping back behind the bar.

"Morning, Lem," Yuri said in passing to an older man propped against a mop. Lem gave a brief nod, his eyes wary.

Evan resumed wiping down the bar, glancing at Margaret. "Well, now, it's early, but I'd say 'tis about time you gents brought someone to brighten the place. Was startin' to wonder, what with all that time ye spend holed up in the back room…" He chuckled, then caught Margaret's expression and cleared his throat. "Ah—beggin' your pardon, Miss."

Margaret said nothing.

Yuri pulled out a chair and gestured for her to sit. "I think it best if you remain here while Thomas and I have a little chat." He smiled faintly. "Oh, and Margaret—do stay put, won't you? I'd hate to disrupt your morning with any… unpleasantness." His gaze flicked to Thomas.

Margaret's glare could have cut glass, but she sat, arms folded tightly.

"Drink?" Evan offered.

"Juice," Yuri said. "And something for the lady."

Margaret held his gaze a moment longer before dropping heavily into the chair.

Yuri turned his attention back to Thomas. "Shall we?"

Without another word, he led Thomas down a narrow corridor with a door to the restroom on the right and another facing it. Yuri pushed open the left door and motioned Thomas inside.

The room was dim and thick with the stale scent of smoke and beer.

A round card table stood at its center, surrounded by chairs.

Above, a lone bulb cast its meager glow. The barkeep followed them, dropping off the classes and ensuring the door closed on his way out. Back in the main room, Margaret watched Evan return behind the bar. She stood. "I think we're being robbed," she said. "Can't you call the police?"

Evan sighed. "Robbed? Don't reckon so, Miss. Those two have been coming here for the better part of—" He glanced at Lem.

"Six months," Lem supplied.

Margaret didn't like that answer. "If you won't, I can have someone here before they are out."

Evan raised his hands in surrender. "Miss, I run my business, feed my family, and try to survive this war. But I'd strongly advise you to stay put."

Margaret locked eyes with him, her jaw tight. Then, with a huff of frustration, she picked a chair and sat back down in a very unlady-like manner.

Meanwhile, inside the back room, Yuri removed his coat and draped it over a chair. "Now then," he said, settling into a seat. "You've landed yourself in a bit of a mess, my friend."

Thomas remained silent, irritation stirring beneath his skin.

Yuri studied him for a moment. "Something's… off. You're too calm. Normally, you'd be spinning excuses a mile a minute." He leaned forward. "So tell me—why have you failed to contact your handler for two days? That's not good for you, Thomas."

Thomas's exhale was slow and measured. "I'm afraid you'll have to start from the beginning. Because I haven't the faintest idea who you are."

Yuri laughed loudly, shaking his head. He leaned back in his chair, his vest strained against his oversized waist. "You don't know what?" Swinging forward on the chair, he grabbed the glass before him. While looking at Thomas over the top of the glass, Yuri managed a chuckle and a sip of apple juice simultaneously. He made a face, "I thought you English had beer for breakfast?"

"I wouldn't know."

"That's good, very good. I never thought you had a sense of humor, but a guy in your position should get to the point."

"Okay, just what's my position? It's certainly my first time being robbed by a gentleman who frequents Seville Row."

"Сократите дерьмо or, as you say, cut the crap, Watson. I'm the only friend you have right now. You're persona non grata in the rest of the world. You know, that's not bad English for a dumb Russian on his third language. Did I tell you I also speak Italian? I spent eight years in Italy, a great country with beautiful women and magnificent food. It's a bad combination as the women get round like Russian women. The problem is that Russian women keep getting round. It's a curse."

"Well, you'll have to stick with English. I'm afraid I'm not as well-traveled as some in this room," Thomas said. "Look, I don't know you. I don't know what to say. I think I hit my head. I don't remember, and you'll have to take that for what it is."

The personality change sparked Yuri's curiosity. Thomas never addressed a question head-on. He always managed to wiggle out the side and change the subject if it didn't suit him.

"You remember where you live. You remember that very… how should I say it?... strong woman you charmed into marriage. By the way, this woman," Yuri said, motioning toward the other room, "is special and not a normal woman. Italian women throw things if they don't get their way. Russian women starve you to death. This woman convinces you she's right. I've heard these conversations."

Thomas didn't like Margaret pulled into whatever was going on. "Why would you care?" he said.

"You don't think we would pay handsomely for your services and not watch you?

Thomas looked at the man and said, "Look, I don't remember."

Yuri became very serious. "It's a lie, a stupid lie." He stared at Thomas and said, "You're mine, Mr. Thomas Watson, and I have to decide what to do with you, so you better give me a reason to be your friend."

"What's your name?" Thomas said, knowing he had heard it earlier.

"Are you serious?" Yuri bellowed.

"Look, are you going to tell me or not?" Thomas said, his voice a little higher than before.

"What a stupid question. Yuri, of course. Enough of the games."

"Yuri, I need you to tell me exactly what trouble Thomas is in before we can get anywhere."

"This is a joke with words. You're Thomas. Why are you wasting time?"

"Will you tell me, or will we continue in these circles?"

"You speak of Thomas, yourself, like you're not here."

"Look, answer the question, will you? What did Thomas do to make him persona non grata?"

"Okay, for your entertainment, I'll play this little game. Time is short, and there's a need for certain informations. Thomas is, I mean, you're, an officer working for the NKGB."

Thomas said, "The Russian Intelligence, a resident spy?" His voice rose as he spoke.

"Yes, the same agency that paid all the money for informations about a secret project Hatcher Ltd. might be working on for the government. You made the agreement, took the money, and broke the deal. Now, the way I have it figured, you're either tired of living, or you just got a better deal from MI-5 to uncover your case officer, which isn't good for Yuri. So now, you may have both of us in trouble. Things aren't in a good way, Mr. Watson. You've been absent from your work for over two days without informing us, which has raised some questions."

Thomas worked to comprehend what he was hearing.

"What's curious, Mr. Thomas Watson, is that you're not acting like a man on the run. I watched the two of you before I interrupted your morning meal. To be honest, you act more like a man in love. The supposed hit you took must have been a mind-altering event, as you've never acted in such a way to your Margaret or been so direct with me. It's all for the best, as she was much too good for the old you."

Still trying to grasp the situation, Thomas said, "So I'm a spy? I don't remember that, and you'll have to believe me. I walked out of a bathroom, married to Margaret. Almost everything else is blank."

"Almost?"

"*All.*"

"Enough," Yuri said gruffly. "I don't believe you, but it doesn't matter. I can help you, but you don't see it. You need to give me all the informations you have, or I'll leave, and you're on your own. I need it now before it doesn't matter and the invasion takes care of everything. Lists will be exchanged; people will disappear." Yuri slammed the table for emphasis.

Thomas shot back with equal energy. "There won't be an invasion. Herr Hitler won't conquer England. I'm certain of it."

It was the first pause in the conversation. There was an unusually long silence as the energy between the men dissipated, and Yuri tried to size up the man in front of him. Things were becoming confusing. He leaned back again, put his hands in his pockets, and, in a normal tone, said, "Oh, I see. You'll guarantee this, but you're only an army of one. So it is then the choice is yours."

Yuri stood up, took his coat, and carefully laid it on the table. Looking into the small wide mirror at the top of the coat rack, he became enamored with adjusting his hat. Satisfied with the fit, he stepped back casually as if they had been discussing the weather.

Thomas looked at the coat half hanging off the table's edge, creasing right through the pockets. "Where's the gun?" He asked.

Yuri was surprised at the question. "Thomas, I told you before. I'm trained in firearms but have seldom ever had to use one. I wouldn't unless there was no other alternative. In fact, I'm surprised the trick worked. Other people use guns. For me, there are other ways, better ways. I'm a diplomat, not a thug."

Thomas wanted to establish some defense and said, "Now, that's one thing I remember. I think I know my way around guns." The thought felt true for some reason, so he went with the threat.

Yuri said, "That's a surprise. How could that be? When we struck our agreement, I asked you if you needed a gun, and you said you wouldn't know how to use it."

"Sorry, I don't know the answer to that."

"Watson, you've always been a strange man—very strange. Today, it appears, is no different. Life is strange, but I tell you, as this case progressed, it became undeniable that even if you had truly wanted Margaret Hatcher, she deserved better than you. But now she won't have you, so it doesn't matter."

Yuri shook his head, pulled back the latch, and opened the door. "It's over; you've made your choice."

Chapter Thirty

Thomas is a Spy

Yuri stepped from the cramped little room where the hushed words had been exchanged and strolled back into the pub's main hall.

"Evan, my thanks. We're square again."

Sitting at a small table, Margaret rose to her feet with something close to defiance.

"You see, Mrs. Watson," Yuri said, turning slightly as Thomas emerged from the dim hallway, "here he stands, safe and sound."

"Margaret, everything is fine," Thomas assured her.

She fixed Yuri with an unforgiving glare. "Don't lie to me, Thomas."

Yuri chuckled, unable to suppress his amusement. As he approached, his voice still tinged with mirth, he said lightly, "You know, Mrs. Watson—Margaret, if I may—I watch many American gangster films. James Cagney, now there's a man who understands power, strength, and how to take what he wants. To him, you'd be what they call a 'tough cookie.'" He laughed heartily. "Not a bad—how do you say it—style?"

"Quality," Margaret corrected.

"Oh yes, quality. Not a bad quality, especially considering what's ahead for your country."

Yuri studied her for a moment. He had grown to admire this woman and reached out a hand, but Margaret stepped back. Accepting the rebuff with a respectful nod, he touched the brim of his hat with two fingers. "A good day to you, madam." And with that, he strode out the door.

The sky above greeted Yuri as he stepped outside, pale and indifferent. If it were fair, it might explain why things remained so confounding even after meeting this man. Instead, the air was thick with unease, and Yuri could sense the storm brewing. He crossed the street and walked up Chiltern Avenue toward Amersham Station.

Moscow had sent a man into his domain without his knowledge. They had even dangled before him the promise of a comfortable retirement—a dacha, a pension, a peaceful ending. But things were not falling neatly into place. This Thomas Watson, a mere nuisance initially, had evolved into something else entirely. A mystery. He knew far more than he let on, or he knew nothing. Either way, he was dangerous, and Yuri had no taste for unknown variables in his double life.

The scene was set. Tomorrow, it would all come to a head—or would it?

Thomas and Margaret watched Yuri's departure, a mixture of confusion and awe settling over them.

Hands planted firmly on her hips, Margaret turned to Thomas. "Now is the part in the gangster picture where you tell me, quick and sharp, what in blazes that was all about."

Thomas took her by the arm and said, "First, we must get out of here."

He reached into his pocket, but Evan, the barkeep, waved him off. "You're on account, Mr. Watson. There's no need for that. Besides, I'm even now."

"Account?" Margaret thought. She glanced at Thomas, her eyes demanding answers. They stepped into the street, and Thomas said, "Let's wait until we're back at the house."

He needed time to unravel what had just transpired. That morning, he had been speaking to Margaret of things yet to come. Then a Russian appeared, declaring him a spy who had reneged on a deal and was now in dire straits. Old Thomas, new Thomas—it hardly mattered. The problem had landed at his feet all the same. Whatever fate awaited him because of the old Thomas, one thing remained clear—he had to get to Bletchley. Britain's fate depended on it.

***

Margaret sat stiffly on the couch, one leg crossed over the other, her foot swinging in a steady, agitated rhythm. She was waiting for an explanation, and from the look in her eyes, her patience was wearing thin.

"Margaret," Thomas began carefully, "the man said I was a spy."

She blinked, utterly dumbfounded. "A what?"

"He said I was a spy. And that you had no idea. He claimed I was paid handsomely to pass on information about your father's work for the government."

Margaret stared, her expression unreadable. The silence that followed was the loudest thing in the room. Margaret Watson, for once, was speechless.

"Margaret," Thomas said gravely, "why did you marry him?"

Her eyes snapped to his. "We discussed this at the picnic." Her tone was clipped. "It was after my mother, and I had the most dreadful row imaginable. I wanted to spite her, and marrying Thomas was the surest way to do it."

Arms folded, foot still swinging, she continued, "At first, he doted on me, catered to my every whim. Exactly what I needed at the time. And I didn't tell him everything either. He didn't know I was a 'Hatcher'—whatever that was supposed to mean. Not that it meant much at the time. I only let him into that circle after Mother and I patched things up."

Thomas exhaled. "I'm sorry, Margaret. But I think he knew exactly who you were."

"I don't believe that. He never gave a damn about my past. That's what I liked about him. I had walked away from being a Hatcher. I was ready to leave it all behind. He never pushed to know." She paused, frowning. "Though … he did change. We were getting through it. I thought we were making progress when, well"—she threw her hands up—"you walked out of the bloody bathroom."

"Margaret," Thomas said gently, "he married you for the information."

"No," she shot back. "It was my idea to get married."

Thomas spoke carefully. "Either way, he took the Russian's money. He was supposed to pass along the intelligence, but he stalled. They kept pressing, and now I—I haven't reported anything. So they've grown suspicious."

Margaret's face darkened.

"That man said my time was short," Thomas continued, "but he didn't say how short. For now, I think we're safe. But this complicates everything. My priority remains unchanged—I have to get this information to Churchill. The rest we can handle later. At least, I hope we can."

Margaret's jaw tightened. "Are you still going to Bletchley?"

Thomas sighed. "If you have a better idea, now's the time."

She folded her arms tighter. "No. And you're not going alone. I'm coming with you."

Thomas groaned. "Margaret, be serious. It's hard enough getting myself through the door—let alone with an entourage."

"An entourage?" she snapped. "I assure you, Watson, I am no one's entourage."

Thomas pinched the bridge of his nose. "Margaret, if you stay behind, it's safer. Less attention is drawn to me."

She narrowed her eyes. "That's a trick, and you know it."

"Will it work?"

"Damn you, Thomas," she muttered. "You know the only thing that would keep me here is your safety."

"I know," he admitted. "But I don't want to be hurt either. I'll find a cab—safer than the train."

And so, Thomas left for Bletchley alone. Margaret, outmaneuvered, sat fuming. Something about all of this sat wrong.

As she reflected, her thoughts drifted to the other Thomas. How had she not seen through him? She had led the marriage, but looking back, he had followed her every cue. It all made sense now—his willingness to accept her unusual demands, even the hurried nuptials.

"What was Daddy working on that interested the Russians?" she wondered.

A sick feeling settled over her. The old Thomas had deceived her, and it made her feel unclean. But the new Thomas … that was different. He was different. And despite the chaos, one thing was clear—what they had now was real. It was love, pure and simple.

Chapter Thirty-One

Yuri Thinks He Knows

Yuri left Amersham Station, bound for the embassy. He barely noticed the world around him, his thoughts consumed with making sense of his meeting with Watson. It wasn't until the doors slid shut and the train pulled away from Chalfont & Latimer that he realized how lost in thought he had been.

He glanced about the carriage as he waited.

"Approaching Chorleywood," a clipped voice intoned over the speaker.

As the train doors opened, the station master barked, "Mind the gap, people; move along."

Yuri lingered, allowing the departing passengers to clear before stepping onto the platform. After a few paces, he turned back, slipping a hand into his coat as though searching for something. In truth, he was watching—cataloging. A novice might make the mistake of hanging about too conspicuously, pretending to be absorbed in some mundane task. A professional, however, knew that losing a tail was preferable to exposing one. Satisfied that no one had lingered behind, Yuri strode up the stairs and out of the station, melting into a small throng of Londoners carrying parcels, bags, and a sense of purpose. For them, this was just another morning during the Blitz. For Yuri, it was the beginning of something uncertain.

Trained to avoid the unknown, he bristled at its presence now. His mind worked quickly, the pieces falling into place. He had decided that Watson was a double-agent, but he likely wasn't working directly for the British. That placed the Hatcher woman in grave danger. If Watson's loyalty was only to profit, it would explain the absence of political conviction. More likely, Watson's true objective was to discover what intelligence the Russians sought, assess how much they already knew, and then sell the information to the British. And the British, no doubt, would pay handsomely for anything regarding the elusive Hatcher machine. That would explain why Watson had been ineffective in gathering intelligence—he wasn't genuinely trying.

Yuri had expected this of the Thomas he had recruited. But the Thomas he had encountered that morning was an entirely different man. Something was off, and he needed to uncover what it was.

Regardless, Moscow Center had no patience for loose ends with an invasion looming. They wanted Watson removed. More than that, they wanted the London station run by someone fresh from the new Soviet school, steeped in Stalin's doctrine, with unwavering loyalty to the man who called himself Uncle Joe. Stalin was purging once more, clearing house, and Yuri had no illusions about where he stood. Just days ago, Trotsky had been assassinated. Nearly all of Stalin's original government was gone. The military had been gutted. The Foreign Service had been spared—mostly. But Yuri's file painted him as too independent, too prone to thinking for himself. He knew what awaited him back in Moscow. There would be no dacha, no comfortable desk job.

His survival depended on discovering whether Watson was indeed playing both sides. If Watson disclosed Russian intelligence to the British, the Soviets would have him killed before he reached Glasgow. Yuri needed to maintain his façade, report to the embassy as ordered, and keep Moscow from turning its gaze toward him. He might avoid his demise if he could convince them he followed orders.

Reaching the street, he scanned his surroundings. Barely twenty feet away, he spotted what he needed and strode toward it, fishing in his pocket as he went. The red wooden telephone booth stood waiting. He stepped inside, deposited his coins, and dialed a number from memory. He memorized every case number and every contact. He kept nothing on his person that could be used against him if searched. It had saved his life in Italy when he had walked out of a police station unscathed, his diplomatic immunity intact despite the authorities' certainty that he was involved with a deported national.

Yuri pressed the receiver to his ear.

Meanwhile, Margaret sat in her parlor, her mind still wrestling with her decisions. The thought of waiting idly for Thomas was unbearable, and she had to act. She crossed to the hall tree, snatched up her coat and scarf, and moved toward the door with a determined stride. Just as she reached for the handle, the telephone rang. She hesitated, staring at it, letting the double ring sound twice before lifting the receiver.

"Hello," she said cautiously.

"Margaret, this is Yuri, the person that you—"

"I know who you are," she cut in.

“Well then, is Thomas there? I must speak with him. It’s urgent,” Yuri's voice carried a sense of duty and urgency.

Margaret hesitated. “He’s not available.”

“Not available or not there?”

“And why should I tell you?”

“If my instincts are correct, this concerns all of us. Put him on the telephone.”

Margaret gripped the receiver tightly. She had no idea where the Russian was, nor did she want to be within his reach. “He stepped out. He’ll be back shortly.”

Yuri was not easily deceived. Margaret Watson was sharp, and he knew full well that Thomas was nowhere near. “Margaret, Thomas is in danger. You need to tell me where he is. I may be the only one who can help him.”

“You’re lying.”

“No, you’re lying. But it doesn’t matter. You’ve no choice because either I can protect him, or I am the one hunting him. Either way, I will find him. And you will tell me because you love him and wish to keep him safe. Either he’s gone somewhere I don’t know, or he’s at Bletchley Park. I heard you say it as I walked up. Which is it?”

The word Bletchley sent a jolt through her. It shattered the rhythm of their exchange and was not lost on Yuri.

The line went dead.

Yuri stepped from the phone booth and quickly returned to the station. At the ticket counter, he nodded briskly. “Bletchley Station, please.”

The older man behind the counter regarded him sourly. “Well, there’s a Bletchley township with a rail station. That will be a long, unpleasant ride,” he grumbled. He turned, reached for a large, wall-mounted map, and propped it against the bars.

“You’ll need ter start with the Varsity Line connecting Oxford an' Cambridge. It goes through Bletchley. Are yeh sure yeh wan' ter stop there’s not much there i know o'.

Yuri, pressed for time, merely nodded. “Yes. Quickly.”

Buy all your tickets here, an' bob’s your uncle—all that’s left is waitin’ fer the righ' train.”

The clerk clacked at the ticket machine keys three times. The tickets emerged. He handed them to Yuri and then gestured to the platform as a train rolled to a stop.

“That’ll be yours, sir. Bit o' luck, I’d say. Hope the rest o' your day runs that smoothly.”

Yuri hurried aboard and took a seat at the back. As the train lurched forward, he exhaled, his thoughts racing. Luck alone would not untangle what had once been a straightforward intelligence operation.

Chapter Thirty-Two

Bletchley Park

Between Oxford and Cambridge, sixty miles northwest of London lay the township of Bletchley. A minor stop on the route to Birmingham, the industrial heart of the country, it held little significance—except for what transpired behind the walls of the Bletchley estate. The station took its name from the grand estate built by Sir Herbert Leon in 1882, now repurposed by the government in 1938 to house the wartime headquarters of the Government Code and Cipher School. The location connecting two of England's best universities was no accident.

The estate boasted a stately Tudor mansion and numerous outbuildings—stables, a groom's house, a dairy, and a spacious car park—all hastily converted into offices starting in August 1939. As the demand for cryptographic work exploded, the estate grew, with rows of fabricated huts springing up to accommodate the overflow. This peculiar collection of buildings, the occupants relocated from London, became the nerve center of British intelligence.

Bletchley remained unremarkable, except for the extraordinary work unfolding at Bletchley Park. Within these unlikely quarters, mathematical and technological minds converged, decoding German transmissions and laying the groundwork for one of modern history's most significant advancements. Long after the war, when the names of decisive battles became public, this hidden place would be recognized as a battleground in its own right—where the war was won.

Here, Thomas had arrived, determined to bring his information to the right people. After much persuasion, a reluctant cab driver had agreed to bring him from Amersham. Thomas had him drop him at the station to ease suspicions, which only heightened the man's doubts.

Paying his fare, Thomas passed the ticket counter, glancing left. Above the tree line, the chimneys of the mansion loomed. Directly across Sherwood Street, a worn footpath led through a small wood—no more than two hundred yards, he guessed—to the Bletchley Park grounds.

Crossing the road, he entered the path, the trees quickly enclosing him in a hush of nature. Halfway through, the world of war and secrets momentarily faded, the green canopy offering a rare moment of peace. He slowed, breathing it in. But the path, like all things, reached its end. Wilton Avenue stretched ahead, leading directly to the mansion gates.

Approaching the entrance, he took in the grand, if somewhat faded, Tudor archway. The elegance of its past was still visible, though years of government use had left it in disrepair. Surprisingly, there were no guards, no imposing fences, nothing to suggest the magnitude of the work done here.

Inside, just beyond the entrance, the Music Room had been repurposed into a modest reception area. Three tall windows, their panes crisscrossed with tape against bomb blasts, faced the front. Once lined with fine bookshelves, the far wall now housed a haphazard array of military cabinets. The silk wallpaper, still intact, bore the weight of government occupation. Three stark military-issue chairs sat under its grand coffered ceiling and, dominating the room, a large metal desk.

Behind it sat a woman of rigid composure, her hair in a neat perm, rimless spectacles perched on her nose. She spoke crisply into a telephone, feigning indifference while scrutinizing his every move. As she set the receiver down, she tidied a stack of papers, sliding them purposefully into a drawer as if to shield them from his view.

"Can I help you?" she asked.

"Yes, I believe so." Thomas thought for a moment and said, "My name is Dunning. I'm looking for a Mr. Alan Turing."

She repeated the name, her brow furrowing in thought. Reaching for a frayed manila folder, she flipped through the pages, struggling to find what she sought. After a moment, she looked up. "I'm very sorry, Mr. Dunning. There's no Alan Turing listed here at the academy. Do you know his department?"

"No, I don't. And I wouldn't expect you to grant me an audience with him directly, given the nature of his work. I'm more than willing to undergo an interview regarding my intentions. I have information that may be of significant use to Mr. Turing's efforts."

She did not waver in her duty to keep outsiders at bay. A true Praetorian Guard, she stood, resting her hands lightly on the blotter. "Well, in the absence of more information, I can offer very little, Mr. Dunning. If there's nothing else, I can summon you a cab, or the railway is a short walk away."

Thomas knew it wouldn't be easy. No one just walked in and spoke to the minds behind the war's deepest secrets. His only advantage was starting early. A request like his could take weeks, even months.

"No, but I do appreciate the offer, Miss—?"

She hesitated, then relented. "Mrs. Stimson."

"Well, Mrs. Stimson, at the risk of being a bother, I must insist on speaking to someone. The matter is of the utmost importance."

His insistence drew an icy stare, the sort that belonged to a schoolmistress of the strictest order. Arms crossed, she said in clipped tones, "Mr. Dunning, I could ask you to leave. But that won't be necessary, will it?"

"You could, Mrs. Stimson. But I won't be leaving until someone assesses my information."

Without another word, he turned and sat in a well-worn chair, reaching for a magazine.

For twenty silent seconds, she studied him, her fingers tapping the desk. Finally, she spun on her heel and disappeared through a side door, closing it with deliberate force.

Fifteen minutes later, she returned, her composure intact. "I said there was little I could do. However, I have found someone willing to speak with you. Follow me."

She led him through a side corridor, out of the mansion, and across the grounds to a long, narrow hut. Inside, a dimly lit long hallway stretched ahead, lined with doors bearing simple numbers. Not a soul in sight. After passing five doors, she opened one.

"Please have a seat, Mr. Dunning. Someone will see you shortly."

"Thank you, Mrs. Stimson. You've been most helpful," he said with a knowing smile.

She left without a word. She was not accustomed to losing.

The room was a classic interrogation setting—a single table, two oak chairs, and a bare bulb overhead. A mirror installed on one wall, undoubtedly one-way. Thomas paced, folded his arms, and unfolded them. He knew he was being watched.

After ten minutes, the door creaked open. A slightly built man entered, moving with measured slowness, not out of infirmity but as if his world operated at a different pace. Wire-rimmed spectacles magnified his boyish face.

"Mr. Dunning?" he asked, extending a hand. "Alan Turing. My apologies for the confusion. You see, you can't find anything on a never updated list. I take it you got past our guardian at the desk?"

Thomas shook his hand, eyeing him with quiet suspicion. Through the fog of his memory, he wasn't optimistic that the man looked like Turing.

Thomas said, "Even after all my insistence, I'm surprised you're sitting here."

Turing, appearing somewhat disinterested, nudged the wireframe of his spectacles higher upon the bridge of his nose with a long, slender finger. “Yes, quite possibly,” he said. “However, how precisely may I be of assistance?”

Thomas leaned back in his chair, one hand resting idly upon the table as he studied the man before him—this Mr. Turing. After a measured pause, he said, “I want to help.”

Turing gave a slight nod, already turning back through several well-thumbed pages in a yellowed notebook he had brought along. He paused at a blank one. Reaching into his shirt pocket for a pencil, his brow creased briefly in puzzlement as he inspected the tip with a practiced eye.

Thomas cast a fleeting glance at the mirror, then spoke deliberately. “The war is going badly. There are things I can do to aid the work being done here.”

Another nod from Turing, this time more an acknowledgment than an invitation to continue. He leaned forward and penned the date at the top of the fresh page, saying nothing.

Thomas pressed on, sensing the need to command the man’s attention. “The German high command employs a machine—Enigma—to encrypt orders transmitted to their field commanders. This establishment is engaged in breaking those ciphers, and I have information that may accelerate your efforts.”

Turing settled back in his chair, crossing one leg over the other, and in precise, almost mechanical script, wrote *Mr. Dunning* beneath the date.

“Would you like me to continue?” Thomas asked.

“Oh, yes, quite,” Turing replied. “Do go on, Mr. Dunning.”

This fellow hadn’t the faintest, but there was no turning back now. “The Germans swap one of five cipher rotors in their Enigma machines daily. To decipher intercepted messages efficiently, your machine must be adjusted to accommodate the ever-shifting configurations.”

Thomas paused, gauging the effect of his words. None.

“You’re attempting it with patch cables,” he continued, “which—while functional—are intolerably slow. Meanwhile, across the Atlantic, the Americans are struggling with a similar problem in constructing a device for computing artillery tables. Your machine requires a stored program that can be altered in minutes rather than hours. That, Mr. Turing, is what will make it truly practical. I can help with this.”

Turing regarded him impassively. “I’m afraid you may be mistaken, Mr. Dunning,” he said at last. “I’m neither engaged in any such work nor acquainted with any such machine. I can assure you that—”

The door swung open mid-sentence. A broad-shouldered man poked his head in, clad in a baggy tweed jacket, a tie rather strained about his thick neck.

"Devin, that'll do for now," he rumbled. "Mr. Shane wants you over in Hut Twelve, Room Two—another visitor to be seen. But first, the operator's holding a call for you in your office. Best not keep her waiting."

Thomas exhaled, relieved beyond measure. This man wasn't Alan Turing.

Devin's frail figure rose stiffly, collecting his notepad without a glance in Thomas's direction. He shuffled out, his posture sagging with quiet resignation. "I do wish you'd all make up your minds," he muttered.

Devin's role at the Park wasn't particularly illustrious, but he expected, at the very least, a modicum of respect. He could leave if he wished, but women—who worked for lower wages and with far fewer complaints—were swiftly filling the jobs that had once belonged to men. It would have been a different story if he had been in the military. But with his eyesight, there had never been a chance.

Chapter Thirty-Three

Bletchley Park Station

Still grumbling, Devin trudged down the corridor to his office a few doors away. He lifted the receiver, and the operator's crisp voice came through. "Mr. Fletcher, you have a call."

"Yes, put it through."

Yuri heard a voice, "Devin Fletcher here."

"Are you alone? It's Yuri?"

Fletcher straightened, glancing about as if he had been caught in some guilty act. "Wait," he said, lowering his voice. He crossed the small office, opened the door, and peered into the hallway. Seeing no one, he shut the door firmly before returning to the line. "What the hell are you doing calling me here?"

"Because I pay you," Yuri said, his tone clipped. "This is important, so shut up and listen. There's a visitor—name's Thomas Watson. Has he been through today?"

"No."

Irritation flared in Yuri's voice. "No? That's all?"

Fletcher exhaled, glancing around again, his fingers fidgeting with his spectacles. "That's all."

"Well, Mr. Fletcher, that's not all," Yuri said, urgency tightening his tone. "Find Watson. Make him leave the Bletchley complex now. I don't care how."

"And just how am I supposed to do that?" Fletcher asked.

Yuri spoke slowly, deliberately. "I don't care."

"I don't even know who he is—"

"He arrived in the last hour. He'll be looking for someone important. He'll have to be screened. That's your job. That's why I pay you—to keep track of who's coming and going. So, anyone new in the last hour?"

Fletcher hesitated. "Two people. One was a WAAF—she's here for training. The other… well, he's not your Watson."

"Why not?"

"Because that's not the name he gave. What do you want me to say?"

"What name did he give?"

Fletcher flipped open his notepad, his eyes landing on the scribbled entry. "Dunning. Only new arrival I know of."

"Did it occur to you he might be using a false name? Describe him."

"Tall. Light brown hair. About one-eighty."

"Was he wearing a bluish shirt and khaki trousers?"

Fletcher hesitated. "Ah…"

Yuri's patience thinned. "Fletcher."

"Yes," Fletcher admitted, his grip tightening on the receiver. "That's probably him. He wanted to see Turing, but they took him elsewhere." A lie, but one he told reflexively, shifting in his seat, aware of how guilty he looked even though no one was watching. "I don't know where, but someone didn't like what he had to say. He knows too much. Even if I wanted to help you, I couldn't."

"Devin," Yuri said, his voice lowering, "you've been on the take for over a year. Now it's payback time. Find him, or he's a dead man. And if that happens, I can't promise your future will be any brighter. Do you understand?"

Fletcher swallowed hard, shifting the receiver to his other hand, his palm damp with sweat. He wiped it on his trouser leg. "I'll find him."

"Tell him he's in danger. Tell him to meet Yuri at the station—quickly."

"And if I can't?"

Yuri let the silence stretch, then hung up. It was a long shot, but he had no other choice. He couldn't risk slipping into Bletchley himself. The place looked deceptively open, but appearances were misleading. He clenched his jaw, scanning the station once more. He had to determine where Thomas's loyalties lay, and fast—before it was too late.

In his office, Fletcher stared at the wall, his mind racing. What the hell was he supposed to do? He opened his desk drawer, pulled out his pocket calendar, and flipped it open with shaky fingers. The rest could stay—he'd take only what mattered. For appearances, he grabbed his notepad and strode purposefully out the door.

He moved swiftly toward the back of the building. He had no plan, only the gut-churning certainty that he couldn't stay. Everything was falling apart. That Russian bastard could start talking to the wrong people.

"I can't believe this is happening to me," he thought bitterly. Selling names of new arrivals had seemed harmless—easy money for something anyone could see just by watching the front door. He had four children, and his government salary barely kept them fed. He had never imagined this would escalate or thought the danger would reach his doorstep. Now, the very family he had tried to protect was at risk.

He pushed through the back door and fled, desperate to outrun the mess he had created.

Chapter Thirty-Four

Bletchley
Meeting Dr. Turing

Thomas watched silently as a towering, bouncer-like figure entered the interrogation room, followed by another man who moved behind the now-vacant chair at the table. A brief, knowing glance passed between them before the large man exited, closing the door behind him.

The newcomer pulled out the chair and sat, his thick shock of brown hair appearing to defy any attempt at order. His dark, steady eyes locked onto Thomas, the look of an erratic but brilliant professor betrayed only by the dreadful sweater he wore. Most importantly, Thomas recognized him- the man he had been sent to find, who held the key to the Allies' victory.

"Mr. Dunning, I've been briefed on your discussion with my colleague," he said, gesturing toward the mirror. His right hand rested on the table as though bridging a psychological gap. "Well, it seems today is your lucky day. My name is Alan Turing." He extended his hand, firm and deliberate. "I suppose I should say the real Alan Turing. Forgive the theatrics, but you haven't exactly wandered into a picture house, have you?" He smiled faintly. "I was pulled from a meeting in one of the other huts."

His gaze studied Thomas. "Given your comments, you seem well-informed, so I must ask—have we met?"

"No, we haven't," Thomas assured him, "but I am keenly interested in your work."

Turing leaned forward, intrigued. "Ah, so you're interested in mathematics?"

"Not particularly," Thomas admitted. "But the sum of your work appeals to my sense of history. One day, people will look back and judge it as among the most important contributions to shortening the war."

Turing's eyes narrowed. "And how would you know that, Mr. Dunning?"

"Well, Alan—if I may—you're more than just a mathematician. You're one of the few in the world with the intellect to devise an entirely new approach to sorting vast quantities of data. You've created an algorithm capable of identifying relevant segments in encrypted messages. Am I correct?"

Turing's face betrayed nothing. Encouraged, Thomas continued, "What makes your work extraordinary isn't that you solved the problem, but how. Your method speeds up the process by eliminating the information that can't be relevant, thus leaving a much smaller set that can be productive—instead of the other way around. It's like arriving at the right place by not going everywhere else. A process of elimination—what you call exclusion."

Turing's expression darkened. "That's rather unsettling, Mr. Dunning." He turned toward the mirror, then rose abruptly. "If you'll excuse me, I need to have a word."

At that exact moment, the door opened wide into the room, and the bouncer was in the doorway. The large man's head was turned, so he wasn't looking into the room but listening to someone outside. With the slightest nod to the mystery person outside, he looked at Turing and said, "Continue for now."

Turing exhaled and resumed his seat. "Apologies," he said, lifting his hands. "But you must understand, this is disconcerting. To my knowledge, no one—not even my staff—fully grasps these concepts, let alone articulates them with such clarity. To prevent leaks, our work is heavily compartmentalized. Beyond that, due to secrecy restrictions, I haven't published my findings. With the pressure we are under, I've barely been able to put any of it to paper."

The man hesitated, frustration flickering in his eyes.

Thomas was aware Turing had addressed the frustrating thoughts before. "Alan, it must be hard. I can only imagine."

Turing nodded. "Yes. But enough about me—let's return to you, Mr. Dunning. The fact that you know any of this is both intriguing and, frankly, alarming. Just what is it you want?"

Thomas saw his opening. "Doctor, my primary goal is to convince the government that I possess critical intelligence regarding the impending invasion. To establish my credibility, I offer you information that could aid your work. Once I've proven myself, I ask only one favor."

Turing raised an eyebrow. "And that favor is?"

"If, through my assistance, you find my information credible, I would like your help in presenting it to those with the authority to act. I have no direct access to them, but you might. But we must move quickly—time is running out."

Turing leaned back in his chair. "Mr. Dunning, I am merely a mathematician. Few in military command even know I exist. And, if I may be blunt, given the secrecy of my work—hypothetically speaking, of course—how could you possibly offer anything useful?" He shook his head. "Actually, I believe you may have already answered that."

His voice trailed off. Thomas noted the exhaustion in his face, the toll of secrecy and relentless pressure. The weight of knowing that every day lost meant losing more lives. Turing did not need another burden.

"Alan, all I ask is that you try me," Thomas said. "Your team has built a machine to crack encrypted messages, but you're struggling to make it work efficiently. That's where I come in."

Turing's fingers drummed the table. "You do enjoy your surprises, Mr. Dunning. Yes, we have a machine. But with that knowledge, you've crossed into a rather murky area where everyone is an enemy until proven otherwise. You realize you've put yourself in quite the predicament."

Thomas nodded. "I do. But am I wrong?"

Turing sighed. "No. The machine—Bombe, we call it, after a dessert—has limitations. I see its potential, but the problem is speed. We can't decode messages fast enough for them to be useful. My team and I—mostly telephone engineers—are desperate to improve its efficiency. We've added more huts, more teleprinters, but we're at a technical impasse." He studied Thomas. "How could you possibly know about this?"

Thomas took the gamble. "Because I also know the German encryption device is called Enigma, and the intelligence you extract is known by the codename Ultra. No one in the British military knows it exists outside of a handful."

A long silence followed. Turing's gaze bore into him before he finally exhaled. "Who are you?" he asked, his voice tinged with caution and curiosity. "And how do you know all this?"

Turing stared at him, his expression unreadable. The silence stretched before he slowly shook his head in disbelief.

"Alan?" Thomas prompted. "Alan, the world will reflect on your work as a revolution in managing and distributing knowledge. After the war, monumental advancements will arise from your work. You will be regarded as the father of modern computing. What you create here will lay the foundation for something that will change the world—something called the Internet, the free exchange of information. But that's a story for another day. What matters now is this war. And we must act."

Turing blinked. "You speak with unnerving certainty, Mr. Dunning. Again, who are you? How do you know all this? Surely, you must have known that revealing such knowledge would place you in a… precarious position."

Thomas knew what the future held for Turing—the brilliance, the seclusion, the unrelenting mental battles. He would lock himself away for days, running long distances to burn off the pressure, struggling against a society unwilling to accept him. It was an undeserved fate for one of the greatest minds of the age.

Leaning forward, Thomas spoke as if confiding a great truth. "Your work is vast, Alan, and I urge you—to persist, even in the darkest moments. Even when you believe it will drive you mad."

Turing chuckled the first hint of mirth in his voice. "Mr. Dunning, some might say I've already crossed that line." He sobered quickly. "But you have my attention. Where does this lead?"

"I knew sharing this information would raise suspicions, but I saw no alternative. For reasons beyond explanation, I am aware of your work. That knowledge led me here."

Turing studied him. "For reasons beyond explanation?" His voice carried a note of skepticism.

"What matters is that I may be of help. I can't assist with your equations, but the key to improving the Bombe's speed is not mathematical—it's mechanical. The solution is to accelerate input. Right now, the machine is set using an enormous patch cord panel. It takes a team of women hours to configure it for a new code. The settings trigger a relay to adjust the drums."

Turing's eyes narrowed.

Thomas said evenly. "You need an automated input system using a half-inch punched paper tape used in stock tickers—containing pre-set instructions. Instead of manually adjusting the patch cords, the tape would control the relays electronically. The holes correspond to binary values, just as the patch cords do now. Feed the tape through a light source and optical sensor, and the machine reconfigures itself instantly. Setup time is reduced to minutes, not hours. It's the same principle used in Jacquard's loom to weave intricate patterns—only instead of a needle, you use light. Are you following?"

Turing sat motionless, absorbed in thought. Then, almost imperceptibly, a small smile flickered across his lips.

"A program," he said. "This is… fascinating." His fingers twitched as though yearning for a pencil. "And how would you ensure—?" He cut himself off, gaze dropping to the table. Silence stretched between them, but Thomas could see the pieces aligning in Turing's mind.

Then, as if jolted by revelation, Turing ran a hand through his unruly hair, straightened, and said, "Yes... yes, of course. Optical relays to replace the manual patching..." He shot to his feet, pacing rapidly. He reached the far wall, stopped short of leaning against it, then turned on his heel and pointed a finger at Thomas. "A switch! A high-speed patch connection! My engineers have been working on an advanced relay switch—far faster, far more precise. It's dreadfully expensive, intricate beyond measure. We installed them, but we still rely on manual patching. We never considered integrating the new relays with a better way to input the settings."

Thomas exhaled, allowing himself a small, victorious smile. He had achieved his goal—he had impressed Alan Turing. It was a monumental first step, and he allowed himself a slight sense of optimism. More importantly, he had taken the first crucial step toward changing the course of the war.

Chapter Thirty-Five

Bletchley
Dr. Turing

Turing was beside himself. "How absolutely fascinating."

He turned to Thomas with a broad, almost childlike grin. "There are a few problems to iron out, but that's a magnificent piece of thinking." He stepped closer, his eyes gleaming with excitement. "How would you like to see what we're working on? I think I can arrange a—"

The door to the room swung open with unnecessary force, and a large man in civilian dress stepped inside.

"Mr. Dunning," he said firmly, "you're to come with me. Another interview has been arranged."

Thomas frowned. "Who might that be? And why?" He turned to Turing, and at that moment, both men understood—it was over. Neither wanted it to end so abruptly.

Turing rose and faced the man. "I don't think you quite grasp the situation here," he said sharply, throwing Thomas a knowing glance over the man's shoulder.

The man remained unmoved. "He's said some rather alarming things. He needs to come with me."

Turing's voice rose with frustration. "No, no, I insist. What he's telling us is critical. You don't understand."

As they argued, Thomas acted swiftly, reaching into his coat pocket. With a small, precise motion, he pulled out his cab receipt and placed it on his knee beneath the table. Keeping his movements smooth, he reached for the abandoned pencil left by the first Mr. Turing.

"Please, Mr. Turing," the man interjected. "This is not your concern. I have my orders."

Turing, ever perceptive, caught a glimpse of Thomas scribbling over the man's shoulder. He stalled. "Where are you taking him? Will I see him again? I must see him again. You people can't control everything if we're to make real progress here. I demand to know where he's going!"

Turing turned to Thomas, his expression helpless.

"This way, Mr. Dunning," the large man said, stepping out and expecting Thomas to follow.

Thomas locked eyes with Turing and quickly mouthed, "Can we talk?"

Turing knew at once—this was serious. They weren't just moving him. They were taking him away. And once he was gone, there would be no coming back.

When the man realized Thomas wasn't behind him, he reached back, clamped a firm hand around Thomas's arm, and pulled him forward.

Thomas resisted for a fraction of a second, seizing the opportunity to clasp both of Turing's hands in what seemed like a desperate plea. The grip was firm, lingering—and just enough time for Turing to feel the cab receipt pressed into his palm.

The pressure on his arm forced Thomas to let go. As he stepped backward, he called out, "I'll find a way to contact you, but don't stop your work."

Turing knew the truth. They wouldn't let that happen. Perhaps, if he was lucky, he might see Thomas again—in prison.

"Dunning!" the man barked.

Thomas almost shouted, "Perfect the tape input. It's the key to the output!"

Turing watched as Thomas was led out through a back door of the building. Slowly, deliberately, Turing opened his right hand and saw the scribbled words: "Crown Inn."

Hopeless. It was hopeless. It wasn't going to happen.

As he was ushered outside, Thomas's stomach sank. Two young Royal Marines stood waiting, their uniforms impeccable, buckles polished to a mirror shine. Both carried sidearms. In another moment, Thomas might have admired their double-creased shirts, which were remarkable for wartime. But their rigid posture belied the fact that they had no idea who he truly was or his intentions.

One marine took the lead while the other followed behind, their silence more unnerving than any interrogation. War heightened suspicions; it was best to assume the worst.

"Where are we going?" Thomas asked, but none of the men answered.

His mind raced. He took in every detail, his heightened senses cataloging anything that might prove helpful later. They passed an old horse barn, its weathered wood darkened with age. It stood apart as if its former pungency kept the other huts at bay. There was no worn path leading to it. Most of the surrounding huts were windowless, hiding the secrets of war and the minds that unraveled them. The narrow footpaths twisted into a confusing maze.

Beyond two huts, he spotted a car park. Across from it, an open common.

One marine opened the door to a squat building, motioning him inside. The other marine followed, closing the door behind them. The civilian, speaking into a bulky radio, strode ahead.

Another small room, another interrogation. The setting was the same—plain table and chairs—but there were two windows this time. One faced the hall, its blinds drawn tight. The other, small and multi-paned, overlooked the cluster of huts and, in the distance, the stables.

It was all so unassuming, so ordinary. Yet he knew better.

A faint but persistent murmured hum of voices drifted through the building. No one was visible, but the place was alive.

Everything was unraveling. This was not how he had imagined things unfolding. Worse, if he vanished, what would become of Margaret?

The marine who had entered with him stepped forward. "Palms against the wall. Feet back." He said.

Thomas complied.

"Anything I should know about?"

"No."

It was the first time since entering that "Mr. Dunning" had disappeared from the conversation. The formality was gone. Both marines, he thought, reported directly to and had received training from Mrs. Stimpson.

The marine reached into Thomas's pocket, retrieving the return cab fare and slipping it into a worn envelope with a clasp. Thomas had left anything identifiable behind at Margaret's, so no one could trace him back to her. Traveling without identification in wartime was a gamble, but it had been necessary.

Then, chaos erupted.

Window panes shattered. Glass rained into the room.

The marine gasped, staggering backward. Blood seeped between his fingers as he clutched his leg.

Without thinking, Thomas started dropping to the floor. His palms met shards of glass as he hit the ground beside the wounded marine.

The young man panted, pain wracking his body.

Thomas ripped open the marine's shirt, easing his breathing. "Hold on, son."

He worked swiftly, yanking the man's tie free and looping it around the wound. "You'll be fine," he assured, tightening the makeshift tourniquet. "It's gone through clean. Help's coming."

The second marine burst in, gun drawn. "Eddy?"

"I'm—" The wounded man gritted his teeth. "I'm okay."

The civilian followed into the room, barking into his radio. "Hut 14—gunfire—marine down!"

A second volley of glass exploded—more gunfire.

"From the barn, sir!" the second marine shouted. "Dutch door on the right. Saw the flash on the second shot."

"Cease firing!" the civilian snapped.

"Sir?"

"We might hit our own."

Commands flew over the radio. The grounds were being secured.

Thomas lay still, mind whirring. Whoever had fired knew precisely when he would enter. They had come for him.

But why wait? Why not strike outside?

The British suspected him. They were about to detain him. But they wouldn't kill him. They needed him alive.

No, this wasn't the British.

This was about Margaret's Thomas. About the Hatchers. About the Russians.

Yuri's people thought he was here to expose them. And they intended to stop him.

Chapter Thirty-Six

Bletchley Railway Station

At the station, Yuri paced restlessly, his steps carrying him to and fro between the telephone he had just used to speak with Devin and the ticket counter at the far end of the platform. The chances of Watson appearing were, at best, remote.

Near the ticket counter, he caught sight of an older man shuffling towards him, his shoulders bent beneath the weight of a great, battered bag. His clothes, worn and rumpled from months of hard living, told their sorry tale. Like Yuri's, a face carved by time and hardship peered out from beneath the brim of a tattered hat. Yuri shifted slightly, half-turning as though to walk away—but his feet would not carry him.

Behind him, a wavering voice croaked, "Kin ye spar' a gift, sir?"

For the briefest moments, its sheer absurdity struck Yuri like a thunderclap. Here was life in all its tangled, illogical splendor—countless lives unfolding side by side, some interwoven, some brushing against one another for a fleeting instant, and others never touching. A spy chase, war secrets hanging in the balance, a man's life possibly at stake—yet this poor devil stood in the midst, seeking a few meager coins. A twist of fate, a strange, impossible alignment of two separate stories meeting at their seams, and both, somehow, equally true.

Without a word, Yuri reached into his pocket, withdrew a pound note, folded it once, and pressed it into the man's hand.

Then, without another glance, he veered onto Roche Gardens Road, skirting the edge of the complex, his eyes scanning the grounds beyond. It was a fool's errand, but it was his only lead. He had no notion of what he sought—no certainty of what he might do should he find it. He walked, observing, listening—until the sharp wail of security sirens suddenly split the air.

Chapter Thirty-Seven

Bletchley
The Common

The interrogation room had descended into chaos. Thomas crawled forward, peering out into the hallway. The first doors swung open, confirming what he already suspected—confusion would soon reign supreme. A tide of people flooded the corridor, drawn by the shouts and commotion.

He glanced at the injured soldier, whom he had helped into a half-sitting position against the wall. The man was conscious and alert. The fellow on the radio now eyed the window, his gaze tracking towards the barn. The second marine hurried to his comrade's side.

With the soldier in good hands, Thomas slowly rose and slipped into the hall unnoticed. Armed security guards came tearing toward him, and for a split second, his entire body seized with dread. But then they rushed past, utterly unaware of his involvement. He stepped swiftly toward an exit door that led away from the stables and slipped outside, pulling it closed behind him. He'd sort through the mess later; right now, the priority was getting clear of it. A few hours ago, his plan had seemed merely difficult. Now, it bordered on the impossible.

The rhythmic stomp of heavy boots pounded against the pathways, orders ringing out in sharp bursts. The air was alive with urgency, yet all Thomas could see were office workers scurrying in every direction. He had to move fast—this window of opportunity would not last long. Oddly, a sense of calm washed over him despite the tightening noose around his options. It was the same peculiar certainty that had guided him all along, the same unbidden instincts that now dictated his every move.

He hurried past groups darting between the huts, taking a sharp left to veer away from the stables. Just as he rounded a corner, he glanced back. More soldiers appeared from the opposite direction, focusing on sealing off the stable yard. A logical response, of course—but any shooter bold enough to strike so close would be clever enough to have long since vanished.

Thomas turned and ran, knowing that, in the chaos, he'd draw no attention. Others were fleeing just as he was. He moved swiftly past them, heading for the last hut and the car park. Keeping low, he ducked between the rows of vehicles, finally kneeling at the farthest edge.

Across the road lay a neighborhood common, nearly a block square, dotted with towering trees and dense shrubs. A five-foot stone wall bisected the green, stretching diagonally before halting some sixty feet from each corner. In its center yawned a wide, wrought-iron archway. Thick hedges lined the path on either side of the wall—a promising first refuge.

But reaching it was another matter. Thomas would have to cross the road in full view before vanishing into the greenery. If he managed that and could slip unseen across the common to the far street and disappear into the warren of houses beyond. He had no time to hesitate.

Drawing a deep breath, he straightened, then, with deliberate ease, he crossed the street, his eyes flicking about for any sign of danger. The shooter's location was still a mystery—until he knew where they were, he was far from safe.

On the other side, he was startled by a sudden *brrrring!* Behind him. A boy on a bicycle shot past, ringing his bell in irritation at the pedestrian who had blocked his way. The lad muttered something, but Thomas scarcely heard him over the hammering of his own heart.

Reaching the thick hedge, he ducked behind it, pressing between the foliage and the wall. He knelt, trying to control his heavy breathing, forcing himself to calm. Through the branches, he saw an elderly couple emerge from the park. They had not noticed his dash into the greenery. Good.

His only chance now was to edge along the wall, hidden by the dense shrubs, to cross the common. However, the archway at the center presented a problem. To cross it, he would have to expose himself.

Weaving his way forward, he finally arrived at the gap. He could hear the increasing commotion over the shooting at Bletchley. But right now, that was not his problem.

He looked left but failed to look entirely around the wall to the right. He sprinted across the opening—and collided with a man.

The impact jarred his shoulder, the force of it nearly knocking him off his feet. Both men staggered back, stunned, eyes locked for the briefest moments.

Thomas took him in at once—tall, broad, a full face beneath a simple hat and a civilian overcoat. But the flash of recognition in the man's dark eyes told Thomas all he needed to know. He had been identified. The man had seen a photograph of him. Thomas rightly sensed he wasn't part of Bletchley's security.

The stranger's hand darted inside his coat, prompting another one of Thomas's subconscious reactions. In one continuous motion, Thomas grabbed the barrel of the gun that emerged to control the direction of any fire and drove his elbow hard into the man's midsection.

The stranger doubled over, cursing in a thick accent—Russian. Another quick jab to the temple, and the man crumpled onto the paving stones.

Breathless, Thomas knelt beside him, prying the pistol from his limp fingers. It was a Tula-Tokarev 33 25mm revolver with a Bramit silencer and an eight-shot clip. Not the weapon of an ordinary soldier.

His escape across the common had been apparent—anticipated.

Cursing under his breath, he searched the unconscious man. A thorough pat-down yielded only a slip of paper hidden in the lining of his coat—a telephone number. Thomas tucked it into his pocket, then hauled the man off the path, rolling him face down into the hedgerow.

Reaching under the man's coat at his back, he could feel the magazine pack attached to his belt. Upon snapping it open, three clips fell out—all full.

A distant thought prompted him to have a full clip in a defensive situation. Thomas turned the gun to the side and ejected the existing clip into his hand. Pulling the top action back created the spring motion that loaded a shell and cocked the mechanism. All of it produced entirely too much noise.

A short time ago, he was talking to Turing about computers. Now, he was behaving and feeling like a spy on the run. Thomas looked at the gun in his hand. He wasn't sure how he knew how to handle the situation, but the fact that he could was a comfort. Perhaps Margaret's Thomas was more than just an opportunist. "Or," Thomas wondered, "maybe we just acquire the needed skills when needed." In any event, he needed to get out of here and fast. A movement beyond the trees caught his eye. Another man. Was he working alone, or did he have a partner?

"Does he know where I am?" Thomas wondered.

He saw the movement again, but it was moving away. Thomas thought the casual cadence in the steps wasn't normal for a person charged with adrenaline or fear. The second man didn't know there was a problem, but the man's care in staying out of sight behind the trees belied his true intentions.

Staying low and moving from bush to bush next to the wall, Thomas made it to the far end closest to the street. Before standing up, he set the safety on the Krupp, pushed his overcoat aside, and stuffed the gun down his waistband at the back. It wasn't comfortable.

With a hand on the stonework, he pulled himself up and looked to the other side of the clearing. There was nothing. He looked back toward the second man; he was gone. Thomas wasn't sure it was safe, but he had to vacate the green, cross the street, and blend into the people milling about the neighborhood houses and shops. Between the end of the wall and the street, there was another tall tree next to the pavement. Its sizable trunk would be his next cover.

Dashing from his position as he neared the tree, he dove to the ground. A shot cracked through the air as he landed, causing the bark to explode next to his face. He rolled behind the trunk away from the sound of the shot, his heart hammering. This was terrible cover—too exposed. Another shot could easily find its mark. He reached behind for the gun, mind racing.

He surveyed everything in sight and listened with complete concentration. However, the only noise was the strained sounds of a car pushed to its limits, combined with the sound of terribly abused tires. Still lying on the ground, he turned half over toward the nearing commotion—just in time to see the approaching vehicle.

His body tensed in terror. An Austin lurched over the curb, door flying open.

"Get in!" The driver yelled. "Thomas, get in!"

He blinked. The driver—*Margaret?*

Half-in, half-out, of the car, another bullet pinged off the roof.

"Go!" he bellowed.

"Where?" she shouted, jamming the accelerator.

"Anywhere!" He barely got the door closed as she sent the car hurtling forward.

Trying to get low, he slid down in the seat as his knees slammed into the dash. "Argh.... God, that hurt," he said.

"Hurt? You could be dead right now," Margaret said, fighting the wheel and shifting gears. "Fine bit of pitch you found, Mr. Watson."

"What in bloody hell are you doing here?" Thomas said. "How did you find me?"

"Actually, I thought I was lost, hopelessly following some impossible directions. Then I see you run across a park, fall on the ground, and pull a gun out. What was I supposed to do? "You, sir, have a *lot* of explaining to do."

A voice from the back seat said, "I would say my directions were spot on, wouldn't you, dearie?"

Mrs. Somerville clutched her handbag in the back seat with a delighted grin. "Well, now," she chirped. "Isn't this all terribly exciting?"

Thomas turned sharply. "Mrs. *Somerville?* What the *devil* are you doing here?"

"What *do* you mean, dear boy?" she said, clutching her handbag primly in her lap. "After all, it's *my* car."

"I mean—*both* of you—" Thomas stopped, rubbing a hand over his face. "Never mind." He grabbed the door handle for dear life as Margaret took a sharp corner at forty-five miles an hour.

From the shadows, a figure watched Thomas enter the vehicle. Angrily, he pulled out a pack of Belomor Kanal's and lit a cigarette. Sirens were blaring; Bletchley security was making their way to the park. It all meant he wasn't happy. He might have lost two men, but he didn't care. He pulled away; next time, there would be no mistakes.

Watson was now in the wind.

Margaret didn't look away from the road as she spoke. "The Russian rang after you left," she said, voice tight. "Wanted to know where you'd gone. He said he urgently needed to speak with you. I told him you weren't available, and straight away, he asked if you'd gone to Bletchley."

Thomas frowned. "How would he know that?"

"That's exactly what startled me," she said, throwing the gear stick into another brutal shift. "He must've overheard us talking. Or maybe he caught something in my voice because the moment I hesitated—he was gone." She shot him a sideways glance. "He said he wanted to help. Said it more than once. I didn't believe him."

Thomas thought back to Yuri's coat left on the chair that morning, his remark about weapons, his insistence that he was a diplomat, not a thug.

"I don't think he was the one shooting at me," he said.

"Thomas," Margaret said, voice taut, "why would someone be shooting at you?" Her grip on the wheel tightened. "I knew I shouldn't have let you go alone. That's it. I'm never letting you out of my sight again. I'm responsible for at least part of this mess."

"Margaret, we can discuss that later," Thomas said. "Right now, we need to disappear. We can't go back home. They might have ministry contacts—trace the car's number plate."

"Not possible," came Mrs. Somerville's voice from the back, utterly unbothered.

Thomas twisted to look at her. "What do you mean?"

Mrs. Somerville beamed. "Well, dear, after Margaret rang me this morning, I had my good friend Vernon Bartlett remove the plates and replace them with an old set Charles had nailed to the garage wall years ago. Poor Mr. Bartlett—he'll do *anything* for a lady."

"*Anything?*" Margaret asked, arching an eyebrow.

"My heavens, woman," she said with a giggle; he also does what I ask him not to do." Mrs. Somerville clutched her handbag to her chest with giddy delight. "Besides, isn't this exhilarating? I haven't had this much excitement since Charles and I stayed at that darling little inn by the coast and—" She paused, her expression wistful. "Ah. Well. Oh, Charles," she said fondly, gazing at some distant memory, "may God bless your lovely soul."

Margaret sighed. "I'm taking us to Mother's. Her house has a security detail, and she's on the Home Guard's watch list." She turned the car onto the main road, shifting to a steady speed.

The wind whistled through the bullet hole in the roof.

Only now did Thomas realize he was still clutching the pistol. He turned it over, examining its weight.

Margaret flicked her eyes toward him and stared. "Thomas—where on earth did you get that?"

He looked up, still bemused. "The fact that I *know* what it is surprises me." He frowned. "And the fact that I know how to *use* it is beyond my comprehension right now." His gaze flicked back to the two women. "Which brings me again to the question—what in God's name are *you* both doing here?"

Margaret's hands tightened on the wheel. "I'm a schoolteacher, not a criminal," she said, exasperated. "I didn't know what I would do when I got here. But after the Russian rang off, I felt you'd be in trouble." Her lips thinned. "That'll teach you to leave me behind."

A silence stretched between them. Then, quietly, she added, "Thomas, you could have been killed." Still gripping the wheel, she said, "If you loved me, you wouldn't take such risks. Running through gunfire—bullets flying—"

"Loving you would be wonderful," Thomas said, still watching her, "if only I understood what drove you to be here. Maybe then I'd understand why I know what I know."

Margaret's jaw tensed. "Blast you, Thomas Watson; you're not making sense, let alone doing yourself any favors later if you know what I mean," she muttered.

"I know what she means," Mrs. Somerville chimed in from the back.

Thomas exhaled, rubbing his temple. "Fine. The favor I need now is for you to take me to the Crown Inn. But first, we need to drop Mrs. Somerville at the station."

Mrs. Somerville gave a scandalized sniff. "Afraid not, Professor. It's my car, and I—"

"Mrs. Somerville," Thomas interrupted, "some people want me dead. And being around me is dangerous."

Mrs. Somerville buttoned the top of her coat, utterly ignoring him.

Then, in her sweet time, she said, "Well, that's that. I suggest we turn left at Addison Road. It's safer not being the direct route one might expect."

Thomas turned to Margaret. She merely shrugged.

Mrs. Somerville raised an eyebrow, smiling slyly. "Couldn't hurt."

Chapter Thirty-Eight
Bletchley
Common

Yuri's mind whirled. He had placed little faith in Devin—neither in his ability nor inclination—to deliver the message to Thomas.

Keeping to the shadows, he made his way to a corner opposite the common and stepped into the shelter of a bus stop. He needed to gauge the form this alert would take. As he did, his eyes caught movement—it was Watson, dropping behind a tree, then sprinting into a waiting motorcar. A man lay sprawled upon the walkway near the archway while another figure—his back turned—raced down the street. Moments later, Bletchley security personnel swarmed the park. Yuri stiffened. He had no desire to explain his presence.

He turned on his heel and hurried towards the station, his only thought to reach it before security locked it down. He must avoid scrutiny—blend into the throng—before boarding.

At the station, he slowed his pace as he neared the sheltering structure of the platform; he crossed casually, laid a firm hand upon the coach handle, and pulled himself inside. Moving down the aisle, he cast a wary glance through the glass before slipping into an empty compartment. The door slid shut behind him. He exhaled. Thank God for round-trip tickets.

Hardly had he settled when the platform began to drift past the window. Two uniformed men burst into view—one running, flinging an arm skyward, the other, seizing the stationmaster by the sleeve. The stationmaster reacted at once, wrenching himself free and shaking his head with a vehemence that sent the peak of his cap quivering. The guard was demanding he stop the train. But a train well underway? Not in this country. Not on a continent where the measure of a civilization lay in the precision of its rail schedules.

Held before departure? That was another matter.

More security men arrived, but as the commotion faded from view, Yuri could see only the heated gestures of their argument. They would call ahead, of course—to the next station. But whoever received the order would be armed with nothing more than a verbal description. Yuri was now a hunted man.

Yuri's gaze drifted to the empty seat before him. What a devil of a mess.

Had the shooting been a British operation? No, that made no sense. The British had already seized Watson. He was far more valuable alive than dead. No, this was not their doing.

The order to kill Watson could only have come from Russian security.

Moscow had assigned him the task of eliminating Thomas. And yet now, it seemed another had attempted it in his stead. A rogue Russian operative? A second measure, in case he faltered?

This had been brute force—clumsy, unsubtle. Back in Russia, where men grew up battling the ferocity of winter, the notion of brute force was ingrained in the very sinew of their being. This, however, was brute force wielded without refinement, a crude affair, hastily stitched together, its underlings disposable. Someone lurked behind the curtain, but who? And did it even matter? Unless, of course, they had targeted the wrong man.

That was the trouble—he had no plausible reason to believe it, yet the thought gnawed at him. One thing was certain: matters were spiraling beyond control, and Yuri's instincts thrummed with warning. If he could discern no apparent pattern to the day's events, he must vanish for survival.

Yet another certainty gripped him: if Thomas was in danger, so was his wife, Margaret.

If there remained even the slimmest chance to act, he must act. He needed information—critical information—and he knew precisely where to find it.

Chapter Thirty-Nine

Crown Inn
Milton Keynes

"That's it there," Thomas said, gesturing toward the Crown Inn, a two-story brick building opposite another village common. The Inn sat directly down Shendly Brook, which began as Bletchley Lane within the government compound. Built in 1850, the building had once featured an extension on its left side—a butcher's shop that had long since disappeared. Now, the structure housed several flats, one of which was rented by Turing. Below them, the first floor was home to the Burnt Oak pub, known for its generous pours and the largest snooker table in the village.

Thomas stared out the car window, his thoughts drifting back to the commotion at Bletchley. He winced, picturing the absurd sight he must have made, dragged down the corridor by armed guards. To Turing, it must have been nothing short of pathetic. Thomas did not doubt that his knowledge of the project had fascinated the scientist, but it had also made him a wanted man. He had been warned not to cross the line. Given any choice, he wouldn't have done it. But that was then, and this was now.

Margaret eased the car around to the rear of the inn as if they were stopping for the night. It also kept them out of sight from the street.

"What now?" she asked as she pulled into a space beside a gleaming red Lagonda—the preferred motorcar of every well-to-do country solicitor. Thomas's gaze dropped to the wire-spoked wheels, polished to a shine too perfect to have been done by the owner's hand. He thought, "It must be nice to have enough money for others to tend to such details while you glide through life unbothered."

In the silence left by his hesitation, Mrs. Somerville leaned forward, fixing Thomas with a look. “I could use a cup—anyone?”

“Mrs. Somerville, this is no time for tea! I’ve made us all enemies of the state, and such normal pleasures have gone the bye.”

“Mr. Watson,” she said, tapping the back of his seat, “I should think you’d be far less conspicuous if you were accompanied by two ladies taking tea—particularly if one looked like your mother. Besides, I’m dreadfully dry.”

Thomas sighed, but before he could protest, Margaret cut in. “She’s right. We can move to another table or take a walk when the man arrives.”

He exhaled sharply. “Even though I’m putting both of you in danger, you’re completely ignoring my attempts to keep you safe.”

Mrs. Somerville turned to Margaret with a knowing smile. “He’s quite quick off the mark, isn’t he?”

Margaret placed a steadying hand on Thomas’s arm. “It doesn’t all have to rest on your shoulders. We’re not looking for trouble, but if we can help, we want to.”

From the backseat came a dry voice. “You can add me to that list. But more to the point—besides keeping you alive—what exactly *is* this little adventure?”

Resigned, Thomas relented.

Upon entering the pub, he instinctively scanned the room, though he wasn’t entirely sure why. It was nearly empty at this hour, save for a pair of sharply dressed gentlemen hunched over towering stacks of papers deeper than a pint. Selecting a table at the far end of the room, they took their seats.

The waitress appeared, rubbing her arms against the chill. “I know it’s a bit brisk, but we’ve got a distributor’s special on Pimm’s No. 1.”

Thomas considered ordering one—something to steady his nerves after the past few hours—but decided his wits were more critical than the comfort of a drink. As he hesitated, the waitress glanced over her shoulder toward the bar. “Arthur, couldn’t this be the gent Alan was on about?”

A burly man behind the counter, balancing three clean mugs in each hand, looked up. “Are you a Mr. Dunning?”

"Yes… yes, I am."

Margaret shot Thomas a questioning look but remained silent.

Arthur wiped his hands on his apron and stepped around the bar, lowering his voice as he leaned in. "Alan Turing's a close friend of my family. He rang ahead—said I should call 'im if you showed up."

Thomas let out a breath he hadn't realized he was holding. "Please—yes. I'd be in your debt."

Arthur's grin widened, revealing a pronounced gap between his teeth. "Come along, then," he said, waving them toward the bar. "You can have a word yourself." He wove through the tables, leading Thomas to a small wooden shelf protruding from the wall. "Only phone for the whole place, so don't be long."

He fished a scrap of paper from his pocket, scanned it, and picked up the receiver. "Ellen? Yes, Wellington 4397, please—and there's a drink in it for ya if you don't put it on your log."

Thomas heard a woman's voice on the other end, though he couldn't make out her words—only a burst of laughter.

Arthur rolled his eyes. "Ellen Bromley, I've got me reasons, and I'd better not 'ear it comin' 'round, or there'll be 'ell to pay."

He shot a weary look at Thomas, then turned back to the receiver, speaking in a low, deliberate tone. "No, you're not gettin' a short room let neither. No—get me the number before I call your Mum about this nonsense."

A few seconds passed before he handed Thomas the phone with a shake of his head. "In me line of work, there's a lot to be known in a small village."

Thomas took the receiver, and after a brief ring, a voice answered.

"Hello, Alan Turing here."

"Alan, this is—" Thomas hesitated, weighing his options. It's best to sort that detail later. "Mr. Dunning. Are you alone?"

A sudden, startled exclamation came through the line. "Great God," Alan said, his voice louder than intended. Then, lowering it, he asked, "Are you all right? Were you hurt?"

"No. By the narrowest of margins, I managed to avoid someone's attempt on my life. The last one today, I hope."

"I can assure you, it wasn't the British," Turing said. "But I'm baffled as to who it could've been. You aren't mixed up in something, are you? Given what you've just told me, you could be of interest to any number of unidentified factions. I suppose none of them are good chaps and certainly not the sort you can see coming."

Alan glanced around his dimly lit Bletchley office, stretched the phone cord taut, and walked over to close the door.

"Well, they were plenty visible today," Thomas said. "They shot a hole in the car that got me out of there."

"At least you're in one piece. Where are you? Security's tense at the compound—talk of heads rolling and careers ending. They're swarming the huts and the surrounding neighborhood like ants after honey."

"Believe me, this is not how I wanted to start my day. I'm at the Crown Inn."

"Well, splendid—that saves us a great deal of trouble. Are you parked round back?"

"Yes. We've only just arrived."

"Stay inside. I've got a car, and I can be there in a few minutes—but we won't have long. Are we all set, then?"

"Yes. There's much to discuss—including my request for your help."

"Don't know about that," Turing mused. "But I would love to chat about the other matters. I'm on my way."

\

Chapter Forty

Crown Inn
Milton Keyes

Alan Turing emerged from the back near the kitchen and walked straight to the table where Thomas sat alone. Margaret and Mrs. Somerville had taken seats a few tables away, but that was as far as Mrs. Somerville would go.

Thomas rose, extended his hand to Turing, and then nodded towards the women, the only other customers in the room. "My protective contingent. Best they not be introduced."

"Of course, of course." Turing smiled at Margaret, nodding. "Ladies."

He was nervous, slightly on edge, as he removed his gloves. "I live here, you see. Came in the back way."

"I know," Thomas said. "That's why I chose this place."

Alan studied him, a look of deep concern crossing his face, one Thomas was beginning to recognize. Turing unconsciously shifted his hat on the table, debating whether this was worth the risk.

"I gave it some thought," Turing said. "The danger of coming here. But with the invasion, the increased bombings—well, the whole lot is on the line. Still, I can't for the life of me understand how you came by this information. Not just where I live—but the technical details."

"As you said, we don't have much time." Thomas cast a glance at the other table. "I don't want to put anyone else in harm's way if I can help it, so let me get straight to it. As I said, I gave you that information to win your trust, but now I see it was clumsy. As you pointed out, some of it only you would know. As for the source—" he hesitated, "—that's complicated. But if it helps win the war…"

"That's why I'm taking this chance," Turing said. "People's lives are at stake. One deciphered message, caught in time, could save a ship and its crew."

Thomas, eager to move beyond Turing's doubts, leaned in. "I need help delivering information just as important—something that would benefit the prime minister and the country. *Our* country." The last words lingered on his tongue. "All I need is ten minutes."

"As I said, Whitehall doesn't even acknowledge I exist, and I've no influence—none. Let's be honest; I've met Churchill twice, both times in crowded rooms. That doesn't mean I won't try, but I want to be deadly honest."

"An interesting choice of words," Thomas said.

Turing smiled at that, breathing fully for the first time since they sat down. Thomas studied him, weighing the man before him. "You'd be surprised by the visibility and admiration you engender—now and later. But your work is so advanced and vital that public recognition won't come soon. It'll remain classified long after the war."

"Recognition isn't my concern. My heaven is to return to university, bury myself in pure research." Turing looked off, lost in thought. Then, as though struck by an idea, he turned back. "Oh, yes, I had a question. What did you mean by 'keep on it even if it drives me mad'?"

"Nothing. Perhaps a nod to history—how every great thinker was once called a heretic, at best, and a madman at worst. Newton hid his work on calculus for ten years before revealing it to avoid the inevitable row from the church."

Both men laughed.

"Perhaps *you* have run afoul of the church," Turing mused. "You speak as though you're providing information from the future. That would be most distressing to men of the cloth." His voice was light, but his eyes were sharp. "However, I've chosen to put that aside, as what you're saying is intriguing. I spoke with my staff, and they grasped the importance immediately. My most brilliant engineer started speaking faster than I could listen, then hung up to try something. Marvelous people, but I think they're exhausted by the constant pressure."

Thomas placed both hands flat on the table. "So we come to the Bombe—your wonderful machine. As I said at Bletchley, it all comes down to speed—modifying the machine quickly to match the day's encoding wheels. Once the patch settings are entered, the core setup will function. At least… that's how I remember it."

He realized what he'd said.

True to his word, Turing ignored the slip. "We know speed is the problem. We've tried modifications—faster electrical switches—but they've only been marginally effective."

Thomas narrowed his eyes. "Can you resolve the wheel combination when the Germans change it?"

"Yes," Turing said. "I designed a mechanical logic engine. It grinds through possibilities using brute force, applying the exclusionary scheme you mentioned at Bletchley.

Thomas felt the conversation accelerating. "So the first problem is the wheel combination, which you have solved. Next, you can set the Bombe switches to translate the messages now that you know the proper wheel combination for the day. I mentioned an optical reader. An array of light-sensitive switches. Have those been invented yet?" He knew he'd done it again.

Turing didn't miss it but pressed on. "Yes. Vacuum photo-electric sensors. Professor Reginald Jones wrote a classified paper on them with the team at Clarendon Laboratory at Oxford, suggesting they might work. They're experimenting with them for…" He stopped.

"RDF," Thomas said. "Or radar, as the Americans call it."

Turing froze. "You *cannot* know that." His voice was barely above a whisper. "Apart from what I'm working on, it has the highest security clearance in all of England. Stealing the Crown Jewels is easier than accessing that project."

Thomas's voice hardened. "Ignore *why* and focus on *how*. You *must* obtain those optical sensors—arrange them four across, perpendicular to the punched tape. Adjust the tape width if necessary, stagger them, or use lenses—whatever it takes. What's the output of the logic engine?"

Turing blinked. "The switch settings for the day's wheel combination."

"Yes, but—paper? Physical settings? Lights?"

"Oh—paper, from a teletype machine, listing each switch on the Bombe and its setting."

"Perfect. Then, dismantle the teletype. Use the signal from the logic engine that drives the printing keys to punch the tape. It'll take some rigging, but it can be done."

"I just got it," Turing said suddenly, his voice sharp with realization. "All too often, things seem simple once they're known." He leaned in. Turing tried to stand up but then sat down in a mindless need to express what was going faster through his brain than he could convey. It appeared he expressed deep thought or excitement with constant movement.

He gestured wildly in the air, "Mr. Dunning, we can take the signal generated by the tape running over the light switches and run it through a conversion board where each signal is amplified with enough current to trip the relays on the Bombe. It will be ugly and messy, but it can be done quickly. Each electrical switch will set itself from the signal fed from the amplifier board. We *bypass* the slow manual patching entirely!"

Thomas stared at him. "I'm not sure I follow."

"It's okay, as the rework is relatively minor, so it shouldn't take long. With your tape idea, we go from teams of our girls manually setting the patch positions by looking at each line on a hundred sheets of paper to a direct electrical setting, which is almost instantaneous.

He scrambled for his hat, missing it the first time, and stood.

"I must get back to Bletchley for my usual beating befor the committee. "Except—his face was radiant." He threw his arms up, laughing. "—not after *this*. Today has been… interesting. Historic, perhaps."

"You're confident?" Thomas asked.

"Yes, it's all coming together in my head. Right before they whisked you away, you came out with some fascinating things today."

Thomas said, "I remembered your first Bombe was to begin full operation this month. I knew the information would be helpful. As I mentioned, I believed that with your help, I could reach someone in Whitehall."

"But you said 'remembered' just now. Quite the feat, that—recalling something which hasn't yet come into existence."

"Ah, well, it's a peculiar knack of mine, you see. Though I confess, it does raise certain concerns."

Turing's gaze sharpened. "I say, what is your source? How do you do it?"

Thomas gave a slow shake of the head. "Can't say for certain. The knowledge comes from somewhere. As you observed, the oddest part is that it feels less like foreseeing events and more like recounting history." He leaned back in his chair, observing Turing.

Turing studied him for a moment before speaking. "If we set aside everything we know of how the world works, your source suggests but one explanation—you've come from the future."

Thomas gave a half-smile. "Perhaps. But if that's so, how? And, more to the point, why?"

"Oh, that's simple enough," Turing replied matter-of-factly. "To tell me—at precisely the right moment—that I must use an optical reader, just when the higher-ups were beginning to lose faith in my ability to increase the machine's speed. Some would rather see great halls filled with legions of women grinding away on mechanical calculators. They're uneasy about the idea of electrical or mechanical assistance to thinking—though they've no qualms about the assistance of block and tackle when loading a ship. Perhaps you were sent to set them straight?"

Thomas lapsed into thought, his expression darkening. "I know one thing for certain—the war is going badly and will only worsen. With the best intentions, some within the War Cabinet may even consider surrender."

Turing sobered at once. "Good Lord. Will they? Will we surrender?"

Thomas hesitated, then shook his head. "No. At least, I don't believe so. But I can't be certain. That's why I need your help."

Turing exhaled, rubbing his brow. "Ah, yes—this Whitehall business. See here, I'll do everything within my power to secure you an audience with someone of rank, but I can't promise anything beyond that. As I told you, I'm merely a scientist and not one the brass has particular faith in at present."

Thomas pushed himself to his feet. "But you'll make the calls?"

"Yes, as soon as I arrive. Then I will set my team to work."

"Please remember, I don't have much time. How will I contact you to know if you've been successful?" Thomas said.

"That could be a problem, as there are no outside phones where I'm headed. All calls must be routed through a special exchange. Besides, Bletchley denies I exist, let alone forwards my messages."

Turing dropped his head in thought, then brought it up, saying, "I'll manage to find a phone somewhere and leave a message with Arthur here at the Inn. You can call him. Yes, that's it. The message might be a little cryptic, but I call in frequently, so it shouldn't arouse special attention."

Thomas offered his hand and said, "Then good luck to you, Alan, as I know you'll be successful, although you left me a bit pale at the last part."

Turing shook his hand, gripping his hat in the other. "I know why you told me these things. But the larger question is how you know them." He studied Thomas. "Are you mad or a heretic?"

Thomas laughed. "Perhaps both."

Turing settled his fedora, turned toward the back room, and paused. "Get somewhere safe, preferably far from here."

Thomas nodded. Turing pulled on a glove, pushed open the kitchen door, and disappeared.

"Thomas?" Margaret's voice came softly from behind him. "We heard most of it. Do you think it will work?"

Mrs. Somerville placed a steadying hand on Margaret's elbow. "Kitten, we haven't many cards to play, and there's no use holding them to your chest. Mr. Watson, I thought you handled that marvelously."

The mention of Watson made Thomas stiffen. "Damn it all. Turing still knows me as Dunning."

"Who's Dunning?" Margaret asked.

Without answering, Thomas rushed to the back door, flinging it open. His eyes darted across the car park, but his heart sank as he spotted Turing's car turning onto the street. He shouted and waved, but the vehicle slowly disappeared.

"He's going to set up a meeting for Dunning. A wanted man," Thomas muttered, frustration tightening his jaw. "It's all for nothing."

He stood alone in the cold air, mind racing. He thought of the young marine who'd been shot because of him. They'd be searching for him now—everywhere. And Turing was right. He, Margaret, and Mrs. Somerville had to leave the inn.

The woman stepped outside.

"I don't see any choice," Thomas said. "We must disappear for a bit, play the last card we've got—Margaret's mother's house. They'll be watching your house in Amersham, so we can't return there."

"That's *our* house," Margaret corrected.

"I knew that," Thomas replied with a grin.

"Just making sure," she said, tugging playfully at his coat sleeve.

He turned to Mrs. Somerville. "As for your safety, I think you'll be all right. But no one would know you were involved if you hadn't insisted on coming along."

Mrs. Somerville lifted her chin. "Thomas, dear, we've been over this before, and I daresay my contributions outweigh any inconvenience I may have caused."

"I won't argue that," he conceded, "but you still put yourself in danger. That's my concern—and my responsibility."

"Perhaps," she said lightly, "but the danger was equally *my* concern."

Thomas frowned, uncertain of her meaning.

Margaret stepped in. "She means me, Thomas. She was worried about *me*."

Mrs. Somerville gave a satisfied nod. "Well, at least someone here has a good head on their shoulders."

Thomas's tone softened. "I'm concerned for you. That's all. I don't see why that's so bad."

Mrs. Somerville studied him. The frustration in his voice was impossible to miss. It had been a long day for all of them, but especially for him.

"If I might say, Mr. Watson," she said, "up until a few nights ago, I wouldn't have given tuppence for your neck. But something's changed. It's as though you were switched at birth—but it happened to you as a grown man." Her voice lost its usual teasing edge. "Despite it all, I'm very grateful for your concern. Very grateful."

Thomas sensed the shift in her tone. "Look, Mrs. Somerville, perhaps I was a bit over the top."

She scoffed. "Don't apologize to me, young man. I could take you out in a second." The words might have been convincing had she not chuckled at the end. "In any event, may I suggest you drop me at a cab stand?"

Margaret and Thomas exchanged a glance.

"It's simple," Mrs. Somerville explained. "You two need the car. I don't drive, and I don't take the rail late at night, so I often take cabs home. It won't raise suspicion. But if you go tearing through town trying to dump me at my house, then all hell will break loose. I'm afraid your days in my little flat are over."

"She's right," Margaret said. "They'll be watching. Whoever *they* are."

Thomas exhaled. "I know it wasn't the British who tried to kill me, but they don't like what I told them. I've no doubt they'd love to continue our conversation. The only thing working in my favor is that they're looking for Dunning. The problem is, whoever did try to kill me knows my face. And judging by what that man Yuri said this morning, I'd wager they're Russian."

Margaret moved close, slipped her arm through his, and looked up at him. "Thomas, Mr. Turing was right. We need to leave."

Thomas gazed at her, the day's events crashing down on him. He pulled her into a firm embrace. "I'm sorry, Margaret. I never meant for this mess." He pulled back slightly, gripping her shoulders, his voice quiet but confident. "I love you."

Margaret rose onto her toes, flung her arms around his neck, and kissed him, her feet lifting clear off the ground.

Mrs. Somerville watched with something between amusement and nostalgia.

"Are you busy later?" Thomas said to Margaret in a knowing tone.

Mrs. Somerville clapped her hands together. "For God's sake, you two—set a mind to it and stop carrying on like teenagers in heat."

Thomas smirked. "Jealous, Mrs. Somerville?"

She shot him a glare. "Absolutely not, Mr. Watson. But there's a time and place for everything—and *now* is the time to leave." Then, glancing at Margaret with a mischievous grin, she added, "Although you never told me about your day at the picnic. And, yes—I could be jealous."

Chapter Forty-One

Turing's Office
Bletchley Park

Alan Turing left the Crown Inn and turned sharply onto the street, guiding the motorcar towards Hut 8. While Huts 3 and 6 played no small role in the decoding effort, Hut 8 housed his office, and that was where he was bound.

Upon arrival, he gathered his belongings from the front seat and strode briskly towards a side entrance marked Administration Offices—Employees Only. He pushed open the door and stepped inside.

To his left sat a young woman, neatly dressed, her dark brown hair immaculately arranged, her posture poised with impeccable manners. Beside her desk teetered a stack of papers she was valiantly trying to keep from cascading to the floor.

She looked up with a bright smile. "Good evening, sir." No names—per regulations.

Turing nodded and removed his hat as he passed by.

When Turing initially discussed managing the project, he insisted on having complete control. He proposed creating a second backup Bombe machine at an off-site location because Bletchley Park was too prominent, making it vulnerable as a potential target. He later discovered that funding for this off-site location was routed through a private company to conceal financial trails. Eventually, Turing learned that Hatcher Ltd managed the lease and security for this privately owned location. The decision to involve this specific company in the project had been made far above his pay grade.

However, Turing was aware of the political influence wielded by the Hatcher family and the fact that they had a daughter. After careful consideration, he concluded she did not know of her family's business involvement. Nevertheless, he remained concerned about her safety—specifically, the possibility that someone might target her to gain access to confidential information.

Although Turing personally vetted every worker assigned to his top-secret operations, he entrusted the monitoring of the daughter's safety to MI5 under the condition that they would keep him informed. After some time without any updates, he discovered they were going directly to Churchill's office. Given his workload, he was relieved, though he was surprised how far up the chain of command their project had visibility.

Upon entering his office, Turing found Gordon Welchman already waiting. Welchman was another Cambridge man, another brilliant mind recruited into their vital work.

"Gordon, look, I must apologize for that telephone call," Turing said as he removed his coat. "In hindsight, it lacked substance."

Gordon laughed heartily. "Oh, I wouldn't say that! I haven't seen you so animated in ages—it was contagious. Whatever you were worked up about certainly grabbed our attention. I even instructed the team to clear their desks and their heads. Whatever was coming needed their full focus."

"Gordon," Turing began, "I doubt it warranted quite so much drama."

"No, Alan," Gordon replied, chuckling, "you wouldn't."

Turing smirked. "Fair enough. We have a mountain of work ahead, but I must make a telephone call before I join the fray. It's a matter of keeping my word. After that, I'll be right out to terrorize the troops. It's quite the story. You'll want to hear it."

He reached for his notebook and the number of Churchill's office. The Prime Minister had once pressed it into his hand, declaring that any matter of absolute urgency should come directly to him. The success of this phone call was anything but straightforward. However, Turing had committed.

He lifted the receiver and dialed.

The line rang twice, then twice more. After a long pause, a polished young voice answered, promising to relay his request if he would hold. Turing, never one to waste time, began drafting instructions for his team while he waited.

Meanwhile, in Whitehall, a newly appointed junior file clerk approached Colville's desk woefully uninformed about office protocol. It was her turn on telephone duty, and she was entirely unaware of the gravity of the person holding the line.

She leaned in hesitantly. "There's a gentleman on the line wishing to speak with Mr. Churchill."

The response was swift, sharp, and utterly dismissive.

Colville barely glanced up. Irritation flashed across his face as he ignored the girl and instead barked across the room, "Mrs. Nell! I've a situation that demands your immediate attention."

Mrs. Nell, composed as ever, was on her way.

Colville jabbed a finger toward the bewildered clerk. "Be so good as to inform this young lady," he said, voice thick with exasperation, "that the vast majority of the human race would dearly love a word with the Prime Minister. And her duty to ensure they do *not* succeed."

Mrs. Nell regarded the trembling clerk with cool detachment before reaching for the slip of paper in her hand. She then turned back to Colville, her voice as measured and unflappable as ever. "As always, Mr. Colville, your insight is unimpeachable. I shall see Miss Denton receives the orientation we didn't have time to give her this morning, as she started on one of your assignments immediately."

Miss Denton stood stiffly at attention, understanding—without fully comprehending—that she had just blundered into the very heart of an ongoing power struggle. She did not yet grasp the internal workings of Whitehall, but she instinctively recognized two opposing forces: one ruled by sheer, frantic energy, the other by steady, immovable resolve.

Colville was like a trapped bird—darting, dive-bombing, rattling the office into a frenzy before perching only long enough to resume his chaos anew. Mrs. Nell, on the other hand, was a mountain. Unshakable. Unmoved. A woman who executed her duties with methodical precision, entirely immune to theatrics.

She turned to Miss Denton with quiet authority. "If you please, Miss Denton, kindly put the call through. I shall be along shortly."

Miss Denton all but fled, eager to remove herself from the field of battle.

Mrs. Nell waited precisely the appropriate amount of time before speaking again. Then, with a faint smile, she said, "Your instincts are sound, Mr. Colville. It is indeed imperative to filter such interruptions. However, some among the masses do occasionally get through."

At that very moment, the forwarded call rang beneath Colville's hand. The sudden buzz made him flinch.

Mrs. Nell presented the slip of paper and arched an eyebrow. "And it appears Dr. Turing is one of them."

Colville stared at her. He was acutely aware that he had been deftly managed—yet again—and that this was far from the first such occasion.

He exhaled, his chair tilting back, and with an air of forced good grace, said, "You're absolutely right, Mrs. Nell. I am, as always, grateful for your assistance."

Knowing she'd won the day but not wanting to demonstrate the slightest sign of improper decorum, Mrs. Nell replied, "You are most welcome, Mr. Colville."

Chapter Forty-Two

Turing's Office
Bletchley Park

Turing sat at his desk, his left elbow bracing the notepad as he jotted down notes, utterly absorbed. He was well into the fourth item on his list, momentarily forgetting that he was still on hold with Churchill's office.

"Dr. Turing, how are you today?" came the familiar voice of Jock Colville. "We don't often have the pleasure of speaking."

Turing blinked, shifting his focus back to the call. "Quite true," he said. "As you know, we're keeping our heads well below the parapet until we've something redeeming to report." He hesitated briefly before taking what he knew to be a long shot. "Might there be a possibility of speaking with the Prime Minister? I can't claim to have redeeming news, but I *do* have something rather intriguing."

"I'm afraid he's engaged at present," Colville replied smoothly. "In conference with Lord Beaverbrook, and they'll be dining in. Shall I arrange for a return call?"

Turing considered his promise and duty balanced against his pressing desire to get on with his work. A message might suffice.

"If you would," he said. "This morning at Bletchley, I had an extraordinary conversation with a Mr. Dunning. In short, he demonstrated knowledge of my project—detailed knowledge—some of which, to my astonishment, may constitute a breakthrough. The curious thing isn't just that he knew our secrets, but he imparted *new* information—secrets that, until this morning, did not exist." He paused. "I admit that all sounds rather convoluted."

Colville, mid-sentence in his notetaking, stopped writing.

Turing pressed on. "At the very least, it's unusual. At worst, deeply unsettling—except that he was *right* in his recommendations." He bent the truth ever so slightly. "Mr. Dunning made it plain that this information was merely an overture—an effort to gain my cooperation in delivering even more vital intelligence directly to the Prime Minister. It does not concern my work, but he insisted it was urgent and of the highest consequence to the war effort. He made me swear I'd do what I could to secure an audience with Mr. Churchill, that he might tell his story himself. I assure you, I wouldn't be making this call were I not convinced of the caliber of what we discussed. I feel duty-bound to try."

Colville glanced down at the place where his notes had faltered. "And what, Doctor, shall I put down as the subject of this request? That an unknown civilian wishes to disclose to the highest authority certain secrets which, by all accounts, do not yet exist?" His tone was not unkind, but his incredulity was evident. "With the greatest respect—how am I meant to frame such a thing?"

Turing exhaled. "Mr. Colville, I know my standing within the administration is hardly stellar. Even knowing that I am prepared to stake whatever influence I possess on ensuring this man is taken seriously—or, at the very least, given the opportunity to make a fool of us both."

There was a silence. Neither man spoke.

Turing shifted. "Very well, then. I acknowledge the... unorthodox nature of this request. I'll handle it myself. If I can secure a meeting, I'll take full responsibility."

Still uncertain what to make of the entire exchange, Colville hesitated before replying. "Very well, Doctor. I'll be in touch, and with luck, we'll see you tomorrow."

"Thank you," Turing said and replaced the receiver.

For a moment, he sat motionless, drumming his fingers lightly against the desk. None of this sat easily with him. He commanded an entire unit of the finest minds, working at the edge of an uncharted science backed by an almost limitless budget. Their efforts had produced work of staggering complexity—genuine scientific breakthroughs—but none of it, thus far, had been enough.

They'd been digging in the same hole for months to find the prize, and then, out of nowhere, a stranger appeared, dug a completely new hole, and found the very thing they had been searching for.

And somehow, impossibly, he had done so using information that *should not have existed.* Turing and his team had already discovered some of it. Some, Turing alone, had known. But the rest... the rest had come from nowhere at all.

His team had held the pieces. Dunning had rearranged them—into something far greater than the sum of its parts.

But why? Why do such a thing, knowing that the British authorities would view it with intense suspicion?

One thing was certain: they would need to determine the *source* of this knowledge. Harming the man was out of the question—he was far too valuable. But detaining him?

That was another matter entirely.

Chapter Forty-Three

Milton Keynes

The group arrived at the taxi stand at the top of High Street in Milton Keynes, where a fare was always certain, given the steady stream of patrons from the restaurants and shops. Their purpose was to see Mrs. Somerville safely on her way home.

Thomas stepped out first, offering his hand to the older woman as she emerged from the Austin. "Not sure how things will unfold," he said, "and I can't say when we'll be able to get back to you."

"Then let me stay," she declared, eyes twinkling. "I'd rather not miss any of the action."

Margaret smiled at her, a look both affectionate and amused.

"Oh, don't give me that look," Mrs. Somerville giggled. "I wasn't born yesterday, you know. And don't you worry about me?" She patted the stout handbag tucked firmly beneath her arm. "This may look like an ordinary handbag, but I assure you, it's a lethal weapon. There are moves I haven't even shown you yet."

Thomas laughed. "Then it's a good thing I eventually grew on you."

"Good, my dear sir? That's putting it mildly. Now, off with the both of you!" She shooed them towards the car with a dismissive wave of her hand.

"It's a bit of a ride," Thomas said. "Can I help with the fare?"

She scoffed. "You want to give me money? I've got plenty of money. The trouble is, there's nothing worth buying because of this bloody war—oh!" She clapped a hand over her mouth, eyes twinkling with mischief. "Pardon me! That sort of language never escapes my lips—well… hardly ever."

Thomas grinned.

"Now, be off," she continued. "And when you do call, mind who might be listening."

"Isn't that a bit dramatic?"

She fixed him with a knowing look. "No, Mr. Watson, being shot at is dramatic. Or have you forgotten that already? Now, go on!"

With that, she turned towards the street, scanning the stand. Spying a lone cab idling in the queue, she brought two fingers to her lips and let out a sharp, piercing whistle that made Thomas flinch.

"*Cabbie!*" she bellowed. "Wake up, you're on the clock!"

Margaret and Thomas climbed back into the Austin, watching her march towards the taxi in that unmistakable way—one arm clamped firmly around her handbag, the other swinging high as though she were leading a royal parade.

Thomas settled into his seat, eyes following her down the street, a quiet smile playing on his lips.

Women, he thought. What amazing, wonderful creatures.

Margaret, seated beside him, caught the subtle tilt of his head, the faint, knowing smile. She said nothing, sitting still, her silence impossible to ignore.

Thomas sighed, finally turning towards her. "What?"

"You know what," she said smoothly. "Just like you know cricket."

"It was a harmless thought," he replied, "about the most dangerous of subjects: women."

Margaret narrowed her eyes. "Thomas Watson, you don't know danger. Not until you've seen me properly cross." She leaned in, her voice carrying a playful edge. "Now take me to a hotel, buy me dinner, and wipe that smile off your face."

Before he could respond, she slid closer, pressed a quick kiss to his cheek, then just as swiftly retreated to the driver's side.

Thomas blinked. "What was that?"

Margaret's only answer was the engine's roar as she threw the Austin into gear, shooting past the taxi stand where Mrs. Somerville was now banging on the cab's roof, rousing the driver with the vigor of a general rousing troops for battle.

Chapter Forty-Four

Whitehall
War Rooms

Churchill sat in silence, the heavy receiver back in its cradle, his mind troubled by the grim report he had just received.

Two U-boats had ambushed Convoy SC 2, sinking three ships. All hands lost. The other casualty, though not of flesh and blood, was no less a blow—an essential cargo vessel carrying military provisions, including a vast quantity of tinned meat he had personally ensured would be sent to bolster morale.

The attack had come while the submarines surfaced, evading British ASDIC's detection. It was a brazen maneuver and, worse—an effective one. Hitler's Kriegsmarine was tightening its grip on the Atlantic lifeline, slowly strangling England's connection to North America.

A sharp knock at the door broke his thoughts.

He exhaled, rubbed his brow, and barely glanced up as the door edged open. Jock Colville, ever observant, had waited for the signal—the small light on Churchill's telephone—to flicker off before entering.

"Prime Minister, may I interrupt with a curious update?"

Churchill's voice came too loudly, irritated but weary. "Only, Mr. Colville, *only* if it is bloody good news and not yet another weight for these shoulders to bear. Answers, Colville! That is what I need. Answers to the—"

Churchill stopped abruptly. The silence that followed was unsettling, even by the standards of the War Rooms.

When he finally spoke again, it was with measured calm. "I would, however, be most happy to entertain the details of your curious update, Mr. Colville. You may proceed."

In an unusual move, Colville stepped fully inside and closed the door behind him.

"This comes from Mr. Maston, sir—head of security at Bletchley. There's been… an incident at the compound."

Churchill frowned. "What sort of incident?"

Colville consulted his notes. “A man—calling himself Mr. Dunning—arrived at Bletchley, seeking Dr. Turing. He survived an apparent attempt on his life by an unknown assailant, then managed to evade both the attacker and our security forces, who attempted to detain him. They did, however, apprehend another unidentified individual.”

Churchill raised an eyebrow.

“There’s more,” Colville continued. “This Dunning, almost certainly an alias, displayed an alarming degree of knowledge regarding the Ultra project. Naturally, this caused great consternation among those at the site. Quite beside himself, Dr. Turing made it clear to Mr. Maston that this man is valuable. He insists Dunning’s knowledge could directly assist the project.”

Colville closed his notebook and exhaled sharply. “Frankly, sir, I find it hard to believe that any unknown figure—this Dunning or anyone else—could possess the expertise required to be of use in Dr. Turing's efforts.”

Churchill leaned back, fingers steepled in thought.

. “I spoke with Turing this morning regarding this Dunning, and he insisted he be allowed to talk to him. But even more urgent was his insistence on a meeting with you directly.”

A ghost of a smile touched Churchill’s lips. “Perhaps Dunning is an angel,” he said. “God knows Turing needs one.”

He sat forward, eyes keen now. “Regardless, nothing is more critical than this Turing business, Colville. The success of the Ultra project must be secured at any cost. See if you can fit him in.”

He reached for a cigar, rolling it between his fingers as he spoke. “Jock, see to it that Dr. Turing has immediate access to this Dunning—if we can find him. I want no excuses. No obstacles. This infernal effort at Bletchley must be set on the right course. It can save lives—let alone the bloody country.”

Colville gave a sharp nod. “Yes, sir.”

“Furthermore,” Churchill continued, “instruct Mr. Maston to properly secure the Bletchley compound. I never believed in his fool notion of keeping a low profile as a means of protection. The place should have been locked down ages ago.”

“I’ll see to it at once, sir,” Colville said, already moving.

Churchill took a slow draw from his cigar, exhaling in a thin stream as the door clicked shut behind his private secretary.

The war was not just being fought on the seas or in the skies. There were battles, too, in shadows and whispers—and *this*, he knew, was one of them.

Chapter Forty-Five

Yuri Visits Pavel

Yuri's legs were beginning to protest, the silent torment of anyone who had ever stood watch. He had been waiting outside Pavel's second-story flat for nearly two hours. If he was to untangle this mess, he had to speak with Pavel. The man always knew things—too much, more often than not—but Yuri had always trusted him. Still, loyalty was a fickle thing, and Yuri was no fool. He knew that a telephone call was out of the question. If Pavel was not alone, it could be the end of both of them.

A sliver of light leaked through the blackout curtains. Yuri had hoped his extended stakeout would reveal whether anyone else was interested in Pavel's movements. It turned out someone did. He had spotted a lone officer posted at a distance. That gave Yuri some confidence in Pavel's loyalty.

The officer—leaning against a doorway between rounds—lit a cigarette. He made a pass every fifteen or twenty minutes, disappearing into the shell of an abandoned building in between. A reasonable hiding place, though not ideal. His line of sight covered the primary approaches but not the back of the building. Yuri had been studying him, recognizing his height and his distinctive gait.

It could only be Sergei—one of Yuri's men. *Аист человек*—"Stork Man," as they called him. That he had been given such poor vantage points suggested he was following orders, not issuing them. Someone had placed him here deliberately.

Yuri had no intention of forcing his man to make a choice he might regret later. Instead, he moved at the opportune moment, slipping around the back of the building. He had been through this entrance a hundred times before.

Up the stairs and down the hall.

He peered through the rough, translucent glass of Pavel's door, searching for movement, a shadow, anything out of place.

Nothing.

Could Pavel be inside, held at gunpoint? Or worse?

Yuri rapped his knuckles against the wood. He heard movement and stepped aside.

"Who is it?" Pavel's voice.

Lowering his tone, Yuri answered in an acquired English accent. "Sorry 'bout the hour, mate. No offense, but I was expectin' a lady, ya know. Am I early?"

Silence. Then, the sound of the latch turning.

The door cracked open. Pavel's head appeared, eyes scanning the corridor, first one way, then the other. Yuri's attention fell to Pavel's arm—held stiffly behind his back.

A pistol?

Pavel motioned him inside, bringing the revolver forward, thumbing the safety back into place.

"Did Аист see you?" he asked.

"No," Yuri replied. "I trained him, remember?"

Pavel frowned. "Then why is he the only one here?"

"My guess? He's following bad orders."

Pavel exhaled sharply and gestured toward the kitchen table. "I have hot tea."

"No, my friend. I won't stay long."

Pavel wrinkled his nose. "By the way, that was a dreadful accent."

Yuri grinned. "It fools the English—sometimes. Anyway, I had to be sure you were alone."

The tension eased. The men embraced a bear hug that carried unspoken relief.

"How are you?" Pavel asked.

Yuri let out a breath. "To be honest, my friend… I don't know."

Pavel's expression darkened. "Yuri, the knives are out. I don't know much, but I was told—more like warned—to stay here and not speak to anyone. That meant you."

"Who gave that order?"

"A very dangerous man from Moscow Centre."

Yuri described Joseph.

"No, no," Pavel said. "This guy's mind and body are like one of Stalin's tanks. He has the authority and mental capacity to take 'devious' to another level."

"Tell me what you can."

Pavel nodded. "I was following Watson and his wife in the countryside last night. I heard he was bound for Bletchley in the morning, and that didn't sit right. He had no business there—unless he meant to speak to the British authorities. And if he did, what could he say but things that would compromise Russian security?"

Yuri listened in silence.

"I went back to the embassy to telephone you," Pavel continued, "but before I could, a colonel from the NKVD walked in behind me."

Yuri stiffened. "NKVD? Name?"

"Viktor Grigoryevich Krivitsky."

Yuri's jaw tightened.

"I've never seen him before," Pavel said. "Not in the halls, not anywhere. But he knew things—too much, too precisely. And he was casual about it. Like an assassin who prefers subtlety."

"Go on."

"He asked what I was doing. I told him I reported to you, and that he should know the standard procedure. That's when he took out his papers—with great satisfaction and arrogance, I might add—and declared that *he* was now in charge. He said he wanted to know everything. There was no way he could have known I had been tailing Watson, but he knew his name."

Yuri's fingers tapped lightly against the edge of the table.

"He made it clear," Pavel said, "that I now reported to him. And when I mentioned Watson going to Bletchley, his interest sharpened. Too much. I suggested we contact you, and that was the end of the conversation. He told me I was off the assignment. He said that he would bring you up to speed personally. He boxed me in, Yuri. It left me no room to maneuver. Then he told me to come here. To stay here. To disappear."

Pavel checked his watch, then moved to the window, parting the drapes just enough to see the street below.

"He's still there," he muttered. "Sergei. I expect Krivitsky put him there deliberately, knowing I'd see him."

Yuri barely heard. His mind was turning over something else.

Pavel said, "I'm sure he chose that place because I can see him. Sergei is a good man. Another thing, since I'm on vacation, you must assume my field duties, as I can't. Especially the 'Actor' drop off."

Pavel's face was grave. "Where do we stand, Yuri? Where do any of us stand?"

Yuri met his gaze. "For now, you follow orders. If you get the chance, tell the others to do the same. My guess is he's in over his head, and his ego sees some opportunities he can capitalize on."

"I don't think so," Pavel said. " Yuri, he's not just opportunistic. He's dangerous. Be careful."

Yuri thought about what the Ambassador had said about them sending an officer and things becoming unpredictable.

The telephone rang.

Yuri remained still. Pavel hesitated, then picked up the receiver.

A voice barked through the line. "Pavel. This is Comrade Viktor. I want Watson's address."

"It should be in the file at the office," Pavel replied.

"I *said* I want the address. I am *not* at the office, but that shouldn't matter. Get me what I want."

Pavel could hear it—the strain in Viktor's voice. Something had gone wrong.

"Of course, comrade," Pavel said smoothly. "I'll get my notes."

His coat hung in the entryway. Retrieving his pocketbook, he flipped through the pages, found the address, and turned it toward Yuri—a silent question in his eyes.

Yuri thought for a moment. Whoever Watson was, he wouldn't be foolish enough to return home. They'd likely end up at her mother's estate.

Yuri gave a slow nod.

Picking up the receiver, Pavel read off the address, after which Viktor immediately rang off.

Yuri exhaled. "He must be going to the Watson's house. Someone tried to kill Watson today. At Bletchley. Two gunmen."

Pavel's eyes widened. "At Bletchley? In broad daylight? It was him, Yuri. It had to be."

Yuri stood. "Then I need to find him. Has he filed with the embassy? Do we know where he's staying?"

"Sorry. Yuri, I don't think the embassy even knows he's here."

Yuri exhaled, deep in thought. "That's a shame," he muttered. "Since I know he's going to Watson's, I could turn over his place or confront him when he returns. One way or another, I'll find him. I have to."

He moved toward the door, then turned back to Pavel. "Listen, my friend. If you have to play along, follow his orders. Play his game. But if you must shoot—miss. Do you understand me?"

Pavel grinned. "Of course. I learned from the master." He clapped Yuri on the shoulder. "I'm almost the best."

Yuri smirked, giving him a return slap. "Almost? That's like saying you *almost* dodged the bullet. Do you have a torch?"

Pavel chuckled as he stepped to a cabinet above the sink, retrieving a torch and tossing it to Yuri. Then, without a word, he crossed the room to the fuse panel, pulling it out from the wall by a few inches. Reaching into the hidden space, he extracted a cloth bag.

From inside, he produced another pistol and set it on the table. A moment later, he pulled out a few more items. Yuri reached for three passports beside a bundle of British pound notes and Russian rubles. He flipped open the Spanish one and looked up with a knowing smile.

Pavel grinned proudly. "As I said, I learned from the master."

"Yes," Yuri said, closing the passport. "Almost."

Pavel eyed him thoughtfully. "I know how you feel about guns, Yuri, but you can't walk into a meeting with a man like this armed with nothing but an order of fish and chips." He nudged the pistol forward. "Come on. You know I'm right. It's clean. Not registered here."

Yuri picked it up, turning it over in his hands. The machined edges along the squared barrel, the deep crisscross pattern on the grip—it was a solid weapon. He thought about the contents of his locker, about what lay ahead, and with a sigh, he slid it into his outer pocket.

"There are two clips in there," Pavel added. "Be careful."

Yuri shrugged. "Won't matter if I can't find him."

Pavel exhaled. "Just remember, he's ruthless and arrogant. A dangerous combination."

The sentence barely left his lips before his expression shifted. Something had clicked into place. Without another word, he bolted past Yuri to his jacket hanging by the door.

Yuri watched as Pavel frantically searched the pockets. Then, suddenly, he looked up, beaming.

The kind of grin a man wears when he's just found the telephone number of the only girl in ten years who told him to call.

"I think he's here," Pavel said, holding up a book of matches. "Without thinking of the consequences, the arrogant bastard threw it at me."

Yuri plucked it from his hand and turned it over. The front bore a logo with the words Old Plough Inn. He flipped it open and scanned the address inside.

"Fifty-two Parson's Mead," he read aloud. He nodded. "I think I should go."

Pavel strode back to the window, parting the drapes. "Sergei's just now walking over the bricks—heading into that wreck of a building. If you're going, go now."

Yuri pocketed the matches. "Then it's settled." He pulled the door open but paused. "I'll contact you when I have answers. If I don't remember… play the game."

Pavel gave a firm nod.

Then, without another word, Yuri stepped into the night.

Chapter Forty-Six

Viktor Sets Up Watch

Viktor knew he'd planned the operation well. The embassy's knowledge of the layout and uses of the different huts at Bletchley was essential to the plan. There were guards everywhere, but every hut had a specific purpose, and only one held the security team that would interrogate Watson. He also had a roving team in a car covering possible escape routes, which ended in the park shooting. Nevertheless, at the end of it all, they missed the critical shot. Only an incompetent idiot would miss at such a distance.

He'd taken a chance. Success would have meant being honored for his bravery and assertive action, but it failed. Viktor needed to change what could become a messy failure into a success. Keeping a resident spy from going to the British, thereby compromising the entire in-country effort, would make everything right. He still intended to stop Watson but needed to do so quickly.

Viktor shouted at Dimetry, the embassy officer who was driving. "Stop at the next phone box." He got out, made a short call, and returned to the car with a slip of paper with an address. Viktor gave the driver the paper and said he needed to be there in a hurry.

Viktor's mind raced as the driver pulled up two houses short of Margaret's. He didn't expect Watson to be there but hoped the man might be that dumb, so he had to cover the possibility.

Viktor and Dimetry slowly walked up to a side window. The lights were off, and the blackout shades were open. It appeared no one had been here during the evening, and it was empty. Viktor quickly approached the front door and told the officer to pick the lock. He did so quickly, and they both rushed into the house with guns drawn, checking all the rooms.

Viktor angrily shouted, "Check the backyard and alley."

Flipping the lights on, Viktor could barely control his anger. He needed to get Watson now. His next attempt had to be successful. He would report the initial unsuccessful attempt, blaming the inept shooters, and when he'd straightened it all out, he would bask in the glory of Moscow's admiration. The first step was finding the couple. In addition, he needed to return to his room at the inn because the other idiots in his group would be calling for instructions. The last thing he wanted was some half-wit wandering around, getting caught doing something stupid.

"There is no one out back," Dmitry said. Comrade Krivitsky, we must turn out the lights or draw the shades, as the local warden will ask questions. He'll know we don't live here."

Viktor ignored him and ordered, "Stay here and set up observation from across the street or somewhere, but don't let anyone see you. If they show up, break in and hold them. If Watson tries to escape, kill him and leave. If not, I want to question him about Bletchley."

The officer did not reply. Dmitry, one of Yuri's men, was caught up in something, but he didn't know what. The colonel's credentials were enough to make him obey any order, but this wasn't going smoothly. Being very careful with every step, he asked, "Do you want me to call you if they show up?"

"Of course, you idiot."

"Comrade Krivitsky?" The officer said hesitantly.

"What could you possibly not understand?" Victor almost shouted.

"I'll need a number to call if you won't be at the embassy."

Irritated, Viktor wrote a number on a slip of paper he found on the dining table. Looking over at the telephone shelf in the wall, he also noted that number, just in case. He handed his number to the man and said gruffly, "You can get me here. Keep trying. I'll send a man to relieve you in a few hours."

"Yes, comrade."

Viktor opened the door and said, "If Comrade Stakova shows up, put him on the phone to me immediately. At gunpoint, if you have to."

"But…"

"You've your orders. Follow them!" Viktor barked.

The door slammed shut. Dmitry had been in the country for over two years and knew how the embassy worked. At all costs, it avoided this kind of visibility in the community. If Yuri knew the orders Viktor was following, he would have his badge. Unfortunately, this comrade jerk outranked Yuri. The officer heard Viktor start the car and loudly speed away, certainly drawing the attention of anyone in the area. Dmitry thought, "This man might have the credentials, but it doesn't mean he knows his way around in the field."

Quickly turning off the lights, the officer walked outside to see if they'd raised any suspicion. The deserted street and the houses on either side appeared to be deserted. He started looking for a good place to set up his post. He needed a cigarette but decided to wait until he could get himself hidden. He had a photo of Watson and a description of his wife. In a blackout, knowing what they looked like would be useless unless they entered the house.

Viktor grabbed the wheel tightly and retraced his route back to the embassy. From there, he was sure he would recall his path back to the inn where he was staying. He struggled with driving; it was black, and every vehicle was upon him quickly. He knew he had to return to be there when his fieldmen called his room. He had Joseph look over Yuri's place in case he showed up, which was unlikely.

Chapter Forty-Seven

High Street—Milton Keynes

Mrs. Somerville spotted the cab driver sitting motionless, lost in thought. His mind was far from the empty streets of London, calculating for the third time how much he could send home to his family in Bangalore. No matter how he figured it out, the sum always fell short of his promise. The nightly bombings kept people indoors, cutting into his earnings. The only remedy was longer hours and greater sacrifice—his only solace, the knowledge that his toil provided for those he loved.

A sharp whistle pulled him from his thoughts. He threw an arm over the back of his seat, peering through the rear windscreen. An older woman approached confidently. A moment later, a thunderous knock on the roof made him jump. He swung the driver's door open and stepped out, hurrying around to assist.

"Madam, it's late," he said with concern. "Not safe for you to be about. Please allow me to—"

"No need, young man," she interrupted, waving him off with a gracious hand. "I can manage quite well, but it's a lovely gesture."

Mrs. Somerville pulled the door shut behind her. "How wonderfully warm it is in here," she murmured appreciatively.

His first fare in an hour. He was grateful. His heritage instilled a duty of care towards his passengers, especially one traveling alone at this hour. "I mean no offense, madam, but you ought not to be wandering alone after the blackout."

"You're Indian?" she asked.

"Yes, but—"

"How delightful. I hardly think of India, so far away."

"It depends on perspective," he replied. "It's here that feels like the far side of the world."

"Quite right. How narrow of me." She leaned forward. "Take me to 128 Chesham Road, Amersham."

"Yes, Mum." He pulled down the gearshift, setting off.

She studied him for a moment. "Sounds as if your heart is still in your homeland."

"My family is there, and I am stuck here, unable to return because of the war. The borders are closed. I must stay to earn, yet some stranger decides I may not see my wife and children." He touched the brake as they rounded a corner.

She understood something of separation. There was a gentleness about the man, and she could not recall the last time a cabbie had made an effort to open her door. "You've chosen a perilous trade—driving blind through the city, avoiding collisions in total darkness."

"It's not a choice so much as what's left to a foreigner like me. The work others refuse is all that remains."

Mrs. Somerville turned to the passing streets, their windows blacked out. A home guard stood on his rounds, his torch beam searching a parked car. She thought of Margaret and Thomas and prayed for their safety. None of this had unfolded as she would have wished. The world had set off in its own direction, making a dreadful mess of things.

She recalled the day the man arrived at her door, flashing a badge and requesting a moment of her time. Over tea, he spoke of England's need for help. Then, to her astonishment, he produced a letter—from Churchill himself. It warned that a young woman from one of Britain's finest families might possess sensitive knowledge. The wrong people might be interested, so her safety was paramount. In reality, she was just a teacher. Still, even the possibility made her a hostage threat. However, due to her personality, confining her against her will or even having her followed would be counter-productive.

The authorities knew Somerville owned the house next door. Would she consider letting it to the woman in question? The tenants had already agreed to relocate, with the government providing a modest subsidy. They had not been given an explanation, nor had they asked for one. War had a way of weaving peculiar stories into the fabric of everyday life.

She had been instructed to place an advert and wait for a Margaret Hatcher to respond. No one else was to be considered. Her sole duty was to keep watch and to report any threats. At first, she had felt a keen sense of duty, a purpose in aiding someone of value to the war effort. But somewhere along the way, Margaret had moved into her heart and stayed there. Mrs. Somerville only hoped this little security charade would not damage their friendship. Would Margaret believe her when she said it had begun as a patriotic endeavor but had become much more personal?

"It was easy to love Margaret," she mused. In many ways, the girl embodied all the qualities one admired—a lively spirit, an enlightened mind, an independence that defied her station. Beneath it all, however, was a quiet longing to be cherished for who she was, not for the name she bore.

Drifting back to her youth, the former Miss Leeds wished she had been like Margaret. But she had belonged to another era. Her generation of women had been lost. She had nothing to show for it but the memory of Charles—the one thing she had come into this world to find and the one thing war had taken from her.

The cab came to a halt, pulling her from her thoughts. She fished in her handbag, glancing at her house.

"Just a little farther, if you please. To the next walkway." She checked the meter and handed him the fare.

Across the street, Dmitry had relocated to an empty house under renovation. It afforded him a perfect view of the target's home and the street before it. He had scarcely settled in when a car approached. He could not make it out without streetlights until it passed directly before him. A cab. His pulse quickened as it braked in front of the target house—only to lurch forward and stop at the neighboring residence.

He felt disappointed and then curious. As the door opened, he shifted for a better view, and a woman emerged. She did not match any of the descriptions he had been given. The driver and passenger exchanged words.

Mrs. Somerville leaned into the cab's window. "Sanjay, that covers the fare and a little extra. It's not much, but send it home. I'm no queen, but you are certainly a gentleman, which is rare in these parts. If I need you again, can I call the company?"

Sanjay beamed. "Of course, Mum. If I'm free, they'll send me."

He moved to exit the car, but she waved him off. "I can manage the steps, but I'd be most grateful if you'd watch until I reach the door."

"Of course, Mum," he said.

Dmitry observed from the shadows. The driver stood by his car, watching the woman climb the steps.

Mrs. Somerville paused for an unknown reason. She turned slightly to see a shadow retreat behind a wall. She thought, "Thomas might be right. Are they watching Margaret's house or hers? She unlocked her door, waved to the cabbie, and stepped inside. She made her rounds, looking across the street before drawing the curtains against the night.

Weariness pressed down upon her as she readied for bed. The day's events settled heavily upon her shoulders. Had she upset Thomas? He had changed; that much was clear. But what weighed upon him? She straightened the blankets, pulled them to her chin, and sighed deeply.

Margaret had become like a daughter to her. That, she knew, was the direct result of who the young woman was. There was no doubt that she must leave the message. There was no choice left for her now.

Tomorrow would change everything.

Chapter Forty-Eight

Yuri Goes To Viktor's Room

The Olde Plough Inn wasn't far from the embassy or Pavel's flat. Yuri knew Viktor was at Margaret's and had a window of time, yet he walked briskly, cursing the absence of a cab.

He reached the inn's entrance and pressed the door open. A rush of noise met him—raucous laughter, shouting, the general din of a pub well into the evening. The ground floor bustled with patrons, thick smoke curling toward the ceiling. The rooms for let were upstairs, but first, he needed information.

A sign reading "Rooms" hung over a high counter. Yuri approached and glanced about. Behind the bar, a man was pouring two pints, balancing the glasses in one hand while the other gripped the polished handle of a Mackeson Stout pump. The barkeep met his gaze with a nod, signaling he'd be over.

When the man finally stepped up, Yuri placed his embassy credentials on the counter. The gold medallion caught the light, and the innkeeper eyed it warily.

"Yes, sir? Fine credentials, those. Are you with the police?"

"No," Yuri replied smoothly. "Russian Embassy. I'm working with the British authorities, tracing one of my countrymen who may be here illegally. It's merely a formality, but the British insist on an answer. The invasion has everyone a little… jumpy. Is that the word?"

"Jumpy, indeed," the man said. "For you, perhaps. For me? I'm just plain scared. What can I do for you?"

"I believe the man has checked in here, but I don't know the room. Have you had anyone with a noticeable accent book a room in the last twenty-four hours? And did he leave his passport at the desk?"

"Of course, gov'ner. It's the law." The man scratched his chin. "Aye, I think I know the one. Something off about how he spoke, but he handed me a British passport all the same."

He reached into his pocket, producing a set of keys, then turned to unlock a cupboard behind him. "Looks like wood, but it's got a metal lining per regulations. Keeps things proper."

A voice from the end of the bar called out. "Lyle! Forget all that; my mate here desperately needs a Scotch!"

"Hold onto yourself. Can't you see I'm busy?" Lyle snapped. "Business before the likes of you!"

The drunken patron lifted his glass and bellowed, "Did ya hear that, lads? I'm takin' me business elsewhere, I am!"

The pub erupted in laughter. "Where'll ya go, Scotty? No one else'll have ya!" someone shouted, bringing the house down.

Lyle smirked and placed a British passport on the counter. Yuri flipped it open, studying Viktor's face for the first time.

"Well, the passport looks in order—though it's likely forged. We have eyes on him, so I know he's not in his room. I'm afraid I'll need to look around up there."

The innkeeper frowned. "Not sure I can allow that, gov'ner. I don't make a habit of breaking the law, y'see."

Yuri tapped the passport. "I understand. But MI5 isn't pleased they overlooked this one. They'd prefer to keep it quiet, so there'll be no questions. Politics, you see. I just follow orders."

Lyle hesitated, then slid a key across the counter. "Number Six. Top of the stairs, end of the hall before the back escape."

Yuri pocketed the key and made his way up, senses alert. He paused before Room Six, back pressed against the wall, listening. Silence. He slid the key in and pushed the door open, letting it swing wide before stepping cautiously inside.

A faint, unfamiliar odor lingered in the air. He flicked on his torch. As he navigated past the bed toward the window, his foot struck something under the bed, and he looked down—a suitcase. Drawing the blackout curtains, he turned his torch downward, retracing his steps to the open door before shutting it and flipping on the ceiling light.

The bed was toward the wall beside the window, near the entrance to the small loo. He knelt by the suitcase, knowing it wouldn't be a serious hiding place but checking nonetheless. Standard Russian issue. Double-lined. Just clothes and personal effects. He replaced everything as he found it.

Viktor was too seasoned to carry anything incriminating. If there were something of value, it would be well hidden—or buried near a tree somewhere.

He ignored the mattress, where Viktor would only hide something he wanted to be found. Given the age of the inn, Yuri was surprised at the private loo. Viktor would have had to request the amenity. "It was small," Yuri thought, clambering up onto the seat of the toilet and shining the torch into the top of the tank. He crouched under the sink, its pipes ancient and rusted, checked the tiles for looseness and examined the baseboard for tampering.

His image in the cabinet mirror above the sink caught his eye. The streaks from the corroded silver crossed his face. It was a snapshot of where he was today, and the picture wasn't pretty. Viktor was a problem; only a few times in Yuri's career did he have to get his hands 'dirty,' as they said, in the field. It wasn't his preference, but he was more than capable, if not usually willing.

The hinge resisted as he swung open the mirrored door. He saw three empty glass shelves coated in dust—except one. The middle shelf bore a faint fingerprint as if it had been removed recently. The back panel had two empty screw holes. Someone had tried removing the cabinet, though how recently, he couldn't tell.

"Sloppy work," he thought. "Not what one expects from a rising star of the Party."

He set down the torch, gripped the cabinet's edges, and rocked it gently. It came away immediately, revealing a crisp, sealed envelope pinned to the back wall.

Due to the small space, he placed the cabinet on the floor outside the bathroom. With the torch's light, he looked carefully at every aspect of the envelope, then carefully pulled the tack and took it off the wall. He opened it.

His breath caught as he unfolded the letter. Moscow Center. Viktor's orders.

He read to the bottom, exhaling slowly. Despite the grim news, he had a clear picture for the first time since meeting the Ambassador. Planning was far more manageable when one knew what one was planning for.

Moscow Center felt the invasion was imminent and German soldiers would soon be on the ground. It wouldn't take long to discover the decrypting machine. Knowing it was compromised, the Germans would design a new machine, rendering the old one worthless. Despite the non-aggression pact between the two countries, Stalin deeply distrusted the German leader. This made obtaining information on Hitler's intentions towards Russia the highest priority. If England were soon to be occupied, the Germans would take a different attitude toward the Russians. Moscow needed a high-profile operative in London, not a diplomat. The Watson operation, now considered useless, was to be terminated. Viktor was to have Yuri kill Watson, and Viktor was to kill Yuri. It was business as usual, Moscow-style.

He slid the letter back into the envelope, pressed the tack precisely where it had been, and ensured the angle matched Viktor's placement. Then, he reinstalled the cabinet, wiped any stray fingerprints from the mirror, and collected the bits of wall plaster that had fallen loose.

With the lights off and the curtains open, he eased the door open an inch, listening. The pub hum drifted up the hall. Satisfied, he stepped out, locking the door behind him.

He had nearly reached the staircase when the sharp crash of breaking glass split the air.

Chapter Forty-Nine

Olde Plough Inn

While Yuri was searching the room, Viktor strode through the inn's front door, moving purposefully. He scanned the crowded bar room, disdain curling his lip. It was intolerable to be forced into a place like this as a cover, a typical dive, instead of accommodations befitting his rank.

The barkeep caught sight of him immediately, recognition flickering across his face. Viktor noted the expression, filing it away. The man had seen him before. No doubt he remembered his check-in.

The barkeep finished serving a customer and moved toward the counter. "Evenin', sir. Can I help?"

"My key," Viktor said curtly.

The man set his bar towel down with careful deliberation, his movements slow, almost measured. Something in the gesture unsettled Viktor. He couldn't define it, but his instincts pricked with warning. The innkeeper turned, unlocking the key cabinet. As it swung open, he reached inside for Room Six's key.

Viktor's body tensed.

"Where's the other key?" he demanded, voice cutting through the low hum of conversation.

"Sir?"

"The other key to my room," Viktor snapped. "All the others have two keys. Where is it?"

"The maid may have it," the keeper said, knowing that the other man might still be upstairs and didn't want any trouble. "Can I pour ya a tall one on the house?" He started walking over to the bar, but Viktor didn't move.

The barkeep offered again. "A pour on the house, Sir?"

A figure stumbled from the back of the room, weaving past Viktor and Lyle, still fastening his trousers as he made his way to the bar.

Scotty, as he was known, had just returned from the loo and took his usual seat, slouching into his stool. Scotty heard the barkeeps offer a free drink and looked at Viktor.

"Not takin' it, eh? Mighty strange," he muttered, resting his head on his hand. He misjudged the counter, and his elbow slipped, sending him lurching forward. He landed too close to Viktor, reeking of cheap ale.

"I'd be takin' it, mister," Scotty slurred. "Not likely you'll see another offer like—"

Viktor shoved Scotty aside, stepping swiftly toward the stairs leading to the rooms. Scotty reeled back, colliding with a table laden with mugs. It tipped beneath his weight, sending him sprawling to the floor. The table followed, crashing onto its side. The sound of breaking glass filled the air as eight or nine empty mugs shattered against the stone.

The room erupted. Chairs scraped against the floor, voices rose in protest, and suddenly, everyone was standing.

Yuri froze as the commotion from the other side of the stained-glass doors at the end of the hall sent a chill down his spine. He looked at the key and decided not to chance returning it. To his left was the noise, and to his right was the escape door leading outside that was likely unlocked. He moved quickly, gripping the doors knob, twisting—it gave way. He slipped through, closing it behind him as he hurried down the back stairs into the cold night.

Viktor ignored Scotty and stormed past the innkeeper, key clenched in his fist. He headed to the door that opened to the hallway of rented rooms. The noise from the pub swelled behind him as angry patrons cursed and shouted. Without hesitation, he slammed through the door, scanning the dim hall ahead.

He moved fast.

Yuri, now in the alley, knew he had only moments. He couldn't clear the passage in time—if Viktor stepped outside and looked, he would be caught in the open. Thinking fast, he wedged between a lorry and the wall, squeezing into the narrow gap. From his position, he could see the stairs through the side and front windows of the vehicle.

He held his breath.

The door at the top of the stairs burst open. A dark silhouette appeared against the night, scanning the alleyway. The figure hesitated and leaned over the railing, eyes searching the tight confines of the passage below.

Then, just as quickly, he turned and retreated inside.

Viktor reached his door. Something was wrong. The missing key and the tension in the barkeep's face were all wrong. He wouldn't take chances.

Without hesitation, he kicked the door in. It flew open with force, the frame splintering. He swept the space with sharp, measured movements, gun drawn, arm steady. The dim light from the hall spilled inside, revealing a room empty of life.

Slowly, he lowered the weapon.

In two strides, he reached the loo. He flicked on the light, his eyes immediately darting to the mirror. The edges were clean—too clean.

He stood in front of the mirror, looking at the edges. "Clean," he thought. Opening the mirrored door, he cursed at his careless tradecraft as he saw the fingerprint on the glass shelf and the empty screw holes. He yanked the cabinet out of the wall, with the glass shelves jostling inside, and saw the envelope but wasn't satisfied.

Moving closer, he examined the lower corner of the envelope tacked to the wall and saw it still aligned perfectly with one of the plaster laths running horizontally. Still, he wasn't sure. He'd been sloppy with the fingerprints and screws, but the missing key was still the only evidence that someone might have been there.

Then the phone rang.

The shrill sound jarred his already raw nerves. He turned sharply toward the open door. Beyond it, angry, drunken patrons slurred and were moving down the hall. The innkeeper pushed them back toward the pub, attempting to calm the growing agitation.

Viktor's eyes locked onto the barkeep.

The look that passed between them needed no words. The innkeeper understood his warning. He gave a nod and turned, ushering the protesting crowd away.

Meanwhile, outside, Yuri didn't linger. Carefully, he untangled himself from his hiding place, muscles aching from the strain. Keeping low, he moved quickly, keeping his eyes on the stairs as he slipped into an adjoining street.

He knew exactly where he was going.

Chapter Fifty

Room at the Inn

After dropping off Mrs. Somerville, Margaret and Thomas knew they had to find a place to hide and get some much-needed rest before facing Margaret's mother the following day.

Margaret drove on, keeping in the general direction of her mother's house. Twice, they pulled over to check if they were being followed. They found nothing but empty, darkened roads lined with blacked-out houses each time. Their new reality was constant vigilance until Thomas could set things right and reclaim their lives.

Thomas studied Margaret as she focused on the road, shifting with practiced ease. Today's chaos wasn't his doing; he was sure of that. But it was his burden to bear, and in carrying it, he had put Margaret in danger. The thought of someone out there trying to harm her made his blood run hot. He wouldn't allow it.

"Thomas," she said, breaking the silence, "something's been bothering me."

"Could it be my charming habit of brooding in silence?" he quipped, hoping to lighten the tension of the past hour, which had felt like something out of a spy novel.

She ignored his attempt. "After you left for Bletchley, remember I told you the Russian called?"

"Yes?"

"He was the only person besides me who knew you were going. Since the British didn't try to kill you this morning, that leaves only one possibility—Yuri. All we need to do is turn him in, and we're safe."

Thomas kept his eyes on her. "First, there was the one who shot at me. Then, there were the two in the park. This is bigger than just Yuri. And second, do we even know who he actually is? Who do we turn in? Have you got an address? I'd love to visit him while he's sleeping."

"Right, Thomas," she scoffed. "And what would you do?"

He caught her eye and said, deadpan, "Whisper in his ear."

Margaret smirked. "Thomas, you couldn't hurt a fly." She glanced at the road, then back at him, her tone suddenly curious. "I think."

Silence stretched between them. Thomas glanced out the rear window. "I'm fairly certain no one's following us. Let's find an inn."

Margaret slammed on the brakes. Thomas lurched forward, bracing against the dashboard. "What the—are you all right?"

"Of course, I'm all right," she said breezily. "You said find a place, and it was right there."

She shifted into reverse, backing toward a stately house that had been converted into an inn for the duration of the war.

At the desk, the matronly innkeeper gave Thomas a long, suspicious look as he signed in as Mr. and Mrs. Thomas Watson for one night. Her eyes dropped to his left hand, noting the absence of a ring.

Upon catching the glance, Margaret said smoothly, "He never wears one."

"I'll need to see your identity cards," the innkeeper said, her expression unreadable.

Thomas knew this was a problem. Being without an identity card was against the law, and he'd purposely left his at home.

"I was robbed today," he said without hesitation. "My wife has hers—it matches the address I wrote down. I know it's unusual, but we need a favor."

Margaret produced her card. "We're on our way to my parents' house in Fernhurst, Surrey. Hatcher is my maiden name."

The woman's gaze lifted sharply. "Sir Ian Everett Hatcher?"

"Yes," Margaret confirmed.

The innkeeper's face softened with recognition. "Your father helped out a close family friend, a man who nearly lost his life in a mill accident—must've been before you were born, young lady: a fine man, your father. We don't forget those kinds of folk. Not many left like him anymore."

She fiddled with a small dish of matches on the counter before finally nodding. "Well, I suppose I can look past it—this time. Not for you, mind, but for your father. None of my business anyhow. That'll be three shillings, paid in advance."

As if Thomas's lack of an identity card wasn't enough, the woman's skeptical glance at the hotel register showed she wasn't entirely convinced of their marriage. Margaret's attempts to maintain her dignity took another hit when she had to borrow a nightgown.

"You can leave the key in the box and the nightgown on the bed in the morning," the woman said, eyeing them over her spectacles. "Or tonight. Whichever."

Inside their room, Margaret sighed heavily and collapsed backward onto the bed, the borrowed nightgown dangling from her fingers. Thomas recognized the signs—she had reached her limit for the day.

He lay beside her on his side and said, "We need food. And at dinner, there will be no talk of today's events. Across the street, I saw a stuffy-looking restaurant with a full car park. It can only be a good sign. What do you say?"

Margaret rolled toward him, wrapping her arms around his neck. "You said you loved me today. In front of Mrs. Somerville."

Thomas smiled. "Could mean it's true, then. What do you think?"

"It better be true," she teased. "My reputation won't be worth a glass of water in this town come morning. You'll have to do right by this unfortunate girl." She pouted dramatically.

"Oh, I don't think you're so unfortunate," he said. "That whole 'Lady Hatcher' act was rather convincing."

She raised an eyebrow. "It wasn't an act. Besides, you weren't exactly useful back there. We'd have been on the street if not for me. I saved the evening, and now you owe me dinner. Kiss me, sir."

"As you wish, my Lady Hatcher," he said mockingly, catching her wrist and pressing it to the bed before she could protest with a swing. Then, before she could say another word, he kissed her—rather thoroughly.

Margaret didn't object. Not now. But knowing her, Thomas suspected there were no guarantees about the future.

Chapter Fifty-One

Yuri to Safe House—Leyton High Road

It had taken Yuri over an hour to reach Euston Station near Regent's Park. The air raid sirens had sounded earlier, sending people scattering for shelter, and now the station sat nearly empty. It made blending into a crowd impossible, and he decided it was best to wait up the street. He stood with hands in his pockets, watching the station from afar. He would move when the all-clear sounded and things returned to normal.

Eventually, the long, wavering note of the all-clear siren filled the air. A shopkeeper across from the station raised the rolling security panels on his newsstand, the clatter breaking the stillness.

Yuri strolled over. "You're open late."

"Gotta be open when ya can, I say. Lucky for me, people still read."

Yuri stood at the stand, scanning the magazines. Now and then, he tilted his head as though taking an interest in a particular cover, only to glance away again. After a moment, he handed over a shilling for the weekly in his hand and stepped into the street, seizing the opportunity to scan for movement in both directions—traffic, faces, anything out of place.

He glanced down at his purchase. *The War Illustrated.* Staring back at him was a black-and-white image of two helmeted civil defense wardens peering through the gaping hole in a bombed-out church. Across the top, bold lettering read, *Nazis Target Church.*

"It's only going to get worse," he muttered, stepping onto the curb.

A station teeming with people, the clatter of luggage, the hiss of steam from an engine—it was all strangely comforting. He moved toward a shop offering travelers biscuits and tea, but his true destination lay just beyond: six long rows of metal station lockers. He took a slow, measured circuit around them. The first two rows housed small compartments, barely large enough for a child's schoolbooks. The third row and beyond contained larger lockers meant for luggage.

He slid his hand into his coat pocket, fingers closing around cold metal. As he reached the locker he sought, he withdrew the key and fitted it into the lock. The door swung open. Relief washed over him. Nothing had changed.

Two leather bags sat where he had left them nearly three years ago, gathering dust. He pulled them onto the floor, a fine cloud rising in the air. Lowering himself to one knee, he unzipped the smaller of the two. Inside, neatly packed, were clothes, money in several currencies, a rail pass, and multiple passports—each linked to a different escape route—his other identity. Slipping the handgun from his pocket, he nestled it into the bag's depths and zipped it shut.

The second bag was longer and slimmer. It contained more clothes and money—just in case he lost the first. But despite its unassuming appearance, it was the heavier of the two. Inside rested a Lee-Enfield Mk I rifle, standard issue for the British Army.

Yuri was no stranger to the shifting tides of life or the tradecraft of his profession. Nothing ever remained the same, not with the people involved. Change was inevitable. The only way to survive was to be ready. Within days of arriving from Italy, he had made these arrangements. He had also secured a flat on Leyton High Road, far from the embassy's quarters near the docks. Ostensibly, it was a personal retreat—somewhere to disappear when he needed solitude. In truth, its primary purpose was to act as a secret, safe place for him to go in case of trouble from any faction.

The cabbie barely glanced at him as he hefted the bags into the boot. He settled into the back seat, "Twenty-three Frederick Place. Do you know it?"

"Indeed, sir. 'Bout twenty minutes—provided the German bastards are done for the night. Travelin' late, are ya? Hard to hear the sirens on the train."

"They started after we pulled in," Yuri replied absently. His mind was already moving ahead, calculating. "Been a long day. I think I'll close my eyes a bit." It was enough to silence further conversation.

The journey passed in a blur. When the cab rolled to a stop, he felt sure he hadn't indeed drifted off. A mistake. He had to be more careful.

"Here we are, sir. You sure this is the place?"

"Yes, that's it." He eyed the man. "How do you drivers remember so many streets?"

"Born here, sir. Still live in me Mum's house. Streets stay the same—it's the world tha' changes."

"Yes. Indeed." Yuri reached for the door handle as the driver stopped

The bags hit the pavement with a dull thud. He paid the fare and offered a brief nod. "Good night."

"Good night to ya, sir."

Yuri lingered. He fussed with the bags, waiting. Only when the cab faded into the darkness did he move. He turned the corner, stepping onto Leyton High Road.

To his right, the vast common stretched into darkness. Without the city's glow, it felt as though the world ended just thirty feet away. But from his flat's window, the common remained unmoved by day, a fixed point amid London's turmoil. Commons also don't move, he thought with a wry smile.

He turned into an alley behind the buildings lining Leyton High Road. The rear entrance of his flat awaited. After two trips up the narrow staircase, the bags were inside.

Only then did he allow himself to relax.

The flat was sparsely furnished, but that had always been the point. He was sure no one—no one but Pavel—knew of this place. Until now, he had kept nothing here that could be traced back to him. Anything incriminating had been stored in the station locker.

But things had changed.

He sank into the oversized leather chair, the day's weight settling into his bones. He thought of shifting alliances and the dangerous gaps in his knowledge. In espionage, the rules were simple: tie up loose ends, protect your people, and extract cleanly.

And above all else, never leave behind a mess.

Messy operations attracted attention, which led to investigations that had a habit of uncovering things best left buried—never a good thing in the spy business.

Chapter Fifty-Two

The Fox Restaurant

Margaret and Thomas crossed the unlit road quickly, keeping to the shadows. Thomas gestured toward a building at the far end of the street, its structure barely holding after a recent blast. There was no fire but severe damage. The area bustled with movement—official torchlights crisscrossing through the dust-filled air as rescue crews arrived. Wardens rapped on doors, ushering people from their homes, their voices sharp with urgency. Brightly colored ropes marked the perimeter, keeping onlookers at bay. Within that secured zone, a cluster of men in authoritative uniforms stood in grave discussion. A bomb disposal unit—Sappers, they were called—would soon arrive to deal with the unexploded device.

Thomas shook his head. No amount of money could ever be enough to hover over an active bomb and defuse it by hand.

Considering the chaos of his life, it was almost normal to have dinner just outside an evacuation zone, a potential disaster smoldering in the background. He pulled open the door of the restaurant for Margaret, and they stepped into a world far removed from the devastation outside.

Warmth greeted them first from a fire crackling in the great hearth. The air smelled of roasted meat and fine wine. Except for a uniformed officer dining with a lady, there was little to suggest a war was on.

The Fox had long been known for serving what others could not. Rumor had it the proprietor had an arrangement with the officer's commissary, though no one cared enough to question the origins of scarce delicacies. Soft lighting bathed the restaurant in an amber glow and hushed conversations over polished china and delicate crystal. Here, society's upper crust still dined with civility, the war an unwelcome but distant guest.

"No fish and chips here," Thomas mused.

Margaret shushed him. "It's romantic, don't you think?"

"Your mother's sort of place."

"She loves it."

"You could have mentioned that sooner."

Thomas glanced about. The walls were covered in paintings, each depicting a variation of the same theme—fox hunting. Masters of the hunt, flanked by their red-coated assistants, galloped through rolling countryside, packs of hounds in pursuit of their cunning quarry. The riders' backs were ramrod straight as they soared over hedgerows, followed by a dutiful staff prepared to serve an extravagant lunch, regardless of the hunt's outcome. It was all rather traditional and, to Thomas, a delightful waste of time.

He took their coats to the cloakroom, placing their gas mask containers alongside several others. Some had been fashioned into fashionable accessories, tucked into large handbags, strapped to umbrellas, or covered in cheerful fabric. If one had to carry the wretched things, why not make a statement?

Upon returning, he found Margaret speaking with a man impeccably dressed in a tailored Italian suit, hair slicked back, his practiced smile one of effortless charm.

The maître d' clasped his hands. "My sincerest apologies, madam, but your mother's table is occupied. We weren't expecting you. However, I do have a most agreeable table by the fire. Quite private, quite perfect."

Without awaiting a response, he swept his arm toward a secluded table. They passed the soldier in uniform, and he guided Margaret to her chair at the table, carefully sliding it into place. Then, the smile vanished, and he turned, eyes locking onto one of his waiters with a glare that could shatter glass. He delivered his silent command with a mere tilt of his chin before instantly restoring his genial expression to Thomas and Margaret.

With a graceful bow, he said, "Andre will see to your every need."

As he vanished, Thomas chuckled. "I see why your mother likes it here. But why would you? That man is as phony as a wooden nickel."

"What's a nickel?" Margaret asked.

Thomas hesitated.

Margaret had learned to move on when his thoughts drifted. "She enjoys the ambiance, the menu, and the small fact that she has an account here."

"I thought you refused family help."

"I did," she said, intently arranging her napkin.

Thomas studied her. The relationship with her mother was more complicated than she let on. There were feelings there, indeed, but she fought them. Why?

Andre was, in fact, at his best, exuding far more warmth than his superior. Over dinner, they flitted from topic to topic, conversation moving rapidly. For once, they were simply Margaret and Thomas, untethered from their predicament. Thomas found himself watching her, wondering what lay ahead. Whatever the future held, he was becoming sure it must include this woman—this whirlwind of energy now waving her arms, recounting a story about Churchill and her mother.

Her mother had invited Churchill to dinner, expecting a polite decline. To her astonishment, he accepted. The guest list had been thrown into turmoil. Usually, an invitation from her mother was a prize, elevating any event to a spectacle in the social circuit. But Churchill's acceptance outflanked her entirely. Arriving with flowers, he charmed the guests, led conversations with ease, and toasted the hostess warmly, proving yet again that charm, when wielded deftly, was a powerful tool.

Across the room, at another table, Edith Bresto had never dined at The Fox before. It was far beyond her means.

In uniform, Paddy, finishing his meal, signaled the waiter. "Yes, you can take them away. Have you any champagne?"

"I'm very sorry, sir, but not this evening. The supply, sir," he said with a knowing smile, "is rather… irregular."

Paddy laughed, "Yes. I understand. The officers' club struggles with the same."

Feigning surprise, the waiter said, "Now, isn't that an incredible coincidence?"

When they were alone, Paddy looked across at Edith, holding her gaze. For a long moment, neither spoke.

Edith wasn't sure where the evening was going, and for once, she didn't care. His voice over the telephone had been different—rushed, urgent. He, the ever-confident fighter pilot, had changed.

"How was your day?" he asked.

Edith leaned forward, resting her chin on her folded arms, looking at him silently.

He stammered. "It's a simple question, one asked all over the country. I just wanted to know if you're happy."

She hesitated. "I'm sorry, Paddy. You, of all people, know how war rewrites the rules. Some don't even make it. Can we talk about something else?"

"I hate this war," he said, his voice rising. "It changes everything. People want to live their lives, and some bloody kraut decides he's better than everyone else."

Edith sensed he was different tonight. He was holding something back.

"You need a break," she said, studying him closely. "However, did you manage to leave? And on my night off, no less. You must be frightfully clever."

"My squadron leader granted me forty-eight hours," he replied, flashing a weary smile. "Though he made me promise I'd spend most of it sleeping because of my recent schedule."

Cradling her teacup in both hands, she took a sip, then smiled. "Well then, perhaps we ought to return you to base in good order, as your commander surely knows best."

He looked into her eyes, his grin boyish, teasing. "I told him not a wink if I can help it."

She chuckled. "I daresay it's not such a terrible crime to steal a little of a man's sleep, but you must do your best to ignore me now and then and promise to get at least a few winks."

Paddy shut one eye and smirked. "Does that count?"

She nudged him under the table with her foot. "Not in the slightest, you brute. Is that all men think about?"

"Mostly," he admitted, the smirk deepening. "'Cept me, of course."

"I don't believe you for an instant," she quipped, shaking her head. "And it is quite clear, Captain Hemingway, that my morals fly considerably higher than yours."

She waited for his customary swift rejoinder, a quip to match her own. Instead, silence settled between them. He shifted in his chair, his gaze distant. Either he hadn't heard her, or he had chosen not to respond. Instinct told her to leave it alone.

"Edith?" He said slowly, absently turning over the salad fork resting on the table.

A cold sensation crept down her spine. She had never heard him speak in such a tone. Setting her teacup down, she studied him. Something was coming. She could feel it. Was he being grounded? Had the accident left some unseen wound? Was he drifting away? Panic flickered at the edges of her thoughts, a slow-growing unease settling in her stomach.

"It's all right," she reassured herself. "Whatever it is, we'll face it together."

He exhaled sharply, then spoke. "I told my commander this leave meant more to me than anything. If he didn't grant it, I'd be going anyway."

Edith heard the words, but their meaning took a moment to settle. For so long, she had waited for some sign that she was more than a fleeting part of his life. That they shared the same depth of feeling. She loved him—God, she loved him. But the unspoken rule of never grounding a flyboy had always kept her at arm's length. She had learned to enjoy him one step away. And now, this.

Paddy shifted, his left hand appearing atop the table. Edith met his gaze and found his eyes uncharacteristically glassy, uncertain. Nervously, he glanced away before looking back at her. She held her breath.

Pushing past the emotion in his voice, he said, "There's only so much time in this world before we become nothing more than a footnote in history. We search and search and *sometimes* know when something is right. When that moment comes, one shouldn't hesitate, for life is a winding, unpredictable road."

He reached across the table, his fingers curling over hers.

Taking a steadying breath, he continued. "If we were reading this in a novel or watching a play, the words would come out perfectly. But it's just me. So here goes... Edith, I love you more than life itself."

He opened his hand. Resting in his palm was a gold ring, three petite sapphires set in a row. She stared, transfixed, before her gaze traveled upward. A single tear traced its way down Paddy's cheek, disappearing into the starched fabric of his uniform.

With all her might, Edith fought to steady herself—not the tears—they were beyond her control—but her composure. It was a battle she promptly lost, emotion cascading through her in waves, leaving her utterly unable to speak.

"Will you marry me?" he asked.

Across the room, Margaret paused mid-sentence, her father's beloved country estate momentarily forgotten. She peered over Thomas's shoulder, catching sight of a woman quietly crying, a man clasping her hand as he slipped a ring onto her finger. The man cut a dashing figure in his blue flight uniform.

"How terribly charming," Margaret said, gesturing discreetly toward the couple.

Thomas turned to follow her gaze.

Margaret continued watching, absorbing the scene wrapped in the quiet romance unfolding before her. After a moment, she sat upright, her voice a whisper of wonder. "Thomas, that man is proposing marriage at that table." She sighed softly. A few tears fell onto the pristine white linen. "Good heavens, how she must feel."

Thomas kept his eyes on the scene. "Are you certain he's proposing?"

"Of course," she replied. "There are very few moments in life when a woman cries and smiles all at once."

They lingered long enough to see the couple embrace before disappearing out the door. A short while later, Thomas and Margaret left as well.

Back in their room at the inn, Thomas found that, for the first time, they settled into bed with an ease that had never quite been there before. He watched her, this perfectly wonderful woman beside him, and knew, deep within, that there would never be another Margaret in his life.

Lying side by side, he slid an arm around her, cherishing their quiet closeness. The day's events had woven something special into their time together, unspoken yet profoundly felt. He was just about to tease her about her scandalously lax morals, perhaps suggesting they prove the innkeeper correct, when he heard it—that familiar, steady breathing.

She had fallen fast asleep in his arms.

Chapter Fifty-Three

The Hatcher Estate

Thomas opened his eyes to morning darkness due to the black-out curtains. Almost simultaneously, he caught the sound of movement—deliberate and unmistakable. A presence that should have been beside him had vanished. Without stirring, he said, "Margaret?"

"Thomas?" Her voice was crisp in response.

"What are you doing?"

"What most people do when they rent a room for the night. I'm getting ready to leave. Care to ask me anything more challenging?"

"Uh-oh," he groaned, rolling his eyes before dragging the pillow over his head.

Margaret strode across the room, deftly snatching the pillow from his grasp. Then, with exaggerated cheer, she yanked back the covers and chirped in an unnaturally high voice, "Good morn-*ning*, Mr. Watson, internationally known criminal and rogue spy—or have you forgotten? We have a rather serious problem to tackle, and it won't be solved with you lazing about."

Thomas peeked out with a smirk. "What happened to last night? Does all that romance and devotion vanish with the morning? I've survived gunfire, and I ship out tomorrow to some distant land to fight an unjust war. You could make this soldier a very happy man. Come back to bed?"

"What romance and devotion?" she countered.

"Last night," he said, grinning. "Before we drifted off, it was wonderful. Don't you remember? It was heaven." He stretched his arms wide, beaming.

"There was *no* last night," she said primly. "And with that nonsense, you are well on your way to damnation. We've only one option left, as I see it, and we might as well determine if it works. You asked for my help, and I can think of no greater sacrifice than approaching my mother, hat in hand. Now, up with you." She punctuated the command with a playful whack of the pillow.... Soldier."

The drive from the inn to her mother's estate occurred during a resplendent morning with the crisp air tinged with the scent of early blooms. Their earlier jousting had given way to a thoughtful silence. Margaret pondered their safety—the Russian had already made clear his ill intent. Thomas, for his part, sifted through the layers of information, concluding that contacting Churchill remained his only course of action. He gazed out as the suburban landscape gradually surrendered to the rolling countryside.

Margaret drove, her hands steady on the wheel. Thomas reached out, resting a hand on her knee—an easy gesture in the confines of the small car. She turned, meeting his gaze, her face radiant with a smile.

"*Was* there a last night?" she asked, her voice barely rising above the engine's hum.

Thomas merely smiled.

"I thought so."

After a pause, he asked, "Do you mind driving?"

"Not in the slightest," she laughed. "Especially when considering the alternative. Do you mind being a passenger?"

"No, I don't mind at all," he replied, eyes shining. "Especially when I'm in the hands of one so capable."

Margaret stole two glances at him between watching the road, marveling at the duality of the man beside her. "We're getting close," she said.

They ascended a series of gently rolling hills. As they crested the final rise, the Hatcher Mansion suddenly emerged, dominating the horizon. Thomas stared in astonishment at the grand edifice standing alone at the end of a sweeping drive, a structure that looked like it had been plucked straight from Whitehall.

The estate's iron gates, open during the day, framed the entrance. Home guards patrolled within sight, ever vigilant. Margaret slowed, waving at one of them—George Alton, a uniformed figure she recognized instantly. By trade, he was the estate's livery smith, offering his service to the guard on odd days.

Thomas, still dumbfounded, absorbed the spectacle before him. A thought surfaced, unbidden from the depths of his mind, the sort of orphaned thought that filled his days. As they neared the mansion, he said, "Over the meads of our pleasant land of England, there lie spread the stately seats of her nobles."

"What?" Margaret asked, half-distracted.

Since the 1700s, the community of Fernhurst had been regarded as the countryside. Yet, with the ever-expanding reach of the Empire's capital, its serenity had been steadily encroached upon. Though still a sanctuary for the exceedingly wealthy, Fernhurst remained a bastion of privilege—where lineage, fortune, and tradition dictated the order of society.

The Hatcher Estate originated in a land grant awarded to Frederick Hanover, Duke of York, in 1815 as a royal hunting ground. Frederick, the second son of King George III, had played no small role in the taxation disputes that led to the loss of the American colonies in 1776. By the 1820s, he had constructed an imposing country retreat with vast French gardens and extensive outbuildings, a beacon of nobility in the greater Hempstead region. Upon his death in 1827, Sir Lawton Everett Hatcher, a prosperous businessman with close ties to the royal family, acquired a portion of the reserve along with the mansion complex. After years of residence, he and his wife retired to a cottage in Scotland, passing the estate to their son, Ian Everett Hatcher I—Margaret's grandfather. Now, Margaret represented the fourth generation to occupy a home originally designed for royalty.

Beyond the mansion, rolling hills blanketed in dense, fertile woodlands lent the land a natural, undulating charm, strikingly contrasting the smooth, even plains to the northeast. Though only a fragment of Frederick's original holdings, the estate still encompassed nearly 700 acres, including the surrounding moors. Beyond the manicured gardens, the land remained untouched, watched over by a dedicated caretaker tasked with maintaining its wildlife.

The crushed rock drive split into a grand, divided entryway stretching nearly 400 feet. A regimented formation of meticulously shaped shrubs stood between its lanes in straight, disciplined rows, each exactly five feet high, ensuring an uninterrupted view of the estate's magnificence upon arriving.

The mansion itself, a neo-classical triumph, loomed ahead. Its three stories were sheathed in locally quarried limestone, now bearing the graceful marks of time. The entrance was adorned with a Greek cornice, re-carved with permission from the Crown to bear the Hatcher family motto: *Famulus Regis Et Patria*—Latin for *Serving King and Country*. Four stately Doric columns stood in solemn symmetry, flanking the grand black door at the top of an impressive stone staircase.

Thomas exhaled, his voice barely above a whisper. "My God, Margaret."

Chapter Fifty-Four

Hatcher Estate—Margaret's Memories

When the Austin rolled to a stop before the grand façade of the mansion, it gave a weary sigh, like a runner reaching the end of an arduous race. Thomas glanced at Margaret, then gestured toward the imposing structure beyond the car window.

"This is your house?" he asked.

"No," Margaret corrected. "This is my mother's house. Mine's in Amersham."

She continued before he could respond. "Now remember, we saw her only last week. Took the train over."

"You said your mother doesn't like me."

"That's an excellent place to start. As I told you, you walked into her life without her consent. You are why she was robbed of hosting the grandest wedding event of her life, stripped of her moment in Society's limelight. Though the idea was entirely mine, she blames you for our little elopement. Now that I think about it, you should be ashamed of yourself."

"Why did you want to go it alone?"

"Because the event and the groom's suitability became far more important than my happiness. But that's neither here nor there. To her, you're the outsider and the one being held accountable. If she follows true to form, she'll order a drink shortly after you arrive—some tonic to steady herself for the ordeal—and then begin prattling away nervously."

Thomas raised a brow. "You're joking, surely?"

Margaret merely shrugged.

They ascended the stone steps, Thomas pausing momentarily to take in the sheer scale of the door as Margaret reached for the bell pull. "You gave all this up for me?" he asked.

"Don't start, Thomas; this will be difficult enough as it is. What shall we tell her?"

"I suggest we play it by ear. Let the pieces fall where they may."

Margaret's nerves betrayed her. "Thomas, you're not taking this seriously. We need her help, and you—of all people—must ask for it. That requires a strategy, a way to ease her into even considering it."

The door swung open before he could respond.

"Too late," Thomas muttered.

"Pardon, sir?" The young maid at the door, dressed immaculately in black with a white lace pinafore, peered up at him curiously. A ruffled cap covered her forehead, its ties neatly knotted at the back. Then, spotting Margaret, her expression brightened.

"Oh, ma' Lady, what a pleasure! I do beg your pardon; Alistair asked me to attend the door. Come in, come in. Let me take your wrap and things. Lady Hatcher is currently detained. Is she expecting you? She has a guest—Mr. Portman, the solicitor."

She lowered her voice. "He usually doesn't linger, but he's been in her private office for a good spell today."

Voices carried through the corridor from deeper in the house, and soon, a man emerged and caught sight of Margaret.

"Marion, my hat, if you'd be so kind," he said in a deep, measured tone.

Marion half-curtsied and said, "Excuse me, Miss; I must fetch Mr. Portman's things."

"Mr. Portman," Margaret said. "How lovely to see you and on such a wonderful day."

"Margaret, my dear, as gracious and beautiful as ever. I must be brief and apologize as I am under direct orders, and the timing is quite short. It is, however, always a delight. He bent to kiss Margaret's cheek, and with hat in hand, he made his way to the open door, rushing past Marion and having never acknowledged Thomas being there.

"No, Marion," Margaret replied. "We didn't ring ahead. But it will be all right. We'll wait in the drawing room."

Thomas shed his coat, along with their masks and hats, and followed Margaret inside. The thought struck him—how odd it was that a daughter needed to arrange an appointment to visit her mother. Even more so that she had to knock. He wisely kept the observation to himself.

There was still no sign of 'Mother.'

Margaret nodded to Marion. "We'll see ourselves in."

The mansion's interior was every bit as grand as its exterior. The entry foyer soared two stories, its marble floors gleaming ivory, each tile set at an angle. To the right, a sweeping rosewood staircase curved elegantly toward an open balcony above. Directly ahead, above an arched opening, hung a grand tapestry—a sprawling verdure scene depicting a fox hunt. To the left, the ceremonial stateroom, where

Frederick once entertained, boasted Louis XVI marquetry cabinets, an imposing fireplace, and a portrait of Sir Lawton Everett above it. The ancestral coat of arms flanked either side of the mantel.

Most of the furniture lay draped in white linen, a silent testament to the war effort that had stripped the household of its usual staff. Thomas had thought he understood class divisions. He was, evidently, quite mistaken.

Margaret caught his pause as he took in the room. "Almost everyone's off working in munitions factories or assembling aircraft. The house is too vast for what staff remain, so entire wings have been closed off."

They continued into the drawing room. The space, at least, still bore signs of daily life. A warm fire crackled before two divans, separated by a low glass table. Unusually large windows dominated the right-hand wall, offering a breathtaking view of the sprawling estate. Outside, a kitchen garden and a small glass hothouse stood beyond a distant outbuilding. Thomas moved to the window, surveying the manicured expanse of green. Near a group of trees, an older man, accompanied by a younger apprentice, carried a woven basket. The older gentleman paused, stooped to pluck a single leaf from the ground, studied its underside, then carefully placed it in the basket.

Margaret joined him, taking his arm and leaning against him. "That's Ned Pomeroy, our head gardener. Been with us since before I was born. One of the few who became, as Father used to say, 'working family.' He and Father had a peculiar arrangement. They'd vanish for hours, pretending to 'inspect' the gardens. In truth, they'd smuggle a bottle of Scotch and an old folding table, hiding away in the hedge maze, solving the world's problems over cards. Father used to boast he lost enough to fund Ned's daughter's schooling. And when she qualified as a full nurse at Wembury Medical Academy, no one batted an eye."

She pointed toward a small ornamental structure with an unmistakably oriental flair. "See that? That's a garden whimsy. Back in the day, the aristocracy competed to build these little architectural follies—utterly useless but splendidly extravagant. Father had this one transported from some manor up north, then spent months reconstructing it here. One of his favorite projects."

Her grip tightened playfully on Thomas's arm. "It was rather special to me, too."

He sighed. "And why is that?"

Margaret grinned mischievously. "Since you ask, I had my first kiss under that roof. Poor Nigel." She sighed.

She drifted into the memory. "We were walking in the garden, under strict observation from this very window by Mother. She was uneasy about me strolling alone with a boy, especially after I warned her that if she didn't relent, I'd throw a fit right before him."

Thomas feigned shock. "You? A fit? I don't believe it."

"Of course, I knew she couldn't bear the thought of any unbecoming behavior returning to her friends with their perfectly polished daughters. My only concession was agreeing to stay within sight."

She smirked at the recollection. "Just as I saw Mother repositioning herself for a better view, the heavens opened. A sudden downpour sent Nigel and me running for cover beneath the whimsy's roof. That, naturally, set off an all-out alert. In a panic, Mother ordered Mr. Pomeroy— arming himself with an umbrella—to retrieve us immediately."

Margaret laughed. "The dear man took his time, claiming he'd misunderstood making his way to the potting shed. According to Mother, he was squandering precious minutes."

She shook her head, eyes gleaming. "So there we were, alone, out of sight for the briefest, most precious moments. Poor Nigel, shifting on his feet, staring at his shoes, fumbling for words. He started to say something, but I didn't give him the chance. I rose onto my toes and kissed him mid-sentence. I was fifteen, utterly starry-eyed, and convinced I was in love."

Thomas tilted his head. "And he tried to kiss you again?"

Margaret nodded. "He was about to. I wouldn't let him."

Thomas folded his arms. "That's the problem with women. Just because they're in control doesn't mean they must behave like it."

Before she could respond, a voice from the doorway interrupted. "Lady Hatcher, may I?"

A tall, impeccably dressed man stood at the threshold—Alistair, the butler, exuding an air of quiet authority. Margaret all but leaped forward, embracing him with a kiss on both cheeks.

"Alistair! Where on earth have you been? You weren't here last time, and the evening ran away before I could ask after you."

Alistair turned to Thomas with a measured gaze. "Welcome, Mr. Watson."

Thomas extended a hand. Alistair shook it firmly, then hesitated, studying their clasped hands before looking back up with a quiet, curious smile.

Margaret interjected sharply. "Oh, Alistair, when Mother isn't about, do call him Thomas, won't you? Now, tell me—where did you disappear to?"

"I had to ask Lady Hatcher for some personal time as I finally located David. Thank the heavens, he was one of the rescued survivors at Dunkirk."

"Oh, Alistair, that's wonderful news! What happened? Where was he found?"

"At a recovery hospital where they sent the boys, but in all the chaos, the records arrived much later. He was in a dreadful state. The doctors called it 'shell-shock,' but I think he was just a frightened lad thrust into war, never prepared for its horrors. They were lucky to be alive, let alone make it home."

Margaret's brow furrowed with concern. "How was it possible to get so many soldiers off that one beach?"

"He caught a ride with three others in a small pleasure craft—one of the hundreds Churchill called upon to bring our boys home. He said an older man and his son were just offshore, waving a hat to get someone's attention. David and his mates left everything behind and swam out. The man turned out to be a master seaman. Together, they battled the rough waters, bailing constantly. A little worse for wear, but safe they are."

Alistair lowered his gaze. "It's coming to light now that over thirty-five thousand soldiers were left behind. They fought inland, holding off the enemy, ensuring those on the beach could escape. No rescue boats came for them. Heroes, the lot of them. They helped save my boy and half a million others. His mother would strike me down from heaven if I had let anything happen to him. God rest her soul."

Margaret exhaled. "What a somber, tragic tale. Those boys are the reason we'll see another day. And thank God, all is well with David. We must be grateful."

Then, without thinking, she said, "Alistair, I want you to meet Thomas." It was perfectly natural, given he'd never been here in her mind. Realizing her blunder, she clapped her fingers over her mouth. The butler, to put it mildly, looked perplexed.

Thomas, smiling, interjected, "Alistair, some things require explanation. But now isn't the time."

"Of course," Alistair replied with a perceptible nod. "If I may be excused, Lady Hatcher should be along any moment."

Margaret watched him closely. "Why do you stay here and endure, Mother? You could serve as the King's valet at Buckingham with your qualifications. You'd earn a fine increase in rate, too."

Alistair hesitated. "Ah, your father… well—" He stumbled slightly over his words before finally offering a small, knowing smile. "I think now isn't the time."

He bowed slightly, stepped back smoothly, turned, and left the room.

Margaret sighed. "He was Father's valet and is now the head of the household—but so much more than that. When I was younger, he cared for me with a devotion I never truly appreciated."

"He's fiercely loyal," Thomas observed, sensing the emotion in her voice.

"There was one time—Father was away at the factories after a roaring row with Mother, and I stormed off to my room. In the dead of night, I slipped out through the service entrance and tried to run away."

She hesitated, the memory vivid. "After a while, I realized how dark, cold, and frightening it was. I hid in a doorway, hoping for dawn, when I heard Alistair's soft, calm voice calling my name. He was careful not to startle me. He slowly emerged from the shadows and explained it wasn't safe for a twelve-year-old girl to wander the roads at night. He had followed me for nearly a mile, staying just out of sight. Aside from Mr. Pomeroy and Father, he was the only person who could have convinced me to return. Mother never knew. From then on, when things got tense in the house, Alistair and I would exchange a knowing wink. He'd wag a finger, side to side, silently reminding me to behave."

Thomas shrugged. "I'll keep that in mind next time you wink at me only to vanish."

"That, my good man, will never happen."

She moved toward a tall, glass-fronted cabinet, its shelves lined with meticulously arranged objects. Most were wooden, some with metal fittings—old and well-used. Thomas stepped closer, eyeing the collection, but his thoughts lingered on Margaret's last remark.

"You called me 'my good man.' Isn't that a phrase typically exchanged between men?"

"Typically," she replied airily. "Ought to answer your question, Mr. Watson—typically."

He looked at her. "Indeed, it does, Mrs. Watson."

Shifting his attention back to the cabinet, he peered at the oddities. "This is quite a collection. What am I looking at?"

"My father's collection of weaving tools. Some are centuries old. Though I had little interest, I was made to learn the history of every spindle, shuttle, and bobbin. Whenever he acquired a new piece, I got the full lecture. Go on, pick something."

"Oh, I can't resist," Thomas said. He pointed to three thin, flat wooden boards, each about five inches wide and twelve inches long. Threads along the edges bound them together but allowed them to move independently. The boards were perforated with a grid of holes in a six-by-twenty-six pattern. With a smirk, he said, "Tell me about this one."

"That's an easy one," Margaret replied confidently. "In 1801, Jacquard used punched holes to control the pattern on his loom. You might say," she added, with deliberate emphasis, "he was to weaving what Gutenberg was to printing."

Thomas folded his arms, his satisfaction evident.

"You look insufferably pleased with yourself," Margaret noted.

"That's a good story," he admitted, "but only partly correct. You get a B+."

"Rubbish. I don't get anything but A's—more than you can claim. Anyway, how would you know? You were the one who asked, remember?"

"Don't ask me how I know; I thought we agreed not to go into that anymore. You said Jacquard was the first to use punched holes in a weaving machine. He wasn't."

"Was, too."

"Was not."

Margaret glared at him. Thomas stood tall, adjusting his coat, and brushed away an invisible speck of lint. "Jacquard was the first to use punched wooden cards strung together, which made him famous. But," he paused, savoring the moment, "a man named Basil—something—used punched holes in stiff paper seventy years earlier."

"Did not."

"Sorry," Thomas chirped. "You lost the contest."

Margaret stepped between him and the cabinet, jabbing a finger into his chest. "I didn't lose anything because you had the wrong answer. Which means," she declared, "this conversation is over."

Chapter Fifty-Five

Mrs. Somerville's Home
Amersham

Shortly after rising that morning, Beth Somerville firmly closed the kitchen cabinet doors, pressing them against their latches. She lingered for a moment in the quiet hush, reluctantly acknowledging that a decision must now be faced. With measured determination, she reached for a pen and notepaper from the modest telephone shelf, setting them purposefully upon the dining room table. Drawing a chair nearer, she paused briefly before placing pen to paper, aware that her words could alter the course of her life down a path she scarcely felt ready to tread. Her original intention in agreeing to help had long since faded; what began as patriotic duty had evolved into an earnest desire to protect Margaret, whom she cherished as dearly as a daughter.

The government had been explicit. Should Beth suspect Margaret to be in peril, it was her solemn obligation to promptly send word. The gentleman had assured her the rest would be handled without fail. Yet, was Margaret truly endangered? Today, Beth felt convinced of Thomas's genuine affection for Margaret, though merely days before, she had regarded him as a crafty opportunist skilled at hiding darker motives beneath his charm. Even then, she hadn't believed Margaret to be directly threatened. Margaret earnestly sought to build a life with someone she trusted and sincerely cared for.

Beth felt heavily burdened by the choice before her. Would alerting the authorities ruin Margaret's newfound bond with Thomas? Privately, Margaret had admitted suspicions that Thomas concealed secrets, yet she remained undeterred in her pursuit of love and security. Margaret believed determination could conquer all obstacles—as it had her own formidable mother. At least, so Margaret presumed.

Beth stared at the empty page before her. At length, she reluctantly conceded that Margaret's proximity to the recent shooting changed everything. The man had plainly declared that if Margaret faced danger, so too did England. Irritably shaking her head, Beth began to write:

To: Dacha
Believe Princess is in danger and awaiting instructions.
Actor

With careful precision, she folded the note into a plain envelope, wrapping it securely in wax paper and placing it alongside a small piece of chalk in her handbag. Moving briskly to her bedroom, she knelt by the bed's right side, fumbling briefly until she grasped the hidden item she sought. Swiftly returning to the front room, she took a warm muffler from its hook but paused abruptly. Where had she put her mask? "Always here," she muttered impatiently, scolding herself for the oversight. It must have been left behind in the cab.

Beth settled on the divan, thoughtfully peering through the front window curtains. A faint smile appeared as she recognized the car pulling up outside. She quickly gathered her belongings and rose promptly to greet Sanjay at the front door.

Sanjay observed closely as Beth approached the vehicle.

"Good morning, Sanjay. Delighted you could make it. Your dispatcher wasn't terribly encouraging. I must get to Camden Town Station."

"You mean just past Euston, Mum?"

"Yes, that's the one. Never been myself, but it's opposite a park, I believe."

"Shall I drive you to Amersham station or directly to Camden Town, Mum?"

"Young man, I can certainly find my own way to Amersham's railway. Take me straight to this address—or as near as possible."

"Camden Town isn't exactly respectable, Mum."

"I'm well aware. If the choice were mine, neither of us would set foot there, but urgent matters compel us where we must."

As they journeyed, conversation resumed from the previous evening, touching gently upon war, family, and how Sanjay spent his rare leisure moments among friends. Soon, they neared their destination. Sanjay slowed the vehicle cautiously, easing past the station towards the street indicated.

"Is this the spot?" he asked uncertainly.

"I believe so," Beth answered, rechecking her instructions. "Look there, Sanjay—the small park across the square."

"Begging your pardon, Mum, but may I ask your business here? That green's notorious for unsavory sorts."

"Sanjay, you're a perfect gentleman, and your concern does you credit. Trust me, though, you're better off not knowing. Besides, it's probably someone's crude sense of humor."

Beth understood perfectly well why such an obscure meeting place had been chosen. The gentlemen in charge likely never anticipated sending a lady of her years to so dubious a locale. She frowned slightly, gazing thoughtfully through the window.

"Sanjay, I must ask your assistance. Could you accompany me briefly?"

"Certainly, Mum," he replied immediately, stepping from the car without presuming to offer her assistance, respecting her independence.

Holding tightly to her handbag, Beth was grateful for Sanjay's reassuring presence.

"Just over to that bridge," she directed.

Together, they crossed onto the deserted common, relieved by its emptiness. An ornamental bridge spanned a dry streambed strewn with rocks and was usually waterless except during heavy rain. At each end stood aged gas lamps, long fallen into disrepair. Beth approached the left lamp post, gripping it cautiously and peering anxiously downward. The steep bank dropped sharply, offering few footholds; descending appeared challenging, returning impossible.

"Sanjay, might you place this envelope beneath that dark stone there?"

"Certainly, Mum," he obliged readily, swiftly climbing down to conceal the envelope.

"Ah, youth," Beth said aloud, "just as one masters life's lessons, the strength to act fades. Many thanks, Sanjay."

"Might we leave now, Mum?" Sanjay suggested anxiously, glancing around.

"With pleasure. Just one last favor—would you mark an X, about six inches high, on that letterbox facing the station?"

Curiosity flickered briefly in Sanjay's eyes, yet he silently accepted the chalk.

"I know it's peculiar," Beth admitted, "but afterward, our errand will be complete, and we can retreat comfortably to your warm cab."

With that simple gesture, Mrs. Beth Somerville, Margaret's devoted friend, had irrevocably set the future in motion. Returning home now to await a response would be arduous indeed—the uncertainty of how and when word might arrive troubled her profoundly.

Chapter Fifty-Six

Turing's Laboratory

After yesterday's phone call to Colville, Turing remained at the lab, working tirelessly through the night alongside his team. Hours slipped quickly by as they diligently integrated the new ideas supplied by the enigmatic Mr. Dunning. Though initial skepticism lingered, it gradually yielded a hopeful understanding that his suggestions might hold the key to their troubles.

Obstacles persisted, undoubtedly. Foster faced particular difficulty converting the teleprinter to accurately punch holes in tape, aligning precisely with the original written commands. Determining how best to instruct the electrical switch that regulated the drum's position was equally challenging. Yet, in a stroke of ingenuity, Gordon devised the idea for a conversion board—though as a purely experimental model, its construction was an exercise in trial and error. Nonetheless, the moment had arrived to test the core idea despite not yet having input from the teleprinter crew.

"Are we ready?" Turing inquired, looking around the room. His colleagues nodded in agreement.

For this preliminary test, they'd installed a single set of wires from the electrical switch inside the hardware cabinet to the conversion board's output side. Another set extended directly from the board's input terminals to the newly constructed photocell assembly.

Gordon positioned himself behind the cabinet to observe the switch's response while Duncan stood by the conversion board, ready to intervene if necessary. Turing carefully slid a piece of paper, manually punched with a single instruction, between the photocells. Three sharp clicks followed, signaling the relay had moved the drum precisely into position.

"Whoa!" Gordon exclaimed from behind the cabinet.

"You all right there, Gordon?" Foster asked anxiously.

"Bloody hell," Turing muttered in astonishment. "It actually kicked the switch."

Glancing at the punched paper, Turing called out, “Gordon, can you read off the settings?”

Gordon responded from his unseen position, “Set one is twelve, set two is nine, and set three is fifteen.”

“Exactly right!” Turing cheered, raising his arms triumphantly. “Precisely as designed, lads!”

“Too right, Doctor,” Gordon agreed heartily. “Now we need to build the wire harness to link the switches to the conversion board.”

“A valley of wires, Gordon,” Turing said, “and each needs thorough testing.”

Duncan inspected the board’s underside and said, “We’ll need mechanical expertise. Can we get clearance for some additional hands?”

“I’ll see to it,” Turing assured him, “but first, another quick test. Gordon, remove your hands from there for a moment.”

“Why?” Gordon replied cheerfully. “I think I might marry this beauty—fallen in love, I have.”

Ignoring the humor, Turing again inserted the paper between the cells and waited. Silence ensued. “Nothing this time,” Turing noted with satisfaction.

“Naturally,” Gordon called out knowingly. “You fed it the same instruction twice.”

“Bravo, Gordon. That is exactly why I brought you aboard. If the first switch worked correctly, repeating the instruction will serve as a parity check, costing us nothing in cycle time. Any discrepancy would reset the switch to zero. Eventually, we might discard the parity check altogether—but not just yet.”

Turing knew they’d eventually require a real coded message complete with wheel settings, but for now, progress was palpable. Once Foster's teleprinter was operational, another team would convert wheel settings into the punched tape required. The room brimmed with cautious optimism—they were finally, indisputably, moving forward.

Chapter Fifty-Seven

Meeting Mother
Hatcher Estate

Margaret was not particularly pleased with Thomas for implying she had lost, especially when she clearly had not. Yet, before they could reconcile the matter, Thomas became aware of the sharp click-click-click of heels briskly crossing the marble tiles. Lady Hatcher was approaching; her presence seemed to precede her, filling the room with a specific formidable energy. Thomas felt uncertain—how was he to approach this legendary figure? Suddenly, his plan to seek her help felt dreadfully foolish. He needed a new approach, something Margaret's old Thomas had never attempted. However, it would all be a guess at best without knowledge of what had been tried before.

Still unseen, Lady Hatcher called out, "Margaret, dear—is that you?"

Shortly thereafter, she emerged from the entry hall and entered the drawing room, greeting her daughter with noticeable reserve. Although pleased to see Margaret, she placed her hands gently on her daughter's shoulders and held her at arm's length. Thomas was struck by this subdued greeting, realizing such restraint must be considered proper amongst England's upper classes.

"What marvelous timing," she remarked. "Marion has just laid out breakfast. You must both join me—I insist."

Margaret interjected, "Mother, I know it's early, but we must discuss something."

"Yes, yes, come sit," Lady Hatcher said, dismissing Margaret's urgency with practiced ease. Guiding Margaret toward the divans facing the fireplace, she rearranged a few embroidered pillows before settling comfortably. Folding her arms and crossing her legs, she prompted, "Well, then?"

An awkward silence stretched out briefly before she turned to Thomas, almost as an afterthought, and politely asked, "Oh—ah, Thomas, how do you do today?"

Thomas joined them carefully, scrutinizing Lady Hatcher's posture and mannerisms for any clue to assist him. Yet she remained entirely inscrutable, like studying the reverse of an unknown painting, revealing nothing useful.

"Very well indeed, Lady Hatcher, thank you," he responded amiably. "And yourself?"

Lady Hatcher briefly looked from Thomas to Margaret, whose hand lightly touched Thomas's knee, accompanied by a faint, forced smile.

"Well," Lady Hatcher replied crisply, "apart from how the war has clipped our wings in previously unimaginable ways, I suppose I'll manage. That new day-girl I hired with such enthusiasm lasted scarcely a fortnight before leaving to change linens at the Navy hospital. I even offered her more money, but apparently, I missed the point entirely. Honestly, I fail to understand young people nowadays."

"There will be others, Mother," Margaret reassured her.

"Perhaps," she replied doubtfully. "Meanwhile, we've had to close all guestrooms but one—thinking you might need it—and without help, more rooms will inevitably follow. At this rate, I'll be confined to my bedroom all day."

Trying to contribute thoughtfully, Thomas remarked, "Things appear difficult everywhere, I'm afraid." The observation fell flat. Wincing inwardly, he attempted a swift recovery: "How fares the business? Surely the war has boosted orders for your textiles?" He shifted uncomfortably, removing a decorative but inconvenient cushion. Only then did he notice Lady Hatcher's silent, puzzled stare.

"How very odd, Thomas," she began slowly. "You've never shown the slightest interest in our actual business operations, much less the order rates. Previously, your incessant probing into our company's specific projects and locations was more irritating than helpful. What, may I ask, prompted this sudden change? And since when have you taken to addressing me as Lady Hatcher?"

Summoning Marion with a gesture, she instructed, "Marion dear, kindly have Alistair prepare me a gin and orange." Returning immediately to her authoritative demeanor, Lady Hatcher exchanged glances with Margaret and Thomas.

"In here, Madam?" Marion asked politely.

"No, I shall take it with breakfast," she clarified.

"Mother, it's not important," Margaret said hastily. "Thomas was simply being polite. You disliked it immensely when he called you 'Mum,' claiming he had no right despite our marriage."

"And rightly so, young lady; I scarcely knew the man."

Desperately trying to redirect the conversation, Margaret asked quickly, "Why was Mr. Portman calling so early? I don't recall him ever rising before midday."

Lady Hatcher's attention returned swiftly. "He came by for my proxy signature for a board vote scheduled this morning. I never attend those meetings anymore—they're frightfully dull and always thick with smoke. Men and their cigars—it's positively ghastly. I once proposed banning smoking when I was present. Mr. Campbell took me aside to explain, as if imparting some tremendous masculine secret, that smoking was essential to their thought processes. Utter nonsense, naturally, but I acquiesced; he has, after all, managed admirably through some difficult times.

"In any case, one of our factories was severely damaged during the bombings. Mr. Campbell called the meeting to authorize a short-term repair loan, as all our working capital is currently in inventory. Your father always had an instinct for knowing when someone was ready for greater responsibility—giving Mr. Campbell that chance was sheer brilliance. Frankly, I don't know how I'd cope without him."

Thomas ventured carefully, "Perhaps Mr. Campbell could contact the War Office? After the initial raids, I understand they've made long-term funds available for critical war factories. Sir Walter Mildmay, the Chancellor, stated it was their highest priority, promising swift action without bureaucratic delay."

Thomas hoped this would be helpful, but Lady Hatcher merely regarded him blankly, neither hostile nor approving—simply inscrutable. She turned slightly away, absent-mindedly adjusting the precise folds of her dress.

"Ready, Ma'am," Marion announced, entering the room and breaking the silence.

With breakfast called, Margaret's mother rose swiftly from the divan and maneuvered gracefully around the glass table. She slipped her arm around Margaret, gently steering her daughter toward the dining room. Thomas, left momentarily alone, quickly followed.

"It's simply delightful to have you here, dear. Will you be staying in your usual room? I've had it prepared just in case."

Trailing behind, Thomas allowed himself a quiet smile. He had settled on a plan. Clearly, the other Thomas had never attempted to earn Lady Hatcher's respect or even genuinely engage her attention. Every word he uttered felt slightly misplaced. To succeed, he needed to win her regard—ideally, her respect.

They proceeded down a grand corridor, turning left into an unexpectedly charming surprise—a sunlit day room serving as an informal dining area. At its center stood an imposing rectangular table encircled by substantial, carved chairs. Alongside, an expansive glass partition separated them from a lush solarium. Hanging baskets, brimming with vivid blooms, cascaded from the iron supports, brilliantly illuminated by sunlight filtering through the glass ceiling. Some freshly watered plants dripped gently onto the wet tiled floor, suggesting Mr. Pomeroy had made a timely escape. The scene resembled a vivid Monet painting, just shy of perfection.

Having swiftly arranged two additional place settings, Marion moved the central floral arrangement aside to facilitate conversation. With considerable effort, she drew back a chair for Mrs. Hatcher, who sat down smoothly, remarking, “Both of our footmen are lost to the war effort, forcing us to discard some centuries-old custom about male servers exclusively tending the dining rooms. Truly, this war has unsettled both society and tradition.”

Margaret sighed gently. “I'm certain only those facing the same challenge would even notice.”

Ignoring this remark, her mother briskly issued directives. “Margaret, you'll sit here, and Thomas, you'll take that seat there.”

Spotting an opportunity, Thomas boldly interjected, “Actually, I’d prefer Margaret sat here beside me so she might enjoy a splendid view of those lovely flowers. Such a delightful arrangement deserves proper appreciation.”

Mrs. Hatcher paused briefly, appearing momentarily confused or perhaps believing she had misheard. Thomas sensed he had finally gained her attention.

Alistair entered silently, placing a drink before Mrs. Hatcher, who promptly took a somewhat indelicate sip before resuming the conversation as though entirely unaffected. “Marion, darling, please instruct the kitchen maid to return to Fortnum & Mason for more of that excellent black tea and those delightful small jars of caviar. The ladies will expect such luxuries this afternoon.”

“Yes, Ma’am,” Marion replied dutifully.

Returning her attention to the table, Mrs. Hatcher addressed Margaret, "It'll certainly surprise them, a pleasant break from the usual cakes and biscuits. I know they'd prefer lunching at the Strand or the Berkley, gawking at dashing wing commanders or smart young Guards officers. However, it's my turn to host today, so they'll have to content themselves with luncheon and cards here.”

“I'm sure they'll be delighted,” Thomas offered politely. “How many are expected?”

Ignoring his inquiry, Mrs. Hatcher raised her hand, motioning elegantly toward the flower vase. "Marion, would you kindly rotate that vase so we might enjoy Mr. Pomeroy's splendid orchid?"

Marion adjusted the vase carefully under Mrs. Hatcher's watchful gaze, who, once satisfied, remarked warmly, "Marvelous."

"Thomas, there are six of us—there have always been six," Margaret's mother said absently, her hand reaching for her drink again.

Thomas was confident his previous self had rarely, if ever, shown this much interest.

"Now, Margaret, you shall have those fluffy eggs you adore, and Thomas, those dreadful bangers you favor—a taste you share only with Alistair, the sole reason we keep such things about the house."

Thomas looked toward Marion with polite determination. "If possible, I'd greatly prefer an omelet with oregano. If available, Margaret would be positively thrilled by a cream cheese turnover with strawberries."

Marion's eyes widened considerably. Clearing her throat delicately, she glanced from Thomas to Mrs. Hatcher, then finally to Margaret, who sat demurely smiling with pleasure, hands neatly folded in her lap. Beyond that, Marion stood frozen and speechless.

Thomas inwardly groaned, thinking, "I've done it again."

"That sounds absolutely divine," Margaret enthused, breaking the awkward silence. "Do you actually have them? How on earth have you found strawberries during wartime? I wager Uncle Ned must be cultivating all manner of delicious secrets in his victory garden."

Chapter Fifty-Eight

Mother's Other Side
Hatcher Estate

Lady Hatcher signaled Marion from the dining room but paused abruptly as her fingers brushed her glass. Instead, she carefully returned her hand to her lap, lowered her gaze, and touched the napkin gently to her lips. Then, for the first time since Thomas had stepped through the front door, she fixed her eyes on him, deliberately holding his attention.

Lady Hatcher's late husband often remarked that the head of a significant business must possess clarity and the courage to face issues directly. He admired her greatly—not for what she eventually became but for who she had been during their early marriage.

Then, with the unmistakable authority and precision of England's ruling class, Lady Hatcher announced, "I must apologize to you both. I've deliberately misled you regarding Mr. Portman's presence here this morning."

Both Thomas and Margaret detected an immediate shift in her manner. Gone was the familiar society hostess, replaced by a more serious and commanding persona.

Thomas thought, "I was right—Mother has two distinct faces. One is the cultivated socialite, insulated from harsh realities. Now, I sense we are about to see the other." Perhaps, Thomas mused, this decisiveness was what first drew Mr. Hatcher to her.

Margaret, clearly noticing the change, sat upright with widened eyes, visibly startled.

"Marion!" Lady Hatcher called out sharply.

Having barely left, Marion swiftly returned, halting abruptly at her employer's raised hand. "Close the door, please."

"Yes, Ma'am," Marion replied, quickly closing the double doors.

Lady Hatcher resumed calmly, "Mr. Portman was not here returning a paper to the board, as I earlier suggested. He has an appointment at the War Office to finalize contracts of utmost secrecy, in which our company agrees to offer vital assistance at the government's highest request."

Turning to Margaret, she added gravely, "It's precisely the kind of service your father and grandfather repeatedly provided for Crown and country."

Leaning slightly away from the table, Lady Hatcher addressed Thomas directly. "Thomas, I am troubled—or perhaps intrigued might better describe it. Something does not add up. In our short acquaintance, you've never addressed me as Lady Hatcher—not last week, nor any time prior—yet today you did. Remember early on, during our private meeting; I specifically mentioned that 'Helen' was more suitable, emphasizing tone above formality."

Margaret immediately protested, her voice rising sharply, "Tone? I don't recall that conversation. Why wasn't I included?" Her apparent agitation prompted Thomas to give her a gentle yet firm look, silently urging restraint.

Undeterred, Lady Hatcher continued firmly, "Thomas, you seldom join our conversations unless you are seeking information about company projects. Otherwise, you feign polite interest. You offer no real opinions because you seem to have none, and you certainly never present contrary ideas. You're always very careful to avoid any behavior that may place you out of favor. I've always felt such an exchange would lead to your revealing more of yourself than you're willing to share. The affluent develop sharp instincts about such insincerity; thus, I've always considered you somewhat contemptible—a shameless opportunist."

Margaret shot from her chair in outrage. "*What?*" she nearly shouted.

Thomas gently grasped Margaret's dress, easing her back into her seat. Her fury kept her seated only momentarily before she began rising again. Thomas touched her shoulder, speaking softly, "Margaret, it's I who must endure this—let her finish. Please, two minutes more." Margaret's grip tightened painfully on Thomas's leg beneath the table.

"Thank you, dear," Lady Hatcher said calmly. "I must confess I overheard your conversation just before I entered. Margaret, you spoke as though Thomas were a stranger visiting us for the first time, revisiting thoroughly covered details. If you recall, we were all at the glass cabinet when it was first discussed. Moreover, you've always eaten those awful sausages, Thomas—except once, when Alistair consumed the last. Then there is your sudden grasp of specific company projects and knowledge of information that remains a state secret for another two weeks."

Margaret and Thomas exchanged a silent glance, feeling uncomfortably exposed and embarrassed.

Turning thoughtfully to Margaret, Lady Hatcher continued, "Margaret, Sir Walter Mildmay has not yet announced the program

Thomas referenced. Its existence is so secret that even he, as Chancellor, has yet to be informed fully until approval is finalized. Only a select few in government have authority to withhold information from elected officials, yet Thomas speaks of it openly."

Slowly setting her napkin aside, Lady Hatcher gazed unwaveringly into Thomas's eyes, briefly looking toward the terrace before returning her attention to Margaret. The silence was thick and palpable.

Then, with remarkable calm, she stated plainly, "You are not Thomas, are you? I understand it defies logic—perhaps you're a twin, an imposter, or even an actor. I simply know what I've observed."

Thomas glanced nervously at Margaret, who nervously tucked a strand of hair behind her ear.

Realizing the seriousness, Thomas thought carefully. Lady Hatcher was no idle socialite; she was perceptive, intelligent, and determined. Her daughter, family business, and country were at stake, and she demanded clarity.

Taking a deep breath, Margaret blurted out, "Mother, that's precisely why we're here. We desperately need your help—something that could help save England and win the war."

Thomas marveled briefly, thinking, "Like mother, like daughter. Both direct to a fault." Margaret had previously spoken of easing her mother into the situation, but now she'd plunged headfirst.

Margaret continued bravely, "Mother, Thomas isn't exactly Thomas—not the one we knew, anyway."

Lady Hatcher raised her eyebrows, sipping her gin and orange coolly. "That's intriguing indeed. Care to clarify?"

"Several days ago," Margaret explained cautiously, "the Thomas we knew simply vanished. Another person—a different Thomas—stepped into my life. I married our Thomas because he displeased you. We'd have no issues if this Thomas had been mine from the start. But what's more difficult is... Thomas, perhaps you should..."

Thomas took over hesitantly: "Helen, I recall nothing from a few days ago. I simply possess knowledge of events yet to occur, especially relating to the war. Somehow, I know details before they're public. That's how I'm aware of the Chancellor's upcoming announcement."

Lady Hatcher remained calm, revealing nothing, prompting Thomas to continue.

"Lady Ha, I mean, Helen, I can't explain my knowledge, but I know this: England will stand firm, inspire Europe, and defeat Hitler with America's assistance."

Lady Hatcher scoffed, "The Americans? They're isolationists and wouldn't offer two pence for England's survival."

"Currently true," Thomas agreed, "but soon they'll be forced to join after Japan attacks Pearl Harbor and Hitler declares war on America. Giving Roosevelt a reason to get America involved in Europe. Right now, Hitler is determined to conquer England. Given the poor state of the RAF, the moment is closer than anyone will know until after the war."

"Preposterous!" Lady Hatcher exclaimed. You can't possibly know what people will be thinking after the war. You can't know this!"

Having to defend an impossible situation, Thomas said, "I don't know how; I just know. I'm also certain that we will win the war. However, other than not surrendering, I'm unsure how."

"Mother," Margaret said, "he predicted the bombing of the civilians in Berlin the day before it was in the paper. He told me exactly what was going to occur. He doesn't know how it works, Mother, but I truly believe he's correct."

"Helen, very shortly, the war cabinet will try to force Churchill to consider some type of surrender."

"Nonsense!" she said.

"No," Thomas insisted earnestly. "On September seventh, the war cabinet will debate the issue in the face of overwhelming odds. The debate is close, but Churchill's persuasive determination ultimately prevails, as he has no intention of even considering surrender. But the decision is not guaranteed; we can't leave it to chance. I must speak to Churchill and convince him not to waver. I have information he might trust, and it might just tip the scales in our favor. England's survival depends on it."

Chapter Fifty-Nine

Breakfast
Hatcher Estate

Sitting at the end of the table, Lady Hatcher struggled to make sense of the extraordinary information presented to her. The situation was peculiar—this wasn't the familiar, tiresome Thomas, but rather someone different, improved even. Yet, she thought, could any good possibly come from such a fantastical story? Then again, Margaret seemed to genuinely bond with this new Thomas in a way that had always been elusive. Perhaps the strange shift in Thomas was acceptable if it meant Margaret would finally find happiness.

She turned sharply to Thomas. "What makes you think Churchill will believe your story? What makes you think I believe it?"

Thomas spoke earnestly, "Because we simply can't afford not to. We must not take the risk."

Lady Hatcher pressed further. "And why should I accept your word?"

Yesterday, I was nearly killed at Bletchley Park—someone tried to shoot me. Margaret managed to get me away in her car at the last moment."

"What utter nonsense!" Lady Hatcher retorted. "Who on earth would want to harm you?"

Thomas shook his head gravely. "I honestly don't know. Perhaps they knew I'd come—though how or who 'they' are, I haven't a clue."

"Lady Hatcher," Thomas insisted, "have you read today's newspaper?"

"No," she admitted coolly. "Mr. Pomeroy interrupted my morning routine."

Thomas straightened, his tone confident yet urgent. "British bombers attacked a factory near Berlin yesterday evening. Perhaps it was Militarily ineffective, but it was a crucial political strike—Churchill directed it. He declared it an example of Britain's resolve."

She stared at him skeptically. "How could you possibly know that?"

He met her gaze squarely. “What would I gain by inventing such a tale—other than risking your doubt about my sanity?”

Lady Hatcher coolly responded, “I’ve considered that possibility already, Thomas.”

“Do I appear confused or unstable?” he asked evenly.

“No,” she conceded cautiously, “you do not. Yet, it remains preposterous.”

“Perhaps so,” Thomas admitted, “but what possible motive could I have?”

Lady Hatcher lifted her hand abruptly. “Marion!”

Marion appeared promptly at the doorway. “Yes, Ma’am?”

“Fetch this morning’s newspaper, would you?

Marion curtsied slightly and hurried away, leaving behind an anxious silence. The quiet grew oppressive, weighing upon them until Marion returned, a newspaper in hand. Lady Hatcher swiftly scanned the front page and then the details beneath.

“You won’t find mention of the airfields being in poor shape,” Thomas assured her.

Lady Hatcher ignored him momentarily, engrossed in reading. Finally, she looked up sharply. “Remarkable,” she murmured. “Everything is exactly as you described. There must be a reason you know this.”

Margaret leaned forward anxiously. “Mother, I know it sounds unimaginable, but Thomas has convinced me—he truly knows events before they happen. I can't explain it, but he has convinced me beyond a doubt.”

Lady Hatcher studied Margaret’s earnest face and sighed. “But even supposing this is true—and it's a significant supposition—what would you have me do?”

Margaret interjected urgently, “Mother, you're the only person we know with high enough connections to arrange a meeting with Mr. Churchill.”

Lady Hatcher raised an incredulous eyebrow. “My dear girl, surely you don't imagine I can simply pick up the telephone and arrange an appointment with Winston Churchill?”

“Mother. If Thomas is correct, we must act immediately. Even if Churchill dismisses him, we must try. Thomas has information Churchill may find helpful, and he needn't tell anyone the source.”

Lady Hatcher considered thoughtfully. “Margaret, Churchill is notoriously stubborn. He will not entertain war advice from a friend's widow, least of all one involved in textiles.”

Lady Hatcher's eyes flickered thoughtfully between them. Yet, here you sit, discussing matters that are not public knowledge. How can I reconcile such discrepancies?"

Thomas calmly replied, "Helen, I understand your doubts, but what matters is preventing disaster. Britain is at a crucial juncture. Churchill will soon face significant pressure to surrender."

"Nonsense!" she exclaimed sharply. "Churchill would never surrender."

Thomas persisted steadily. "On September 7, due to the critical state of our defenses, the cabinet will debate surrendering. Churchill's passionate resolve turns the tide, but the decision will be razor-thin. Any added persuasion might prove critical. That's why I must meet him—I possess knowledge that could tip the scales in our favor."

Lady Hatcher appeared genuinely troubled. "But you've said we'll win the war. So, why panic?"

Thomas explained earnestly, "I don't know if History is inevitable. Decisions could swing either way. Even a tiny influence could prove decisive. That's why I must speak with Churchill—persuade him to stand firm."

Lady Hatcher silently considered this before turning to Margaret. "And you believe him, dear?"

Margaret nodded emphatically. "I do, Mother. He predicted the Berlin bombing precisely. He knows things no one else possibly could."

Lady Hatcher took a deep breath, then carefully placed her napkin aside, studying Thomas intently. "Very well," she said with resignation. "Perhaps we must take this seriously after all."

Margaret leaned over gently, covering her mother's hand with her own. Startled briefly, Lady Hatcher nearly withdrew her hand but allowed the gesture to linger. Margaret spoke softly, earnestly, "Mother, I've no illusions about how absurd all this sounds. I've never known Thomas like this—honestly, it's as if he's another man entirely. Yet he seems genuine, and I trust him. Perhaps logic isn't at work here, but we must take him seriously. I need your help, Mother. Will you help us?"

Thomas stared in astonishment, scarcely believing what he had just witnessed. In mere moments, Margaret had clearly outlined their improbable circumstances, devised a sensible approach, and—contrary to every instinct she'd previously shown—openly sought her mother's aid.

Lady Hatcher visibly moved regarded her daughter with newfound consideration. Perhaps this resolute, forthright Margaret was what her husband had always seen—something she'd missed entirely in her fixation on Society's approval. Margaret had never truly needed Society's endorsement or even her mother's support until this very moment.

With a softened expression, Lady Hatcher said, "Yes, of course, dear, though I'm unsure the question is not whether I will help rather than if I even can help. Honestly, what should I say? That my son-in-law reads tea leaves and has inside information on the Luftwaffe's next target?"

Margaret calmly insisted, "No, Mother—just secure Thomas a meeting. Let him explain things to Churchill, and he can make his judgment. Surely Churchill owes you something for all those years with Father?"

"Oh, he owes me indeed, though I rather doubt he remembers, given his particular condition on numerous occasions." With that, she reached decisively for her gin and orange, then raised her voice, "Marion, you may come in—I know you're hovering."

Marion promptly appeared, "Yes, Ma'am?"

"Fetch me the telephone and Winston Churchill's number from my directory, please."

"Oh, Mother, thank you!" Margaret exclaimed softly.

Lady Hatcher turned pointedly to Thomas. "You realize, young man, if you're mistaken, it could affect countless lives at the factory and beyond. Are you quite sure of what you're saying?"

Thomas replied unwaveringly, "Yes, I am sure—though I can't explain how I know."

"Given the stakes, I wish you were confident about both points," she murmured.

Marion swiftly returned, carrying the phone and directory. Lady Hatcher donned her glasses, dialed deliberately, and waited with an expectant gaze fixed firmly upon Thomas.

"Connect me with Mr. Churchill, please. Yes, you may. This is Lady Hatcher. No, it's not merely important—it's critical." Her irritation mounted, and she continued sharply, "Young man, I am fully aware that he's busy fighting a war—I'm not daft. Inform him I have valuable information. Immediately, please." She glanced towards Margaret with visible exasperation.

Margaret mouthed silently, "Thank you."

Turning back to the receiver, Lady Hatcher added crisply, "Young man, Churchill is always in a meeting. I hardly expect him to be lounging about discussing cinema attractions. Inform him immediately who's calling and remind him he is in my dept for any number of reasons. That's right—do it now. If not him, get me Colville at once."

An uneasy silence filled the room, tension growing with each passing moment. Lady Hatcher sat rigidly, determined to outwait the hesitant young man on the other end of the line, fully aware of the turmoil her insistence must be causing.

At last, Churchill's familiar voice clearly said, "Lady Hatcher, it's Winston. To what do I owe the pleasure on this busy day?"

"Winston, I apologize for troubling you," she began firmly, "but I have a most unusual request. Could you spare fifteen minutes to meet privately with my son-in-law?"

Churchill paused briefly before replying, "That's all? Barnes implied you had valuable wartime information—not that I wouldn't gladly entertain your request regardless."

Lady Hatcher retorted dryly, "Winston, you haven't changed a bit."

"Oh, but I have," Churchill chuckled warmly. "I've stopped dipping my cigars, doctor's orders to reduce brandy intake." He continued, "Helen, you've brightened my day, but could you perhaps elaborate slightly? If you give me specifics, I promise prompt attention."

"I'm afraid it's not suitable for the telephone," she insisted. "My son-in-law, Thomas Watson, must explain personally and privately."

Churchill sighed audibly, "We're rather pressed currently—perhaps a fortnight's delay?"

"Winston, we don't have a fortnight Lady Hatcher asserted strongly. You're busy precisely because the situation is dire. Winston, in all the years that you corrupted my husband, I didn't complain, nor have I ever asked you for a favor other than for you to try harder at making the ashtray, a request that I might add consistently went ignored. Grant Thomas just fifteen minutes, not because he's family, but because he might genuinely aid your efforts. Remember, Winston, this is my bloody country too."

Churchill chuckled gently, "Lady Hatcher, I've never known you to be short of words; I see this time, there is no exception. While admittedly responsible for certain adjustments to your dinners, such history scarcely grants unlimited privileges. Besides, your husband was responsible for many dubious anecdotes likely to mar my legacy."

"Mr. Churc*hill*," Lady Hatcher intoned slowly, drawing out each syllable purposefully.

Churchill relented humorously, "Helen, I yield to your formidable persistence. Through years of delightful friendship, I never did determine who among us was more obstinate. I'm glad to have finally discovered the answer. Have him contact Colville promptly. I will meet him as soon as possible—you have my promise."

"Mr. Churchill," she said, realizing she'd indeed been successful, "your gracious consideration is beyond reproach."

"As is my respect for the Lady," Churchill concluded, and, as was his habit, immediately rang off.

Turning calmly to Margaret, Lady Hatcher announced, "He instructed Thomas to call Mr. Colville immediately."

Margaret clasped her hands together, overcome. "Mother, oh, thank you so much!" Without thinking, she rose impulsively and kissed her mother's cheek before swiftly retreating to her seat, suddenly shy.

Thomas wondered anxiously how Lady Hatcher might react. The brief silence held tension, yet, with surprising grace, Lady Hatcher softly responded, "Why, thank you, dear."

Chapter Sixty

Thomas and Viktor

After Lady Hatcher's telephone call, Thomas rang up, asking to speak to Mr. Colville. Being told he was away, Thomas could make the appointment with Barnes, who already knew the particulars. "Should make for an interesting meeting," Thomas reflected quietly.

The three concluded their breakfast on a distinctly more pleasant footing, Thomas discoursing earnestly upon his further thoughts regarding the war. Margaret's mother seemed genuinely intrigued, though Thomas suspected she scarcely credited half of what she heard. Seeking to steer the conversation elsewhere, Thomas asked about Margaret's childhood—an unfortunate misstep, as mother and daughter clearly recalled the same episodes quite differently. Nonetheless, the remaining time was not nearly as fraught as the awkwardness he'd encountered directly upon passing through the large black door.

Lady Hatcher departed soon after, explaining that her afternoon would be occupied with preparing the ladies' tea.

Margaret and Thomas were keen on having some quiet time together, and Margaret's bedroom was ideal for that purpose. Apart from routine attention by the household staff, the room remained as Margaret had left it upon her decision to move away. Despite the tensions, her mother hoped that her daughter's absence wasn't permanent.

Situated conveniently between the bustling social rooms below and the servants' quarters on the top floor, Margaret's bedroom occupied a privileged position on the family's second floor. Several large windows overlooked the grounds, admitting far too much sunlight in the early hours, as Margaret claimed. It was an impressively sized room—almost half as large as the house she rented from Mrs. Somerville. The décor was marked by framed photographs, charming stuffed animals, and decorative cushions embroidered brightly with whimsical themes. Apart from the vivid floral pattern of the canopy on the impressive four-poster bed, there was little to suggest this was ever a young girl's room. Indeed, the overall tone matched the rest of the house, all neutral silken wall coverings and substantial furniture. Plush indeed, and likely difficult to forsake. Later, as dusk fell and shadows danced from the low fire, the room became softly luminous.

Margaret busied herself rummaging through a dresser drawer as though her past—or perhaps some clue to the future—might be concealed in a neglected corner.

Standing quietly by a window, Thomas stared unfocused across the grounds. His mind returned to the puzzle at hand, a frustrating jumble that seemed always beyond his reach. From his back pocket, he withdrew and unfolded a small slip of paper.

"What's that?" Margaret asked, nearly slamming shut one drawer, finding nothing of interest, and moving briskly to the next.

"A loose end that's bothered me all day," Thomas replied thoughtfully. Showing her the scribbled note, he continued, "A phone number—but whose, exactly? I found it on one of the chaps in the park. Except for the gun, that was the only thing he had."

Margaret stared at him, silent.

Holding the scrap aloft, Thomas spoke earnestly. "If we're to see this through, we must discover who exactly wants me dead."

"That's easy enough, surely—it's that fellow Yuri."

"If it were that simple, why give me the chance to explain myself back at the bar? Besides, something doesn't feel right. I can't picture Yuri behind the shooting. He wouldn't resort to a gun unless forced, and he had other choices."

"Thomas, besides being scatterbrained, you're being monstrously naïve," Margaret replied impatiently. "He believes you possess information about some blasted machine and is quite ready to kill for it."

"But I do know something about a machine."

"What? That was the old Thomas. Not you. Or have you forgotten again? Please, tell me you're not—"

"No, my senses haven't left me. This information differs from what the old Thomas knew—perhaps in nature or the source itself."

"Thomas Watson, I promised to help so we could move past all this and find a normal life. But I cannot help unless you begin to talk sense. There is a point where you do begin to make sense—right?"

They exchanged a long, meaningful look.

"Thomas, answer me."

"Margaret, the Russians think I'm someone else, a spy they engaged to acquire information on a secret project your family's company is undertaking—something even your mother might not know about."

"Trust me, my mother knows everything. Or have you forgotten whose daughter I am?"

"And what of your secret midnight escapades and Alistair finding you at the doorstep?"

"Well—almost everything, perhaps."

"Regardless, the Russians want this information, and providing it seems the only way clear of this mess."

Margaret's eyes rolled dramatically. "And you believe they'll become harmless kittens once you've handed it over?"

"No, but I have a plan."

"You have a plan? I thought we were following my plan—a quiet life once everything's settled."

"Margaret," Thomas said, gripping her hand gently. "Think carefully: It's precisely the same plan—only with a twist."

"Twist?" Margaret retorted. "You'll know 'twist' by the time this is over. Now kiss me."

Thomas emerged from his thoughtful reverie, smiling, "Now, that's a plan."

"But there's a twist," she added playfully, "and it involves you not making that call."

"That's pure blackmail," Thomas protested good-naturedly.

With arms dramatically spread wide, Margaret declared triumphantly, "Welcome to the eternal conflict between women and men, dear boy. When it truly matters—we win."

Quickly leaning forward, Thomas slipped the paper deftly between two fingers, took her face gently in his hands, and kissed her deeply. He meant it as a swift raid, but Margaret pulled him down and straddled him, pressing both hands firmly upon his chest.

"You absolute bounder! That's no way to treat a proper lady. You can't say and do as you please and expect me to keep falling in love with you—or stay in love." She paused thoughtfully. "Either way, Thomas Watson, your brain's quite addled." She rolled gracefully off him and onto the bed.

Sitting up, Thomas carefully placed the slip of paper beside the telephone on the bedside stand. He briefly regarded the number, then turned his gaze back toward her.

After Lady Hatcher's phone call, Thomas called, asking for Mr. Colville. Informed he was out, Thomas could make the appointment with Barnes, who already knew the story. "It's going to be an interesting meeting," Thomas thought.

The three of them finished breakfast on a much more pleasant note, with Thomas explaining his other thoughts about the war. Margaret's mother appeared genuinely interested, although she surely had trouble believing most of what she heard. Thomas tried to change the subject by asking questions about Margaret's childhood. The subject did not go over well, as Margaret and her mother had decidedly different memories of the same events. Overall, the remaining time wasn't as uncomfortable as the disaster he'd encountered immediately after walking in the big black door.

Lady Hatcher left to prepare for the ladies and her tea, explaining it would take much of the afternoon.

Margaret and Thomas wanted to spend time together, and Margaret's bedroom was the perfect place. Except for the staff's attention, the room remained as it had been when Margaret had decided to leave the family. Obviously, her mother did not believe it was permanent.

With the social areas occupying much of the bottom floor and the service staff living quarters up on the third floor, Margaret's room was in the family living area on the second floor. Several windows overlooked the grounds and, according to Margaret, let in far too much light in the morning. The room was large, almost half the size of the house she rented from Mrs. Somerville. The décor included pictures, stuffed animals, and brightly stitched, theme-based pillows. However, for the most part, there was nothing to indicate it was a little girl's bedroom, except for the four-poster bed whose canopy was a vivid flower pattern matching the bed cover. Instead, the room used the same motif of neutral silk wall coverings and heavy furniture as the rest of the house. All very plush and, one would think, hard to leave. Later, the low flame in the fireplace and the onset of night cast a wonderful flickering radiance about the room.

Margaret was busy exploring a dresser drawer as if her past or clues to her future were in a hidden corner.

Standing at one of the windows, Thomas was locked in an unfocused gaze. Again, he was turning over events and trying to assemble the picture puzzle. It would get close, but it was always beyond his ability to locate the final few pieces. From his back pocket, he removed and unfolded a piece of paper.

"What is that?" Margaret said, almost slamming one drawer shut, finding little of value, and moving on to another.

"It's a loose end that's been at the back of my mind all day."

He showed her the scribble, saying, "It's a phone number, but the real question is, whose phone number? I found it on one of the men at the park. Except for the gun, that's all he had on him."

Margaret just looked at Thomas without saying a word.

Holding the piece of paper up, Thomas looked at her. "If we're going to get to the bottom of this, we need to know who wants me dead."

"That ought to be simple. It's that Yuri character."

"If it was that simple, then why did he give me a chance to come clean when we were at the bar? Besides, there's a feeling that I get. I have a hard time thinking he was responsible for the shooting in the park. I don't think he would use a gun unless he didn't have a choice, and he had choices."

"Thomas, besides being scatterbrained, you're now being monstrously naïve. He wants the information he thinks you have about some bloody machine and is ready to kill for it."

"But I do know something about a machine."

"*What?* That was the old Thomas. Not you, Thomas. Or don't you remember again? Please tell me it's not you. I mean old…"

"No, I haven't left my senses. It's not the same information that the old Thomas had, or at least it's not the same kind, or the source is different."

"Thomas Watson, I made a promise to help so we could get past this and to a life we can call normal. I can't do it if you don't start making sense. There's a point you start making sense—right?"

They exchanged looks.

"Thomas, answer me."

"Margaret, the Russians think I'm someone else, a spy they hired to get some information about a project your family's company is working on, something you or perhaps even your mother doesn't know anything about."

"I can assure you my mother knows *everything*. I grew up as her daughter, remember?"

"What about your sneaking out in the middle of the night and Alistair finding you on the doorstep?"

"Well, maybe almost everything."

"Anyway, they want the information, and giving it to them is the only way I can think of to get us out of this mess."

Margaret's eyes rolled back with her head in an unmistakable gesture. "You think they're all going to turn into harmless stray cats after you give them the information?"

"No, but I have a plan."

"You have a plan? I thought we were following my plan. The one that has us leading a simple life after we get this straightened out."

"Margaret," Thomas said. He grabbed her hand. "Think for a minute: It's the same plan. It just contains a twist."

"Twist," she said. "You won't know 'twist' when this is over. Kiss me."

Thomas emerged from his deep thoughts, saying, "Now that's a plan."

"But there's a twist," she said smiling, "only if you're not going to call that number."

"That's sexual blackmail."

With arms stretched wide, Margaret said, "Welcome to the real world of women versus men. When it counts—we win."

Quickly leaning forward, he slipped the paper between two fingers, grabbed her face with both hands and kissed her. He had intended it as a hit and run, but she pulled him down and straddled him, with both hands pushing on his chest.

"You sod. That's no way to treat a proper woman. You can't just say and do what you want and think I'll fall in love with you. Or stay in love with you." She stopped and thought a moment. "Either way, your brain is messed up, buster." She rolled off of him and fell onto the bed.

Sitting up, Thomas put the slip of paper on the bed stand, where a phone was. He looked at the number and then at her.

"Margaret, I've got to ring," he insisted. "How in heaven's name will we sort this if we sit about doin' nothing'? Besides, whoever answers might just shed some light."

"Light my foot," Margaret snapped. "What'll you tell him, anyhow?"

"Well, that rather depends on who picks up, doesn't it? I'll feed him whatever he wants to hear. Let's at least discover who we're dealing with." Thomas already had the telephone to his ear, dialing swiftly. "It's ringing now; it's a direct line."

Thomas heard a click as someone lifted the receiver, followed by an angry shout. "Where the devil have you been, you idiot? I've been waiting. It was supposed to be a clean hit, not some blazing shootout right in broad daylight. What in blazes went wrong?"

There was a short pause, and Viktor's voice demanded sharply, "Answer me. Who's this?"

"What business have you with Mr. Dunning?" Thomas ventured.

"Dunning? Who the hell is Dunning? Who is this, anyway?" Viktor barked back impatiently.

Thomas pressed again cautiously. "Then what is it you want with Watson?"

A stunned silence came from Viktor, broken eventually by a grim tone. "You're in considerable trouble, Watson. How'd you get this number?"

"That hardly matters. What do you want from Watson?" Thomas shielded the mouthpiece and whispered urgently to Margaret, "It's not Yuri, but he sounds very Russian."

"What d'you think?" the voice sneered. "We want what we paid for—and handsomely at that. Your arrogance has stirred up powerful enemies. Moscow isn't pleased, Watson. We want details on that machine."

"Where's Yuri, then?" Thomas demanded.

"Comrade Stakova's finished. Moscow is displeased with him as well. I've been sent directly from headquarters to mop up his mess before the Germans tie our hands—or worse."

"So you're the one who tried to kill me?" Thomas asked coolly.

"You amateurs," Viktor mocked disdainfully. "So very childish, indeed. Chatting with the British? What did you expect us to think? You played your game and chased your money and your girl, but talking to the Brits can only mean trouble for Russia. We're hardly allies, or have you spent the war in a bomb shelter?"

With conceited assurance, Viktor moved to clinch it. "Many things remain unsettled. Your only chance now is to meet me and surrender the information."

Thomas intentionally let Viktor finish his threat before replying. "Wouldn't it be childish to stroll straight into your trap? Given what's already happened, you'll forgive my caution. If we meet, I shall select the time and place."

"Fine, but move swiftly. Moscow doesn't wait. I require explanations for your jaunt to Bletchley and the intelligence you've been withholding."

"I can give you both," Thomas responded evenly, "provided my safety and that of my wife is assured."

Viktor's voice hardened. "Thanks to your escapades, your choices are few. Hand over the information, then leave England quickly."

Thomas hesitated thoughtfully. "That will prove difficult."

"Being dead is far more difficult, I assure you."

Feigning amateurish uncertainty, Thomas pressed, "Can you truly guarantee our safety? Can you get us clear of the country?"

After the invasion, they'll eventually find out you were playing both sides with information they think is critical. You don't have a connection to German intelligence. Consequently, the Germans will see you as an enemy of the state, and, of course, this isn't good for both of you. I'm the only one who can get you out of the country. But only after I'm satisfied with the information you must provide."

"You speak alarmingly good sense," Thomas conceded. "When the Germans arrive, they'll hound down anyone suspicious. That's precisely why I'll agree to meet."

Viktor interjected sharply, "How do I know your chosen place isn't a trap?"

"What d'you mean 'so *you'll* know'? I'm the one who must fear treachery—I believe I've been clear enough about that already," Thomas retorted firmly.

Realizing he lacked leverage, Viktor grudgingly conceded. "Very well, but it must also be secure from my perspective."

"It is," Thomas assured briskly. "Richmond district—you familiar with it?"

"Certainly," Viktor answered curtly. "I've studied the area thoroughly—unlike you amateurs."

"Here's the deal. I'm only going to do this once and at a specific time. It has to be tomorrow morning. It's a place I stayed during some tough times when there was little money. Everyone knows everyone, so taking over a flat for any observation or deploying anyone on the side streets will be very difficult. The whole neighborhood will be watching. The people there are very suspicious of the authorities. Any actions of this nature will make them think it's directed at one of them and act accordingly. It's on Richmond Hill Road. Any cabbie can find it. A green in the middle of a housing terrace is visible as you crest the hill. The road ends there, and you can have a look about. It's right out in the open. You must meet me in the green at precisely 11:30 a.m. If you change it, the deal is off. Is that clear?"

"Curious," Viktor remarked, fumbling in his coat pocket for cigarettes. "I understand precision never suited you before. Why now?"

"You'll understand once you've seen the information," Thomas responded crisply. "You must arrive first, alone. If I spot anything suspicious, this intelligence will quickly become valuable elsewhere. My car might not be the first you see—so shoot up the neighborhood prematurely, and you'll ruin everything. There won't be a second chance.

Bring two open tickets on the Pan Am Clipper to Lisbon and two entry visas in our names."

Viktor chuckled grimly, "And how exactly am I to procure visas so swiftly?"

"Don't play games," Thomas snapped. "Your embassy can conjure visas at will. Do you agree or not?"

"It appears I've little choice," Viktor growled reluctantly. "You've covered everything. I want information, not your heads. Assuming I'm satisfied, I'll tell my people to let you reach the airport. But remember, your problems won't vanish in Lisbon. Nazis swarm there like flies."

"Leave the rest to me. Just be punctual." Thomas replaced the receiver firmly.

Margaret's face darkened. "You're really going to meet him—with no information? And besides, I'm not going to Lisbon."

"Don't fret," Thomas reassured gently. "We're not going anywhere. No need to, remember? The Germans won't invade."

"Thomas, you simply can't meet this man. He's an assassin, ruthless. Nothing good will come from it unless you eliminate him entirely from our lives."

Thomas met her worried gaze calmly. "Precisely."

Chapter Sixty-One

Margaret's Bedroom

Hatcher Estate

After Thomas phoned to arrange the Richmond appointment, there was nothing else but to wait. He and Margaret enjoyed the unexpected respite, their lives having become unceasingly hectic since that Yuri fellow first appeared beside their table. They passed a leisurely afternoon wandering the grounds, Margaret recounting more stories from her childhood whenever they chanced upon a secluded bench or a charming grove of trees. Eventually, they arrived at the now-famous pagoda, Margaret giggling softly as they circled the familiar structure.

"Enjoying the memory of your first attempt at controlling men, are we?" Thomas asked teasingly.

"First?" she retorted.

"Forgive my presumptuousness for thinking there had been no earlier occasions for you to wield a woman's ethereal power over the weaker sex."

"Thomas, you are a dear soul, but I strongly advise against continuing down a road that leads only to bruised ribs." She leaped in front of him, one hand clenched while the other pointed directly at his side. "Right there, bruised, you follow?"

Thomas spread out both arms, his body forming a cross, and said, "Strike me. Strike me now. Punishment gladly take I, for fair lady's favor outweighs the fate of lessor souls! He barely got out the last two words before giving in to laughter and realizing his soul best flee.

Back in their room, Margaret kicked off her shoes and flopped onto the bed in a manner practiced from years past. "You ought to feel privileged, Thomas—the other Thomas never got this far."

"As far as—er—?"

"Watson? Even your mind cannot be that twisted."

"Oh, indeed it can," he replied with a broad grin.

She sat up sharply to clarify. "Not in this room. I would never let him in here."

"Is this still about pagodas?"

"I would rather not discuss it."

"Excellent," Thomas declared, "because we need to change the topic and address some matters."

"No," Margaret moaned, flopping back and clutching a small embroidered pillow. "I simply refuse."

A moment later, she asked softly, "Mother really did change, didn't she?"

Thomas was lost briefly in his thoughts and remained quiet. He was considering how best to handle what was inevitably coming.

Realizing her words lacked clarity, Margaret clarified, "I meant from how I described her. She transformed from a hollow socialite, the perfect companion for the owner of this grand house, into a military contractor baron. It makes no sense. Why did she not show me that side when I was young? It could have changed everything."

"Is it not plain enough?" Thomas replied.

Margaret quickly turned towards him, eyes sharp. "Plain enough? Would I be asking if it were plain?"

"Perhaps she was not that person then. Perhaps she rose to meet the challenge. She adopted that persona to safeguard the family's reputation and business. Yet she never saw reason to abandon the comfortable façade of the empty-headed hostess. She chose both worlds."

"My mother is no empty-headed woman, Thomas. I would be careful choosing your next words."

"Why are you cross with me?" he asked gently.

Margaret frowned in confusion. "I suppose I was defending her."

"There are worse fates," Thomas replied.

"It is your fault, Thomas. All your wild stories turn my life topsy-turvy. You are why I came here seeking help."

"And look what came of it? Were you not watching your mother's face when she let you embrace her and even thanked you? When did that last happen?"

"I honestly do not know," Margaret whispered, rolling away to stare blankly.

"Margaret?" Thomas said gently.

"Oh," she groaned, covering her face with the pillow.

"We must speak about tomorrow," Thomas continued firmly. "You must remain here. It is too dangerous. I will see Churchill alone."

She threw the pillow aside. "Oh, indeed you will—not likely! We are in this together. Remember where we are—asking my mother to believe you are someone else entirely. Then, expecting her to risk ridicule by admitting it publicly."

"That does not lessen the danger. Our arrangement never meant putting you at risk. I would sooner not find answers at all than risk losing you. Truth be told, I cannot imagine life without you."

Margaret met his gaze, noting his seriousness. "Sweet words, Thomas, if you mean them. Say what you please; I am not listening." She turned away, hiding again beneath her pillow.

Thomas looked at her concealed form. "Things grow more clearer now—or focused. Feelings become tangible—"

Muffled beneath the pillow, she interrupted, "What nonsense are you talking about?"

He smiled at the stubborn girl before him.

She tilted the pillow away slightly. "Not that I care. I was not listening anyway."

"Well, it's important, so you might want to try. Take the government's finance deal we discussed with your mother. The reasoning and purpose are clearer to me. What Turing is doing is clearer, and when I have these thoughts, they're starting to become connected."

Still, Margaret ignored him. Changing his tactic, Thomas remarked casually, "Do you know that radio will eventually come with a moving picture that will show the person talking?"

Margaret's eyes widened. "Thomas, you cannot say just anything! Next, you will have tea kettles flying over the moon instead of cows. Or the King inviting me for dinner! See, I can do it too."

"I'm trying to point out that some of what I can remember might help us. And that something is changing. The feelings and visions are much clearer. There definitely won't be an invasion, and England will maintain its independence after the war. Women help win the war by working beside men and instead of men, in many cases. Women's role in society changes forever."

Margaret's face was unreadable. "I know things are changing. But, tell me, where did the tough fellow on the phone come from? Combined with your gun in the park, it seems I hardly know you. Yet you remember Richmond Hill Road and forget we are married!"

"I read it somewhere, or I simply knew it."

"Right, have you forgotten you'll see Churchill tomorrow morning? Remember the little phone call my mother made?"

"There is time enough," Thomas assured.

"No time, Thomas! Besides, there is no confounded secret information for you to offer."

Thomas smiled softly. “I have something but will not hand it to him—just test a hunch from afar.”

“What will you do, send the other Thomas? The rascal I foolishly found appealing?”

“Do you not find me appealing?”

“Thomas, behave!”

“I am sincere about the Richmond meeting. Let me attempt it—what is the harm?”

Margaret grabbed the telephone. “I am ringing Mrs. Somerville. We have much to lose.” She dialed but received no answer, and concern flashed across her face.

“She is too clever to wait around,” Thomas reassured gently.

“Is she afraid?”

“Everything she does has a purpose. Trust her. I will check tomorrow. Can we sleep now?”

“Thomas, you said that like you were a little puppy. How cute. The answer is no. I mean, we can go to sleep but not to bed, and you can blame yourself. I warned you.”

Thomas sighed warmly. “If you insist—though bed is surely required for sleep.”

“None of your clever games,” she warned.

“You win, Margaret—sleep it is.”

“Truly?”

“Indeed.”

“What if making love were my true intention?” she teased.

Thomas laughed softly. “Margaret, you are always hard to get—no playacting necessary.”

Chapter Sixty-Two

Safe House

Like the first day, Yuri began his second morning at the safe house by sleeping late. Sleep had proven elusive since the day of the shooting. Missing a single night from his apartment would not have aroused suspicion; however, being absent for two nights, particularly with Joseph stationed at the embassy, would undoubtedly signal something amiss. Yuri had pieced together what he could—at least those details directly concerning him—but still faced a lengthy list of obligations to his people.

It was a bitter truth that all things, both good and bad, must come to an end. What had he gained for dedicating his life to the service of his homeland? His country's undying gratitude had manifested as a contract on his life. He blamed Stalin far more than Russia itself.

The first day of his escape plan was filled with several crucial tasks, including securing a new British passport and exit visa. Britain had recently altered its documentation laws, necessitating updated passports and visas. The ones Yuri had stored away were obsolete. His Russian civilian and diplomatic passports and those from other nations remained valid. Sometimes, diplomatic status drew unwanted attention, necessitating travel as a civilian.

Typically, he would have secured his British documents through official embassy channels, creating a potentially dangerous record. Instead, Yuri turned to an underground contact favored by operatives across many governments—a man known solely as "The Printer." Renowned for forging near-perfect official and commercial documents, The Printer was cautious, enforcing a stringent protocol designed more for secrecy than scheduling convenience. An appointment ensured that operatives from competing nations would never cross paths—a scenario detrimental to his livelihood.

Yuri spent most of the day navigating the intricate security procedures that confirmed his identity as a returning customer. First, he placed a chalk mark on a designated lamp pole. Two hours later, he stood near the domestic ticket window at Hampstead Heath railway station, a crowded location allowing The Printer safe anonymity while observing. If all appeared secure, The Printer would dispatch an innocent boy to deliver an envelope containing the address of a second location in another part of the city.

The actual face-to-face transaction occurs only after carefully inspecting this secondary meeting point. Payment was always upfront, strictly in Swiss francs. The Printer was not someone to deceive lightly; dire stories circulated about those who compromised his security. You followed his rules or faced permanent consequences.

Though the passport and visa were completed swiftly, the process consumed most of Yuri's day. Late in the afternoon, he stopped briefly at a newsstand, keenly aware of his surroundings. Newspapers displayed prominent headlines and noteworthy stories yet curiously omitted any hint of the extraordinary events now dominating his life.

"ИРОНИЧЄСКИЙ (ironic)," Yuri said quietly, frustrated at not knowing the equivalent English term.

Finally leaving his flat, Yuri embarked upon a mission that he could not explain to anyone. Viktor's relentless obsession with capturing Thomas had changed everything. Glancing thoughtfully at the common across from his apartment, Yuri moved deliberately toward the first phase of his carefully planned exit.

Chapter Sixty-Three

Mrs. Somerville's House

The double ring of the bell startled Mrs. Somerville. She placed the kitchen cloth on the counter and went to the phone. The voice on the other end asked if she was alone and safe. It was all charming but unnecessary, given the situation. Then, the caller gave her the correct code word to verify his identity.

The voice said, "I have your note," and then gave brief, detailed instructions for a meeting.

"That's odd," she thought. "It's so close."

Mrs. Somerville knew she'd been asked to follow the procedures exactly, but she was still mistrusting and hesitant. Margaret was in danger and hoped the note she'd written and dropped off would protect her, but there was no way of knowing for sure. She didn't know why the British government had asked her to keep an eye on Margaret. It was all very casual, with no pressure or compensation, and they'd said she could stop at any time.

Ultimately, her continued participation was based on the friendship between the two women from different eras. As far as Thomas, she didn't know what side of his multiple personalities to believe. Unlike the other, the new side put Margaret first, even over his own gain. Indeed, both sides of that man were in one body, but their minds had grown up on different planets.

Mrs. Somerville balanced these thoughts like a performer spinning plates on the end of a pole. Which one would wobble with the weight of deception? Making her decision, she grabbed the notepad and pen to write a message to her young friend, just in case she came by and started to worry. She wanted to be extra cautious. How could she ensure that it was getting to Margaret and only Margaret? She couldn't just write it out for the world to see. Things were too strange and unpredictable.

Frozen for a moment with pen in hand, she looked at the sideboard. That'll do it. She smiled and quickly completed the steps that solved the thorny problem. She checked her handbag for money and keys and headed for the door.

Chapter Sixty-Four

Hatcher Estate

Margaret's mother wanted him to take the driver and the Mulsanne, but he felt uncertain of the day, not wanting the burden of a driver stuck smoking and polishing the Bentley's fenders for hours. He decided to stay with Mrs. Somerville's trusty motorcar. However, he had to admit it was a beautiful and tempting offer. Alastair had come out with him to the garage. He told him that the Bentley was the ninth off the line in '33, their first year in production. Margaret's father was a complete child when around the car. Alistair related one instance where Sir Everett Hatcher managed to coerce a friend of his wife's, who was leaving after tea, over to the car. She was one of the stuffiest, most insolent of his wife's social circle, and he proceeded to bore her to death with a tour of its sparkling motor.

"Really, Mr. Hatcher," she said, "couldn't you just pursue the hunt and play polo like the other gents? I can assure you. I've no interest as to a turbo-charger thing."

She'd taken the bait and, with a broad grin, Sir Hatcher reeled her in. "Why Lady Winthrop," he said while adjusting the front of his trousers, "it's what every decent gentleman should have under the bonnet—don't you think?"

With that, one of the last remaining pillars of Victorian society huffed out a very guttural sound. Aghast, she snapped her umbrella into full bloom, turned her full dress with the other hand, and directed herself back to the safe confines of decent company.

During this time, Churchill was sitting in the back seat testing the glassware. He said, "Well done, lad. Well done. Your heralded career in mixed company is now nonexistent."

Thomas and Alistair laughed, but the story ended when Margaret came into the garage, saying she and Thomas weren't quite finished with their conversation on whether she should stay at the house.

Thomas proceeded to present what he thought was a reasonable case. "Margaret, if nothing else, you're safer out here than in the bombing areas. On top of that, I don't want Viktor or someone finding me, which would put you in harm's way. I can't have that."

"You can't have that? When did you think it was yours to have?"

It was the first serious disagreement in an excellent start to a day. In the end, driving off, he felt the gearstick vibrate as it searched for the proper site to eliminate the pain. Glancing at the wing mirror, he saw Margaret grow smaller, standing with hands on her hips and imaginary steam coming out of her ears, like in a cartoon. He was definitely in love.

Chapter Sixty-Five

Whitehall War Rooms

Churchill had just concluded a meeting with the home secretary and a few of his key people. Colville entered to continue orchestrating the leader's day and deliver an important message. Colville was holding his notorious clipboard in his left hand while trying to flip some pages with his right, two fingers doubling as a paper clip for yet more paper. Colville, realizing something, stepped back to close the office door for privacy. Churchill was certain that this man's unlimited but well-disguised patience, unique sense of order, and complete dedication to the job at hand made him one of the more important figures of the war.

"Yes," Colville started, "Director Petrie placed a rather high priority on this. There was gunfire at Bletchley involving a visitor named Mr. Dunning. Security has arrested two men without identification, but only one was armed. Mr. Dunning, for unexplained reasons, managed to escape. Details are still coming in, so it's a bit sketchy. This Dunning knew enough about the Ultra program to raise serious concerns. They have full a manhunt out."

"Why wasn't I informed yesterday?"

"I can't fully answer that. I'm sorry. I can check into it right away."

"Don't bother. The director has his own problems. Keep me up on it."

"Also," Colville paused, avoiding eye contact, "Prime Minister, we must address a rather bothersome matter. It's the appointment you promised Mrs. Hatcher, who rather abusively got through to you directly during my off-duty hours. My sincerest apologies. Perhaps you have noticed Corporal Barnes is no longer on staff."

"Yes, yes…" Churchill said slowly. "I wouldn't be too hard on the corporal, as he went to battle completely unarmed with an unusually formidable opponent. There's a long list of brave and capable men who've battled and lost to our Lady Hatcher when she finds the need to emphasize her position. None of us has fared well, I'm afraid. Let's see him back for another try."

Churchill's tired mind willingly wandered at the name of Hatcher, providing visions of much simpler times, including the sport of teas and stuffy dinners and garden parties with even stuffier people. He longed in his heart for the return of an era seemingly lost. However, it wouldn't include his dear friend Everett if it were to re-appear.

"Your schedule, sir, is extremely tight, given your expressed desire that the visit to Uxbridge not be endangered. Actually," Colville said, as he flipped back to the last sheet and paused to read Barnes's note, "it's not specifically Mrs. Hatcher. The corporal's notes indicate it's with her son-in-law, a Mr. Watson, married to her daughter, Margaret."

"Really," Churchill muttered, his eyebrows lifting as he leaned back in his chair.

To Colville, this wasn't a good response. He carefully studied the man before him for signs that threatened his schedule. He observed him wandering in thought, not his typical manner of gnashing out information for a clear decision.

Churchill's memory served up another vision of his lost era. His memory smiled, remembering an evening when little Margaret stole his bowler, only for him to find it later that evening in the library, cocked atop a magnificent bust of the Duke of York. The footstool used to accomplish the act gave the perpetrator away. While drumming his fingers on the desktop, the great man took a moment to savor a growing outward smile.

At Churchill's request, some of the projects his friend Everett worked on were vital to the Empire. Thus, his company became an unofficial but very valuable and essential part of the government. Late one evening, alone in the library, Everett had addressed his friend after a long pull on his cigar.

"Winston, I know this. Some won't appreciate our efforts for the king. My friend, I'm a husband and father and don't want to leave anything to chance."

That evening, Churchill had promised Margaret's father to protect Margaret and her mother, regardless of his position in government.

Many, inside and outside the country, would have liked to curtail Hatcher's influence, and it would appear they were successful. It was still a government secret, but the crash investigation revealed evidence of an internal explosion before the plane crashed. Churchill dearly missed his old friend and stridently wanted to keep his promise to look after his wife and daughter. He also shouldered a heavy burden, harboring the guilt that he might have contributed, even in the slightest, to the loss of a great man.

"Prime Minister?" Colville said, looking up over his papers, waiting.

Churchill returned to the moment, saying, “I’m afraid we will need a bit of your magic, as I must see this Mr. Watson, if only briefly. It’s a long story that can be told only over a two-hour cigar.”

“But he could arrive at any time, sir,” Colville said as he turned to the door, trying his best not to show any irritation. Once again, he would need to rearrange the constant train of dignitaries who felt access was their right piled up at the door. Many of the upper class who entered the military found it hard to accept that their rank, or lack thereof, limited their station's usual civilian access and privileges. There were times, Colville felt, the PM didn’t fully appreciate his efforts in dealing with the many inflated personalities that insisted on access to his schedule. In his most diplomatic manner, he constantly persuaded them that the war's outcome did not depend on their getting face time with the prime minister.

Mid-step, he heard Churchill say, “Jock…?” Colville stopped. “How is your little girl?”

Taken a bit off stride, Colville said, “Well, ah… she’s doing fine, Prime Minister. Despite our best efforts, she continues to run the household at her leisure.” Colville paused, begging the question of the great man’s newfound interest.

Duly prompted, Churchill looked up and said, “It’s just sometimes the level of work obscures what’s truly important. I may forget to ask of such things; it’s not that I’ve forgotten. Your efforts are exemplary, with a yoke that wouldn’t be present with another man occupying the rather small confines of this chair.”

“Thank you, Prime Minister,” Colville said. “We’ll make due, sir.” He continued to the office door. “Once again,” Colville thought, “the man’s timing was impeccable.”

Chapter Sixty-Six

Margaret Calls Mrs. Somerville

Margaret didn't think losing an argument meant defeat. Losing didn't mean it was a bad idea; it just meant you lost the argument. With that in mind, as soon as she saw Thomas drive off, she went upstairs to ring Mrs. Somerville again. She stubbornly let it ring well beyond what was practical, indicating her concern. She decided to be driven into Amersham to check on Mrs. Somerville before taking the underground to join Thomas at the Ministry.

She rang the garage, where Brenan, the chauffeur, picked up the line.

"Brenan, I need to go into Amersham this morning. Don't bring the car around; I'll come to the garage."

"Lady Margaret, I can't do such a thing as her Ladyship has instructed me against doing precisely what you're asking. There was no mistaking her meaning and the consequences of letting you leave the grounds…" Brenan explained into the phone.

Margaret said, "Brenan, you dear man. I'll be down in a second."

Brenan's pensive look met Margaret as she approached the garage. He was placed in a sticky situation and wondered how he would handle two direct orders—the mother's order, carrying the weight of authority, and the daughter, who was an insurmountable force.

Margaret saved him the trouble. Tapping his shoulder with a smile, she walked right past him and got into the driver's side of the service staff's lorry, saying, "Brenan, where are the keys?"

"Lady Margaret, this is most disturbing, as I see no positive outcome for you or myself."

Margaret, showing impatience, said, "Brenan, if you don't say anything, who'll know? None of the house cars will be missing, and we go out via the service road."

The man was silent.

"I can't drive into Amersham and just leave the lorry, as I'm going into London proper and coming back with Thomas. You need to drop me off."

"There are still the issues of directives, ma'am."

Margaret moved into the passenger seat, looked at the chauffeur, and pointed at the seat beside her. "Quickly," she said, "I'll make do with Mother if there's a fuss."

Chapter Sixty-Seven

Amersham—Mrs. Somerville's Home

Less than a minute before Margaret's call, Mrs. Somerville had traveled well down the walkway of her home. She was off on a mission she hoped would ensure Margaret's safety. She crossed the street and headed in a most unusual direction. Back in her dining room, the phone rang, filling the empty space with the sounds of concern from its caller. Now, well across the street, Mrs. Somerville wouldn't know Margaret was calling and thus would miss the opportunity to explain her actions and to tell her friend to stay at her mother's. As a result, there would be no contact, and events would take their course.

The man who had called Mrs. Somerville to give her directions looked at his watch, knowing time was short. Passing through the shop door, he entered another world dominated by the aroma of baked goods. "It's very curious," he thought, "that just a whiff can send my mind back to the farm where my father planted the grain and my mother used it to make every baked good imaginable." His mother mastered getting all the children to eat the same thing daily by pretending it was something new. The pleasant memory of his boyhood returned over forty years later in England, of all places. "In some ways," he thought, "time doesn't exist, or how can I feel like I'm next to my mother, in her kitchen, putting my hands on the hot bread, and still be in London?"

"Can I help you?" Emma Saxby called from the back of the shop as she reached into an oven wearing an oven glove. "Bread rolls are coming out right now. The kids love them." Emma looked at the man with a jovial note and added, "Big kids too."

"Just the thing," the man said.

Mrs. Somerville, busily making her way to the bakery, was pleased to see only one person there, which would make things a bit easier. The man was sitting at a table outside, facing the other way, looking rather seedy and unkempt. Again, doubt drifted into the thoughts controlling her actions. Her pace slowed as she approached him, stopping behind, a few steps short. With her handbag held tightly just above her waist, she spoke the password: "Princess?"

The man threw his chin over his shoulder, and his body followed. A scowling, questioning look distorted his face. Standing up, he quickly downed the rest of his tea and, with hardly even an attempt at pleasantries, said, "Missing your wits, lady? Do I look like a bloody princess?" The jerking of his body followed a mumble as he promptly stomped away.

"Well, that went well," she thought. "Now, what do I do?"

Inside the shop, the man paid and took the bag sitting on the glass display case. As he rolled the top of the bag over, he could feel the warmth from within escape, holding it closer to his face to catch the aroma. At the same time, he saw movement outside the window. A woman approached a rough-looking man sitting outside at one of the tables. After a few words, the man got up and walked away. Still holding the bag up, he looked back at Emma and said, "Thank you. What a nice shop you have."

"Good day to you," Emma said, followed by a light-hearted, "Mind the bombs now."

The man politely acknowledged her comment as he looked at a picture he'd pulled from his coat pocket. With a moment's glance, he moved to the shop door.

Mrs. Somerville, still surprised at her encounter, saw another man appear. The man closed the shop door behind him and walked over, closing the distance in just a few strides.

The man, bag in hand, laughed and motioned to the figure walking away, saying, "Did 'princess' confuse him?" He offered her the seat the man vacated. "Please," he said, positioning the empty chair to facilitate conversation.

Mrs. Somerville looked at the chair next to the table but remained standing.

"As you wish," he said, nodding to the other chair. "May I?"

She nodded and watched him sit down and unwrap the top of the bag.

With his nose firmly planted as far down into the bag as possible, he took two deep breaths and said, "Do you bake?"

Mrs. Somerville, still standing, answered, "Why are you offering me a job?"

The man laughed as he took a roll from the bag and tore a piece from it. "No, I understand you've done quite well on your own. However, there are some things more important than money."

Mrs. Somerville watched as the man stuffed the piece into his mouth. Then, he reached up and handed her a note written in her handwriting.

"Mrs. Somerville, I'm Dacha," he said. "My real name is Yuri Stakova, and I'm the person who's very grateful that you are looking after Margaret Hatcher."

"I don't think so," Mrs. Somerville said. "I may be old, but I know enough to expect a British secret officer or something to sound like one. Your accent, it's Russian or something, not that your name wasn't my first clue."

"Who said I was a British officer?" Yuri said. "Besides, do all British officers have to sound like one?"

"No, but the man who interviewed me on the phone said he was from MI5. He told me that after any drop-off, I would get a phone call the next day to arrange a meeting. The person on the phone, who said he was Dacha, also sounded British," she said. "There's logic to this; I'm not just rambling on, you know."

"Something like this, perhaps? I want to thank you for the compliment," Yuri said in a British accent. With a charming look, he continued, "It's hard sometimes to get just the right rhythm, let alone the accent."

Mrs. Somerville stared down at him in shock and thought, "Good God, had she been working for the Russians all this time?"

Returning to his native accent, he continued, "It's tough to judge a foreign accent, listening through these ears," Yuri said, pointing to his head. "I know you have questions. It will all become clear, but at this moment, we must address important matters."

"You bet, like why would you, a Russian, be involved in protecting Margaret Hatcher, a British citizen? Besides that, why would I agree to assist a bloody foreign country, pardon my language? I don't even know if you're who you say you are."

"Mrs. Somerville, how many 'Dachas' do you have in your life that also know your contact identification, 'princess,' and happen to have a note, written by you, to me and whose instructions created this meeting."

Yuri's smile waited for a response.

Mrs. Somerville didn't say anything but sat down.

"I also handle her husband, Thomas Watson, another Englishman who happens to be a Russian spy. At least, I think so; today, I'm not so sure. He was supposed to be getting information from Margaret."

"What?" She leaned forward, putting one arm on the small table. "Let me get this straight. As a passionate British citizen, I'm watching over a child who couldn't possibly have a drop of information anyone could want. Moreover, *I'm doing it for the Russians*?"

Mrs. Somerville was beside herself. "But wait," she put her finger in the air like a schoolteacher, "as a ridiculous aside, you think her husband is one of *your* spies—but you're not sure? Hells bells, I'm confusing myself. You look bright enough to know that no sane person, and with you, I'm assuming a lot here, would be in such an upside-down position. So," she said, throwing her handbag onto her lap, "although there's little you could say that would convince me why you would do such a thing, and why would I continue to help you?"

"Why does anyone do anything? Usually, it's a devotion to your principles."

"That, my dear sir, is a dapper pile of horse crap. I'll give you one more chance."

Yuri leaned back and broke into a laugh. "Mrs. Somerville, there are no national boundaries when it comes to beliefs and principles that are branded into your life by the force of pain and agony."

Mrs. Somerville silently looked at the man, thinking of her and Charles. "Perhaps we have one thing in common," she said. "So what do you believe, Mr. Stakova? Whose side are you on? Because right now, I'm a traitor."

"With my belief in freedom, I think you should consider me on the British side," Yuri said. "In my country, they stole freedom from the hands of our children before they could feel the choices it provided. I've seen firsthand the horrors of those who wished to impose their will on others. No one can take back the terror already taking its toll there, but your country has this chance to stop the terror that lies before us. This man, Hitler, is no different from the tyrant that's killing my homeland, except Hitler is worse and German. If one is to be unjustly ruled, it's only slightly better from the hand of Stalin. The world must stop both Hitler and Stalin. I have no love, as you say, of England, but I know your government is against both monsters. That's why, as you say, I'm upside down."

He paused and looked at her.

"The man knew his heart," she thought. At the same time, Mrs. Somerville knew he hadn't answered her question about her being a Russian spy.

Yuri put the bag down. "Time is short, and we must come now to the urgent matter. You've done a great job, and your country is grateful, but there are never secrets forever, and this one is no different. You might be in danger and must leave to a safe place."

"In danger, from whom?" she said. "We've covered most nationalities, so, just for humor, why not throw in the useless Americans?"

"Danger is danger; it matters, not the source," Yuri said. "Is there someone watching the Watson's flat?"

"Yes," she said slowly. Poorly, I might add, if I can figure it out."

"All the more reason you can't return to your house until I've taken care of some tasks that will set things right."

Mrs. Somerville looked at the man before her. "Since we're into questions, I have one. How do I know you're not the danger? My interest is in Margaret's safety, and what keeps me from going directly to the British authorities?"

"My interest is in everyone's safety, and we must do it my way as time is short. You're free to go to MI5, but some in MI5 don't know we exist due to how this is structured. It's a time of war, and how will you explain agreeing to look after a fellow citizen for the Russians? Not just any citizen, mind you, but someone whose family manufactures military equipment for the government?"

"What?" Mrs. Somerville wasn't happy.

"It's the truth, I must say."

Anger was in her voice. "I don't believe it. But it doesn't matter. I didn't ask for this."

"Beth, can I call you Beth?"

She didn't respond.

"Beth, I didn't ask for this either." Yuri was searching inside his coat, feeling for the lining pocket. He handed her an address and two keys to the Leyton High Road apartment. "You must go there and stay until I can get there. Don't open the door to anyone except me unless there's a phone call or you hear the code name Princess. Yes? Do you feel comfortable doing this?" Yuri said.

"I don't know," she said.

Yuri thought momentarily and looked across the street to the pub where he and Thomas had talked.

"Mrs. Somerville, may I ask you a question?"

"I'm the one with questions."

"How is your relationship with Margaret and Thomas? Do you know them well?"

"Margaret is like my own daughter. You'll never find a purer heart. Thomas? Figuring that one out is a little more difficult."

"Please," Yuri said, "could it be he has put on another of his many coats?"

She smiled; it was the first real evidence this man had provided to prove that he was who he said he was. The curious question made her a lot more comfortable.

"Well, Mr. Dacha, it's apparent you're also confused about who the real Thomas Watson is. Margaret said it was amnesia, and there it must lie, as I don't have a better explanation. However, I can assure you that the heart of the Thomas, whom she originally married, doesn't beat inside the man she's with now. I'm not sure how this can be true, but it is," she said.

"I, too, am not sure, but I agree," he said. He'd picked up the bag again, and another piece of bread muffled the words. "That's why we must do something to save them both. However, you've done your part and must go to the rear door of this flat, not the front entrance. I don't think it's being watched, or I wouldn't send you there, but you can never be too careful. Inside, you'll find some of my things and some food. You must promise to go directly there, do you promise?"

"No," she said. "Not until I take a few passes at the stations, ensuring no one is following me. That would be obvious, even to the old lady next door. You're not very good at this spy stuff, are you?"

Yuri crumpled the now-empty bag in his hands as he smiled. "Do you know where Margaret and Thomas are?"

"No, they dropped me off the day of the shooting. I think they were going to go to her mother's."

"I saw you pick up Thomas at Bletchley. Were any of you injured during the shooting?" He studied her face and said, "No, Beth, I wasn't responsible for that, but I know who was, and *he* is the danger, and I must say, a danger to us all."

Yuri rolled the watch on his wrist and started to stand. "I'm late and must go."

She looked at him, "This is so strange and diffused."

Yuri looked at her quizzically.

"Unclear," she clarified.

"Oh." Yuri nodded and looked again at the same sky that had betrayed him a few days before. "It's the nature of the business."

"What business?" she said.

With a pleasant but serious expression, he looked down at her and said, "Freedom, Beth, freedom. Now, I can't protect you unless you promise me that you'll go to the flat after your precautions and stay there. To do the things I must do, I need to know where you are and that you're safe. If it makes you go, you may tell your close friends inside," he nodded to the bakery, "but no one else, is that clear?"

She looked into his eyes briefly and said, "Okay, but if you don't help Margaret, *I'll* be the danger. Is that clear?"

With that, he smiled, touched his hat, and headed toward the railway station.

Beth watched him walk away. After the phone call from Yuri, she knew the meeting would be at Emma's. After that, she wasn't sure what would happen. That's why she told Margaret in the note that Emma would know where she went. No one could know where Emma was located except Margaret, so that wouldn't endanger Emma and Stewart.

She re-read what she'd just finished writing and returned to the shop. "Emma, dear, if Margaret shows up here looking for me, can you give her this note? I think she might be in some danger."

Emma was concerned. "From that man outside? He's the same man who talked to them the other morning."

"Talked to Margaret and Thomas together?"

"Yes, just after you left," Emma said. "I went into the back, and when I came out, they were gone. Didn't think much of it. Did I miss the mark?"

Mrs. Somerville thought for a moment. This information didn't clarify anything and only made the issue harder to understand. He was supposed to be protecting Margaret. Why would he talk to both simultaneously if he directed Thomas to work with Margaret for information? She considered her options. Finally, something genuine in the manner of the Russian solidified her decision. She turned to Emma, "If Margaret shows up, can you ensure she gets to this address? She'll be safe there. It's where I'll be, but I would feel better if she had someone to accompany her."

Emma took the note. "I'll take care of it. You take care of yourself."

Her husband was listening and said to his wife, "Ya should arm her with a bag of y'ur hard rolls. Blame potent as a rock if…"

"Mr. Saxby, that'll be enough out of you."

Emma was concerned. "How long will you be there?"

"I don't know until things clear up, whenever that might be. I should tell you not to give that address to anyone else."

Emma had a worried look. "You let me know how you are, or I'll be in a fit of worry."

"No need to worry about me. You've got problems of your own," she said, looking at Stewart.

Emma looked at her husband, who was walking into the back, and said, "Beth, love is a mysterious force in this universe. I'm hoping someone figures it out someday."

Chapter Sixty Eight

Mrs. Somerville's House

Sitting in the back of the car, Margaret was waving a finger, "Brenan, pull over here and drop me off. I don't want to be too close."

The driver, who had eventually agreed to take her into town, did as instructed but wasn't happy. He'd had an excellent job for over ten years, and he knew it. Some didn't have a job, and he wasn't interested in giving someone a reason to sack him.

"Miss Margaret, if Lady Hatcher finds out I brought you into town, she'll have me 'ead."

Sitting beside him in the front seat, Margaret touched his shoulder. "Nobody is going to find out, I promise you. Just go back and don't say a word. Not even to Alistair."

"Too late, I'm afraid. I wasn't going to do this on me own, when everyone else was plain too afraid. Alistair was the one who said he 'ould have me back."

"It's okay; I'll handle Mother."

"Well, I jus' glad someone can." He realized his fear had let that slip. "I mean…"

"Brenan, I know exactly what you mean, and it's okay. She isn't that bad inside, but how would anybody know? Now go." Two blocks from her street, she got out and shut the door.

Margaret stood at the corner bus stop, looking down the alley bypass behind her row of houses. She paused, pretending to rummage through her handbag while stealing glances, looking for any clue that a guard was watching the house. She could safely take her time, as any man would see that the diversion into her handbag was the equivalent of a woman breathing.

Grigory Dorokhin was a rookie officer who reported to Yuri. However, Viktor flashed his credentials and ordered him to watch Watson's house and notify him if they returned. Surveillance duty was an officer's lowest endeavor, and his replacement was thirty minutes late. He stood hidden between two large shrubs across the street from the front of Watson's house. He had a full view of the front door. He figured the families on either side of him had left town as it was too quiet. It was his good fortune not to have to worry about them, and he could smoke without giving himself away. He finished the cigarette and dropped it atop an ever-growing mound of butts. "This assignment was stupid," he thought. There wasn't a chance in hell that anybody would return to a place that was surely being watched.

This Krivitsky, Viktor, or whoever was an arse who could see nothing but his resume always in his face. Who was he, anyway, flashing his credentials and giving orders? Where was Yuri? Thoughts of his boss's safety entered in a fleeting thought. It had been over forty-eight hours since anyone had heard from Yuri, and at the worst possible time. This Victor had mobilized everyone, and Yuri, the girl, and the guy were nowhere to be found.

Margaret started walking up the bypass slowly, feeling the fear grow in her arms and legs. She was going to do this. Without an answer from her friend, she had to ensure she was okay regardless of what could happen. After all, her relationship with Beth and Thomas had gotten Beth involved anyway. It was her fault, and she had to know.

The growth of hundred-year-old trees and shrubs along the back fences had grown tall. These houses were among the first in the township. Stopping behind Beth's house, she stepped into a row of tall bushes out of direct sight of anyone who would enter the bypass. It was almost certain they were watching her place next door and would spot her if she wasn't careful. That meant she had to get Beth's attention and get into her house and out of sight as quickly as possible.

Reaching up, she moved some branches and looked at the back of Beth's house for a few minutes. There weren't any movements or lights, but that didn't mean she wasn't inside. It wouldn't be as simple as seeing her in a window or entering the backyard to empty trash. How could she find out without standing in plain sight and knocking on the door? Margaret heard a man and a woman talking as they entered the alleyway. They entered the second house on the right through the rear gate. Having seen them before, Margaret felt relieved.

Dorokhin's anger grew, and he left before his replacement arrived. He looked at his watch, deciding to finish with a last every-thirty-minute walk around the block before leaving. He casually strode to the pavement from his hiding place and looked up and down as he crossed the road. He had his hands in his pockets, walking casually. There were a few people out, but not many. His instructions were clear: hold them if he could, but don't let them leave the house. If necessary, kill them both and do it professionally and quietly. He knew it was part of his job as an officer, but it rarely happened. He wondered if he could do it if the situation arose.

Margaret looked at the ground around her feet and saw some planting stones. If she could make some noise at the back of the house, it would rouse whoever was inside, friend or foe, while she remained hidden. Margaret reached down and picked up a small rock, heavier than she would have liked. It had taken years, but she'd conquered the stigma of throwing like a girl, and it had come in handy during her childhood, winning the challenges placed before her by stupid boys at garden parties. She even defended herself from a fox in the woods who had decided she was nothing to fear. She got the animal in the flanks, then quickly climbed a tree when the mother fox appeared.

Knowing the object was heavy, Margaret drew back and gave it an extra bit of effort. Her target was the bottom of Beth's back door, a good fifty feet away.

Unfortunately, the extra velocity kept it high, and it sailed right through the fixed pane of glass in the door, taking the side curtain with it. "God," she thought as she ducked out of sight. That's precisely what she didn't want to have happen. Someone could have heard that from St. Paul's, let alone scare the hell out of her friend.

Angry but out of sight, she waited. Nothing happened for several long minutes. If she's not there, where could she possibly be? Perhaps her sister's, but she should have thought of that back home when she had the number. She had to get inside to find out.

She moved to the gate, pulled at the latch, and rushed to the back porch. Using the neighbor key Beth gave her, she opened the door. Stepping on the broken glass, she cautiously entered the house, pausing to listen for any noises and then closing the door behind her. Moving slowly and quietly, Margaret entered the kitchen and headed for the dining room. Thinking of calling out, she spotted a note on the dining room table. She listened for anything before going into the room. After a moment, she looked around the corner, and the house appeared empty. Checking the bedrooms, she returned to the note and unfolded it.

At the top was the name Kitten. Once, her dear friend had used that name when they were joking around, and the name stuck. She said Margaret was a playful little kitten with claws that needed respect.

Kitten,
I had to leave and am not sure when I'll be back.
I wanted you to know. Charles will tell you where I went.
Beth

Charles? Margaret thought a moment. She looked at the photograph of the handsome man in uniform neatly framed and hanging on the wall. Then remembered the conversation they'd been having when Beth opened the drawer, and Margaret noticed the ornate picture album.

Beth had said, "My Charles is exactly where he should be, in heaven waiting for me and in my picture book, always in the top drawer of my sideboard."

Dorokhin rounded the corner, turning into the dirt alleyway. As usual, he passed several houses before arriving at Watson's home. Giving a general look around, he entered through the now-familiar back gate of the Watson's property. Once on the porch, he checked that the back door remained locked. He stood on the porch for a minute, looking across the street to more gates and backyards. "What a lost part of the world," he thought. "Why would the Germans bomb it, needlessly angering the British and causing certain retaliation? The British papers used it as a rallying point. If the Germans were so precise, then they were precisely stupid."

Proceeding toward the gate, he looked at how each owner had changed the look of the originally identical houses. In the process, something caught his eye when looking at the house next to Watson's. The house's back door was ajar, with a hole in one of its glass windows. His training had taught him that anything appearing unusual usually was. His job was to be aware of anything, assuming any part could influence his present assignment. He decided to check it out.

Margaret pulled back on the knobs of the sideboard drawer and saw a velvet-covered photo album neatly tucked into the front right-hand corner. "That was easy," she thought. Picking it up, she was surprised at its weight. She placed it on the table and opened the hardbound cover to discover another note. Anxiously, she grabbed and unfolded it.

Kitten dear,

If you read this, please be very careful. It's not just Thomas in danger; some wish you both harm. I've done what I can to protect you and desperately want to explain how I know. Go to Emma's, where I'll leave a message telling you my location so you won't worry. Please go back to your mother's; it's the safest place.

Your friend,
Beth

As officer Dorokhin approached the rear wooden door, he stepped on a piece of glass that had landed outside on the porch. He looked into the kitchen through the window, and nothing looked disturbed. He couldn't see anyone or anything indicating recent activity, like food on the table. "It's just a simple burglary," he thought, and he was off duty and hungry. He pulled the door shut and started to leave. His shoulders dropped as he acknowledged the standards his boss and friend Yuri demanded. He returned to the door.

Chapter Sixty Nine

Yuri's First Phone Call

Riding into London, Yuri thought it was fortunate he had checked the drop-off. Viktor created a narrow miss, taking Pavel out of the picture. Yuri had a series of things to do before he could disappear. Time was short. He knew Viktor's men were hunting for Margaret and Thomas. In addition, Yuri was the only one who could reveal Viktor's stupidity at Bletchley, thus making himself an essential target for Viktor. The directive from Moscow he'd found in Viktor's room gave the man all the cover he needed to pull the trigger.

Yuri entered the phone box and slowly picked up the receiver. He knew the heavy Bakelite object wasn't all it appeared. It would carry the weight of a necessary disclosure, the key to opening the next door in his life. Yuri's size always made him uncomfortable in call boxes. He turned and looked out the small panes for anything out of place. There was a smartly dressed man across the street. He'd been standing there for several minutes. Yuri started to put the receiver back as a cab approached, taking the man away. He looked the other way to see if a backup existed, but the street was quiet. "Am I being too careful?" Yuri wondered.

"Never," he said aloud as he heard the familiar dings of the change falling. That's the reason he'd made it out of Italy alive. Through the handset, he heard a young woman saying, "Number, please."

"Wytell 2975," he said.

"Good day," she said, but Yuri didn't hear the usual connection being made.

Confused, she returned to the line, saying, "I'm sorry, sir, I don't have that available on my switchboard. Please hold while I get my supervisor."

Upon hearing the number, her supervisor said, "Stella, patch it to my office, please." The supervisor turned the key at the end of a chain, opening the safe. The phone rang through to the small connection board in his office. He answered and said, "Could I verify that number, please?"

Yuri gave it to him again.

The man flipped through a small book. Locating the number, he discovered it was a military switchboard and restricted. He flipped again to the section where each phone number in the Wytell code had a password next to it.

"Sir, I'll need a password to complete the call."

Yuri said, "Ghost town."

The supervisor's attention became more focused. He never thought he would ever deal with this type of situation, and he was happy he'd paid attention in training more than a year ago.

"Thank you," he said, reaching up and inserting the proper cords into the super's board. He listened for a single ring, assuring the connection before an automatic cut-off. The call traveled outside any regular public system, as it was a direct connection and end-lined at a single device.

A large red phone rang twice in a virtually secret, heavily guarded room. The room was the field communications office of an unknown section within the British Intelligence Service. It was located deep inside Blenheim Palace, Oxfordshire. The palace, named after the Battle of Blenheim in 1704, was a key victory for the English over the French. In an act befitting the nation's gratitude, Queen Anne had ordered its construction for the esteemed leader of the victorious English Army. With the gardens still under construction, John Churchill, 1st Duke of Marlborough, moved in, and it was to be the family estate of the Churchills for the next 300 years. It had been the birthplace, but never the residence, of Winston Churchill, who decided, after a bombing and fire, to allow MI5 to occupy the estate.

Officer Erin Kirkway, the field watch commander, waited for the second ring before he answered, "Watch Desk."

Yuri hesitated a brief second before speaking.

"Hello?" the officer said.

"I need to speak to a nine-nine-two contact," Yuri responded.

"Are you in immediate danger?" Kirkway asked.

"No"

"Can you hold for two minutes?" he said. As per regulations, he wrote down the number.

"Yes," Yuri said.

Kirkway looked at the number he'd written down, making sure it was the number he'd heard. His job was to be the field officers' singular contact and write detailed reports. He conveyed operational issues to the bigwigs, literally upstairs if matters dictated. In his three years of service, the last two as watch commander, he'd never made contact with someone in the 900 series.

Officer Flaherty stood, feeling the key hanging from his neck swing back to his chest. He locked the office door from the inside and then hurriedly passed a row of padlocked cabinets. He stopped at the imposing concrete safe with twenty-inch-thick steel and concrete walls known as Blenheim's Box. Running his thumb across the top of the safe's dial, he removed a thin film of dust. He thought momentarily; he hadn't opened the safe in a while. Was the last number twenty-eight or thirty-eight? He cursed, as they wouldn't let him write it down. He spun the safe's dial back and forth, entering the combination, and the handle wouldn't move. He tried again, using thirty-eight. Holding his breath, he pushed down, hearing a loud clang as the resistance gave way.

At the same time, the red light above the door went out, and the green one next to it lit up, indicating the disarming of the explosives meant to destroy the documents inside. Erin shook his head. A bloody light and a piece of wire were the only things between him and permanent retirement.

He continued pushing the handle down until it stopped and pulled back on the thick door. Before him was a series of internal drawers, each two inches high, running the twenty-four-inch width of the box's interior. He grabbed the thumb handle on the one labeled "Nine-Ninety" and, as it opened, looked at three red folders. He grabbed nine-nine-two, pushing the drawer closed with his other hand. On the front of the folder was a large label declaring the contents MI5 C Top Secret – Private and Confidential, followed by some small print threatening to quickly rearrange anyone's normal life if they didn't follow the rules. "As if the explosives weren't enough," he thought. MI5 was Military Intelligence Section 5A, in charge of domestic security, also known as just plain Five. Department B handled the section's field officers—C didn't exist.

He opened the folder and stared at the first page containing the contact information, instructions, and a brief assignment description. In a subconscious act, his eyes grew wide, and his forehead creased to his hairline. The contact list usually contained the officer's handler and a secondary emergency contact. His job was to make a quick connection between the contact and the field officer. Upon reading the file, Erin was astonished; the only authorized contacts were the director general of security and the prime minister. Usually, the men he handled in the field were double-agents, working for an obscure entity called the XX (Double Cross) Committee. They were typically German foreign officers caught spying and, under threat of death, convinced to work as double-agents for the British. To no one's surprise, they usually cooperated, feeding false information back to their counterparts in Germany. However, this call was from a foreign officer who turned to spy on his own government and was in charge of recruiting British nationals for that job. Having thought he'd seen every form of deception, even he had to think twice: "Do all nine ninety's play those twisted games?" He wasn't sure.

Officer Kirkway moved quickly back to his desk and picked up the phone. "Code name?" he asked.

"Treasure," was the reply.

Kirkway said, "Code confirmed. You wish to report?"

"No," Yuri replied, "I need to talk to someone in the file." Yuri wondered if the system was going to work. It had been years since he'd made direct contact, and all communication went through dead drops in the field.

"May I have your general location?"

"London proper," Yuri said.

Kirkway looked at his list of public phones in and around London and said, "Kentish Town Station at the corner of Caversham Road and Hammond Street in two hours. Can you make it?"

"Yes," Yuri said and hung up the phone.

Erin Kirkway was very grateful that upon hearing the nine ninety number, he instinctively gave himself two hours, the longest amount of time regulations allowed to leave a field officer waiting. He needed the time, as the contact list did not contain handlers, but the names on the list were some of the highest and busiest people in government. They weren't easy people to contact quickly, if at all. Also, the file predated the XX Committee, so Kirkway wondered if he should contact its chairman, Oxford don, Sir John Masterman. He concluded he should start with Sir David Petrie, the PM's Director General of MI5, unofficially inform Masterman and then place an optimistic call to the prime minister. He would then cross his fingers.

Chapter Seventy

Thomas at Whitehall

Thomas put his hand on the sandbags stacked higher than his head. It was strangely familiar, matching a scene in his mind, except the picture was black and white. As he drove through the city, he only took a few wrong turns, surprising himself by finding it quickly. After all, Whitehall hadn't changed location, and… what a strange feeling. Where does all that come from? Why would he know how to get to Whitehall? The source felt closer, for lack of a better way to put it, but not close enough. The sandbag was cold. Before him was a stairwell from which he might not emerge. Once he divulged his information, they may find him just as much of a risk as they did his Mr. Dunning. Nevertheless, he had no choice.

He'd descended the steps and come to the guard when it hit him. He didn't have any identification. What could he have been thinking? Dumbfounded, he stood before the guard as the man waited for Thomas to say something.

"My name is Thomas Watson, and I have an appointment with the prime minister scheduled through Mr. Colville."

"Yes, sir, your identification, sir," the guard said as he picked up the list of the day's authorized entries. "Well, let's see, Thomas Watson, you say?"

The guard ran his finger down the page and said, "Yes, Mr. Watson 'ere it is." The guard then looked up, waiting for the ID, and said, "Nice bit of a day today, in' it? With it, I'm stuck between these walls with a draft up me shorts."

Thomas had defensively put his hand inside his coat as if reaching for something when he finally dropped the arm to his side and said, "Well, Officer, I'm afraid I don't have any ID."

"Well, now, Mr. Watson, surely you mus' know it's a crime no' to carry any form of identification and during war, quite dangerous to no' be able to identify oneself to authorities."

"I know, but if you could just call Mr. Colville, he can verify my appointment."

"That's all well and good, Mr. Watson, but how do I know you're the actual person 'ere for the appointment? You're not coming in to flirt with the ladies now, are yah? No, you're coming in tah see the prime minister whose safety and security the lot of us take somewhat seriously."

Thomas was stumped. Given the magnitude of his mission, it was unbelievable that the everyday rules of life and war were restricting his presenting the information.

"Mr. Watson?" the guard said a little loudly.

Pulling out of thought, Thomas said, "I'm sure Mr. Colville can straighten this all out."

"Will Mr. Colville be able tah identify yah on sight?"

"No," Thomas said as he crossed his arms in frustration, "as we've never met, but I could describe him to you." Thomas knew exactly what Colville looked like. He was so close.

The guard's shoulders visibly dropped, and the situation grew less defensible by the minute. He leaned downward for something under the desk and continued, "Mr. Watson, as we are not just on a need and authority basis, we also require every person to be visually familiar with the entry guard or someone else inside. If no, you're heavily searched and must be accompanied by an armed guard."

"I fully understand. I know this is very unusual and you must do your job, so do whatever you must. It's the meeting that's important."

"Of course it is, Mr. Watson, that's the whole of it, is it not? No one asks to see the prime minister and enters through here now. They always go through Ten Downing and the connecting shaft. Therefore, you see that you're in a very unusual position from the top. Given the rest of your story, I would say yah are no' very bright or just plain daft."

Behind him, Thomas could hear someone coming down the steps. He turned to see two more guards and started feeling a little desperate. The guard must have pushed a button or something that Thomas did not see.

"Could you please call Mr. Colville and find out what *he* wants to do?" Thomas now knew he should have brought Margaret as Churchill could at least identify her, but it looked like it wouldn't get to that point.

The guard looked up to the men behind him and pointed toward Thomas. There was a loud snap of a holster as one of the new guards took three steps back, and the other new guard said, "Stand still, sir, like a good gentleman."

The new guard started patting him down, checking all his pockets but found nothing.

Thomas had never felt so stupid in his whole life. Why hadn't he thought this through? He was angry with himself for being so shallow and stupid. Daft, if you like. He could've gotten a letter or something from Margaret's mother. Why did he think he could just walk in, even with the phone call to Churchill?

This time, the footsteps came from below, and a captain appeared. Thomas's hopes dimmed as he ran out of options. The last thing he needed was to sit in a cell for a day, missing the time he needed to get to the prime minister. Today was the day all hell would break loose, and tomorrow was too late.

The original guard had backed away from the guard desk and began explaining the situation to his superior. At the end of his explanation, they both turned and looked at Thomas.

The original guard stood beside the captain during the moment of silence. Thomas sensed this was his last chance. He started thinking through his situation. Someone was trying to kill him, and that put Margaret in danger. He was accused of being a spy in a baffling conversation with a Russian, who might be the person out to get him. He had no facts to support anything in his story, and all he was trying to do was save the country. At that point, his hopelessness turned into anger.

"Captain?" Thomas said forcefully, and the man looked up. Taking a deep breath, Thomas said, "You need to pay attention as you will have to make a decision that might just affect your career. There's no way, at this moment, I can prove who I am. However, I've some time-sensitive information upon which the nation's security depends, and those facts will come out eventually. When it's discovered you didn't follow up fully to the extent within the framework of your responsibilities, your arse will swing from the highest point within sight. I suggest you do what you have to do, but do it. Mr. Colville would be a good place to start."

Slowly, the guard crossed the few steps between Thomas and the captain, making eye contact with the other station guard.

The captain remained calm under the verbal assault and started to say, "You can fully under…"

Close to shouting, Thomas said, "Captain, given my understandably weak position, I've nothing to lose here. Arrest me and pay the price, or get Mr. Colville."

Thomas now had a guard firmly attached to each arm and could feel their strength as his weight shifted from the soles of his shoes. It was all too symbolic of the diminishing hope he felt.

The captain looked at Thomas in a considered manner that had to be admired. His hands moved to the front of his belt as his mind weighed the situation.

Calmly, he said, "Handcuff him."

Colville put the phone down, shaking his head as he realized the day was falling apart. Why did everyone think one could call and see the most important man in the world as if ringing up for tea? He dedicated himself to maximizing every minute of the PM's time, thus, in his way, shortening the war and saving lives. "It was just astounding," he thought. "The nerve!"

The captain stopped in front of Colville's desk and saluted. "Yes, captain, what could it be now?" Colville said.

"Sir, I have a situation at the George Street entrance. A Mr. Thomas Watson insists he has a meeting with the prime minister and is without any identification. Sir, on the verge of normal stability, he insists I contact you to verify his story. Given his desperate situation, I hesitate to bother you, but it's a gut feeling, sir. I have him bound and detained at the desk. Should I just arrest him, sir?"

"Watson?" Colville said, "At ease, Captain." Colville shuffled the papers on his clipboard.

The captain placed his arms behind his back. "Yes, sir, he says it's essential, urgent in fact. If I may, sir, there's just enough wrong with this that something might be right. Sorry, sir, but can you identify him?

"Yes, he's on my list, but I can't identify him, nor can I assure you that the PM can. I'll need to make a call. Bring him down, but keep him bound."

From his seat, Thomas looked around where the guard had placed him. The noise level in the room was high, with banging typewriters, people talking, and phones ringing. Thomas saw the name Colville on the desk from across the room. Since being escorted onto the floor, the man hadn't looked at him during the flurry of activity Thomas witnessed. After two phone calls, Colville had signed a communications folder and stood with his finger pointing somewhere while vigorously talking to a uniformed office worker.

The captain stood beside Colville's desk, his feet apart and arms relaxed behind his back. Behind him across the room, two guards stood at strict attention like bookends on either side of the very suspicious Mr. Watson.

Thomas shifted his weight forward, away from the back of the chair, easing the pain in his wrists. At the same time, he felt a relaxed hand placed on his shoulder. He looked up, and the guard gave him the 'stay seated' look, like one given a child whose time in the corner had yet to expire.

One of the telephones rang, filling the room. It must have been Coville's as he picked up the phone and, smiling into the receiver, looked at Thomas. Shaking his head, he spoke, and after a bit, Colville put the phone against his chest and said something to the captain, who motioned to bring Thomas across the room to Colville's desk.

Colville said. "What's Lady Hatcher's daughter's middle name?"

Thomas didn't know. He honestly didn't know. Thinking quickly, he said, "Her first name is Margaret, and you can confirm Lady Hatcher's habit of ordering a gin and orange every time I'm a guest at her house." Thomas hoped Margaret's mother could confirm the unusual statement.

Dumbfounded, Colville looked at him. An unmistakable look of disgust quickly replaced his confusion. "I don't have time for this." Through a tight jaw and clipped noises, he said, "Need I point out … that wasn't the *question*? Nor point out the question *wasn't that difficult?*"

"I'm sorry, Mr. Colville, it's the only answer I can give you," Thomas said.

Still holding the phone to his chest, Colville looked to the side, trying to contain his anger. He pointed back to the chair, and Thomas and the guards returned to his seat. Colville returned to the phone and quickly performed a 'what's the use' gesture with his arm. After a polite, smiling salutation, he gently placed the phone on the hook as if the phone were a bomb that might explode. He'd just experienced all he wanted of Margaret's mother for the day.

Colville said something to the captain, accompanied by a stern gesture in Thomas's direction. The captain came over to Thomas and said, "Un-cuff him." Looking at Thomas, he said, "Please stay seated, Mr. Watson, and I would mind your manners as you wait." He looked over his shoulder at Colville. "While I'm glad I made the right decision, and I'm relieved my arse will remain on the ground, you, on the other hand, are standing on thin ice."

He looked up and said to his guards, "Back to your posts, men."

Thomas's hands were around a warm cup of tea offered to him by a woman who looked like she was in charge of the office area. She must have spoken to Colville earlier about getting him some tea while he waited. She was utterly indifferent to Colville's brusk manner.

Upon receiving the cup, he looked up and said, "Thank you, Mrs. Nel."

Surprisedly, she said, "You're welcome, Mr…." and waited.

"Thomas Watson," he said, standing.

"Mr. Watson," she said slowly. "Have we met? I'm sorry."

"No, we haven't, but I think I saw your picture once." He remembered seeing a much older, wonderfully soft woman and remembered the name, but again where escaped him.

"Well, you certainly have a fine memory," she said before walking away.

The image in his mind was surprisingly clear. Things were getting clearer overall, except there was no explanation of why the information was there in the first place.

Chapter Seventy-One

Margaret Checks on Mrs. Somerville

Margaret heard glass break toward the rear and pictured someone at the back door. A wave of fear flew through her body and mind. She froze. Her friend always entered the house from the front, which meant it had to be someone else. The note was specific about her being in danger. Out of caution, Margaret knew she should either get out or hide. The front door wasn't an option, as she would be in full view of anyone watching her house next door. Thoughts connected to memories, and she moved to the other side of the room. Dropping to her knees, she opened the louvered doors to the storage space under the stairs. She awkwardly worked herself into the small space and closed the doors behind her, grabbing the fixed slats from the inside.

Dorokhin checked around outside to see if anyone could see him. Satisfied, he slowly pushed the door open and called out in Russian, "Is anybody here?" He moved through the kitchen and, this time in English, called out, "Hello?" He entered the dining room of what appeared to be the house of a grandmother who loved to knit and used a bit too much perfume. Then, to his left, he saw an open drawer and an open photo album on the table.

Trying to hide, Margaret held her shoulder against the wall while bending her legs back in the tight space. Then terror gripped her heart; she'd left both notes on the table, in plain view—unbelievable.

Dorokhin saw the notes on the table, but his English wasn't good enough for him to understand the message. He decided the back door just meant someone had broken into the house. Thinking he heard a sound in the back rooms, he reached for his firearm in the holster under his arm. He slowly moved to the bedroom area and checked out the rest of the house, finding nothing. Coming back out, Dorokhin walked by Margaret twice. She stayed silent despite the cramp beginning in her right leg. She grabbed her calf and bit her lip as the pain and fear brought tears to her eyes.

Holstering the gun, Dorokhin walked over, unlocked the front door from the inside, and swung it open. His replacement, stationed behind the bush, was surprised as they locked eyes. The officer closed the door behind him and headed toward his replacement.

"Why were you late?" Dorokhin demanded.

"I'm not late," protested the new man. "Besides, you were missing when I arrived. What were you doing coming out of the house next door?"

"Someone broke into the back of the house, and I wanted to make sure it wasn't the Watsons trying to hide. You can tell that Viktor guy it was boring."

"You tell him. I'm not even talking to that guy unless I have to."

Inside, Margaret heard the door close and assumed they were both outside since she could barely hear the exchange between the two men. Quietly, she pushed open the door to her little space and straightened out her leg, trying to alleviate the pain. Standing up, she rocked back and forth on the leg while berating herself for being so careless. The officer had undoubtedly seen Thomas's name, and it would be evident that Beth was somehow involved. That's precisely what she didn't want. She didn't think he could link the names to the bakery, so Beth wasn't in immediate danger.

Margaret tried to get to a simple train of thought. Why did Beth know they were in danger, and why on earth was she involved? Margaret thought about dropping her off last night. They shouldn't have left her alone, but she'd learned it was hard to change Beth's mind once she had it set. Margaret had come to see if she was safe, and she wasn't. Margaret knew her next step was to go to the bakery. She cautiously looked out the sheer curtains as the two men argued in the street. The original officer occasionally vigorously waved an arm at one of the houses in his conversation. If she were to leave undetected, it would be while the officers were together.

Margaret thought about grabbing the notes that caused her so much anxiety. They were lying there just below her outstretched hand. However, if she took them and the man returned, he would know someone had been inside. She cursed and made for the backdoor of the house. Slowly, she opened the door and went out, through the back fence, and into the alley. Which way to go was answered when she saw a cab drop off Mr. Bartlett at his rear gate. It was almost directly behind Mrs. Somerville's. As she approached the cab, Mr. Bartlett tipped his hat and said, "Mrs. Watson, good day, and aren't you just the thing to brighten up an already sunny morning."

"Hello, Mr. Bartlett," she said. "Thank you, but I'm in a bit of a fix."

"Well, you came to the right place. What can we do for you?"

She asked the cab driver, "Can you take me to Saxby's Bakery? I know it's not far and not much of a fair, but I'll pay you extra."

Mr. Bartlett answered for his longtime friend in the cab. "Of course, he would for the likes of you, Mrs. Watson, wouldn't you, Emery?"

Emery said, "I can speak for myself, judge; I don't need you to be mindin' my business." Emery looked out of the driver's window and, with the warmest of faces, said, "I would be delighted to take you anywhere you wish."

Emery then addressed his friend with a long, drawn-out "Well?" The judge was still enjoying the reason for his brightened morning. "*Judge*," the cab driver said like a schoolmaster, "even a schoolboy would know to get the door."

Judge Bartlett opened the door and said, "Now, Emery, you behave yourself." They both knew that Margaret's feminine attributes were the subject of many of their frequent discussions in Judge Bartlett's back garden.

With that in mind, the judge added, "You know what I mean? Dust off the gentleman in you and treat her like a lady."

"She *is* a lady, and I don't need you to be tellin' me; I can see for myself."

The former judge, Vernon Bartlett, peered into the back seat and said, "You let me know if this rake is anything less than perfect." He laughed.

"Gentleman, I'm in kind of in a hurry. Can we go?" Margaret said.

"See, Emery, she's giving you the benefit of the doubt."

Emery put it in gear and said out the window, "You would be good to lose my phone number, you old dodger."

"I can't; been in my memory for fifteen years," the judge shouted over the sound of the engine taking off.

"Emery, is it?" Margaret said.

"Yes, ma'am."

Realizing he would take the shortest route, which would take them back in front of her house, Margaret said, "Can you take me to the bakery by going up Chesham Road and around? I don't want to be seen by someone."

"Well, that's sad for most of the world, now, isn't it?"

"Emery, this is very important."

"Yes, have you there in a jiffy."

Emery approached the intersection and turned away from the direct route to the bakery. As they drove away, Margaret looked back and saw the new officer running around the corner at the other end of the alley.

Presumably, the other man was going in the front. Margaret slid down in the seat, thankful she'd considered the consequences of taking the notes.

She approached the bakery and asked the cabbie to drive past it and drop her off. She reached into the handbag slung over her shoulder and extended payment to the cab driver.

"No, Miss, no fare today. But on your next walk around the neighborhood, can I ask you to tell that friend of mine how I was the perfect example of a lady's gentleman?"

Seeing that it was faster than getting him to accept pay, she said, "Yes, of course, I will." He began to open his door. "No, Emery, don't get out; I'm fine." Margaret got out and closed the door behind her.

She walked down the pavement and cautiously looked into the shop window. Inside, there were two of the many children who stopped by every day.

Emma noticed Margaret outside. Having taken care of the young boys, she said, "Out with ya now, both of ya, till tomorrow."

Margaret entered as the boys left. Emma pointed to the rear of the shop with a towel in her hand. Passing Margaret, Emma reached out and turned the Open sign on the front door.

She could hear Stewart and another man talking as she walked behind the counter and through the door into the working part of the business. Emma was right behind.

"Is Beth okay?" Margaret asked.

"Yes, dear, she's fine; she was by earlier."

"Yes, I know; she left me a note saying to come here."

Emma said in a different and more serious tone, "After a conversation with a stranger right outside, she came in and said you might come by. It was quite a serious conversation, but I didn't pay any mind to it except that I didn't know him, which was strange." Emma reached into her apron pocket and continued, "After he left, she came inside and asked me to give you a message, along with this key and address."

Margaret looked at the address. "I don't know where this is."

"Beth said things had changed, and both of you were in danger. If you showed up, I was to tell you to go to the rear of this flat, not the front, and you could find her there."

"Did she say anything about Thomas?"

"No, it was quick, but she made me promise I would get you there. She was concerned, anxious even. Very unlike the woman I've known for years. So, I called Bernie, the warden, and he said he would go with you to make sure you get there safely."

Bernie, who had been sitting at a table speaking with Mr. Saxby, stood up. "Yes, indeed, I'm not sure what's goin' on, but I want ta help."

Margaret smiled, acknowledging his concern and offer. "Bernie, everyone can always depend on you. You're such a dear."

Emma looked at her husband and said, "Can't you see Margaret needs something to drink? Where are your manners?"

Stewart looked up in surprise, saying, "Course, Mum, I was jus' goin'," and bolted for the icebox a few steps away. Stewart soon handed Margaret a cold glass, and she suddenly realized what Emma had already determined. The last few hours were tense for Margaret. She took a long drink of the cold, sweet tea and exhaled. She raised the glass and said, "Stewart, that's wonderful."

She paused in thought. Until the Russian read the note on the table, Margaret was sure Beth was safe and not connected to her and Thomas's troubles. However, Emma said she talked to her much earlier after meeting the stranger. After that encounter, Beth somehow concluded she needed to go somewhere safe and that Margaret should follow. Why? The answer lies with who the person was.

"Emma?"

"Yes, dear."

"You said you didn't know the man. Can you describe him?"

"Yes, he was big, but he had a gentle manner. He had a full face, slightly round, thick features, and was well-dressed. Not the likes of those around here." She glanced back at her husband and Bernie, who was still waiting to help. They exchanged confused glances as Bernie pulled his belt up, to no result, as it retreated to its previous angle.

"Did he sound Russian?"

"He came in and left with but a few words. But, no, he had no accent that I could hear."

Margaret was very concerned and had to understand why her friend thought she needed to go to a safe place provided by a stranger. The physical description fits Yuri's person, but he definitely had an accent. She didn't know about the one Thomas called Viktor. They'd dropped off Beth two nights ago at the taxi stand, and Margaret knew she'd gone home because she'd written and left the notes. Then why didn't she answer any of Margaret's calls? Beth's involvement was a serious concern and changed everything, and she had to let Thomas know.

Margaret had made her decision and stepped toward the man in uniform. "Thank you, Bernie, for being here, but now that I know Beth is safe, there's something I must do, and I'll be okay."

On her toes, she placed a kiss on the man's cheek. Again, Bernie self-consciously yanked at the front of his trousers, trying to bring them up over his full waist.

"Thank you all," Margaret said, moving toward the front of the shop. "You've been wonderful, and I'll be back to fill in the mysterious details."

Chapter Seventy-Two

Whitehall—Thomas Meets Churchill

Thomas had been waiting for over an hour, with Colville routinely coming and going out of the prime minister's office. With the latest emergence, he walked over, saying, "Mr. Watson, the prime minister, will see you now."

As he raised his arm, whose first duty was directional management, he pulled his sleeve back from his watch. "You've exactly fifteen minutes. I'll show you in."

Colville's hand was on the door as it swung open. Thomas stepped in, and before him sat perhaps the most outstanding natural leader the world had seen—or possibly will ever see.

Sometimes, the simplicity of appearances hides the actual impact contained therein. That was the case with the office of the prime minister of England, on whose desk lay, undetectable to the naked eye, perhaps the most challenging task anywhere on the planet. He shouldered the responsibility from an office in keeping with the dowdy décor of the transatlantic telephone room. The low bookcase to his left contained various personal memorabilia items. Layers of maps covered the yellowed wall behind him, and on an ordinary desk were the typical articles of a manager: a two-piece pen set with an open bottle of ink, a blotter, and stacks of files. The only exceptions were a communications box with lighted buttons, red and black telephones, and an ornate wooden box, presumably for cigars.

With a gruff voice, Churchill put down the phone and said to no one directly, "Sometimes, in the course of difficult times, no news is good news."

"Fifteen minutes, Mr. Churchill," Colville said, staring at Thomas. He exited the room.

Thomas glanced back at the door, saying, "He's very dedicated. My name is Thomas Watson." He extended his hand.

The prime minister remained seated. "Sometimes dedication is just not enough. Fortunately, in Mr. Colville's case, it's mixed with a great deal of natural ability. The effort before us needs more people like him." He motioned to a chair.

Thomas withdrew his hand and sat in one of the three chairs before the desk. Details started to drop into place, but they always seemed to be within the structure of the current conversation.

Thomas offered, "Sir, I can assure you that Mr. Colville's place in history is secure."

"Are you a historian or a fortune teller, Mr. Watson?"

"To be truthful, it might be a bit of both, but it's not a good way to start."

"Agreed. It's an area I'll choose to avoid. So, Mr. Watson, how is Margaret?" the man said.

"She's very, very Margaret," Thomas said with a half laugh, hoping to ease into what could be a fateful few minutes.

The man smiled. "Amazing lady that one, hard not to give her a whole battalion of Royal Fusiliers, point her toward Germany and, with a lightened heart, take a holiday. I could especially use her today."

Thomas took the opening, choosing his words carefully. "It will get worse before it gets better."

"That's not an exceptionally bold bet, Mr. Watson," Churchill said. "I find it hard to think you're very good at cards. Time is limited before Mr. Colville fidgets in here, changing the subject and the present company."

Churchill leaned back in his chair before continuing. "Despite your somewhat inept charge at the castle gates, you've managed to see, with a strategic assist, the nobleman that resides within. That assist is a dear relationship with Lady Hatcher through her husband. She's a wonderfully complicated woman who has, over the years, failed miserably at the part of a shy flower but has excelled at being the beautiful rose, which can only be handled by its uninviting stem."

Looking to his left, Churchill rotated his chair and said, "Mr. Watson, it's not often, in fact, never, that I receive a call such as the one I participated in last night. No, I should say I was subjected to last night. So, young man, how do you propose to save England?"

Thomas began, "Prime Minister, this will be unlike any meeting you've ever had."

"Indeed, it already is," Churchill replied.

"First, I must ask for your patience as I try to establish some form of credibility, as, without that, we won't get anywhere. What I have to say involves information I'm not supposed to know and will first appear to imply I'm a spy, which I can assure you I'm not."

"That's comforting. Very comforting," Churchill said, almost absent-mindedly.

Thomas drew a deep breath and said, "I know that at this time, Fighter Command is dangerously short of fighter planes. They're shorter yet of pilots and fields for takeoffs and landings."

"Well, you're a spy that reads the newspapers, I see, how clever."

Thomas ignored the comment. "Later today, you'll go to the Uxbridge facility to catch some of the action, as you like to say."

At first, half-listening or not listening, Churchill looked down, appearing to read a paper atop his desk as the sentence registered. At the mention of Uxbridge, the prime minister's head and eyebrows went up.

"Not many in the Kingdom save Mr. Colville, and my wife knows my schedule. You've moved out of the realm of just well-read to actual spy. I hope you have an explanation." Churchill pulled a cigar with a damp end from his outside breast pocket and rolled it in his fingers.

"I hope to do two things," Thomas said. "The first is to prove I've valuable information that's secret, in fact, not known at this time, and, second, to prove that I'm on your or our side to keep from being shot."

"You better be expedient. Thomas, is it?"

"Yes, today …" Thomas started.

"Young man," Churchill interrupted, "you said 'not known at this time.' Do you mean not known to our intelligence services or not known to me?"

"Not known to anyone, and please give me my fifteen minutes, or you'll think I've taken flight too fancy. Information not known to anyone," Thomas paused and looked directly at the prime minister, then continued, "as it hasn't occurred yet."

Instead of the major reaction Thomas expected, Churchill moved the unlit cigar to his lips and smiled as he said, "You're not the type I would have thought Margaret would have taken a fancy to, flight or not."

Thomas continued in an urgent tone, "I must be quick. Later today, you'll witness the largest German air attack to date, totaling over a thousand aircraft. We will repel the attacks, but at the end of the day, if the Germans were to continue the battle, the RAF wouldn't be able to defend southern England."

Thomas took a breath. "Luckily, the Germans will also suffer extensive losses, and the second attack won't occur. At 18:30, England will essentially be defenseless."

"Please, Mr. Watson, why are you doing this?" Churchill reached over to the box on his desk and pressed a button. "It's heresy. I've honored the request of a very dear friend, and you've chosen to belittle the relationship with this nonsense."

The door opened, and Colville entered the room, excited that he could pick up even a few minutes on his schedule. "Your time has expired early, Mr. Watson," he said as his arm directed Thomas to the door.

"Sir," Colville said, I've Mr. Bixby waiting, and there have been reports of another civilian bombing with casualties, this time in Richmond Hill just across the …"

Thomas rose from his seat a bit too quickly, startling Colville and the prime minister. The adrenalin coursing through his system raised his voice. "Sir, I need you to believe me. Within your government, specifically at Bletchley Park, there's an effort to decode quickly…"

Without even turning to the door, Colville yelled, "*Captain!*"

Thomas spit out the words as quickly as possible: "To quickly decode intercepted Enigma messages. The resulting data is called Ultra, and only a few people know about it, and it will, I promise, stay that way."

At that moment, two men grabbed Thomas and pushed him to the ground, his arms pinned behind his back once again. Unable to brace himself for the fall, he hit his head hard on the floor but turned just in time to land on his cheek and avoid striking the entire front of his face. Thomas grunted at the impact of a knee in the small of his back but managed to say, "… the codes of the German high command."

Thomas increased cadence as the two men picked him off the floor. "You can't decrypt the messages fast enough …" Before Thomas could stand on his own, the men pulled him forward, and his shoes dragged along the wooden floor behind him. He struggled against the two men as they cleared the door. "Lord Halifax will call you later today for a meeting of the war cabinet to be held tonight." Thomas was now almost shouting. "He's preparing the cabinet to adopt a proposal of surrender to forestall an invasion."

"Captain, this is unforgivable," Colville yelled, then added even more loudly, "Get him out of here," followed by "Captain, you're not to leave the building without seeing me. Is that understood?" His eyes rolled, looking up at the ceiling.

Churchill watched the drama unfold, standing at his office doorway. He looked at the man lying on the floor beside Colville's desk.

The captain, down on one knee, locked eyes with Thomas. He thought, "This is a very interesting or very disturbed man." Thomas heard a snap in the background. With Thomas still in the firm grip of the two soldiers, the captain said, "Come now, Mr. Watson, before I'm forced, with no lack of pleasure, to bring you to harm."

Thomas felt the pain in his shoulders as the two men started to lift him. Again, he tried to get his feet in a position to stand.

"*Wait!*" Churchill yelled. Everyone stopped. "Put the gun away, captain."

Chapter Seventy-Three

Yuri's Second Call

Yuri had given himself plenty of time to reach the contact point, and his constant awareness was heightened by Viktor's presence.

Leaving the Kentish Town Station, he walked down Hammond to Caversham and turned the corner. He kept walking, as he did not notice any public call box right away. It appeared as soon as he passed a flower wagon with its large umbrella. As he approached, he saw a young man silhouetted inside the darkly lit enclosure. Yuri looked at his watch. "Five or six minutes," he thought. He nervously paced past the stand, looking at the colors of the flowers. How did anyone come up with flowers amid a damn national conflict? Vividly, the blooms sat grouped in rusted tins, representing one of the divine creations that did not wage war.

"A little pickup for the lady, sir?" the vendor said, pulling a bag out from below a counter.

Yuri drew back to the comment and looked at his watch again. He ignored the vendor and returned to stand beside the telephone box so the young man inside could see his impatience. The figure looked back at Yuri, continuing to talk, staking out his rightful territory, having been there first. "The old man will just have to queue it up," the kid thought.

Yuri could tell by the kid's posture and facial expressions that he wasn't talking to his science teacher but with someone of more personal interest. Yuri was out of time; he needed to do something. He could drag the kid out of the box, which would cause a scene opposite of what he wanted. The flower man would immediately run for the constable. Moving closer and staring through to its occupant, he reached into his pocket, placed a one-pound note against the glass, and waited for the reaction. The lad said a few quick words, hung up, and opened the door.

Yuri extended the money. The kid took it and held it up, saying, "Pleasure doing business with ya."

Yuri said nothing and grabbed the door just as the phone started ringing.

Officer Kirkway had dialed the number and listened to the busy signal. The officer looked at the clock again, confirming it was the right time. He dialed the number a third time, relieved to hear the double ring.

Standing behind Kirkway and putting down the red folder he'd just absorbed, Petrie said, "Is he there?"

"I'm sure, sir. They don't generally ring up here to order tea." Kirkway bit his tongue as Petrie gave him a cold stare. "Sorry, sir," he said, as he thankfully heard the receiver at the other end pick up. He turned and motioned the director toward a second phone.

Director Petrie picked up the second phone and held it to his ear.

Kirkway said, "Watch desk, code name?"

"Treasure," Yuri said.

"Hold for Mr. Petrie, Director General of Security."

Petrie came on. "Petrie here; what's your situation?"

"Hello, director. It has been some time. Have you reviewed the file?"

"I didn't need to, but I did."

"Then you're aware of my unusual situation."

"Yes, very aware."

"Then first things first. Margaret Hatcher is secure at her mother's house. Recent developments have forced me to terminate this assignment, which I'll explain. Moscow instructed me to gather as much information as possible on a suspected project at Hatcher Ltd. I recruited a Mr. Watson for the job. It's all in a previous report."

"Yes, I'm familiar with it," Petrie said.

"Watson proved to be very unstable but somehow married Margaret Hatcher."

Petrie, taken aback, said, "Married?" Are you sure?"

"Yes, and despite the marriage, he produced nothing of value on the assignment. All other efforts at uncovering the existence of such a project have also come up empty. Given his ineffectiveness and instability, Moscow instructed me to eliminate him. The same directive ordered me back to Moscow. However, I've discovered Moscow secretly sent another officer into the country, and this officer has gone rogue."

Yuri continued, "As to Watson, except for possibly placing Miss Hatcher in danger, I had no interest in Watson's destiny until recently, when he changed."

"Where's Watson now?"

"As of yesterday, at the Hatcher Estate," Yuri said. They are both safe, given the estate's private protection. There is a minor issue with a local asset I recruited; she is in the file. The embassy is unaware of her involvement. She lived next door, and her knowledge was limited to reporting anything that might affect Miss Hatcher's safety. Other than that, she knows nothing and is now out of the picture.

An impatient Petrie said, "So Margaret and Watson are safe, and the asset is at the safe house. What about this officer?"

"His name is Viktor Grigoryevich, a colonel in the NKVD, and he's very dangerous. Moscow has ordered me back after eliminating Watson. The real truth is he has orders to kill me, which he'll find is not so easy."

"We can help," Petrie said.

"No, if the trail leads back to British intelligence, it will ultimately point to Margaret, and someone in Moscow will reopen another investigation, putting her in danger again." I must eliminate Viktor, and they must know who was responsible. Only then will Margaret be safe, which was my commitment. I believe I've then completed my end of our agreement."

"Mr. Stakova, we also committed to *your* safety. You must come in."

"No, Mr. Petrie. Moscow Center has decided. Even without Viktor, Moscow would have had a cot in Siberia with my name on it. I can't stay in England. I need to disappear. We both know the rules, Mr. Security Director; you can only be a double-agent once and then can no longer be trusted. To lie once is to lie twice. As you say, I've done my bit, and it's time to move on. It's finished; I'll take your secrets and disappear unless you choose to insist on 'protecting' me. In that event, I'm back in the game and will certainly bargain for my life with what I have. To convey any information to anyone at this time isn't in my best interest, so our incentives are one and the same, are they not?"

"Yes, I guess that's true enough," Petrie replied. "Have you made arrangements? Can we help you there?"

Yuri's smile came through in his words. "I arranged to leave the country the day I arrived years ago. In addition, your government provided the necessary documents at the time of our agreement. Of course, I'll not be using them, as you would then know the name I'm using when I travel. Besides, if you help me, someone must know where I'm going, which is never good. Please, it's not a matter of trust; it's a matter of procedure."

"True, sir, very true," Petrie said. Never try to be clever with someone who has mastered the art of staying alive. Mr. Stakova, I know I speak for the Prime Minister when I say we can't thank you enough."

"Mr. Petrie, if I may, Margaret Hatcher started as an assignment. Miss Hatcher is truly unique, capturing your heart in a single beat. Unfortunately, she'll only know me as the enemy. To me, this matters."

Looking at Kirkway, Petrie said, "If it's of concern, then I'll be sure to address it."

"Thank you. I'll not be leaving right away. As I mentioned, I need to address a few issues before I'm free to travel.

"Such as…?" Petrie asked.

"Housekeeping," Yuri said. "I must clean up some things that affect both our houses; actions I'll take to contribute to Margaret's safety and, perhaps more importantly, to my own."

Yuri thought for a moment before exposing his friend. There is a man at the embassy whom I trust, and he might be of service to your government in the future. His name is Pavel. You might convince him to cooperate for the right incentives, namely political asylum and relocation. However, I can't guarantee this. As to the Russian Embassy, nothing was learned of the special project of any importance."

"One thing," Petrie said, "you indicated something about not trusting Watson until recently. What did that mean?"

There was a noticeable pause before Yuri responded, "This, I'm not sure about." He has certainly changed. He was a complete liar with two faces, not very bright, and not someone you would trust with even worthless things. He was incapable of genuine feelings for Margaret. All he cared about was money. Recently, he changed into a serious man on a mission. He would say interesting things like there would be no invasion and Germany wouldn't defeat England. But we both know that at least the boats will be coming—perhaps any day."

"Well …"

Yuri allowed the man his biased opinion and continued, "That aside, more than one person, including Margaret, thinks the current man isn't the same Watson she married. He might as well be another person. One day, when I pressed him for information, he was completely unaware he was working for me. My ah…instincts told me he wasn't lying. However, he's not a threat to Margaret, so I see no reason for action. Indeed, she's safer with this…new, different man in her life. There, you have it. Don't ask me to explain it as I can't, but I'm one of the believers."

Yuri knew this moment represented the end of a chapter in his life. "Then it's done, director. Thank you and the prime minister for allowing me to oversee Miss Hatcher's safety and a second chance to survive the war. I hope he thinks his decision was the correct one."

"I'm sure he does," Petrie said, listening to the muffled thud as the swinging receiver at the end of the cord gently hit the back glass in the small space.

Petrie hung up the phone. So, one of the most interesting cases he'd ever followed came to an end. He turned to his officer and asked for the file. "Is this all of it?" Petrie asked.

"Yes, sir. It's Section 900. Everything that exists is in that file, and then placed in that safe.

"Fine," Petrie said, placing the file under his arm. "Restore security, and I'll write the debriefing report myself."

He reached down to the log and, confirming it was the current log sheet, tore the almost empty page from the binder. He said, "You're to replace whatever notes you had for earlier in the day from memory, but do *not* refer to anything regarding this file or this phone call. This event never happened. I must be certain of your understanding. Am I clear, sergeant?" Petrie raised his eyebrows, expecting an answer.

The sergeant stood up, saluted the civilian, and said, "Understood, sir, fully, sir. It was just a normal morning."

"I hope so, son. Carry on."

The sergeant closed the door behind the director and locked it. Kirkway walked over to the safe, secured it, then turned to his log and started reconstructing his entries earlier in the morning. In doing so, he considered the consequences of error in his pre-war job as a department store clerk. Any minor failures at the sales counter could result in his being sacked, but here, one slip of the tongue, and he could be shot.

Chapter Seventy-Four

Churchill's Office—Thomas On The Floor

As Thomas lay on the floor, the captain was surprised at the strength of Churchill's command to stop.

"Yes, sir," the captain said, freezing in mid-movement like a figure in Pompeii.

The prime minister walked over, stopping at Thomas's feet. Still rolling the cigar between his thumb and forefinger, he looked down at Thomas for a full ten seconds, then said, "Mr. Watson, a spy with unimagined abilities could, in the remotest sense, know the information you've provided. However, the most beloved Halifax won't call me later for a meeting scheduled for today, as this very morning, he requested a meeting for tomorrow. While meetings of this sort are certainly not out of the ordinary, it's extremely suspicious that you would be aware of something no one else could know. You see, Mr. Halifax and I were alone in my quarters during our discussion. Indeed, I've yet to inform Mr. Colville, whose job it will be to gather the members due to the uneven nature of the morning."

Thomas turned his head as much as he could and said quietly, "I still believe the meeting will occur today."

Churchill turned to the captain, who had returned to normal form. "Release him. You and two men stay down here." He looked up at the room crowded with soldiers and at the anxious stares of every worker. "The rest of you fine people can go back to work. I wish to thank you all for your devoted service. Colville, in here with me, and that would include you, Mr. Watson."

Thomas felt relief saturate his body. He stood with the captain's aid and felt the handcuffs fall free from his wrists. Thomas put his hand up to his face, only to encounter a sting. He winced.

The captain noticed the action and said, "Sorry, sir, I think we couldn't avoid that."

Churchill said, "In a minute, I too will know whether to apologize."

Back in Churchill's office, with an almost uncertain motion, Churchill waved Thomas to the same chair, ignoring Colville, who continued to stand. Churchill also remained standing behind his desk.

Thomas was still breathing heavily as he accepted the seat.

"How do you know about Ultra? My first fear is the secret's been let out," Churchill said.

"No, it's still a secret, and it will remain so throughout the war," Thomas said.

"You've found that the Hatcher Ltd. firm is involved with this. Is that where you got your information?"

"No," Thomas offered. "Lady Hatcher knows of the project but not the details, and Margaret knows nothing." He knew it wasn't entirely the truth.

"Well, then?" the PM said impatiently.

"Sir, I wish to continue recounting this afternoon's events, but you might find it advisable that we continue the conversation alone."

"Bloody 'ell," Colville shouted.

Churchill silently looked at Colville as he searched for a way to move this unusual situation forward and get to the nut of it. "Mr. Watson, do you love this Margaret I hold so dearly? Can you tell me why you would place her in this position? By simple association, this path you've chosen could be doing her a grave injustice."

Waiting, Churchill looked directly at Thomas.

"Mr. Watson?" Churchill said, a clear edge to his voice.

"Why?" Thomas said.

"Why do you love her?" he repeated with irritation. "Tell me, and you should be quick about it," he said, reaching across his desk for his lighter.

Thomas was surprised at the query and wasn't quite sure of what to say. It was as if he knew he had only twenty words left, and they had to be exactly right. "Because she was born sixty years too early," he said. "She should have been born in an era when a woman could be prime minister."

"Good God, man," Colville said in disbelief. "Have you no respect?"

Thomas continued, "Margaret was a woman before her time, as much as her mother was a woman of her time. My association with her and my chosen path should tell you the importance I place on the events coming later today."

The great man stared at Thomas in thought. Still standing in front of his desk, he started toward his chair, saying, "Mr. Colville, could you give us a moment?"

Colville was speechless and stood frozen in his spot.

After sitting down, Churchill looked at his exacting gatekeeper as if a teacher was waking a student sleeping in class. He said, "*Mr. Colville*? Would you be so kind as to get the door?"

Colville, with an astonished expression, left the room without a word.

"Thank you," Thomas said, feeling the pressure ease. After a pause, Thomas said, "It's an odd question."

"If so, I believe it fits quite nicely with some of your odd statements. I thought it an excellent method of finding out if you had your wits about you. The test was to determine if you would continue to blabber about your fantasy world, which, even now, I'm beginning to doubt is pure fantasy. The mere thought, you must surely understand, leaves me in a somewhat uncomfortable position."

Somewhat frustrated, Thomas said, "Mr. Churchill, I don't have a source for the information. I wish I had something clever to say to give you confidence in my intentions. I don't. I woke up one day married to Margaret and don't remember anything before that except…" Thomas stopped.

The man waited.

"Except, if I may, I know some things that have yet to occur." Thomas winced as if in anticipation of being called a lunatic.

"You've already proven one with the statement about Halifax. He's very unhappy with my leadership, and given things are going badly, not completely without reason."

With notable caution, Thomas said, "He wouldn't be unhappy if he knew the whole story."

"And I presume you know the whole story?"

Thomas wasn't sure he wanted to reveal the whole story and decided to stay with the subject at hand. He said, "I know enough, sir. Halifax spent yesterday and most of today gathering support for a resolution, which he'll present at a time he feels will place you in the weakest position and that he hopes will force you to sue for peace as soon as possible."

"This isn't hard to believe, given the state of our defenses," Churchill said.

"Prime Minister, that weakened time will be after a battle later today during your visit to Uxbridge. After today's attack, Halifax will have numbers that reflect the day's battle," Thomas said. "Sir, the numbers will reflect substantial losses. They'll be the smoking gun he'll use to support his position, to sway the War Cabinet to his vision of what's best for England. He'll go into the meeting feeling very confident."

"Well, Mr. Watson, I've the same numbers from yesterday, and I can assure you, it's all he needs. If the next battle places us in yet a deeper state of peril, continued resistance, on the face of it, becomes a position that's ever more difficult to defend. The leader of my ever-present opposition isn't without his grounds nor insincere in his efforts." He mindlessly fiddled with the lighter while looking at Thomas.

"Sir, I believe you understand that events don't always logically flow to the statistics or even the obvious. I know you, and perhaps only you, have a vision for the proper outcome of this war. Moreover, I'm positive you intrinsically possess the personal ability to transfer this vision into reality."

Churchill stopped flipping the lighter over and said, "If things are as bad as you say, a state I'm not altogether ready to deny, Mr. Watson, just how does one play this hand?"

Thomas leaned forward to emphasize his answer. "Prime Minister, it's one of your greatest leadership performances. You convince the cabinet that in the face of logical evidence to the contrary, it's an obligation, bound by the blood of those who've given the highest sacrifice, to defend the Kingdom to the last standing stick. To know that these brave boys preserved the hope of presenting our children with the grandest of humanity's gifts, the opportunity to build upon the best of our civilization."

Churchill stared at Thomas with a look devoid of any sign of emotion. "That was an impressive bit of oratory for one who comfortably resides on the cutting edge of insanity."

Thomas smiled, changing the mood, "I must admit, sir, some of those words may be your own, pulled from my fragmented memory. If credit is due, I suspect it's yours."

Winston's forehead furrowed at the comment. "Again, a memory of today and the future?" Thomas nodded.

"I know that this will not sit well with you, Mr. Watson, but a memory resides in yesterday; of that, I'm most confident."

Thomas continued cautiously, "Currently, knowing the future gives me an unusual look at the present, which will become your yesterday. Moreover, what resides behind *my* yesterday will determine what will occur in your future. My memories tell me you—we—win the war."

"As eloquent as you make it sound, if your memories are correct, what's the problem, Mr. Watson? Let events proceed of their own accord."

"Though I've no logical explanation, I believe I'm here to ensure my memories and your upcoming decisions are the same."

Still, in a quandary, Churchill said, "It's been an intriguing rhetorical exchange, but it doesn't answer the question of why I should not accept the agenda of my foe if it benefits the people under my present stewardship. Mr. Watson, I love the story, but what's the problem?"

Thomas thought, "There it is again. If all turns out right, then what's the problem?" What he would say next would determine if presenting the information would be enough. The response carried the weight of Europe and a free people. He needed to say just the right thing, or it could be lost.

Thomas said, "I'll have to answer your question with a question. Prime Minister, have you decided to fight on despite the condition of the RAF?"

Churchill took the time to light his oft-used cigar but not the time to deeply draw in the smoke and savor the taste he so dearly loved. "Honestly, Mr. Watson, I haven't decided, but if I could stop time, I would, as the more that passes, the murkier this saga becomes."

Thomas waited. "For reasons unknown to me, I think I'm here to assist in your decision to continue the fight so that today matches tomorrow's history."

"Where's here?"

Thomas looked puzzled.

"If you can explain 'here,' you must define 'there,' and we discover the source of your knowledge."

In a wistful tone, Thomas said, "I know not of a 'there.' As I said, it's more information than memories. Our dear Lady of History hasn't seen fit to give me a 'there.' It's a blank."

"A convenient blank, I might add."

Thomas took a deep breath and enlisted a tone he hadn't used in the conversation. "Mr. Churchill, it's a short time until you know whether I'm a fool who deliberately sentenced himself to death for revealing state secrets or someone who wants to be useful. Either way, I think I'm in an unrecoverable position regarding my safety."

Churchill sat down and moved some papers on his desk but was really in thought.

"Sir," Thomas said, "in any event, my well-being pales compared to the losses suffered by the people and the 1200 brave pilots that will die saving Britain."

"The total is 820, Mr. Watson. It's a number I spend considerable quiet time reviewing."

"Twelve hundred is the final total, Prime Minister. It's not over."

"It can't be denied; you're a fascinating man, Mr. Watson."

Chapter Seventy-Five

Yuri Back at the Safe House

After his phone call, Yuri stood outside the call box and again took the time to see if he'd drawn any unwanted attention. The people who occupied the immediate area acted as though they were utterly out of touch with a war that, perhaps in a matter of days or hours, could be marching down this street. He could place a purpose on everyone he could see except a rather large man some distance down the street. He could only see his back as he walked away. Yuri's instincts frowned as the man walked with an umbrella, tapping an odd tempo. The metal tip didn't hit at the proper cadence. This rhythm was the birthright of any Brit, and the exception drew attention. "I must be getting jumpy," Yuri thought. In the distance, he heard the distinctive whine of a Spitfire.

Returning to the safe house, he thought about what was next. Margaret and Thomas weren't as safe as everyone thought. Neither was he, not while Viktor was loose. He wanted to check on Mrs. Somerville and tell her about Petrie's men coming for her. Then, he needed to find out where Viktor was and eliminate him. It was something Yuri seldom had to deal with directly. Other people or clever methods had always been available when such issues arose. Yuri preferred an old-fashioned setup where he tricked the target into committing a crime with informed local authorities taking action.

This time, his target wasn't a fumbling civilian but a focused weapon intent on pursuing his agenda, and Yuri and the Watsons were in the way. It would take a more direct hand.

Yuri had just stepped onto the large common needed to cross toward the safe house on the other side. Unlike at night, in the day, the broad green area didn't look like the edge of the world. Instead, it was filled with hedges, blossoms, and trees. The small patch of land was a calming reassurance that nature continued on its plan despite the tortured paths of humanity.

Just as Yuri pulled open the lapel of his coat to access the key in his breast pocket, he heard a shot. The bullet pierced the open garment directly below his arm and glanced off an unused fountain directly ahead of him. Yuri immediately knew who it had to be and began running for his life, dodging in and around tree trunks, making it harder for his pursuer to take aim. He could hear his feet pounding the ground and, after a few seconds, feel his chest exploding as he ran. He thought of the stairs in the Silvertown Station and wished he'd seen them as an opportunity, not a hindrance.

For years, Yuri had visited the safe house and memorized its surroundings. Thus, he knew the area his opponent lacked. "Shooting in broad daylight," Yuri thought. "Things have gotten out of control." His feet hit the cobblestones just as he spied the opening of the walled pedestrian alley that serviced the rear of the mostly commercial tenants on the block. His escape plan was to enter and go through the kitchen door of a restaurant he frequented. He'd checked out the kitchen long ago, confirming the door was open during the day and well into the night. He would enter the rear and lock the door, warning the employees about a man with a gun on the other side. It would delay his pursuer just long enough for him to escape out the front of the business to safety. It would take too long for Viktor to run around to the front of the building in pursuit, eliminating that option.

Yuri approached the alley, breathing heavily, keeping his head low, and waiting for the next shot. Rounding the corner into the pedestrian alley, Yuri immediately knew he'd made a mistake. Fifty feet before him, workers were constructing a wall between the two buildings, blocking the alley and cutting him off from his escape door on the other side. "The mistake," Yuri thought, "will cost me my life." He knew the only other door on this side of the wall was always locked.

The gunman saw Yuri duck between two buildings. He rushed to the corner, preparing to peek around, but waited for the sounds of running; there weren't any. He looked up and down the street and observed people running from the gunshots and another harmless Brit too far away to matter.

Yuri spun around, knowing his only hope was to make it back out of the alley before the shooter arrived. He would trade certain death for a slightly better chance of the gunman hitting a running target. In two steps, he faced a man standing at the corner of the alley. He was trapped. The man with a complacent smile pointed a gun directly at Yuri's chest. It wasn't the man in the passport photo but one of Viktor's men.

Yuri coughed out the words, frantically buying time. "Moscow knows you tried to kill Watson," he said in Russian.

"Moscow knows nothing," the man said, breathing heavily. "They'll only know if you live. I have my orders." The man raised the gun, the final motion before firing.

Eyes closed, Yuri saw himself in his mother's kitchen, leaning over the table covered with flour and surrounded by the aroma of baked bread. He heard the pistol fire—Yuri felt nothing. In shock, Yuri watched his assailant arch backward, fall to his knees, then drop to the ground with the sound of dead weight.

Yuri was stunned. "Was that a shot?" He moved forward and bent over to retrieve the pistol; a second shot hit the bricks above his head. Chips of brick flew as he raised his arm for protection. "Two shooters," Yuri thought. He backed up to the other side of the alley. With the man's gun in his hand, he slid along the wall toward the street, determined to find out who else was out there. Why weren't they together per their training? He lowered himself at the corner so he was lying on the ground. He wanted to look around the corner from an unexpectedly low angle.

From across the street, he heard, "Dacha, I hope that's you."

Mrs. Somerville, the gentle soul, white of hair, came into sight with an open handbag and gun in her hand. She walked up and looked at Yuri lying on the ground with a most unusual look on his face.

"For heaven's sake," she said. "You're not going to do anyone any good down there."

Yuri's quizzical look turned into a small smile, knowing he hadn't the slightest idea how the world worked but was glad it did for him today.

"Sorry about the second shot," she said, holding the Derringer away from her body. "The first one really scared me. Are you all right? Is he all right?"

"Yes, I am," Yuri said, "and no, I don't think he's all right."

"Oh, God," she said. "Did I …"

"Mrs. Somerville, I owe you my life," he said, reaching for the diminutive weapon. "Let me take this."

She handed over the weapon her husband had given her before he left for the war. "You're alive. That's all fine and good, but will I go to jail?"

Yuri looked at the man on the ground as he touched Beth's back, pushing her. "We need to get out of here. Did you see any others?"

"No, I think he was alone. I watched you both run across the common from the window in the flat. You didn't answer the question."

"Is the flat still safe?" he asked.

"Yes," she said. "I followed all your instructions."

"Then we will go there."

"No," she said, resisting the hand's pressure, "not until you tell me if I'm going to jail. I'm still unsure whose side you're on other than Margaret's."

"Then why did you shoot?"

"Because I knew you weren't very good at this stuff, and I didn't know the other man."

Yuri started to laugh while giving her a renewed push into the street. Yuri looked around and said, "We need to act normal and, no, you're not going to jail. You shot a spy. Is that clear enough?"

"Well, now," she said, "that would be true, regardless of who I would have hit."

"Did you aim?" Yuri smiled.

Beth, quite pleased, looked him in the eye. "Of course I did."

They moved quickly toward the safe house. Arriving at the rear, Yuri started up toward the flat.

"Wait," she said, "I said he was probably alone. Don't you think we should stop a second and make sure? They might see us and know where we're hiding."

"No, there will be authorities everywhere. If there's another, he won't stick around." Yuri thought of the man walking away, who had caught his attention near the phone box. It bothered him that he got careless. "It wouldn't happen again."

Beth shook her head as she started up the stairs. There's a practical intelligence that comes with age, and, in Dacha's case, it was apparent it hadn't yet arrived.

Chapter Seventy-Six

Petrie Calls Churchill

Thomas, sitting in Churchill's office, replied to the man's statement, "I don't want you to think that I'm *interesting*; I want to help."

The distinctive loud clacking of the secure phone at the end of the prime minister's desk severely interrupted the moment.

The man looked at Thomas as he said, "Unless someone is inviting me to dinner on this secure phone, I may be required to ask for a moment of privacy."

"Winston," he said into the phone.

Having returned to his office, Petrie said, "Prime Minister, Director Petrie here."

The prime minister looked up, phone at his ear, and motioned toward the door. Thomas, already standing, made his way out, shutting the door behind him. Immediately catching Thomas's movement and appearance, Colville brightened considerably, excited at the prospect of the meeting ending.

"Are we done then?" Colville said.

Thomas again touched the bump on his cheek while sitting beside the door. He smiled at Colville, moving his head from side to side.

Churchill's body visibly relaxed inside the office, "So, Mr. Director, how is the land of ghosts and shadows, over dim visions of lies and counter lies?"

"The task is getting murkier by the second," Petrie told his longtime friend. "We could use a hand up here if you could find a spare minute."

Churchill laughed. "There is a ten-minute lull in my activities, but it would take me half an hour to ascend the steps and report for duty. The result is that you're on your own again."

Given recent events, Petrie was warmed to find the man in reasonable humor. He said, "Regarding decreasing the time, it might be appropriate to consult your charming wife on the issue of the day's menu."

"Oh, yes, I quite agree; it would be so easy to solve if, indeed, she was the real problem. Alas, we're meant to live life, and it's I who decided to partake of its delights vigorously. Unfortunately, the fault lies at my doorstep and mine alone. So, now that we've covered the truly secret items of State, do you have anything else that warrants ringing me up on this line and scaring the bloody hell out of me?"

"Yes, we've had a report from a series 900 officer. It lists you and me as eyes only. The officer is Yuri Stakova, the Russian we turned and used for Margaret Hatcher's security."

"Yes, yes, I remember," Churchill said, recalling the circumstances surrounding his first meeting with the officer. Three years ago, as British first sea lord, he befriended a man named Yuri Stakova, who was then the liaison to his post from within the Russian Embassy. The position at the embassy was usually a cover for the NKVD station chief, reporting directly to the spy apparatus centered in Moscow. Both of them knew the silent charade that was at play. The Russian liaison was in charge of all covert surveillance and managed a group of specially trained officers operating outside the embassy. This wasn't unique to Russia, as a similar post existed at the British Embassy in Moscow. It was a known but unpublicized fact that every country's embassy performed identical duties. All members assumed their foreign intelligence was mining more gold than the effort underway in their own backyard.

As time passed, the Russian liaison and the first sea lord probed each other in a ritual dance, each searching for more information than was relinquished while conversing through a mighty list of subjects. Each meeting revealed an increasing inventory of mutual interests spawned from the minds of two well-traveled and politically astute individuals. Gingerly, they'd gained each other's confidence, with the mutual interests growing into mutual respect.

Churchill possessed a particular skill that allowed him to remain sharp to the content and continuity of conversations when others thought him vulnerable. Churchill had perceived an underlying story in their exchanges during a particularly hazy evening. The officer detested Stalin and the devastation his policies had brought to the people of his homeland. The first sea lord did not perceive a desire for sympathy or a veiled message requesting the aid of a friend. On the contrary, the officer was extraordinarily independent and very capable.

A year later, the officer was picked up by MI5 for recruiting a domestic within the Bletchley complex. Upon investigation, it was determined the domestic wasn't in contact with any secure programs and, as a result, unable to release any secrets. The domestic had broken the law but was deemed more valuable to support a larger goal. On the other hand, the Russian officer was in serious trouble, and due to their repeated contact, officials informed Churchill. Within hours, Petrie and Churchill were in a secret meeting, presenting the officer with an alternative path to the inevitable. Churchill and Petrie had suggested he work as a British double-agent, offering him the only option to live out the war.

Under interrogation, the officer had revealed one of his primary assignments: to collect any information regarding a secret project. The Russians believed there was an effort to build a machine capable of calculating numbers at a high rate of speed. The officer also revealed the Russian suspicion that a successful family company, Hatcher LTD., was secretly working on the project but couldn't find direct evidence.

Growing impatient, Moscow decided to see if they could obtain any information from the family's daughter. To that end, Yuri recruited a British citizen named Thomas Watson to spy on her. Watson walked right into the embassy, asking to speak to someone of authority. The man demonstrated a complete lack of any political allegiance or knowledge but a stiletto-like focus in requesting rather ambitious amounts of money to utilize his unproven abilities. They'd arrived at an arrangement. As time went on, despite numerous meetings and demands, Watson proved to have nothing to show for the effort and money.

On the other hand, Churchill had a significant problem that several attempts had failed to solve. Since Miss Margaret Hatcher had turned down an offer from Churchill to live at Chartwell, she'd steadfastly refused protection of any kind. Knowing nothing about the family business, she was completely unaware that others might believe her to be well-informed and that her abduction would severely affect the work proceeding at Hatcher, let alone put the government in a difficult position.

With her safety in mind, Churchill covertly established security details, which Margaret inevitably discovered. Artfully combining tantrums and taking advantage of his evident love for his friend's daughter, she convinced him to stop. War was hell in so many ways. He loved her dearly, but serious obligations to his country and her father were before him.

With the double-agent, Churchill saw a solution to his problem. At the time, the Russians were the only party interested in, and thus a danger to, Margaret. Moreover, Yuri was in control of that danger. Churchill had entrusted the Russian with Margaret's safety for the duration of the war.

Very aware that any leak of their secret arrangement would have put the Russian in danger and Margaret as well, Churchill had restricted access solely to the prime minister and his chief of security.

Unbeknownst to Yuri, MI5 had already infiltrated the Russian Embassy and received daily reports on diplomatic traffic. Due to this, Yuri's efforts were limited solely to reporting any threat to Margaret or in the event of his exposure within the embassy.

Churchill switched the phone to his other ear and asked Petrie, "Is she in danger?"

"She could be, but it's very intertwined."

"Give me the untwined version if you would be so kind."

"Remember, before working for us, Stakova hired a domestic named Watson to get into her life, establish a relationship, and obtain any information on the Hatcher Ltd. company? Somehow, Watson married her and isn't as foolish as he appeared."

"Marriage?" Churchill choked out, "Margaret?"

"Yuri recruited another domestic named Somerville, who lived next door, to monitor Margaret's safety. Somerville recently contacted Yuri, reporting the possible danger, and they met in person. While covering the danger to Margaret, they soon found common ground on the issue that this Watson had somehow changed."

"Changed, in what way?"

"Watson claimed amnesia and insisted he did not know about any arrangement to monitor Margaret. Yuri and Somerville are certain that he isn't the same man who married Margaret and know it can't be explained."

"David, of course, you know this is the fully entwined version. Is there an answer to my question of Margaret's well-being and safety somewhere?"

"Yes, we think she's at her mother's house, according to the last report."

"Thank you. Now, let's bring Yuri Stakova in here and get all this straight."

"I talked to him directly, and he's not coming in. He says a rogue Russian officer thinks Watson knows about the project, and the information came from Margaret. This is, of course, concerning. Yuri says it's a messy situation, and only he can address the rogue officer. Yuri indicated that it would fall on us to guarantee Margaret's safety once he did, as he would go into hiding. I said we would take care of the Russian officer. Yuri declined, indicating there wasn't time and it wasn't our battle. Yuri also said he's a marked man with the Russians, and his solution will solve both problems."

"This isn't making any sense," Churchill said. "It doesn't sound like she's safe at all and is in danger. We must bring everyone in until we figure out those loose ends."

"Winston, I'm not sure how to do that. Are you still going over to Dowding's place today?"

"Yes, and since some version of Thomas Watson is outside my door, I'll have him in tow."

"Good, that takes care of Watson; we will work on ensuring Margaret is brought in or is at the Hatcher Estate and have it sealed."

"David, make sure you keep both women safe. Since we also charged Alistair with Margaret's safety, keep him current. This young woman has no idea what her father put in motion. Get Alistair more sentries around the perimeter and make them visible."

Petrie paused, "Who'll tell Lady Hatcher about the increased security, let alone more people on the property? She was very clear about either situation."

"Why you, of course. As prime minister and for the sake of the country, I'm not permitted to put myself in the line of fire."

"*That*, my friend, is a very sorry excuse indeed," Petrie said with dry wit.

Churchill quickly replied, "Also cowardly, I might add, but I also have a rather precious item on my agenda: surviving the war. To this end, I must engage only in items of strategy and refuse the desire to engage in the more uncertain items related to field operations. On the other hand, *you,* my friend, could go down as a war hero." Churchill laughed. "You must approach this as an opportunity."

"It's the going down part I'm worried about," Petrie replied. Both men enjoyed the humor and looked forward to their next unofficial meeting.

Chapter Seventy-Seven

Turing in Churchill Meeting

Thomas returned to the same chair after Churchill's call and was relieved the call wasn't an emergency, delaying their conversation to later. Waiting for Churchill to resume the conversation, Thomas saw the office door open quickly, followed by the prime minister's secretary.

"Yes, Mr. Colville," Churchill said. "This is rather important."

"Yes, sir, I know, but Mr. Turing is here for his appointment. You placed importance on seeing him. He is pretty insistent. "

Winston thought about Dr. Turing, a man he deeply admired but hadn't come close to understanding. In politics, perception was the most critical requirement. Thankfully, he'd been born with the gift of reading people and using the information to further his agenda. Despite this, he was somewhat confounded as Turing, brilliant without question, appeared immune to the normal wiles of an old politician.

Churchill, trying to enter into casual conversation with Turing, found a man who appeared lost, as if studying his words and not comprehending whether they were forming thoughts. He seldom initiated contact and was reticent to a fault, although Churchill had prioritized his project in the war. Nevertheless, unlike most people, Turing never used his access and visibility to his benefit.

Colville said, "Remember he called earlier insisting on seeing you with important information.

Thomas was pleasantly surprised, knowing Turing had expended the effort to fulfill his promise at the pub. Having the respected Turing confirm to Churchill that some of what Thomas had imparted was useful could be just the thing. Anything that would get Churchill to believe his story of Germany's upcoming failed strategy was worth it.

The prime minister looked at Thomas and said, "It would seem utterly useless to have you removed from a highly classified meeting in which you know more than the most trusted in our government."

Thomas leaned forward. "Sir, at the least, Turing might substantiate that the information I conveyed was helpful. It would help prove my sincerity and the accuracy of my claims."

"Mr. Watson, my issue isn't with the sincerity of what you believe; rather, it's the nebulous source that's most disturbing."

He looked up, waving his cigar toward Colville, and said, "Let him in if you will."

"Yes, of course," Colville said as though defeated. "It will mean turning out Mr. Anderson to keep a shred of order."

Churchill allowed him to demonstrate his frustration as a favor to a friend and a priceless asset.

Colville reached behind him and opened the door, exposing Dr. Turing's tall, ruffled, restrained figure.

Churchill rose from his chair, extending his hand. "Doctor, seeing the force behind our efforts at Bletchley is always a pleasure. Please sit down."

"Five minutes, Mr. Turing," Colville said through tight lips. He wasn't at all happy with what had just transpired.

Churchill said, "Mr. Turing, let me introduce …"

Turing's face could not hide the surprise. "Well, Mr. Dunning," Turing said upon seeing Thomas, "what're you doing here? I mean, what a pleasant surprise."

Thomas's body tightened up. How could he possibly forget that Turing still knew him as Dunning?

Colville and Churchill looked at each other. In an incredulous voice, Colville said, "Everyone on God's earth, including every town constable and MI5 officer, is searching for a Dunning right now. You're considered a dangerous armed fugitive who tried to infiltrate the Bletchley site, a state secret, and escaped under a hail of gunfire. And here you are sitting in the prime minister's office."

Thomas put his hands up in self-defense, "Dunning is the name I used to get into Bletchley to meet Dr. Turing. I didn't want to use Watson because it could be tied back to my wife. I went to Bletchley to ask for the doctor's help in arranging this meeting, certain I didn't stand a chance alone. I chose the doctor because I had certain information I hoped would gain his trust. He promised to try to get me that meeting, and, as we can see, he's a man of his word."

Churchill paused briefly, then said, "That appears to be the case, does it not?" Churchill looked at Colville and said, "Thank you, Jock."

Jock Colville just gave in to his utter disbelief. "Sir, this man is dangerous." It was the more courteous version of what he was thinking, namely that the prime minister was being downright reckless with his security. After the earlier incident with the guards, he couldn't understand the actions and decisions he witnessed. "They deviated from everything normal. All he could say was, "Should I notify …?"

"No, and thank you again, Jock; I know you're doing your best today but like all things connected to war … well, it's just not following the plan. Be assured. "You'll get the full story when I do, and hopefully, all these irregularities will sort themselves out."

Colville nodded in recognition of the direct address to his issues and proceeded out of the room.

When the door closed, Turing started. "Sir, who this man might be is irrelevant. I've been trying to tell everyone I know that I must be allowed to talk to him again, and all I've gotten is a cowboy reaction of shooting him on sight. Someone must realize how much Mr. Dunning can contribute to our goals at Bletchley."

Thomas was surprised his attempt to talk to Turing had gone so wrong, and he was the target of a manhunt. After realizing it hadn't been the British who had tried to kill him, he'd figured all he had to worry about was staying clear of the Russians. He hadn't calculated on the local search for crimes against the king.

Turing turned, motioning to Colville's desk outside the door. "First of all, I'm sorry for all the fuss, but I made a solemn promise to attempt to get our Mr. Dunning a meeting with you. Additionally, I wanted to inform you about Dunning's visit to me." He looked at Thomas and continued. "He provided information that's impossible for him to have known and made vital contributions to our efforts," Turing added in a secretive tone.

"It's all right, Mr. Turing. Keeping secrets from our friend here is academic, as he appears to be more informed than any of us. You may speak freely."

"Excellent. The simple fact is that Mr. Dunning has made several stunning suggestions, the nature of which only I would have or should have realized regarding the design of the machine. Recognizing the potential, every one of my people has been working frantically on the different aspects of Mr. Dunning's suggestions, knowing the pressure for a breakthrough. The curious thing, and the reason I chose to trust him, is it wasn't something classified that existed, and he secretly acquired. On the contrary, it was something that didn't exist, even in my mind, let alone on paper, and could have an exponential effect on our efforts. I'm sorry; it's just not coming out right at all. Let me try again."

"It won't be necessary, doctor. It's quite clear enough." Churchill thought for a moment. "What I mean by that is, it's as clear as anything involving our Mr. Dunning here. Everything involving him is both outsized in importance and murky in its origin. If that's the sum of it, you've fulfilled your promise, and depending on how things transpire, I'll endeavor to make him available. Thank you for taking the time."

Turing felt he hadn't been specific enough. "But, sir, the breakthrough, your pressure—I mean, interest, it's the process and switch speed. I mean, that's what Mr. Dunning has contributed." Turing was racing. "We could have a demonstration very quickly."

"We hope so, Mr. Turing. You certainly deserve a positive break, given your efforts. I would very much like to see a demonstration and, even more, be able to demonstrate my gratitude. Shall we now?"

"Yes, thanks again," Turing said, standing. "Mr. Dunning, my boys are like I've never seen them before." The final test run should run shortly, depending on the teletype interface to punch the tape. The test would normally demand my presence, but there was, of course, my commitment. Any modifications will be installed on the second Bombe being constructed off-site."

Thomas was unaware that the second Bombe was being constructed. He said sincerely, "Thank you for coming. At the least, it increases the prime minister's trust in other things we've discussed. I hope the modifications work in short order.

Churchill waited until Turing had stepped out. I've heard enough to warrant keeping you in custody. So, barring any other surprises, you'll need to stay with me for a bit. I hope you can understand."

"It's perfectly understandable," Thomas said, "and, I must add, far less inconvenient than getting shot. However, I want to call Margaret and tell her where I am. She's given to worry, and my absence could create alarm."

Churchill pointed at Thomas with the same finger securing the top of his cigar. "I wouldn't count on not being shot yet, as none of this is in the least rational. Why didn't you tell me you were the notorious Dunning when we started?"

"Mr. Dunning was a wanted man by the British, so I needed to get into the building as myself."

The regular phone on Churchill's desk rang with a very different sound. Reaching over, he looked up. "Excuse me," he said. Into the phone, he mumbled a simple, "Yes?"

"My sincerest pardon, sir, it's Byron Nettleton at Number 10," said the voice on the phone. Thomas started to courteously exit, and Churchill waved him back into his chair.

"Yes, Byron."

"With my apologies, I find this intrusion quite out of order, sir, but a young lady at the front door claims to be Miss Margaret Hatcher. She says she wants to speak to the prime minister and her husband, who's supposed to be with you. Normally, of course, I wouldn't bother you, but she says it's of prime importance, and Lady Churchill knows her, and they're chatting away at the moment. Mrs. Churchill asked me to contact you."

"Asked? Mr. Nettleton? In fact, she gave you a direct order, did she not?" He laughed.

The prime minister's head of house responded, "Well, as only you know, sir, she can be persuasive on the odd occasion she feels the need."

"Graciously presented, Mr. Nettleton. Have Miss Hatcher escorted through the passageway and to my office."

"Very well, as you wish, sir."

Churchill rang off.

"Mr. Watson, we are about to be invaded by a bundle of energy whose match is found solely in the sobering straightforwardness of her remarkable mother. But then, perhaps you hardly need reminding of something you've likely already experienced from both sides."

Thomas creased his brow in confusion. "Margaret? My Margaret?"

"God save us all if there were two of her, sir. At a more leisurely time, I must share a curious tale regarding the mysterious disappearance of my favorite bowler."

Thomas's perplexed expression gave way slowly to speech. "I'm shocked and more than disturbed to hear she's here. I left her with her mother just this morning, explicitly instructing her to stay there. Considering recent developments, I believed it was the safest place possible."

"How long have you been married to her, Mr. Watson?"

"Sir, regrettably, my acquaintance with Margaret has been brief owing to my memory troubles. We're still learning a great deal about each other.

"That certainly supports Mr. Petrie's vague suggestion that you are not quite the man who originally married our Margaret. You're still young, Watson, and you've yet to grasp the decidedly unconcealed powers that women hold over the likes of you and me."

Thomas smiled, shaking his head slightly. "Sir, I fear the provenance of my historical memories and my fleeting acquaintance with the present lie firmly under the authority of our dear Lady of History. Surely that's the influence you're hinting at?"

"Once more, very well stated," Churchill responded, a broad grin spreading across his face. "Yet, Mr. Watson, I'm not entirely persuaded that your Lady of History differs greatly from the good women who so deftly manage our lives today. Each lovely soul is an enduring mystery, leaving us gentlemen perpetually at the mercy of an influence we dare not presume to understand."

Thomas laughed heartily, clapping his hands lightly in mock applause. "Elegantly expressed, sir."

Colville put the phone down in wonder. Security had just informed him they cleared Margaret Hatcher through the passageway from Number 10. At that exact moment, he was sure he heard laughter from the PM's office.

Churchill moved his unlit cigar to the ashtray and back. Eventually, I must confront the notion that you can access knowledge from the ethers. The silence hung until he followed with, "Even if your knowledge is such that it can't be explained, I must address it and determine if I have a source available to me that can help win the war. Given our grave situation, you must understand that I would welcome any source contributing to victory, even an over-perceptive divining rod. However, your knowledge doesn't align with what has worked for the world since its inception—beliefs such as remembering the past and looking toward the future. You've managed to stand this on its head, so it's hard to deliver the trust you're working so hard to establish.

"Sir, I'm as confused as anyone," Thomas said, "but as you say, the stakes are high. Just allow me to prove myself with today's events and thus, in my curious way, help shorten the war. You've everything to gain, and I have everything to lose."

Of that, there is no doubt. As to the opportunity, at this point, you have no choice. Upon your shoulders lie two critical objectives that are mine. Those would be winning the war and fulfilling a promise to a dear friend to keep his daughter from harm."

Colville knocked and started to announce that Margaret Hatcher, without an appointment, was here to see the prime minister who, among other things of note, was trying to save the British Empire. However, it all went terribly wrong as Margaret burst past Colville, now humbled at losing control.

She gave Thomas a peck on the cheek and pulled back, saying, "I just had to see you because Mrs. Somerville is missing, and the Russian who broke into her house read the note with your name on it, and he had a gun and …"

"*Margaret*," Churchill said stiffly, "if you could slow down."

Margaret literally yelled, "Uncle Winnie!" She threw both arms straight into the air as if she hadn't known he was there.

Jock Colville watched another parcel of protocols disappear as Margaret flew around the desk, gave the PM a brisk hug, and kissed him on both cheeks. All this occurred as the man remained seated, not allowing time to rise.

In one breath, Margaret said, "I'm so sorry, Uncle Winnie, but I'm terrified that something's happened that could put Thomas in danger, and I knew he had a meeting with you, so I figured Aunt Clementine was the only way in to see you."

"Obviously, it worked," he said, looking at Colville, who had reluctantly decided that going with the flow was easier than figuring things out. He happily closed the door and stood looking down at his desk, wondering, only half in jest, if the events of this single day would get him fired and sent to the front. Then he thought it was very possible that his desk would *be* the front in a matter of days.

Churchill directed Margaret to the second chair. Thomas placed his hand on her arm. "Why aren't you home? You promised you would stay there."

"I never promised such a thing. You assumed I would stay there, and it's a good thing I didn't. I was checking on Mrs. Somerville because she didn't answer my ring last night or this morning."

Thomas leaned forward. "But how did you get there?"

Margaret's face went blank. "Why on earth would that matter? Anyway, while I was in her house, a Russian came in because I'd broken the back door, and he found a note from her with your name on it that I'd left on the table. I don't know what the Russian understood, but he must have recognized its importance. It ties Mrs. Somerville to both of us and, as a result, puts her in danger.

"How do you know it was a Russian?" Thomas asked.

It has to be that guy Yuri who accused you of spying or something and tried to kill you."

Thomas looked at her face and took a mental photograph. The face that could launch a thousand wonderful thoughts looked at him as if he was completely daft.

"The Russians," Margaret said, "tried to kill you, and the only Russian we've had contact with is that Yuri guy. He said we were in danger unless we turned over some information concerning my father's company. Also, they might be holding Mrs. Somerville hostage, in which case they're the ones in danger," she said, then hit the arm of the chair with her fist. "We need to find …"

Churchill put up his hand to regain control. "Did you say Yuri?"

"Yes," Margaret said, "he said his name when he made us talk to him."

"You just said he tried to kill you," Churchill added.

Thomas shook his head. "Margaret, we don't know if it was that Russian or another one." Was it Yuri in the house this morning?"

"No."

Her answer threw Churchill into a completely different train of thought. This tale proved to be far more complicated than he initially thought.

Thomas said, "Then there's at least more than one Russian involved. I don't think it's Viktor, the Russian I talked to last night. When did you say you saw him?"

Margaret was growing impatient and was sure they had enough information to save Mrs. Somerville without more questions.

She said, "This morning."

"When this morning?"

"Well, it was about an hour ago. Perhaps 12:30."

"I seriously doubt it's Viktor. In fact, I know it's not. His desire for the information I promised to give him is so overwhelming that he couldn't possibly miss an opportunity to get his hands on it."

"What do you mean?" Churchill said, "Wait—do I really want to know?"

Thomas wasn't sure he should tell him, "Because I'm pretty sure he was killed at 11:35."

"You arranged for someone to kill him?" Churchill said, increasing his tone.

"No. I merely placed him in harm's way. Although my memory is somewhat hazy, I recall a black-and-white photograph of a large explosion that occurred this morning at precisely 11:35. The photograph was taken at Richmond Hill Circle. The damaged clock tower, frozen in time, showed the exact moment."

Margaret grabbed both arms of the chair and said, "That's where you told that Viktor guy to meet you at 11:30! Oh, my God, he was bombed! Thomas, that was brilliant." She sat back and crossed her arms, sporting a great big 'I-told-you-so' grin.

Churchill had never presided over any activity with so many disconnected trains of thought, "Wait. We're overlooking something that is inconsistent with the proper order of things. If you told him last night and the bomb dropped at 11:35 this morning, it hadn't been dropped, let alone a photograph taken when you told him. You couldn't have possibly known of the incident."

Margaret said, "He does that a lot, Uncle Winnie. It's something you have to get used to. He also predicted the bombing of Berlin the night before it appeared in the morning paper."

Churchill looked at them both. "Well, all this has distilled down to whether Thomas is a spy."

"What?" Margaret said. "You don't understand."

"Indeed I do. Either I've been presented with the most significant secret weapon in history, or I must try the husband of my ward for treason. Both are fraught with their problems. The only way to determine this is to see for myself how flexing the rules of time works. If it's as Thomas says and this afternoon's attacks are unprecedented, it will prove the integrity of his … dreams or something. At that point, I'll have an entirely different problem.

"Also, given we have dangerous spies wandering about, assassination plots, and God only knows what else, I can't have either of you exposed to danger. Therefore, you'll *both*," he said, looking at Margaret, "follow my orders until I release you."

Still looking at Margaret, he said, "As to you, young lady, you're to promise me," his finger tapping for emphasis on the following two words, "right now—on your father's grave, you'll do exactly as directed until then."

His harsh tone took Margaret aback. No one had ever talked to her in that manner. "Besides," she thought, "I can follow the rules as well as anybody, and all he had to do was ask normally." Nevertheless, she was stunned at the reference to her father.

"Yes," was the only word she uttered. The statement wasn't followed by an explanation, opinion, or any sign of the heretofore required negotiation or discussion. It was indeed one of those rare moments in her brief history.

Churchill was still leaning over his desk, looking at Margaret, when his eyebrows rose, and his facial features slowly rearranged into a look of surprise. "I believe the earth just moved." He said.

"Mr. Churchill, sir," Margaret said formally, "it's not that big a deal."

He paused and continued staring. Margaret finally said, "Yes, I promised, didn't I?"

"As our Mr. Watson, wizard of things forthcoming, has indicated, I'm scheduled for a much-delayed visit to the Kenley operations center at Uxbridge. I'm most interested in seeing firsthand the excellent procedure that Dowding has implemented, but I don't want to distract from his duties. That's the problem with being in this position. What becomes a routine quest for knowledge duly expands into a visit from God himself. Such an event means the floor is polished, and all the lights on the dispatch board, which I've not yet seen, must be removed and dusted.

Both of you'll accompany me until the time sorts this all out. You'll return to my residence now, and Byron will find you something to eat. You'll wait for further instructions."

Chapter Sixty Eight

Lonnie and the Sergeant

Lonnie Garrah walked into the circular hall entrance on her way to the Operations Room. She mindlessly adjusted her uniform jacket, pulling it taut from below the belt at her waist. She was sure the designer was the same bozo who had created Army field tents. In mid-motion, she felt the sensation before looking up and seeing the sergeant avert his eyes. Standing guard at the steps leading up to the observation level was a Royal Marine again in full parade dress at his post. It was all mostly for show for the visiting brass. "Simple, but he did it with such color and," she thought, "with handsome flair." The girls thought he should pose for a recruiting poster, joking about how easy it would be to get women to sign up if he did.

Lonnie stopped her tugging and said, "Sergeant, is there a problem?"

His hand flew to his cap in a military reaction. "No, sir—ah, ma'am, there's certainly no problem." Still at attention, he added, "It couldn't be further from the truth, ma'am." He said it stiffly but with a definite note of comfort and confidence.

As a WAAC Warrant Officer, Lonnie was well above the rank of sergeant in the Army, yet she still felt the sensation despite her formal demeanor. It was like two people making contact, but only at the end of a single finger; the tingle of the energy was forced through the narrow point. She liked this game of flirting from a position of power, although it was against the rules. It wasn't often that a girl found herself in this position, so she decided to play it for what it was worth, just to draw his reaction.

"You realize, sergeant, this isn't the first time I've had to deal with this issue on my way to the control room. Although I might add, I've had the presence of mind to act with proper discretion," she said, returning the salute. "I trust you've been fully briefed as to the issue of fraternization."

Still at attention, he threw his arm to his side. After a pause, with a face masking an internal smile, he said, "Ma'am, military regulations don't cover every possible contingency."

"I'm very impressed. "This implies you've read the entire collection front to back?"

Still looking straight ahead at the opposite wall, his tone changed to a very formal, soft voice as he said, "May I speak freely, ma'am?"

"Go ahead, sergeant; I can't wait to hear what's next."

"Ma'am, fraternizing doesn't directly address the 'issue,' as you refer to it."

"Well, then, how would you put it, sergeant?"

"Freely, ma'am?" he said.

Lonnie nodded.

He turned and looked directly at Lonnie, saying, "Admiration, ma'am...." Sincere admiration."

It caught Lonnie off guard. He said it without even a hint of male sarcasm or bravado, key elements of a man on the make. He said it as if he meant it. Lonnie stood there, aware that the situation had been ongoing for some time. It was different, though, once it was in the open. Now, there was no mistake. On many occasions, her body language included a smile. She hadn't discouraged the 'issue,' and she knew it. Still, there was the war and the awful restrictions it imposed on people in every corner of their lives. In the space of a few seconds, a complete novel had been written in mostly silent, invisible words. Frankly, she wasn't sure what to do. There was certainly the military option, and that was to report him. However, she had actually given him permission. Then, in a fleeting vision, she saw herself invisibly touching the side of his face. She felt the energy.

She chose the middle path.

Lonnie said in a steady conversational tone, "Your thoughts," she swallowed, "are duly noted, sergeant." She paused long enough to perceive his muscles unconsciously relax. He was still looking at her, and it was her play. "He was right," she thought. The hell with it; she'd screwed up once already.

She placed her cap under her arm and said, "That will be all, sergeant," as she stepped toward the door leading to the ops room, ten feet away.

"Yes, ma'am," he said, once again going rigid.

Lonnie took five or six steps. A quick look over her shoulder caught his stare as she walked away. "That was supposed to be all, sergeant," she said through a smile he couldn't see but unmistakably could hear.

"As you wish, ma'am."

Deliberately, Lonnie stopped with her hand on the ops room door and, without turning around, very clearly said, “That’s Andersen, sergeant, Warrant Officer Andersen. I trust you’ll remember that.”

“I certainly will,” he said, “Warrant Officer Andersen.” Though his forward stare had returned, there was no mistaking the tone in his voice.

Chapter Sixty Nine

Drive to Uxbridge

Thomas and Margaret were in the back seat and could see Churchill's car just ahead. Behind them was a car full of men specializing in jackets that didn't fit. As appropriate for the travels of a prime minister, local police blocked all side roads corresponding to this route, making it possible to travel to Uxbridge in the shortest time possible. It was an hour ride that should have taken over two hours.

Thomas looked across at Margaret and smiled. "What a catch," he thought. Margaret moved over and put her head on his shoulder.

"There's something I've been meaning to ask you," she said. Sitting up, she pulled her chin in, pushed her chest forward, and spoke in a deep voice, mocking the prime minister's distinctive delivery. "What happens when," she started, "time sorts this whole thing out?" Then she giggled, sounding normal again. "Do we get to have a normal life?"

"Let's ensure what we have today before venturing into things that might occur tomorrow." Thomas knew exactly where she was going with the line of thought, and she knew he knew, so he waited for her predictable response.

"That's rubbish, and you know it. It's inconceivable for anyone to live without thinking about tomorrow. It's the anticipation of a better day on top of a good day and a great day following a bad day. Who raised you anyway?"

Thomas looked at her, his eyes in thought, saying, "I'm not sure."

She nudged him with her elbow. "Why don't you ever answer any of my questions?"

"I believe sheer volume is the probable cause. Also, I believe that response qualified as an answer to your question."

"Thomas, I'm losing my patience with you and your verbal dancing."

"Patience, pray tell, where and when? I think it's a subject you should not have brought up."

Margaret took a deep breath as she crossed her legs. Unaware of the silent statement her mother perfected, she started arranging the folds in her dress, completely ignoring him. It was vintage Margaret.

"Okay," he said. "You wanted to know when we would have a normal life. Well, right now is a good time to start, but without any of your illogical rules and barriers. Are you with me on this?"

"Oh, Thomas, till death do us part," she said as she put a hand up to the side of his face. "You might be starting to get romantic."

With that, he reached over, grabbed a piece of her dress, and pulled it back, exposing a good portion of her knee. She slapped his hand. The driver instinctively flinched at the sound, glancing into the rearview mirror.

"I beg your pardon; that was hardly the action of a gentleman. Besides, a few brief diversions don't give you the world."

"Diversions? Well, it's the first time I've heard it described that way. By the way, when exchanging vows, did you say 'to honor and serve'?"

"I did not! As far as you're concerned, you'll have to take my word that we're even married. Further, you haven't the faintest idea of what you might have said. I remember your complete compliance at honoring my every wish."

"Now *that*, my dear lady, I believe."

She was reaching for her handbag, and when she came back to face him, she was beaming. "Thomas Watson, you're impossible."

"Excuse me," the driver said, waving for their attention. "We're coming up on the Uxbridge depot. Mr. Churchill has business at the Group Headquarters and wanted me to take you directly to the Operations Center. He'll catch you up shortly." They saw the auto upfront turn right as they turned left into the car park.

"What an interesting building," Margaret said. "Is all that dirt on the side for protection?"

"Yes, it's not perfect, but considerably better than nothing. It would be a sweet target for any German to knock out. They've also reinforced the roof, even though it's several stories underground."

"That's a big hole. Are we going all the way down?"

"I'm afraid that's going to be the case. It's why we're here."

Chapter Seventy

Paddy on the Ground

Paddy had landed after a very boring patrol, checking out a reported German submarine sighting. They didn't fly many patrols, as the system dictated all available planes to be on hand to scramble at any moment. He was sitting in the open air outside the dispersal shack. All but two aircraft were topped off, ready to go. He watched his crew working to refuel his plane. He hoped they were checking out the intermittent restriction in a flight cable he encountered when turning hard left. Of course, it never did it when the crew checked it out. They thought he was a bit fussy.

The pilots waited for the call to action in various states of activity and consciousness at the airfields. Some were napping in chairs, writing letters home, or reading. Paddy was thinking about what he'd said the night before to Edith. She appeared sincerely happy, which hadn't been guaranteed, as most women were sure pilots only truly married the part of the sky they happened to occupy at the time. He thought about how she looked, her slow, confident manner, the smell of her hair, the feel of her in his arms. He'd 'gone and done it,' as the boys would say—committed himself, and, to his surprise, it felt wonderful. He drifted back to his last year at upper school and Annette, his first love, to retrieve the intensity of the dreamy passion that gripped his soul when holding her close.

The pilots waited for the phone in the small disposal shack to ring. With its clamor, everyone's ears would stand at attention, waiting to see if it was a flight update or a scramble. On a scramble, the men, already dressed in flight suits, would charge to their planes. Everyone was locked into the same system and, with it, assigned responsibility.

The daily grind produced a certain informality among the pilots when not in the air. To that end, Auggie gently kicked Paddy's chair, "You look very suspicious today, mate. There you sit with a sappy grin as you stare into the blue. Recalling a fond memory, are we?" Auggie looked the other way, "Gordon, what do ya think, lad?"

Gordon leaned forward in his chair and, in jest, stared hard at Paddy. "Yup, Auggie, I shouldn't have missed it. You're dead on. So that's why he has been walking around here like he forgot we were fightin' a war. Or perhaps our dear friend might have seen the inside of some knickers."

Gordon moved closer, leaning over Paddy and looking into his eyes. Paddy put a hand on Gordon's face, shoving him away.

"Bugger off, the both of ya," Paddy said.

"Yup, that's it all right," Gordon yelled. "Paddy has gotten himself laid; *worse,* he shows signs of being in love. Be warned, lads. Stay out of the way of Number 6 as he might be a daydreamin' up there."

Everyone cheered, raising non-existent pints over their head, shouting, "Only the virile will survive. We want pictures and not the ones ya send yer Mum."

Paddy stood up, waving his arms, and shouted, "I'll have all you ladies contain your fantasies. It's not like that at all. This happens to be the real deal, and I want to enjoy the biggest, most important thing in my life."

"Here, here," another pilot shouted. "Here's to Paddy's biggest, most important thing in his life. And may he find a pair of britches bigger than a parachute to keep it."

Paddy looked over in mock anger, pointed his finger at his fellow pilot, and pulled the trigger, rendering him dead on the spot. He blew off the tip of his finger and sat back down in his chair.

Chapter Seventy One

Arrival at Uxbridge

The car pulled up, and the officer exited the vehicle and opened Margaret's door. Before swinging out, she looked back at Thomas with a giggle and said, "Lookie here, a gentleman," as if Thomas wasn't, and then blew him a kiss with her hand hanging in the air just a second longer than necessary.

"Lucky you," Thomas said. "Only two gentlemen are left, and you have us both; imagine that." It was late, around 4:00 pm, and the sky started to change as if preparing for what was to be a long night. Usually, white contrails would appear and then disappear in the blue between the intermittent clouds. It was unusual not to hear any planes.

They followed the officer, entering what appeared to be a steel door and encountering Officer Templeton of security. He was head of the unit assigned to the complex and took his job very seriously. Thomas remembered that he didn't have any identification. The officer held up his street ID and said, "My name is Handraddy; I understand Mr. Colville has called ahead about two guests."

"These two?" the officer said.

Handraddy nodded.

"Their names?"

"Mr. and Mrs. Thomas Watson," Handraddy said.

Margaret looked over at Thomas, very pleased with the sound of the man's response. The sentry ran his finger down a page and looked up. "There aren't any names for any of you. I'm sorry, I'll need something more than your good looks, sir, as this isn't the dining hall."

Handraddy reached into his coat pocket and pulled out his MI5 identity card. Officer Templeton scrutinized it carefully. He started to write down the details when Handraddy reached over, placing a finger over the box where the officer was to fill in the identification number. "I'm sorry, it's Officer Handraddy, and the credentials are for eyes only."

"I'm supposed to rely on that? I'll get shot."

"Perhaps not, I think," Handraddy said in a monotone voice, "but I fully understand your concern. You may call Director Petrie, the prime minister, or Mr. Colville. It's your option, and no offense is taken. We can wait." He backed up, motioning for Thomas and Margaret to sit on an old wooden bench along the wall directly behind them.

Thomas didn't immediately move, and Margaret said, "What?" Having grown unrealistically accustomed to being on the inside of security protocol, she didn't like her credibility questioned. When these inconvenient matters arose, she merely called the prime minister's wife or someone else, and that was that.

Templeton, clearly frustrated, was looking for some modicum of control. He said, "Do you mind if I at least perform a search?"

"Not at all," Handraddy said, standing back and allowing the still-standing Margaret and Thomas to move forward. "You'll find I'm authorized to be armed in a level three security area, as noted on the credentials."

Margaret had her arms crossed, growing impatient at the back and forth. "You'll also find I'm female."

"Margaret," Thomas said sternly.

Templeton said, "On an appointment without names, a single identification I can't record, I'm supposed to allow an armed man and two unknown civilians into the prime minister's presence?"

Handraddy, maintaining a consistent voice and completely lacking emotion, said, "You may call Director Petrie or the …"

"Okay, I get it; wait here." Still holding the officer's MI5 identification, the man stepped toward the hall.

Handraddy reached out to Templeton, bringing him to a stop. Handraddy said, "Excuse me, sir, but that must remain in my sight. Memorize the number if you must."

Obviously put out, the officer looked at the badge and handed it back. Quickly descending two flights of stairs, he arrived at George's desk. "I'll need this," he said rudely, picking up the phone and dialing.

Due to the poor acoustics, Margaret could hear talking but could not understand anything.

"Yes, sir," Templeton said before putting the phone down. As he walked back up the stairs, he wrote notes of the conversation on paper. After signing a slip of paper and handing it to the officer, he said, "We're all set. Sorry for the delay. I was just doing my job."

Handraddy raised his hand and said in a monotone voice, "No need. We all are, and I would expect nothing less."

Margaret was surprised at the comment, having taken the officer as nothing more than a mechanical robot. Handraddy addressed both Margaret and Thomas with an after-you gesture.

Thomas followed Margaret as they moved forward, nodding to the guard as they passed the passageway and descended the stairs. Margaret looked around. She thought it looked like a giant machine with bolts, wires, tubes, and rust everywhere. Perhaps the icy Officer Handraddy following her was part of the building. After two long flights of stairs, they came upon a table on the landing where George sat next to the phone used by Templeton. The man discreetly stared at Margaret, but having had to deal with it most of her life, she knew when to be flattered and when it should be ignored. The sparkle in his eyes conveyed female admiration, and she saw the man almost jump to his feet, lifting his hat. "Evenin', Miss. Just what this place needed, a bright flower like you."

"And you, sir, with that smile, you could illuminate a railway station," Margaret said.

"Oh, thank you, Miss." He looked at Thomas and back to Margaret. He sat back down and nodded slightly, unconsciously placing his hat over his heart.

"Aren't you a sweetie," she said, leaning over the desk and kissing his cheek. "You could conquer half the world with an attitude like that."

George said, "Templeton gave you the go-ahead, so nothing for me here."

With a purposeful glance, Margaret turned to Thomas and Handraddy, saying, "Looks like we've some work to do, gentlemen." Then, delighted with herself, she walked them arm in arm farther down the hall.

"Sorry," Thomas said to Handraddy. "All this enlightenment has gone a bit too far."

Margaret noticed the first expression of humor on the officer's face. "I saw that," she said. "I definitely saw that, Officer Handraddy. I just wanted you to know it didn't go unnoticed."

"Yes, madam, can I get the door for you?" he said in the dark, even manner of a highly trained officer of death.

"Why, yes," she said, "*Officer* Handraddy, you may, and how kind of you."

Thomas said, "All right, you two, enough of the tit for tat."

They stepped into the connecting ring corridor. To the left was a short flight of steps that led to the glass-enclosed viewing room overlooking the Operations room. Straight ahead was the door to the Ops room. Standing rigid in front of the VIP steps was a guard in parade uniform.

Margaret noticed the guard standing still as a statue—but a very attractive statue. She wondered what she would get if she put the gallantly charming personality of the previous guard into the masculine picture that stood before her—trouble, she decided, lots of trouble.

Handraddy presented the paper to the guard, who glanced at it and said, "Mr. Colville's authority, yes, sir." His hand offered the stairs, and the group proceeded up.

"Two pence for every stair in this place would buy Windsor and then some," Margaret said.

Again, Handraddy opened the door, and Margaret entered a room. Addressing Thomas, Handraddy said, "This is 11 Group Operations Room. I understand the prime minister will be with you shortly."

They looked over a room electric with activity; most everyone was engaged in some way. Handraddy walked over to a junior RAF officer who rose after they entered the room. They conversed briefly, below ear level, in a manner that conveyed an understanding, and the officer left the room.

That concluded, Handraddy reached out to shake Thomas's hand and said, "I'll take my leave, but," obviously glancing at Margaret, he produced a slight but genuine smile, "I wanted to offer the best of luck in your efforts toward the very charming, albeit unique, burden you must bear."

Thomas laughed as they shook hands. "Well, Officer Handraddy, someone must step up in these trying times."

"That's enough, you two," Margaret said. "As for you, Mr. Super Secret Officer, that was a genuine attempt at humor, and you should be reported. Wait, I'll do it myself. What's your real name anyway?"

The officer broke out the first broad grin they'd seen; he replaced his hat, nodded toward Margaret, and silently left the room.

"Cheeky, at the least," she said.

Thomas responded, "Perceptive, at the *very* least. You had it coming."

Their entry had drawn the attention of those in the glass-enclosed room.

One of the senior officers was standing while talking on the phone. He rang off, saying to the man sitting at a control desk, "Two thirty-six is at readiness, 12 Group is getting hit hard." The man was a New Zealander by birth, and with over twenty kills in the First World War, he was highly respected, especially by Hugh Dowding.

An officer approached, saying, "The Churchill party is here, sir.

"Yes, of course." He walked from his position to where they were now seated.

The officer said, This is the Colville party, sir: Thomas and Margaret Watson. May I introduce Air Vice Marshal Keith Park, Commander of 11 Group? Sir, they're here waiting for Mr. Churchill."

"Yes, I see, of course. Sorry, we're a bit busy at the moment. Please find a place anywhere but in there if you don't mind." He said, pointing behind him. "Not sure what the PM has in mind, but I understand he is moments away."

"Most kind of you, and please pay us no mind," Thomas said.

"Splendid then," Park said as he was already focused back on the task.

"Big, isn't it," Margaret said. "And all a hundred feet underground."

"Not quite," Thomas said, procuring a look from Margaret requiring a response. "Okay, it doesn't matter," he said. He waited a few moments and said, "It's fifty feet."

The response was stern, "Thomas!"

Margaret was fascinated; it wasn't as if she'd some previous concept of what she was supposed to see. She hadn't even given it a thought, but before her, did not resemble anything she'd ever encountered.

Almost in wonder, Thomas also surveyed the room below as the different elements came together in his mind. Walking down the tunnel entrance, he wondered if he would recognize the Ops room. To his surprise, it was more than just recognition. He generally understood the workings, as well as what was going to occur in the hours to come. He wondered what it meant. Until now, everything was like educated guesswork, far from the certainty whose presence he could now feel. What did this mean for the future, especially his future with Margaret? It was a concern that was growing stronger. Churchill would know he was right and thus as dangerous as valuable. It would conflict with a normal life, and that *is* what he'd promised Margaret.

Thomas reached for Margaret's arm. "Amazing, isn't it? It wouldn't work without the British inventing radar and untold numbers of spotters on the ground. Remember, back at the house, I said radar would eventually cook your food?"

"That's all I need," she said, "to be cooking a roast and have it tell me where some wayward bomber is flying. I don't think so. Not in this lifetime."

Margaret thought she'd been quite clever and was expecting a humorous acknowledgment. Thomas continued to view the activity below.

"Thomas, do you know what's going on down there?"

"Yes."

"There's no way you could know that, Thomas. You're the one who said it was top secret, which means you've never heard of it, let alone seen it. How does that happen?"

"Up to now, I wasn't sure I was right, but my ability and confidence have grown in the last few days."

Margaret recalled that tear-filled morning when she realized something was very wrong. She looked at him silently. "Do you know what's going to happen in the meeting?"

"No, well, not completely; I mean, I know one of several possible conclusions."

"Did you have any influence on the outcome?"

He took a long, loving look into her eyes as he smiled.

"Thomas?" she said.

"To be honest, we might never know," he said.

"So why are you here? Why the mystery? Why appear in my life? Not that I'm not happy you did."

"To save you from that mess you got yourself into with the other Thomas. You have to admit I'm a *little* more reliable."

It was her turn not to acknowledge a comment begging for a witty reply.

Thomas continued, "I genuinely don't understand how I came to be here, but our lack of understanding about how or why doesn't mean there's no meaningful reason behind it."

Chapter Seventy Two

Control Room

Thomas continued observing the personnel and equipment. He knew that 11 Group Operations room was but one component of an incredibly integrated, totally secret system whose sole purpose was to deploy precious air resources where they could be most effective. It did this by keeping the planes out of the sky until needed, providing the maximum amount of rest, and using a minimum amount of petrol. It required vectoring British fighters to meet a German attack at precisely the right time, position, and elevation. It was a brilliant system designed by Dowding.

Dowding had divided the extensive coastline into sectors, each consisting of its radar stations, ground observers, sector headquarters, and airfields. Thomas knew that some of the pilots weren't even fully aware of the comprehensive nature of the system. During times of battle, it was a hectic atmosphere with analyzed messages distributed and senior officers changing directives, and somehow, they managed it all despite the dire consequences of any error. It took about 200 people from the various services to get one Spitfire into the air and return to base.

Even though the Germans were working on radar at the time, they never fully appreciated the integrated quality of the system that was responsible for their defeat.

Thomas looked down at the Sector Station Operations room. The ceiling was very high, with the room divided into two levels, one where they stood and the one below. The upper level contained Park and his senior officers who, looking down upon the room below, could observe the battle unfold in striking detail. Through the curved glass panes, they peered over the plotting room floor. In the center of the floor was a large map of southern England on an irregular table. Their sector was one of the most important as it covered the routes into and out of greater London.

***

Dowding's system had started with the radar stations along the coast. One of those was the installation in the coastal town of Thurleigh. Being posted at the Thurleigh radar station wasn't something you fought for, though others were worse. It was far enough away from London that a twenty-four-hour leave left little time to play. The local offerings were limited to the Horse Guards pub, frequented by farmers. It made the post enjoyable if you were a grandmother.

Thurleigh station wasn't underground or protected at all. It was a nondescript, weathered building where the four girls staffed the station. The second shift supervisor, prone to being late everywhere, hadn't arrived yet, and they were quietly talking during their duties, which was against regulations.

Audry was barely twenty, slightly built with stunning large brown eyes, and had spent her short life being completely anonymous at school. She was holding a cup of tea just under her nose, making continuous odd noises while taking tiny sips. It was her first day back after a two-day furlough, and she had delicious stories that couldn't be recounted in confession. Her biggest claim was never having spent a shilling the whole weekend, but she wouldn't admit what she had to give up to make the claim.

"I was doing my duty to God and country comforting those poor boys," she said between noises.

Corporal Nancy Hillsend was sitting at her console, wiping the round glass surface of the cathode ray tube. "I don't think God appreciates your efforts, dearie. Anyway, it's *King* and country," she said. Nancy was one of the specially trained WAAFs who peered at the screen of the radar receiver by the hour, waiting for the telltale signs of a raid. Dowding's miracle started here, deep within the Thurleigh and other coastal radar stations. Nancy and hundreds of WAAFs like her were at the front lines of the war, as the radar towers were a constant target of the Luftwaffe.

"Come on, Nance, when did you last have a little fun?" Audry said.

Despite being only a year apart, Nancy looked at life differently. She turned in her chair. "Audry, that's not the point. Eventually, you're…" she stopped talking as Craig bounded into the small building, closing the door behind him with one hand, still fastening buttons on his shirt with the other.

"Nancy?" was his first word.

"Nothing to report, sir. It's all clear," she replied.

"Good, my ride was late again," he said.

No one bothered to listen to what was his overused excuse for what could be a serious violation. He knew Nancy would be there on time, which comforted his supposedly tight schedule. To Audry's annoyance, Nancy was clearly his favorite.

Nancy started filling out the shift paperwork when a flicker from the screen caught her eye. She stared intently at the straight green line with a tiny blip on the left side representing the outgoing signal—nothing.

"That's curious," she thought. Seconds later, she saw the slightest blip on the other side, representing the signal bouncing back. Under the line were marks calibrating the distance between the two. Something was wrong as the line extended past the calibration on the far right of the screen. She'd never seen the radar pick up anything that far away.

"I have a distant contact bearing 125," she said.

"And ..." her supervisor said as he came over.

"Too early to tell the distance, but I've never seen something like this."

The supervisor looked at the empty screen and said, "Am I missing something?"

"Wait, there, there it is again."

"Oh, I see what you mean. How long has it been there?"

"Less than a minute," she said.

"I'll call Beachy Head Station. They're a little closer in that direction." After he returned to his desk, Nancy said, "Sir, I think you should see this."

"What?" he said, coming over again.

Nancy adjusted the vector, barely moving the knob, trying to bracket the echo signal. The system was so new that manuals didn't exist, and practical interpretation was a matter of playing the machine like a violin. Experience proved women were far better at the art than men. She turned one of the attenuation adjustments, which meant nothing to her, but she knew it would steady the line, helping to reveal the blip.

"It's the size, sir. The reason we haven't seen anything that far away before is due to the group size. It's bouncing back more of our signal from farther away, meaning it's unusually large."

"Magnificent, Nance. I think you're spot on. Like I've always said, that head of yours is more than just pretty."

"Beg your pardon, sir? When did you say that?"

Nancy said to Audry, "Contact designated T917-1." It defined the station, month, date, and contact on that date. It was Audry's job to document what Nancy found, regardless of whether it amounted to anything.

Craig smiled at Nancy with the phone at his ear and gave her a thumbs-up.

Nancy wasn't happy. She knew she was smart but didn't like being toyed with by someone with half her wits. He had the job because he was a man.

"Stanton," Craig said, "we have a contact at 125 that's very faint. Can you cross-vector it for distance? What do you mean? My operator has it on her screen; what're you chaps doing over there? Nancy, why? We're telling you exactly where to look, for heaven's sake. This'll cost you a pint, dear boy; get back when you see something." he said as he hung up.

She frowned. "Sir, I can definitely say the contact at 125 is 40+ at 60 miles. I think you should …"

"Call it in…," he said, finishing her sentence. He called Observer Corp. headquarters to report a new raid.

Chapter Seventy Three

Churchill Arrives

Margaret and Thomas moved aside as the prime minister entered the room, passing directly before them. He nodded at them, saying, "I'm glad you both could make it." He added a single word, "Margaret." She knew what he meant. He was acknowledging his surprise at her following his instructions.

Churchill looked around and, addressing the junior officer, said, "Is there another place we can sit where we won't affect anything? We don't want to be a distraction."

"Yes, Prime Minister, we have a separate VIP room up here, and there's a rumor that you qualify." The smile disappeared. "Ah, sir, sorry, sir."

"Relax, my boy; there's an easily discerned difference between a sense of humor and a lack of respect. Can we manage another chair so we can all squeeze in here?" he said, motioning to Thomas and Margaret.

With an unusually discreet and lingering glance at Margaret, he said, "That I can do easily. No problem, sir," he added and stepped out of the room.

Thomas and Churchill looked at each other with half smiles.

"By the way, my dear," Churchill said, putting an arm around Margaret, "could you make yourself available the next time I must address the House of Commons? Your duties would consist merely of sitting next to me holding my notes?"

"That's silly; of what possible use could that be to either of us, more importantly, you?"

Churchill replied with famously dry humor, "Since the vast majority are men, they'd be somewhat distracted, preoccupied, and inattentive to the task at hand. At which point I could, and would, pass any agenda. I admit a tactical move of deception but wholly justified for the greater good."

"Winnie, stop that; you're making fun of me."

Thomas burst out laughing. "I will, sir, only in the country's interest, volunteer my wife as your assistant in just such a situation."

Margaret said, "You're both looking to get me riled, and I'll have none of it," she said.

The junior officer returned with the chair and placed it directly behind Margaret, nervously holding it as she sat down. "Will that be all, sir?"

"Quite indeed, soldier," Churchill said. " You've not only provided us with comfort but perhaps brought a heretofore overlooked political strategy to light."

"Sir?"

"Thank you very much," Margaret said. "Your manners are commendable and will be made known to your superior officer. Isn't that what you said, Prime Minister?"

Churchill, face aglow, nodded to the man.

"Yes, ma'am," the soldier said as he carefully left the room.

"An incorrigible moment, the both of you," she said. "Don't we have a war to fight?"

"Yes, my dear," Churchill said with a glow. "Indeed, you're right."

Chapter Seventy Four

Birling Gap and Flight Control

The Birling Gap forward observation post was part of 11 Group's sector and situated atop the cliffs right on the sea. The post was one of the hundreds of Observer Corps outposts scattered to the South and East of England. When the chaps at Home Chain picked up a raid, their equipment could only follow it up to the coast, as the radar only pointed out toward France. Once the raiders flew over the beach and anyplace inland, it was the job of the Observer Corps to keep track of the raids visually.

Birling Gap's high location provided excellent visibility but exposed it to the elements. Constantly buffeted by cold sea winds, the men's only escape was to duck down inside the circle of sandbags that came up to their chest, drink a large amount of hot tea, or both.

Andrew Tembly, thinking he was partially frozen, had had enough. "Cappy," he said, "stop nick nacking with the pot. It's clean enough, for God's sake. Put the bloody thing on the hot plate, or I'm gonna die out here."

Cappy Barns looked at his fellow volunteer, sitting on the dirt floor with his arms tucked between his drawn-up knees and chest. "Be nothing short of drop-down funny, Andy boy, if you survived combat and died of poisoning from a tainted pot."

"Cappy, Cappy, Cappy, me bones they ache, me nose is frozen, an' I would like a surprising' quiet day to end with a cup, but it has to get here sometime 'fore the bloody war ends."

"Such an ornery cuss. Tis a reason why no one hasn't marry ya. And, at this rate, you're destined ta spend the rest of yer life in a pub, gawkin' at the rest of the world." As he spoke, Cappy held the teapot just above the hotplate, adding to his friend's anxiety.

"God demm it. Put it down," Andy said.

Just then, the headquarters phone rang, and finally, after putting the pot in its place, Cappy picked up the handset. Andy grabbed the logbook and tried to wrap his fingers around the pencil.

"Yes, sir. Ready, sir." Cappy looked at Andy and said, "Bearin' 125 at 20+ at twenty-five miles." Andy wrote this down in big, jerky letters while Cappy said, "Roger, sir. Will report back upon our sightin', sir."

"That was jus' too many 'sirs' for me," Andy said. "You don't even know who he is."

"Well, old boy, tis the reason I'm the important one runnin' this station, and you're jus' a cog in the big wheel at me beckon command."

"Rubbish, stinking rubbish. How long ago were they sighted?"

"Fifteen minutes, so we best be on it." They had only another ten minutes or so, as twenty-five miles went fast at 200 miles per hour.

"Yeah, yeah," came the reply. Andy was now standing, his elbows on the sandbags, holding up a pair of high-powered binoculars. He turned to look at the pot.

Cappy scowled at him. "Ya gotta give it time, man."

Back to scanning the sky, Andy said, "Bit late for the Jerries, don't ya think? Wait."

"Got something?" Cappy said as he moved to the sextant, preparing to map out the details.

"I'm not sure," Andy said slowly, looking at the usual altitude. "Bet it's a false run just to …" Andy went silent. He raised his view higher in the sky and said, "Bloody hell at Christmas."

Their job was to identify the planes as friendly or hostile, estimate their altitude and direction, and provide a count. Andy saw a sight he'd never seen in the distance. He silently handed over the glasses, giving in to his more experienced partner. Cappy took the position, not seeing anything. He dropped the glasses down with a moan. He was surprised Andy was still at his shoulder, as the pot had reached a boil but was no longer on his mind.

"Look higher, man," Andy said impatiently.

Cappy retook the position. Starting again at the horizon, Cappy moved the glasses higher. He adjusted the focus, revealing more planes than he'd ever seen in a single formation. They were spread across the clear sky like black stars. "Mother of God," he said, wheeling around to a sextant-like device to calculate the direction and height. "Mark," he called out, and Andy studied the markings, listing them on the confirming side of the log. Cappy was now cranking on the phone to the filtering rooms at Bentley Priory.

"This is Birling Gap reporting," he said, haste in his voice. "We've hostiles 30+, I repeat 30+ bearing…," Cappy waited for the answer.

"127," Andy said.

"127," Cappy barked into the phone. He turned to Andy. "What's the height? Gimmie the altitude," he said nervously.

"Fifteen thousand," Andy said, having never seen his mate in such a state.

Cappy almost shouted into the telephone. "Bearing 127 at angels 15. Wait for update, do you copy?"

"Why only thirty?" Andy said.

Cappy hung up the phone and returned to the glasses. "Because," he said, "we need more time to count. Get the other glasses. We need to compare our count and phone in again."

***

Things were moving frantically as Cappy's sightings came into Bentley Priory in Stanmore. Additional reports from other spotting and radar stations were coming in. To combine and filter the information down to the most precise possible picture, the threat was assigned to the proper Group's headquarters, which had complete responsibility for oversight and defensive measures.

In this case, the call went out to 11 Fighter Group HQ, based in Hillingdon House at Uxbridge. 11 Group's assignment was to protect London from anything approaching from a south or southeasterly direction. Headquarters dictated to their seven Section Stations the number of planes to put into the air and at what coordinates. By this time, it was looking to be a significant attack.

11 Group Kenley Field was Edith's Section Station and was the only one located at Uxbridge. The other six were scattered within their sector. She was one of several WAAFs seated around the edge of the plotting table. They'd been waiting for action longer into the day than expected and were curious at the delay. Once it started, each plotter was assigned a hostile squadron, and her job was to track them on the plotting table. The controllers directing the attack and the senior officers at the upper level depended on the constantly updated plots on the table.

Edith was busy recounting her materials when she heard a slight gasp as her friend Roxanne finally noticed the ring on her finger.

"Oh, my God, lady," she said. Roxanne looked up at the smile on Edith's face. "Well, that certainly explains the unusually quiet manner attached to that silly arse grin on your face. Let me see that gorgeous hunk ah commitment."

Edith extended her hand. "We'll have to wait to resize it," she said.

Roxanne bent over and, with two hands, brought the ring up closer. "Well, aren't you just the cheeky one? Resized? Listen, lady, it could be square, and are you gonna give a damn? Is it that flyboy of yours?"

"Paddy," she said.

"Oh, no. We warned you, girl, in the strongest terms to protect your heart from those air jockeys." Roxanne moved closer, "But mostly, it's jealousy because we don't have one of our own." Roxy held up Edith's hand and said, "Lay-dees, looky here! Edith's gone and thrown her life away on a flyboy."

"No," said Clair, one of the other plotters. "Edith, you're the smart one, the pretty one; you have your choice of guys."

"Yeah," said another, "you can have a banker or anyone on the ground. Why did you settle for…"

"She didn't settle for nothing," Roxy interrupted. "She's in love, and that's a tad better than what any of us have goin.'"

"Can't argue with that," Clair said. "Congrats, Edith, we're all just jealous."

"Edith, come over here. Let me see."

Instead, Edith put her hand up to her headset as it crackled and looked around the table. The headset came to life with a voice assigning her Hostile G26, the code assigned to a specific group of British planes in a raiding formation. Edith was the senior plotter and was the first to receive any information. After a raid started, the rules dictated no talking except the minimum required to communicate with the controllers. Next to her, Roxy was also listening to the voice in her ear. She moved to her position on the table, and the action was underway. The plotting room came to life as if hit by lightning, with everyone now engaged. The Germans were very organized, creating patterns; everyone knew this wasn't a typical day's attack.

"G26 30+ angels 15, heading 127," the voice said. Edith selected the proper numbers and letters from a tray before her. She then slid them into groves on a triangular wooden block called a marker. 30+ was the number of enemy planes sighted heading on course 127; angels 15 was the altitude expressed in thousands of feet. On top, she placed a small flag showing the raid number and, with a long pole, pushed the marker into position per the grid coordinates. Next to it, she placed an arrow indicating the direction the raid was traveling. G26 would be traced and pursued as a target on its way in from France until it was heading back across the Channel.

"G26 update, now 40+ heading 135."

Edith pulled the marker back and noticed Roxy and Janet were doing the same with their groups. Edith changed the numbers and looked up. All the girls around the table exchanged glances, as they knew the average number in a hostile group was 15 or 20. Roxy started to update her G27 marker and hesitated. Roxy then gathered new numbers and changed them yet again. Edith and everyone else, including the controllers, noticed the 50+ on the marker when she pushed it out.

Edith also got the call to increase her heading to 50+. Since each group was a different group, she and Roxy were tracking more than 100 planes alone. The planes were all heading for London, right through her sector.

She looked up at her flight controller above. His face was long with concern as he stood to get a better look at the rest of the table. He glanced up at the tote board behind Edith, which provided the planes' status, from readiness to engagement with the enemy. The panel provided the officer with the number of British aircraft available and the field in which they were located. Another team of WAAFs kept the board up to date.

Edith could see the increased activity and hurried motions around the room. They'd practiced for this, and they were good at it.

The highly trained flight controllers were adept at matching British squadrons to every incoming group of hostile aircraft. Britain was the world leader in detecting, plotting, and vectoring defensive measures against an air attack. None of the other adversaries Germany faced possessed this skill. However, it was becoming evident that this day would be particularly challenging.

Park turned to Stephen next to him. "Winston would pick a day like this to come for a visit. 12 Group is reporting the same level of incoming hostiles. Their portion split off the main group and is making landfall now."

Park hung up the first phone. Into the other phone, he said, "Yes, thank you for holding. Can you tell me if there are any convoys scheduled through the channel? Yes, I will. Nothing for this afternoon? Thank you." Park rang off.

"It doesn't make bloody sense."

"Let me guess: no convoys, which is the usual reason for a large raid," Stephen said.

"Not until early morning, so that's not the reason for the increased activity. I think we better increase the squadrons on standby. Looks like a major run on the factories."

"Notify all fields. Put the first line on twenty-minute alert, engines running."

"Yes, sir," Stephen called the switchboard and issued the blanket message, which reached each dispersal shack in minutes.

The Headquarters phone rang. Park looked at Stephen, picking it up.

"Park here. Yes, sir, copy that. We'll get to it at once."

Stephen was waiting as Park paused for just a moment in thought. "12 Group reports they're targeting the airfields and not going inland as usual. They already have three fields out of action. Well, at least we know what they're after. Stephen, get the ready planes in the air. We will vector in flight," Park said. "And have each airfield sound an air alert: attack imminent. No, I'll do that; you tend to the planes."

Stephen was already on the phone with his controllers.

Park rang up the field manager's line. "This is Park," he hurriedly told the man who controlled all airfield operations. "Sound air alert: attack imminent. I repeat, they're targeting the airfields—end message."

The Headquarters phone rang again.

"Damn, don't they know we're a tad bit busy?" He picked it up mid-ring, "Park here. Yes, sir, we've given the alert. How many? Good God, right away."

Stephen stopped talking. He put his hand over the phone and gave Park a curious look. He had to wait but a second.

"Headquarters reports more formations fifty miles out, 100+." It was the number they used when there were too many to count.

"Tangmere and Biggin Hill are out, sir," Stephen said. "7 and 20 squadrons made it up at Tangmere and 260 at Biggin Hill, but 137 took it on the ground. Towers two and five are hit and out, making current reports sketchy."

At this point, no one fully understood the gravity of the situation, as everyone was executing specific individual duties associated with their sector. Soon over the Channel, a formation of more than a thousand fighters and medium bombers flew, occupying 800 square miles of space one and a half miles high.

Chapter Seventy Five

Birling Gap and Flight Control

Margaret heard it all unfold and was stunned. Thomas focused on every detail, saying to Margaret, "It's just the beginning."

Overhearing the comment, the prime minister looked at Thomas.

"Speaking of the war, Mr. Watson, what do you think of Hugh Dowding's little organization?" Churchill said, motioning toward the room below.

"It's well ahead of its time."

"An interesting description, I must say. Soon, we will see on what side of history you reside. As for myself, I came to see Dowding's system in action, resulting in our ability to get planes into the air to meet the raids."

"Prime Minister, if I may, this day will test Mr. Dowding's design to its limit and the resources it controls. I understand you're in no position to believe anything I have to say, but it's a fact that England barely survives this day."

"As you have imparted in no small measure in your most interesting manner." Churchill, holding his cigar, stared at this man who had no taste for the usual bounds of reality.

Thomas added, "Sir, it's not this wave that will be the problem."

The prime minister looked at Thomas in silence, approving his continuation despite his reluctance to verbalize it officially.

Thomas knew he was way out of line but didn't see another choice. "Sir, we, I mean you, need to order all inland reserves to start for the coast. They can't help now but can for the next wave."

"On its face,' Churchill replied, "authority is a wonderful tool in the right situation. It's useless when applied to these men, who understand what they're doing far better than I. Mr. Watson, you might not know our strategic objective is …"

"I know, sir. It's not our intent to defeat the Germans but to stay in the game. By default, it's a victory if we can't be beaten. However, right now, the Luftwaffe is assembling its entire force in the Western theatre. Gathering them into some order from the various bases took much longer than expected. It's the reason the attack is starting late into the day. It's a final attempt to destroy the airfields and bring us to our knees. It's vital they realize we can withstand the second and third waves."

"Third?"

"That's what I said. Wave two will come from Norway in the East and the third from France in the South. I'm sorry, but it's true. It all feeds into the cabinet meeting later tonight."

Churchill put his hand up to Thomas as he saw Major Dowding walk quickly into the room. "How does it look, Major?"

Dowding's color and rigid motions belied a man pressed on many fronts. However, composure wasn't something a British soldier misplaced; it was sewn into his being. In steady monotones, he said, "Prime Minister, it appears to be our largest engagement, with about a thousand hostiles at the moment. They're concentrating on the airfields and doing a bang-up job catching our planes on the ground during refueling. But our boys will give them bloody hell; we can count on that." He quickly glanced at Margaret, and before he could make amends, her smile eliminated the need.

"Do we have everything up?" Churchill asked.

"Yes, sir, the lot."

"Reserves?"

"The lot, sir. Every inland plane with a pilot is flying to the coast. Some will be engaging shortly."

"Well done, major. It's up to our boys then."

Churchill and Thomas exchanged looks. Neither had a comment clarifying or explaining what was occurring before them.

Chapter Seventy Six

Paddy Scrambles

Connor had just pulled open a drawer inside the dispersal shack to stow away extra stuff on the top of the desk. "What a mess," he thought. The watch before didn't clean up anything.

RING RING—RING RING.

The clamoring sound drove into his ears. Everyone within earshot of the shack tensed. Paddy opened his eyes and, from a fully inclined position in the upright chair, instinctively pulled his feet back underneath himself and pushed down on the arms to stand up.

Connor stuck his head out of the open window where everyone was sitting and yelled, "Two Section Scramble, vector airborne 100+." He then made his way to the large bell hanging just outside the door, where he made as much noise as possible.

"Let's go, lads—*now*," Paddy said. He looked for everyone in his squadron as they stood and bolted for the flight line. The flight crews using Coffman starters ignited the engines, coughing black smoke. Chief mechanics climbed out of the cockpits as the pilots approached in full stride.

"Devin!" Paddy yelled over the top of the Merlin's pounding noise and choking exhaust. The fresh pilot stopped and turned. Paddy took three running strides, closing the distance. "If you stick close to me, you'll be fine. If you don't, you're not coming back. Am I clear?"

"Yes, sir, I understand."

"Good luck."

Paddy stepped onto the wing and dropped into the seat on top of his parachute, putting his arms through the harness. He grabbed the chest strap of the chute harness, pulling it tight while scanning his gauges; oil pressure and petrol were all that mattered. He plugged in the radiotelephone connector and pulled down on his leather helmet. A thumbs-up amidst the din of the engine noise was the signal for the mechanic to close the side door with a bang no one could hear.

Paddy looked up from his cockpit at ten o'clock in the deafening roar unleashed by the mighty engines. There, the flight crew director held his arms out straight, staring at the boys under the plane, pulling the chocks away from the wheels. He waited until they were clear, then looked up and locked eyes with Paddy, signaling to increase engine speed by rotating his finger around in the air. Paddy gently shoved forward on the throttle, feeling the plane start to taxi. He listened to the mighty engine smooth out into the familiar harmonic sound of a finely tuned warrior ready to go to war.

The flight director dropped one arm, raising the other toward the taxi lane. Paddy saluted him as his other hand pushed harder on the throttle. Soon, he was rolling into position. Reaching back for the canopy, it rolled down its track and dropped into its final position. Paddy pulled back on the locking levers on both sides. He scanned the flight line to see if everyone in his squadron was in position.

Verey lights, shooting into the air from the control tower and dispersal hut, warned other planes that a squadron was scrambling. It was best not to be in the way.

A minute later, Paddy's Red squadron was dashing across the grass airfield, four abreast, increasing speed as they bounced along the uneven surface. Paddy pulled back on the stick, as did the others in unison, the nose of each plane rotating upwards toward the sky. The second, third, and fourth sections of his squadron followed. Each pilot threw the lever just in front of the throttle, causing first the right, then the left under-gear to raise, finishing flush with the underside of the wing. These ordinary people, who happened to know how to fly, climbed upward to meet the enemy. England hadn't yet but would soon fully appreciate their contribution to the future of their nation and the world.

The entire sequence occurred in less than three minutes.

Their course heading had them flying directly for the channel, although that wasn't necessarily their final bearing. Squadron and control designations changed once they were in the air to keep the Germans from obtaining the order of battle information by monitoring the voice traffic. Rabbit squadron today was Fox squadron the next.

"Top Hat control, this is Foxtrot leader," Paddy said. "Squadron airborne and awaiting vector information, over."

"Foxtrot leader, this is Top Hat control, Intercept 100+, angels 15, vector 135."

Paddy brought his plane to the new heading with every airplane in lockstep.

"Copy, Top Hat control, 127 angels 15."

Park was leaning on the desk before him, looking down at the room below. He turned and looked directly at Thomas. He took a few long strides toward his guests.

Churchill addressed him on approach. "Splendid job, Marshal Park. You and your group have indeed made us, yet again, proud."

"I'm not sure we can make any conclusions yet, Prime Minister, as there are indications it's not over."

Park looked at Thomas. "I heard what you said earlier about bringing up the inland reserves early in the fight. Dowding has indeed authorized the very unusual step, but it leads to an interesting question. Why would someone who I think is unfamiliar with even the basics of our system suggest such an unlikely and perhaps an even unknown option?"

Addressing Churchill next, he said, "Mind you, it's an issue of curiosity more than being a prime issue for treason." Park followed with a laugh that put light on the comment but didn't hide his inner concerns.

Thomas wasn't ready for the question.

Churchill responded, "Our dear friend, Mr. Watson, has a unique ability to foretell the future, a skill perfected while being a gypsy in a former existence. At least that's what he told me." Turning to Thomas, he said, "Unless you've another story today."

"No, sir," Thomas said. "I'll stick with that one, as it's the most believable." Thomas also followed with a laugh composed of nervousness and uncertainty.

"Good then, I wouldn't want my Margaret involved with any shady types. He looked at Park and said, "Does that do it then?"

After receiving the clear message to let it drop, Park replied, "Most certainly, Prime Minister. Is there anything we can get you?"

"There's nothing better that you could provide this citizen than what you and your people are demonstrating today. It's most impressive."

Stephen poked his head into the room, "Sir, HQ is reporting new formations and a probable new wave."

"Well, then," Park said, looking at Margaret. "I'm needed, but should you require anything, we can get right to it."

Churchill, always inclined to subtle observation, addressed Thomas, saying, "Another bit of evidence demonstrating the attention our Miss Margaret has over those who appreciate the … let's say …"

Thomas smiled. "The finer things crafted by our Creator?"

Margaret silently but theatrically crossed her arms. She then made a point of looking down at the Operations floor, ignoring them both.

"Well said, Mr. Watson. But if you've any further musings on the task below us, you offer them to me alone."

Sheepishly, Thomas said, "My apologies. My convictions blurted out the information before I prepared for the consequences."

Chapter Seventy Seven

Paddy in the Air

Paddy heard the voice in his headset. "Foxtrot leader, this is Top Hat control confirming your status vector to 135 at twenty miles, hold at angels 15."

"Roger, Top Hat control. This is Foxtrot leader, out," Paddy replied.

He then switched the frequency on his radio to talk directly to his group. "Foxtrot squadron, come to 135 on my turn." Sixteen planes all made their way to the spot in the sky, where dozens of people, in various ways, indicated that it was the best place for this squadron to inflict damage on the enemy. Paddy monitored the planes as they drew together in formation. Something was wrong,

Paddy spun his head from side to side, looking through the canopy. "Blue 4, Devin, where the hell are you?"

"Down on your six, just to your port side."

"Bring it in closer, man, so I can see you and stay there."

"Yes, sir, err, roger." The young Canadian pilot had had just 35 of the expected 100 training hours in a Spit, and it was his first time in combat. Paddy had taken him up, chased him around, and even fired at him a few times to scare the hell out of him. Three months ago, he'd left the family home on the sound in Vancouver, Canada, to much fanfare and, he had to admit, with a bit of swagger. Foolish swagger, he now knew, as he increased speed to close the gap as he was instructed. It was hard putting all the training to use, as it didn't prepare you for the deep fear that locked up your body and mind in combat. The apprehension interfered with maintaining group position, watching the airspeed, listening for instructions, and staying in formation. This was all to be done while scanning the sky, looking for a surprise ME 109 before he starts blasting away at your plane.

"Paulson, pull up; Devin, where are you?" Paddy sounded like an impatient mother trying to herd her ducklings across a busy path.

"Blue 4 in position. Out."

"Keep her steady and close, son."

Paddy was the Foxtrot Squadron flight leader and one of the four section leaders with four planes each. His was Blue section. He was Blue 1, and the pilot with the least experience was Blue 4. If they paired off, 1 would go with 4, and 2 would pair with 3.

They continued climbing to altitude, staying in formation. The flight controllers would provide additional changes to the vector headings if necessary. With Foxtrot and the raiding Germans heading toward one another, closing the gap didn't take long. The idea was to get to the contact point and be in the best position to execute an attack. That's why a speedy take-off was critical. Getting to the point of attack too late would put valuable assets in the open air, and a battle would be missed.

"Foxtrot leader to Top Hat control, approaching position. Over."

"Foxtrot leader, this is Top Hat control. They should be at angels 15 with 100+ to your Southwest. Can you see them?"

"Negative, Top Hat. Out." Paddy pressed the button to talk. "Keep a keen lookout, boys. We should be on top of them any second."

Moments later, Eric, the Red section flight leader, yelled, "I see them, 4:00 o'clock low. Henkel's without an escort. Bloody hell, there are a million of them."

"No escorts, hallelujah," someone said.

"Top Hat control, this is Foxtrot leader. We have bomber formation in sight."

"Roger, Foxtrot leader."

"This is Foxtrot leader to Red flight leader. Look for that escort. They're here; we just haven't seen them yet.

Paddy said to everyone in his group, "Everyone on me. We will execute a dive run through the bomber formation strafing as we pass through. After we break through, everyone banks to the West for another run. Just follow me. Everyone turn West in formation, or you'll end up alone."

Whether a bomber or fighter, it was almost suicide to be a straggler, losing the protection of your group. Staying with your formation was the best way to stay alive, even in a dogfight. A bomber with engine problems would fall behind and almost certainly be picked off.

"Foxtrot leader, this is Top Hat control. Look for fighter escort trailing main body at angels 14."

"This is Foxtrot leader. I see them. Out."

"The escort doesn't know we're here," Paddy thought.

"Red flight, this is Foxtrot leader. Climb to angels 17 and wait for the escort. That should put you coming down out of the sun."

Paddy said, "Roger that out."

Paddy said to his group, "Boys, change of plans. We are climbing to angles 17 before the strafing run.

On the ground, Park spoke without looking over. "Who's making first contact for us?"

Stephen looked down at the board. "Squadron 125, out of Kenley, sir," he said. "Call sign Foxtrot."

"Put it up on the speaker."

"Yes, sir," Stephen called the switchboard and gave the order.

The sector controllers talked directly to their flight leaders, and it came over the speakers. The control room could also hear the individual pilots, as once the battle commenced, they were all on the same open channel.

Edith never got used to it. It was Paddy's voice. And it wasn't the first time, as she'd heard him going into combat numerous times but could never speak of it. She had wanted to tell him last night, but it would have ended their romance with her being shot for treason.

The gunners in the German bombers had now located them in the sky and tried to fill all available space with as much metal as possible.

Paddy said, "Alright, boys commencing run. Stay tight."

They continued their run through the formation of bombers shooting at anything within their gunsights. Pulling up on the other side, they gathered into formation for another run and the inevitable retaliation of the bomber's close support. The ME 109s in the fighter escort wasted no time. The defenders close to the bombers were on them quickly. The tactic of having Red squadron occupy the higher trailing patrol did not work, as on contact, Red found themselves outnumbered three to one.

Paddy lowered his seat so the red dot on this gun sight was in the circle's center. The German escorts were now well inside the British formation, where individual battles were the order of business. Down and to his right, Paddy saw one ME make a pass at Devin, who was on his own. Paddy threw the stick forward and came in from behind. He lined up the sight.

"Blue 4, this is Blue leader. I'm behind you; pull up *now*."

Paddy saw Devin's plane pull up as Paddy's tracers passed underneath Devin's plane and tore into the rear of the German aircraft, missing Devin, who would have been directly in the line of fire. The bullets went through the fuselage and tail, tearing off the plane's elevators. A plane can fly with a lot of damage, but even the best pilot was helpless without being able to maintain level flight. The ME's nose went down, and Paddy saw the pilot release the canopy and jump over the side into the air. He would be picked up by British patrols and spend the rest of the war in a secret POW camp.

"Mayday, mayday. Red 1 to flight leader. Red 3 is hit and flipped over. I think he's out."

A tumbling speck in the sky fell unnoticed until it blossomed into a big white cloud, "Ferris is okay."

No time to think. A violent swerve to the left brought Paddy behind an ME. It started a circular chase, and he knew he would win if the German pilot stuck with it. The Spitfire could turn a tighter circle at maximum Gs, eventually bringing the enemy into his sights.

"Foxtrot leader, this is Top Hat control. New formation 30+ angels 16."

"Roger, Top Hat. We have a visual. Out."

Paddy's group fought through the escort, circled back to the West, and regrouped for the next run on the new enemy formation.

Minutes later, Paddy had his squadron in position, "Foxtrot to Top Hat control. Attacking now," Paddy said in a voice that didn't anticipate the mayhem that would follow.

The air war against a stronger foe continued. The squadrons attacked the formations on their way in and again on their way back to France. 12 Group met the enemy planes getting through to the southwest, and then the process started over. Only after the last threat was heading back was it time to determine if their airfield was in good enough condition to land.

"This is Foxtrot leader. Bang up job, boys. Let's break it off and refuel."

It wasn't going to be that easy. The Chain Home had already spotted another group forming over the French countryside. Momentarily, they'd split apart, starting for the channel, yet another wave in the first attack. It continued that way for most of the day in the most significant effort by the Germans to date.

"Foxtrot, this is Top Hat control. You're cleared to return to Kenley. Mind the restrictions."

The ground personnel had been busy surveying the landing areas and had placed orange indicators marking out the only straight path through the bomb craters wide enough for the returning planes to use. It wasn't great, but it allowed pilots to land back at their original field, where the crews assigned to each aircraft and pilot were stationed. The alternative was a patchwork of backups that worked but weren't anyone's first choice.

The battle dragged on as the sun started to fade. Some of the planes went up for the third time. The sheer number of hours in the air alone would warrant concern, but the real toll on the pilots was being in constant combat. A pilot performing at the top of his game for too long was a recipe for trouble.

Later in the day, a note containing the current numerical status of the battle reached Churchill.

"One hundred and eighty-three enemy planes downed, with our losses under forty," Churchill said. "So far, it's a more than a respectable day."

"Sir," Thomas said, "history will find those casualty numbers will be far different on both sides. It was a sterling effort, but it was serious enough to create tonight's meeting. Göring will also get incorrect information, which proves the British have far more planes than his sources were reporting. Two weeks ago, Göring informed his flight commanders the British had fewer than ninety fighters. To his annoyance, the number will become a point of humor, as his pilots will jokingly claim shooting down the same ninety fighters."

Before he could respond, Churchill received another note. He read it carefully. He gave Thomas a curious look and said, "Mr. Halifax is requesting a call to discuss a meeting to be held as soon as possible." Churchill called an aide and asked him to get Mr. Halifax on the phone. "Preferably that one," he said, pointing to one on the table just a few feet away.

"Yes, sir," the aid said.

In a voice fully recognizing the turn of events, the PM looked up at Thomas and said, "It appears, Mr. Watson, tomorrow's meeting is to be, as you indicated, this evening, after all."

Sensing the moment, Thomas replied quietly, "Apparently so, sir."

The prime minister directed his attention to the floor below and said, "Disturbing to the core is my growing comfort with your 'memories' of things to come that are proving critical but equally outside my control."

Within seconds, the phone rang. Popping back in, the aid looked at Churchill and pointed at the ringing telephone as Churchill said, "Thank you, young man." Churchill picked up the receiver and said, "Lord Halifax, I received your note."

Churchill noted the slight pause of his constant opponent as though he was gathering energy for a fight or trying to constrain an abundance of anger to avoid one. "Prime Minister, we have a set of circumstances requiring the attention of the war cabinet sooner than later. I'm requesting we meet this evening to address the faltering state of our defenses."

Churchill calmly said, "I would venture you're informally with a group of the war cabinet at this time?"

Halifax looked around the room and said, "Well, yes, I am."

"Trying to save the country, as we all are, I'm sure," Churchill said. "It would please me greatly if you could convince the members to meet here at Kenley as soon as the group can assemble. I'm sure we can secure the group conference room at Hillhouse. My duties should allow me to be there at 1800 hours. Bring your version of today's losses and the plan you wish fulfilled."

"Well, yes, I'll do my best, as they're still coming in. Winston, we need to face the escalating losses and our ability to mount a viable defense squarely."

The prime minister replied, "I assure you, all points that warrant consideration will be met head-on. I look forward to discussing our nation's proper posture as we move forward. You'll be there then?"

Of course, Thomas was delighted that the meeting would take place as he predicted. The more significant event was witnessing a master politician take the initiative entirely away from Halifax and make it his meeting, and Halifax knew it.

Halifax could barely get the words out. "Yes, Prime Minister, at 1800 hours."

Margaret looked at Thomas, but not for the reason he thought. She looked at him almost in wonder. "Thomas is right again," she thought, "proving that a normal life wasn't in the near future, if at all."

Thomas said, "Pardon if I'm out of line, but well done, sir, extremely well done."

"Mr. Watson, I've survived being shot at, being held prisoner, the Dardanelles fiasco, and, not the least, being married for forty-three years. I've acquired a few skills I deploy from time to time."

Margaret defensively said, "Winnie, being married hardly compares to the rigors of which you speak. I know that you and Aunt Clemmie are mad about each other."

"Of course, my dear, you're right," he nodded towards her with a smile.

"That's the meeting I was talking about," Thomas said. "It's somewhat gratifying that it will occur, proving that I'm not altogether crazy."

"True, Mr. Watson, but this particular meeting with Lord Halifax doesn't come as a complete surprise, as our paths have been on a trajectory to cross for some time, not regarding discussion of the day-to-day aspects of the war but regarding the much larger question of how I'm waging war. Tonight will no doubt include whether *I should* be waging war?"

Thomas nervously put his hands in his pockets. "It will be a moment far exceeding anything that those in attendance could conceive."

"Have you lost faith? If your version of history has any credence, we're facing a solved problem."

"If you can prevail," Thomas said.

"Given your track record, it would appear in some far corner of the universe; I already have."

Thomas wasn't ready for the man to grant him any credibility. Churchill still had his hand on the receiver, cradled on the phone. He picked it up and dialed. "Mr. Colville, there's to be a war cabinet meeting at Hillhouse. Please secure the use of a conference room for 1800 hours. In addition, I'll need you here as quickly as possible. Please bring any numbers that apply to today's attacks. Yes, that's correct. I'll see you then."

Meanwhile, as the meeting discussion occurred, Margaret listened to the radio speaker's portrayal of the ongoing battle. It was starting to bother her, but she didn't know why. She figured she didn't really want to participate in such detail.

She blurted out, "Thomas, can we turn the speaker off?"

"I'm not sure. I'll see."

Churchill put his hand up as Thomas started out of the room. "Now isn't the time to distract them due to our discomfort. We have boys in the air."

"Of course," Thomas said. "That should have been obvious."

Margaret said, "No, I'm sorry, that's not really the problem." Now standing, she leaned forward, bracing herself with her hands on the glass. She looked down at the room below, feeling something foreign and out of place. A chill ran through her body. She saw the supervisor walking around the table briskly, checking positions and talking to the plotters.

Thomas previously had second thoughts about Margaret as a bystander in the actual environment of a battle. Now, he was sure. "He shouldn't have exposed her to this much reality. However, it didn't change the necessity of his needing to be here, and she'd insisted on not letting him come alone.

He put a hand on her elbow to turn her around. It was stiff, and she didn't move. "I could take you out into the other room if you like," he said. She didn't move.

"Margaret, are you okay?" Thomas asked.

As if in slow motion, she looked directly at Thomas with an expression that wasn't hers. He'd never seen her face convey what it was expressing right now.

She said, "Thomas, I'm scared."

Chapter Seventy Eight

The War Goes On

Paddy's group had made it through the day, losing the one plane and Ferris for the afternoon. Ferris would be back tomorrow morning after being rescued. They were again up in the air, headed for another vector and another effort at defending the island.

Paddy peered through the front of the cockpit at the tiny bits of danger growing ever larger. His group again pulled off the strategic position. They were coming down on the bomber group in attack formation. Paddy looked for his target and a space between the German planes. Given his diving speed, he needed to know precisely his path through the formation before the strafing run.

Paddy's thumb moved to the firing button and pressed. He felt the vibration as a burst from the Browning machine gun erupted. The stream was purposely ahead of the target, and Paddy watched the bomber fly into the line of fire. It was always easier to shoot ahead of the target and let it fly into the deadly path than to try to hit it directly. A pilot needed to do this while considering the moving space that was his pass-through.

As planned, the shells ripped through the air and found their mark. The Henkel's wing first caught fire, then broke off entirely at the wing root. It made the bomber skew in the air like a paper plane. Paddy knew the remaining wing would put the aircraft into a tight spin, creating a force that would pin the crew against the insides of the plane, unable to escape. As always, he thought, "What a waste."

Once through the enemy formation, they veered to the East this time and reformed for another attack. Paddy refocused, swinging his head side to side, and found Devin to his rear on the right. He'd completed the run doing exactly what Paddy had done. They locked eyes.

Again, both pilots were heavy in their seats as they pulled up from the dive to engage as they came around. Paddy encountered a single 109 flying level. He figured it was another boy thrown into a cockpit without proper training. Any pilot with experience knew to never fly in a straight line while under attack. Paddy tried to overtake him, coming around. He knew staying the course would shortly put the plane within range.

"Blue 4, are you with me?"

Devin could smell something that wasn't normal. He looked down at his gauges. "Right here, Blue 1. I'm running hot."

"Stay here. It's almost over."

The 109 saw Paddy putting his plane in a tight turn, moving from Paddy's left to his right.

"Bank right," Paddy said. He felt an uneven force on the stick as it swung over to the stop, creating a tight turn. Paddy took short, quick breaths, tightening the muscles in his midsection. This drove the blood to his head that gravity was pulling away, avoiding a blackout. He fired just as the ME entered his gun sight. He knew he hit it but with no visible effect. "Lucky day for the rookie," he thought.

Both maneuvers caused him and Devin to lose altitude, and he had to return to the bombers. He could see them directly above as they were coming over land. Paddy deduced they were heading straight for Kenley Field. "This is Foxtrot leader. All planes break and head for the bombers. We need to break this up, lads, if we want a place to sit down."

"Foxtrot squadron, I repeat, all units make a run at the bombers."

Once they cleared the formation, they would be very close to the deck as they pulled out. "Blue 4, mind the pull-up or get wet."

"Blue 1," Devin shouted, "109 coming in high. Break left. I'm on him."

Dead ahead, Paddy saw the stream of tracers coming from the diving plane above. He calculated the distance to their impact and then desperately threw his aircraft to the left. The move would put him closer to the deck, increasing his vulnerability, which was why he had a wingman. Paddy kept his eye on the tracers. They were getting close. The plane wasn't responding, or he'd miscalculated. The stick was dead over, but it felt wrong. It needs to go further but stopped, not on the restraint but a few inches short. Paddy took his right hand off the throttle and hit the stick as hard as possible. He felt it break free, but it was too late. He was vertical in his turn, with one wing pointed up to the sky. In slow motion, he saw the holes appear at the tip of the wing as they marched right toward him.

Paddy felt the pressure of the impact and thought his eyes were open, but he wasn't sure. His smeared goggles made it dark. It got darker as the pain set in. He felt sluggish, which was never good in a dogfight. He needed to pull up but wasn't sure if he was upside down. He decided to pull up, and nothing moved. He tried to reach for the canopy, and searing pain through his chest and shoulders hindered any movement.

The pain was quickly replaced by the unfathomable emptiness of being alone as his mind realized he wasn't going home. "Bloody war," he thought, "took her away from me."

"Edith," he said.

"Blue 1, *BAIL! BAIL*! Paddy, get the hell out," Devin yelled. "Can you hear me? Pull the canopy *now*. Paddy! Paddy!"

In the cockpit of Blue 1, the headphones dutifully responded, delivering the message. However, a sound not heard is but vibrating air.

Edith looked at the speaker mounted high on the wall. She'd heard her name spoken into a hopeless void, but the speaker went silent for an eternity right after her name. Edith waited for the words that would define the rest of her life. The background static played the dirge feared by all, and then it came. Devins's young voice struggled, "Top hat control. "This is Blue 4." Then, in hushed, reverent tones, the voice said, "*No chute*. I repeat, *no chu…*" The last word was truncated, a victim of emotion.

"Blue 4, 109 behind you. Break left; break left."

From the speaker came a grunt as Blue 4 slammed the stick over, and gravity slammed him into the flight seat, dimming his sight and crushing his lungs. "Bloody hell," he thought. "Follow your training or die." His midsection went solid as he struggled to keep his head clear. Short breaths, he said to himself, short breaths.

The war went on.

Chapter Seventy Nine

Uxbridge—Plotting Area

Before Devin struggled to deliver the news about Paddy, Thomas had listened to the chatter over the speaker as the pilots' voices shouted positions and the leader's instructions. Back then, he'd marveled at how calm everyone was in the plotting area. Pushing their marks, the girls continued to keep track of the battle. It was almost surreal. Then Margaret stood up beside Thomas, looking very uncomfortable.

Then, they all heard the words "No chute" emanating from the tiny speaker in their area of the control booth. Thomas immediately saw the differing body language of the women in the room below. One woman leaned forward for support against the table, her head bowed.

Margaret silently reached out, grabbing a fistful of Thomas's coat.

The room below spoke volumes in its lack of movement. Thomas sensed something was very different with Margaret.

Deep inside, Margaret knew that something awful would unfold, and to see it come true shook her. It was like an emotional bomb had shaken the place, and time paused inside the room. Everyone's body language first shouted shock, then horror. Everyone within the confines focused on the woman leaning on the plotting table. Margaret could almost feel the woman's agony flow through her own body. She watched from above as the young woman tried to remain upright.

"*Thomas!*" Margaret said, but much louder than she had realized. Churchill's head snapped, surprised at the volume. Pointing down with a finger, she said, "That's her—she was the one in the restaurant last night. He proposed, remember?"

Thomas looked again and agreed. It wasn't as if they'd met, but it made the moment more personal. "I think you're right."

"I know I'm right," she said, turning and heading for the door.

"Where are you going?"

He'd said it, never expecting an answer.

She was gone.

Margaret flew down the stairs to the central corridor, running toward the entrance she'd seen coming in. The standing guard noticed the hurried pace, sensing something was unusual—but what kind of unusual? Was it something that needed his attention or someone in a hurry? She'd been upstairs with the prime minister, but he remembered the paperwork and knew she wasn't just an average observer. However, the Operations room *was* for authorized personnel only.

In two steps, Margaret burst through the room's door and collided with a WAAF officer leaving the room. The officer's face was pained and distant. Margaret grabbed the woman's shoulders, ensuring she hadn't knocked her off balance.

***

Edith Bristo hadn't heard the words from Devin as much as felt them hit her with brute force. It turned the anxiety and tension at listening to Paddy in combat into quiet incoherence. She felt her eyes drop from looking up at the speaker down to the plotting table. Instinctively, she reached onto the table to brace herself when her knees started giving. Her arms weren't strong enough. "Paddy," she thought.

"Edith," Roxy called out. She approached Edith and grabbed her at the waist, keeping her on her feet. Roxy looked to the floor supervisor. He nodded, and she walked Edith to one of the benches. Through the incoherence, Edith fell onto the bench and part of the wall simultaneously. She felt her body move oddly, but it seemed an outer experience. Edith leaned forward, grasping her head with her hands, her elbows on her knees. She tried to compose herself, but she didn't care.

Annette, the plotter closest to the supervisor, leaned over, saying, "Paddy asked her to marry him last night."

***

Lonnie wasn't sure what she was doing when she heard the words from the speaker. They made her heart disappear. She couldn't believe it. "Paddy," she'd said reverently through the fingers at her lips. "Paddy," she thought, the love of her life and center for so many years was gone. Her legs were weak. She moved both arms across her chest as if trying to hold the emotion inside. Hours appeared to pass; she realized she was breathing rapidly, still staring at the speaker.

Lonnie was on the other side of the room when she saw the woman almost collapse. She started over to help, but nothing moved. "Edith?" she thought. "Did they say, Edith?" The fleeting glint caught her eye ten feet away, and she instantly knew. It was on the woman's finger, half covered in cascading hair. Conflicted, Lonnie forced herself to take a step, finally covering the distance. She hesitantly placed her hand on the woman's shoulder and said, "Edith…" and stopped. Lonnie could see her fingers touching the dress's fabric, but they were devoid of sensation. All the old wonderful images and emotions flew through her mind instantly, flashes of events with Paddy that were once hers alone.

Lonnie almost silently said, "I'm so sorry," and she moved her hand up and away.

Lonnie knew Edith didn't know about her and Paddy. She remembered Paddy explaining at the field how much he loved this woman. It was deep and sincere, and it hurt. There were too many divided emotions. A gripping thought took her over: regardless of her sincere sympathy for Edith and the bond all women felt at this time—she didn't belong. Knowing she also couldn't maintain control, she wanted to avoid any misconceptions. She urgently needed to leave the room and quickly made her way to the exit, hoping all eyes were on Edith. Rushing, the closer she got to the door, the higher the feeling in her body. Her face was flushed; she needed to be strong, just another few feet.

Lonnie was looking at the floor when the two bodies collided. She felt off balance, and the woman grabbed her.

***

Margaret said, "I'm so sorry. Are you all right?"

The woman in the uniform she was holding didn't respond. The emotionless look on her face was disconcerting. Margaret looked toward Edith, sitting on the bench and back to the WAAF. Margaret was trying to decide what to do when a tall guard entered the room, appearing right next to them. Margaret was about to ask if he could help her when the guard wrapped his arm around the woman, holding her up. He looked at Margaret and nodded. With that, Margaret took off for the other side of the room.

***

The supervisor had been through it before. Why did this one appear different? "Bloody war," he muttered. "Who was that woman flying by?" he thought. She wasn't in uniform, and he didn't recognize her in a high-security area. He looked up at the room above and saw Winston Churchill standing and looking down.

He caught Parks' eye, who pointed and nodded his approval. The supervisor returned to the moment. He clapped his hands twice and almost yelled, "All right, people, we have planes in the air."

He put down the report he'd been carrying, picked up Edith's stick, and said, "Clair, cover Roxy's squadrons. Janet, fetch another plotter in here on the double."

The switchboard operator reached for a clipboard, plugged in a connection, and started dialing.

***

Margaret kneeled in front of Edith. "My name is Margaret, and I can help. What's your name?"

"Edith." She didn't look up.

"Edith, I was in the restaurant last night and saw you and Paddy having dinner. I know he was taken away, and it's such a tragedy. It was all too obvious he adored you, and I'm sorry I was watching, but I know he proposed. Edith, I know this is a tough time, but you must know that other people, like your family and friends, also adore you. This tragedy will never disappear, but knowing that he came into your life for however long made your life richer. Do you believe that?"

Edith looked up at Margaret through reddened eyes flooded with tears. She nodded.

"Your man will always love you from somewhere. I know that. You need to start supporting that love and see yourself through this, and I would like to help."

Edith was confused. Who was this person? Where was Roxy? She started to drift. In her mind, she saw Paddy underwater, separated from the plane, just suspended there.

Startled, she heard Margaret say, "Do you live alone?"

"Yes," she said, nodding her head.

"Well," Margaret said, "it's not my decision, but I think it's best you not be alone, and you certainly shouldn't stay here. If it's okay, I can arrange to take you to my house by car and driver. Is that all right? It's actually my mother's house. We will be there later, and we will take care of you. I think it's best right now unless you have other ideas or someone to call."

Edith didn't respond. Paddy was fading from view as the water grew darker.

"So, I'll call her with instructions to take you in and wait for me. Will you let me do that?"

"Yes, but why are you trying …?"

"It's okay. There doesn't have to be a reason."

Edith looked around and found Roxy, who understood Edith's confused and questioning look. She'd heard the whole conversation being only a few feet away. Roxy had seen Margaret standing beside

Churchill as the man put his arm around her. It's as good a personal reference as possible, and she said, "Go, Edith, she's right. You need to be with someone and not alone. It's okay." Roxy pointed up at the balcony. "She knows Churchill; I saw it."

Edith looked up at the balcony and saw the prime minister looking down. Their eyes connected as the prime minister stared down at Edith with concern. He said something to the man next to him.

Margaret turned to Edith. "I call him Uncle Winnie. He has known me since I was a child. That's my husband next to him. You'll be very safe."

"But I'm on duty," Edith said.

"Leave that to me; I can take care of that. Churchill bows to no man, but I can make him do almost anything within reason, and if it's not reasonable, I cry."

Edith looked at Margaret. She reached forward, putting her hand on Margaret's arm in gratitude.

"Besides," Margaret said, "we're going to be friends."

***

The remaining pilots in the air were thankful they'd made it through the last wave. They were equally grateful their only problem now was figuring out how to get back on the ground. Here and there, sometimes using questionable and dangerous creativity, they found places to land. A Hawker Hurricane landed in a mature cornfield, harvesting a swath wing-span wide until coming to a rest in an older field directly next to it. The pilot happily jumped off the wing to the ground when heat from the oil cooler started the dry harvested stalks on fire. In the end, the plane and the field were lost. The pilot helped the gathered farmers fight the fire, acquiring minor burns. He would be back in the air tomorrow.

Kenley Field was destroyed. One of the pilots ditched into the Channel and drifted to a stop right next to a Navy rescue ship. The plane sank, but the young, inexperienced pilot was very grateful to be feeling anything, including the terrible pain in his head from hitting the instrument panel. In addition to releasing the canopy, he'd undone his cockpit straps before exiting the plane if it flipped over. He thought it was a good idea at the time.

Someone pressed a gauze bandage on his head, saying, "Hold this, son."

Higher up, a more experienced pilot purposely turned his Spitfire upside down. He fell harmlessly out of the cockpit into a full chute just as his plane's engine sputtered and died over the channel.

Everywhere, smoke billowed from the airfields. Ground crews frantically tried to save anything useful while locating comrades and fighting fires. They tried to stay clear of the ordnance cooking off from burning planes, destroyed ammo dumps, and the arming carts on the tarmac. In all, six airfields suffered severe damage and required at least three days of repair before returning to active flight operations. An additional three airfields were lost for five days or more. Two satellite airfields would be serviceable by dawn.

***

Margaret had taken Edith off the floor and into a room. She called home and talked to Alistair, clarifying that she wanted Edith picked up and explaining all the details. Alistair could hear the personal nature of her concern.

Alaster, in the same tone he'd been using her entire life, assured Margaret that he would take care of everything.

Margaret said, "But we need a car here now, not one from the estate. How are you going to do that?"

"Margaret, I have remarkable security resources that are normally available for your security. I shall address this right away."

Together, Margaret and Edith slowly exited the control room and found Thomas descending the stairs from the VIP area.

Margaret told Thomas, "I'm taking her back to Mother's. Edith, this is my husband.

Holding a tissue at her nose, Edith said, "Thank you both."

As they ascended the stairs, Margaret turned to Edith. "You're going to my house where a man named Alistair will see to your every need. Don't be shy; you can ask for anything. My husband and I will be there later today. I'm very sorry we can't go with you now. There's something important that requires we stay a little longer."

They were now outside, and Margaret grabbed Edith's hands and said, "I trust Alistair with my life. I know this is all very quick, so I want to know if you feel comfortable."

Having gathered herself by this time, Edith was far from being blindly led. "Margaret, I'm deeply grateful, but why are you doing this?"

Margaret was still holding her hands. "Because I can, and if I can, I should. Besides, there was a connection at the restaurant, and sometimes things happen. It's like they come out of the air."

At that moment, a car pulled up with two men inside. Margaret was confused and a little wary. It was too quick, and she wasn't sure the car was for them. Margaret looked at the man exiting the passenger door. He reached into his inside coat pocket, ready to pull out his identification, but stopped when he saw Margaret.

Margaret's worries faded. "Mr. Handraddy, what're you doing here?"

"I'm under orders to escort an Edith Bristo back to the Hatcher Estate."

Edith noted the word Estate, which made Margaret's actions even more curious. "Why would she help me?" She thought.

Margaret asked Handraddy, "Why you?"

"Good question. Someone called someone, and here I am. It was flagged a priority and *way* above my pay grade."

"Edith, this man is a government officer or something. Anyway, I know him. I have to get back inside. There is a meeting I can't miss, and I can't go with you right now."

Edith hugged Margaret and said, "I can't thank you enough."

"Good. Now, remember, you have friends and family who love you."

Edith got into the back of the car. Handraddy closed the rear door behind her and said to Margaret, "Don't worry; we will get her there safely."

Margaret looked at Handraddy, saying, "I hope so, mister big time officer. I can be a handful when displeased."

With a smile, Mr. Handraddy, one of the prime minister's elite bodyguards, said, "Ma'am, of this, there's little doubt."

Chapter Eighty

Uxbridge—Flight Control

After caring for Edith, Margaret returned to the perch above the control room. They continued watching as the afternoon wore on. Churchill knew he had, for better or worse, witnessed firsthand the heaviest attack on his country and knew it was in grave danger. In his hand, unread, were the day's figures, handwritten on pieces of paper. He didn't need the details to know that his country faced a dire situation.

Security had already informed him that the cabinet group had arrived, so Halifax walking in the door wasn't a surprise. The surprise was that he was doing so here, in an energetic huff.

Halifax held up a neatly bound set of papers toward Churchill. "Are you aware of what has occurred today?"

Churchill looked at the bundle of handwritten notes in his lap and found the difference in presentation representative of the two men's differing approaches to life. Churchill was never one for structure. He was comfortable in a changing environment, utilizing his skill in connecting with people to forge a path. In contrast, his associate lived in a world dictated by the logic of numbers, with carefully thought-out paths and proper choices.

He looked up at Halifax and decided to start with a left jab. "Yes, I make every effort to keep up with the efforts of those who wish to destroy our little empire."

"Winston, this is no time for your rhetorical sarcasm."

It had worked. Halifax never acquired the skill of moving his overexposed jaw, leaving it vulnerable to those who wished to marginalize his considerable intellect and sully his usually impeccable manner.

"Truly, sir, it wasn't sarcasm," Churchill responded.

"Winston, the friction between you and me is of little consequence and furthest from my mind. We meet with great concern and fear for our people to discuss our options in ending this ill-fated carnage."

"Tell me, Mr. Halifax, do you mean the ill-fated condition of the Germans? Or of the men still fighting, defending so tenaciously what you find nearly gone? The invaders have also suffered, to an extent exceeding our loss of equipment. In history, an invincible force, even one given to overconfidence, must consider carefully its inability to be invincible. But I'll join you shortly, and we shall sort this out."

Halifax, beside himself, spat out, "Winston, there shall be no sorting if you see what's in plain sight. It should be obvious even to a child."

With a calm manner, the inverted equal of the energy before him, Churchill addressed the distressed man, saying, "I've been called worse."

Halifax huffed a curious sound and stormed out with a death grip on the folders, heading down the stairs and out to the conference room in the other building.

Thomas watched the exchange, fading away from the dialog to a specific notion that entered his mind. The idea brought together the combined and considerable weight of all the experiences within his memory. "Of course," he thought. For some reason, it now all made sense. He must tell the prime minister before he goes into the meeting. There would be no other chance.

"Sir, could I have a minute alone?"

"Son, I don't have a minute. I'm not a fighter pilot, but currently, I have a ME109 on my tail that wishes me harm. Besides, you had considerable latitude earlier today. I listened to your theory. What more could you add?"

With his cane in hand, he reached for his bowler and, before starting out of the room, turned to Park and said, "I couldn't be more impressed with what I've seen today, and I extend the gratitude of the English people. Mr. Park, dawn and dusk have an eerily familiar look about them, save for one is the absence of darkness, and the other the absence of light. Be there no mistake, Mr. Park, at this moment, what may appear to be darkness before us is most assuredly giving way to the ascending light of justice."

Park looked at the man before him. "Thank you," was all he could say.

Thomas turned to Margaret and said quietly, "We need to talk to him now, alone, before he steps into that conference room. It means everything. It's why we're here."

"We?" Margaret said.

"That's right. Exactly right. You're the reason I'm here today. I've always known England needed to avoid surrendering at this critical time, and Churchill argued to continue. What I didn't know was why, in the short term, he felt it was the correct choice. That's now very clear, and I need to tell him.

She looked into Thomas's eyes and saw power, confidence, and certainty. He wasn't searching for clarity as in many previous conversations. Without turning away from Thomas's face, she said, "I will take care of this. "Winnie?"

The man said, "Yes, my dear," pausing his exit from the room.

"Thomas needs to tell you something new before you go into the meeting. I know the pressure you're under, and I'm not sure I have the right to ask this, but you need to give him a minute before leaving?"

To Churchill, the tone was as unmistakable as it was wholly unrecognized. Gone was the little girl who had played the great man like a willing violin. Gone was the young woman who could coerce the smallest favor and generate the largest laugh with the twinkle of an eye.

He looked at Margaret with a respectful gaze. The young woman prone to defending contrary positions to prove a point was giving way to issues on a larger canvas.

"Please be brief," he said.

Thomas felt the moment's pressure and the disparate pieces coming together like a puzzle floating in the air. Could the following few seconds be the reason he'd mysteriously appeared? He was certain the moment was suspended in time, and Nature's laws dictated that the time would be brief.

"Sir, you're right about the Germans having also been damaged and having to reconsider their options. Upon the return of their planes, their combat assessment numbers, although inaccurate, will show they shot down more planes than they thought we had in our total inventory." Churchill kept to his word, letting him talk.

"After the first attack," Thomas continued, "Göring and Hitler were unaware of the extensive damage they've inflicted on our airfields and airplanes. The RAF is at its weakest point in the war, unable to defend against the planned second wave. However, instead of sending more resources to the airfields, Hitler, tired of weeks of Göring's promises of wiping the RAF from the sky, decided more robust measures were needed. He then makes the biggest blunder of the war. Still enraged from the bombing of Berlin, Hitler redirected all bombing from military targets to bombing civilians in London, hoping the extensive loss of life and property would destroy the people's will."

"I know this takes more than a leap of faith, as I'm unsure when he decides. It might be just hours after the last attack; I'm just not sure." Thomas took a breath that caused an unintended dramatic pause,

"However, I'm certain this is a pivotal point—beyond imagine, for the entire world."

Churchill's face tightened. "I'm saddened at the thought of civilians bearing yet a greater burden. However, if what you say is true, not bombing the airfields will provide time for the RAF to recover. It would take but a short time before they could regain decent strength.

"Yes, you have it," Thomas said. "Today, Hitler faces an irreversible situation and a fundamental equation. Hitler knew Göring had failed in his promise, and if he couldn't deliver a knockout blow today, he had to acknowledge it would not be better tomorrow.

Churchill fully understood how the pieces fit. "It's an amazing failure," he said, "as it could well cost Hitler the war."

"Sir, it *does* cost him the war, as the RAF repairs the damage, retakes to the air, and without the constant bombing of the airfields, can concentrate on protecting the people of London. The act preserves the platform for the final blow, the invasion of Europe. Something that would be impossible from the shores of America."

Winston idly tapped the brim of his hat against his thigh. "If that decision is made based on the results of today's damage, this information isn't yet compiled and is not known. We must conclude the decision has, in fact, not been made. Given simple logic, one must again ask how you could know this to be forthcoming?"

"That, sir, I can't explain."

"You mean you won't, again," Churchill said.

"No, sir, I can't. My best explanation is the information isn't mine; it belongs to history."

"I'm afraid, Mr. Watson, that history isn't the owner of anything but the keeper of the past and ..."

"...the steward of tomorrow," Thomas said.

The prime minister eyed the man before him. "Either way, young man, I must move those in attendance to persevere, for they're good men. Yet, to save King and country, they're determined to strike a deal with the devil at the expense of freedom."

"I can assure you," Thomas said, "God saves the King but employs your unique qualities to manage the mortals."

"Mr. Watson, I know you've been right more than wrong. However, I've decided quite recently to fight for continued resistance." The prime minister placed a hand on Thomas's shoulder. With the slightest smile, he said, "Although, I might now fight a little harder."

Margaret threw herself at Churchill, wrapping her arms around his neck and giving him a peck on the cheek. "Winnie, thank you. Thank you for listening because I'm certain that once you have all the information, you always make the right decision."

Churchill's mind took him back to when he was first sea lord, to a critical discussion with his closest friend and confidant. Now wrapped around him was little Margaret Hatcher, all grown up, having unknowingly quoted her own father.

Chapter Eighty One

Cabinet Meeting

***

The war cabinet members crowded into the conference room, each finding their place without a word. The Prime Minister began.

"Distinguished gentlemen, we face an issue of unprecedented gravity; never in the seventeen hundred years of the British Empire could it have been imagined to come upon us. In the coming days, perhaps even hours, our island nation and the Commonwealth shall reach a turning point, rearranging every path toward the future. It falls upon us gathered here—mortals all—to summon whatever Godlike strength we possess as we determine the destiny of our people.

"Today has proven especially costly in a war plagued by disastrous engagements, as the enemy has delivered a heavy blow. In his wisdom, Lord Halifax has called this meeting to evaluate the impact on our ability to protect our citizens. At the outset, allow me to state my position clearly. I firmly believe we must persevere."

Halifax abruptly straightened in his chair and, his voice sharp with urgency, interjected, "Prime Minister, considering today's losses and the disheartening reports of readiness, how can you adopt a positive stance? Under what scenario can you foresee a future for an independent British Empire other than by needlessly sacrificing her people?"

Halifax held up the same papers tightly bound before him. "A mere glance at today's reports compels us to pursue the most favorable peace terms possible if only to preserve our monarchy and civilization. In this weakened condition, England cannot repel an imminent invasion without catastrophic loss of life."

Churchill responded firmly, "I concede the validity of your grim accounting but disagree sharply with your drastic and irreversible solution."

Turning toward the assembled cabinet members, Churchill continued, "Gentlemen, regarding the points made by my esteemed colleague, permit me to offer a few observations of my own. Today, the

Luftwaffe suffered heavy losses comparable to, if not exceeding, our own. Though we cannot sustain such losses as readily as they might, the enemy remains unaware of our true defensive capabilities. They are, quite literally, in the dark.

"Furthermore, our armed forces have repeatedly shown an extraordinary ability to recover from seemingly hopeless situations. May I remind you that we have consistently frustrated German attempts to destroy the RAF, countering each of their strategies. I assure you, gentlemen, the mood in the Reichstag at this very moment is one of reconsideration. They will inevitably alter their approach—and when they do, we shall counter again."

"Counter?" Halifax nearly shouted. "Counter with what?"

Still standing, Churchill placed a clenched fist on his hip and leaned forward, pressing a single finger emphatically on the table. Looking directly into Halifax's eyes, he said, "We shall counter, my dear Lord Halifax, with the indomitable spirit of a free people who have endured hardships before and deserve another chance to defend their liberties. Liberties that have been their birthright, secured through sorrow and sacrifice by their ancestors across nearly every continent. Liberties, which they now defend as caretakers of their century, determined that their children might continue to call this island home and free. That, my dear sir, is the counterweight to the bleak assessment you have so eloquently presented.

"Lord Halifax had we accepted your figures at face value and followed logic alone, we would have ceased resisting at the fall of France or abandoned hope at Dunkirk. What explanation would we offer those young men who fell on foreign soil—that we bargained away the nation for which they made the ultimate sacrifice? At the very least, when we face the judgment of history, let us ensure our efforts match theirs. Let us show ourselves worthy of their sacrifice, that their mothers may hold their heads high, knowing their sons' bravery was avenged.

"That, gentlemen, is the right course—not the easy one, but unquestionably the right one."

Churchill paused, thinking of Thomas's claim of a change in Hitler's strategy. Instead of a blunt confrontation, which he was confident of winning, he decided to get the members to delay their vote for negotiations. With renewed intensity, he proceeded. "Shall we appease again before we even have absolute proof of Hitler's intentions? I say no! I say let Hitler make the next move. It is not our place to act prematurely, but his.

Churchill scanned the silent faces around the table. Fear was evident—the fear of choosing incorrectly, knowing each passing moment of the war could consign them to the wrong side of history. At its extreme, the choice was stark: risk everything for freedom at the possible cost of national ruin or accept survival beneath the subjugation of a ruthless regime.

Employing his unparalleled eloquence, Churchill intensified the moment. "Gentlemen, destiny stands at a crossroads, the past behind us, the future uncertain. The sands in the hourglass are now frozen, suspended between what was behind yesterday and what lies before tomorrow. In this singular moment, a handful of able souls may yet, by the grace of God, pen history in our favor." Raising his voice, he declared, "Do not dwell on the notion that people may perish—rather, consider in your hearts that freedom may die."

The war cabinet shifted uneasily. Halifax sensed the mood shifting, Churchill once again exercising his gift for saying precisely the right thing at precisely the right time. Resolutely, Halifax closed his portfolio sharply.

Recognizing his moment, Churchill placed both hands firmly on the tabletop, leaning forward toward the silent group. "Who among you will preserve freedom for your children's children, as our grandfathers secured liberty on distant shores for us today? Stand now and be counted." With masterful precision, Churchill had changed the conversation from whether to sue for peace to allowing the Germans to make their next decision. Churchill thought, "An idea that seemed the proper thing to do at the least appropriate moment. Who was this Thomas Watson?"

Increasing the tempo of his words, Churchill pressed on. "Who supports awaiting the enemy's next move, responding calmly and resolutely to the unfolding reality—a reality which may yet necessitate the course proposed by our distinguished Lord Halifax?"

Understanding the moment had passed, Halifax felt disappointment tempered by reluctant admiration for Churchill's tactical brilliance. Churchill had won the delay he sought without directly opposing a fellow cabinet member or entirely dismissing the opposition's viewpoint.

An eternity seemed to pass. Secretary Bragdon finally raised his hand, saying, "I favor waiting a short while—but no longer."

Bidden followed quickly, "As do I."

Another long silence ensued as no other cabinet member moved. Churchill's gaze settled on Shawston, whose position relied heavily upon Churchill's support. Finally, Shawston said, "I, too, am for waiting, as I can't go to the hospital and tell my son, who's alive and thus by proxy those who are not, we have surrendered without exhausting every possible angle."

That was four of seven, and a simple majority was the rule. Halifax sat back in his chair. Churchill could feel the silent conflict inside the man as the full-blooded aristocrat faced yet another defeat from the poorly educated son of a minor politician.

The prime minister turned to the War Cabinet Secretary, seated against the wall away from the table. "As prime minister and, as such, chairman of the War Cabinet, I formally request Mr. Collins to notarize the vote and draw up the minutes with the appropriate copies."

Mr. Collins schooled as an exacting solicitor, formally replied, "As per the vote herein, and directions of the prime minister of England, the preceding vote, authorizing an unspecified delay in peace negotiations with those that engage in war upon this nation, shall be entered into the record."

Churchill took in the moment from a mental space outside the room. He believed firmly in the course he proposed, but the conversations with Watson gave him the innermost confidence to argue against the logic of Halifax's case. If Watson were right, the next few hours would offer, in a complete parcel, a devastating day for the population and redemption for the nation.

Chapter Eighty Two

Turing Arrives

With the meeting still in progress, a spirited scene was evolving just outside the Cabinet room door, as Turing had arrived out of breath and in obvious stress.

"I have," he stopped to take a deeper breath, "just come from Bletchley, and thanks to Mr. Watson here, we've decoded a message almost as it arrived. It must be given to the prime minister immediately as the information isn't only timely but astronomic in its value."

Turing handed the note to Thomas. "It's all due to you, old man," Turing said with a smile.

Thomas read the note.

Turing continued, "We were able to reset the machine quickly with the new patch cords installed. By the time we converted the message to the ticker tape, we were ready to go. The old girl took barely twenty minutes to spit out the gold. This will change everything."

Turing was highly relieved at the result but equally concerned at the message. Thomas looked up from the note, also concerned.

Approaching the group, John Colville grabbed Thomas's note and said, "Give me that! This is a security breach, and I'll see you both to jail."

"Really," Turing said, pulling out his pipe. "How so, Mr. Colville? Without Watson here, there would be no message at all."

Thomas said, "Mr. Colville, you must interrupt the meeting without question. We must make sure Churchill is aware of all the facts. There's no other conceivable choice."

"I'll do no such thing and cause such a serious disruption. It's my job to make this call." Thrusting his arm outward and pointing directly down the hall, he shouted in a stage whisper, "Any more of this nonsense, and I'll have you both removed."

Thomas grew impatient, painfully aware that the meeting could conclude anytime. He wasn't sure why or how, but this was the moment it all came together. It was clear now the importance of witnessing the day's battle, the productive meeting with Turing that generated the message, and his eventual success talking to Churchill before the meeting. Up to now, it was confusion in his brain, unwanted thoughts, and un-remembered memories. The pain it had created for Margaret, let alone exposing her to danger.

Thomas's focus returned from a distance. Despite the current situation, he couldn't be positive about the meeting's outcome. With the war possibly hanging in the balance, Thomas said, "Colville, don't be a bloody fool. Rome is burning, and you're majoring in minor things. Read the bloody message, for Christ's sake. If you don't take it in, I will."

Colville looked down at the message, saying, "If you do, you won't see the morning."

Thomas reached for the note and, as Colville felt it starting to slip from his fingers, tightened his grip, then let it go. Colville was stunned.

Turing, a step behind Thomas, moved forward. "Or, Mr. Colville, I will."

Colville looked past Thomas and saw Turing moving forward, looking straight into his eyes, a sight he had never experienced.

"Jock, I mean it," Thomas said.

Turing said, "So do I."

Colville was startled at the unity. He noted the change of events in his mind since Watson had been lying on the floor next to his desk. He could call the security guards, causing a frantic reaction outside the door of a Cabinet meeting. He had the authority, but he would have to explain the consequences, which would all come down to the message's contents.

"Mr. Colville," Margaret's much-needed calming voice said, "I can hardly believe that a man of your experience and responsibility would put regulations over what's surely critical information. The type that, I might add, could very well change the decisions behind that door. We all feel strongly; you must present it before the vote."

"What vote?" Colville said.

"Halifax wants to sue for peace," Margaret said.

Thomas was surprised at her being so confident. He felt she'd never fully accepted the notion of his being here and his curious thoughts.

"That's it then," Colville thought. Whatever magical power little Miss Margaret had over the prime minister would be his protective cover. Without a word and almost relieved at his choice, he put his hand on the doorknob and slowly turned it while tapping ever so slightly on the door.

***

Inside the Cabinet room, with the vote finished, Churchill was still taking in the position he'd carved for himself, a path for which there was neither return nor one desired. At that moment, he heard a faint, reluctant tap on the door behind him.

The prime minister turned to the noise and saw an extended hand holding a note and half Colville's face obscured by the door. The man whispered his sincere apologies. As soon as Churchill grabbed the message, Colville disappeared.

Halifax's frustration had been looking for a target and found one.

"Good God, Prime Minister, it appears you're managing your staff with the same competence you employ running this war." He stood up theatrically, gathering his briefing material.

Colville looked at the group outside the door and said, "You, or we, could hang for this."

Thomas, now far more relaxed, offered, "Surely, given what's occurring behind those doors, you've completely missed the irony of that statement. Without that information and an invasion, we may hang anyway."

Churchill let the message fall to his side in the same manner he had when he received the message of the bombing in Amersham. It was again a stunning turn of events.

Churchill faced the group, holding up Colville's message. "Gentlemen, may I read you an intercept from Bletchley that has just arrived?"

Lord Halifax and his fellow cabinet members sat as Churchill read the words from the stock ticker strips pasted on the paper.

Führer Headquarters
17 September 1940

TOP SECRET

The Führer
OKW/WFSt/Op.No. 662552/43 g.K. Chefs

To Reich Marshal Goering,

Operation Sea Lion was scheduled to begin once we secured control of the airspace over the English Channel and the southern coast. This objective has not been achieved and does not appear imminent. Consequently, the invasion of Britain is postponed until after the conclusion of the Eastern campaign.

You are hereby ordered to immediately redirect all available forces under your command toward targeting the civilian population of England.

Adolf Hitler

Prime Minister Winston Churchill folded the note and placed it in his pocket. Gentlemen, history has ensured that our humble souls shall remain in her favor. With this order, Hitler has abandoned the invasion and will now focus on breaking the will of our people. I hardly need to remind you that the RAF will fully exploit the valuable and, in human terms, dearly bought time that has been granted to us.

A cabinet member removed his glasses and wiped them with his handkerchief. Halifax was still standing by his chair with his notebooks under his arm. Mr. Shawston held back a tear in the silence as the weight of the moment was indeed the same as the world.

Churchill was the first from the room. As the door closed, he could hear the voice of an agitated Halifax arguing about the message's veracity due to its suspiciously prompt decoding.

The prime minister addressed the group gathered just outside the door, locking eyes with Thomas. "The cabinet," Churchill said, "had voted to persevere just as the message arrived. Had they not, I'm sure the message would have changed their minds."

"It might be the message wasn't needed after all," Thomas said with a smile. "It would appear the result rested on a dominant figure with a particular set of skills laying out a plan for victory and skillfully selling it to those who had accepted defeat. It is, however, my opinion that throughout the war, your tenacious grip on the idea of victory virtually pulls it from the nether realm into existence. I believe they call this an important moment in history, certainly in the twentieth century."

"A moment—indeed," Churchill said. They looked at each other, having reached a mutual understanding. Churchill said, "We've much to discuss, Mr. Watson."

Margaret looked at the prime minister, addressing her Thomas with a smile.

"Mr. Watson, it has been a long day for all. I believe you need to take this precious lass home for some rest."

"I'm so very proud of you," Margaret said. She followed with "Prime Minister."

He continued, "Mr. Colville shall arrange a security detail to take you directly back to your mother's, where you'll be safe, as there are still a few things I need to be straightened out." Churchill was thinking of Petrie's report on the rogue Russian officer and Yuri's declining to come in for protection.

"Look, Muffy," Churchill called out; it had been his pet name for Margaret since she was a child.

"Oh, no," Margaret said at hearing the name. "There's never good to come of this."

"That's all the excitement I'll be allowing you today. Your safety is heavy on my mind."

Margaret wasn't convinced. "Is it my beauty sleep or my safety that concerns you? You can't have both."

He returned a stern "do as you're told" look and drifted off to look at the end of his cigar.

"I don't think a caravan is necessary," Watson said, "but I would appreciate you getting us back to your office, where my car can take us back."

"Why is it I've managed a great empire in times of war but can't control the two of you? No, straight back to safety, and Thomas, your car will be there shortly after you arrive. Now, off with you two."

Looking at Thomas, he said to his secretary, "Mr. Colville? Our Mr. Watson will call tomorrow morning for an appointment, as we've many things to discuss. Let's see if we can fit him in."

"Yes, sir," Colville said, thinking appointments were becoming a waste of time. Once formalized, they were now subject to anyone's whims.

Churchill then addressed Colville directly. "And knowing you struggled with the decision to interrupt the meeting, let me say you did the right thing going forward. It took a lot of internal fortitude to make the right decision, and that's why you're so valuable. Now, please take these two and get them home."

Margaret said with a smirk, "Mr. Colville, I believe all's well that ends well,"

"Yes, Miss Hatcher," he said through tense lips as he passed her. "Please follow me so we can get you going."

Margaret, very pleased with the situation, slapped Thomas on the back and pointed her nose in the air as she grabbed his arm.

Chapter Eighty Three

Pavel looking for Yuri

Pavel stood outside Yuri's flat on Leyton High Road and knocked.

Inside, Mrs. Somerville hoped it was Yuri for more reasons than she wanted to admit. She wearily approached the door.

Pavel knocked again. "Yuri, are you in there?"

From behind the door, she said, "Yuri isn't here. Who are you?"

Pavel wasn't expecting a woman's voice; it could only be one person. He replied, "Mrs. Somerville, my name is Pavel, and I'm a friend of Yuri. Do you know when he will be back?"

"No."

"Can I come in?"

"No, you may not. "

"Mrs. Somerville, I'm the only person in Yuri's life who knows about this place. It's his safe house. He has trusted me with a key. If I can prove it by opening the door, will you trust me?"

"No, but I guess you're coming in anyway."

The door opened cautiously.

"Thank you. Is he coming back here, or has he started to leave the country?"

Mrs. Somerville sensed the urgency in Pavel's voice. "I don't know anything, including when he will arrive. He told me to stay here because it was safe.

"He's right. I can't find him; this is the only place I know he would be. When he returns, could you tell him I was summoned to a meeting with the Embassy Director? I must inform Yuri that Moscow has discovered the plot orchestrated by Viktor's uncle. It appears that the orders Viktor was following originated from his uncle in a power play rather than from Moscow. Yuri doesn't need to leave the country; the Director wants to see him immediately to clarify this in person. Can you pass that along?"

"That's definitely good news. I'll inform him."

Pavel glanced at her. “You're his friend; he's mentioned you.”

Keeping her recent inner thoughts to herself, she said, “Well, I wouldn’t say that. We know each other, and he was protecting me from Viktor and his men.

Pavel smiled at a clarification that seemed important and replied, “Of course, that’s the Yuri, I know; I need to go now. Don't forget that the director wants to see him.”

Impatiently, Mrs. Somerville said, “You already mentioned that.”

Chapter Eighty Four

Going Home

The sun hung low as Margaret and Thomas drove through the town. Following the directions, the driver chose the most direct route back to the Hatcher Estate. They were far from the Uxbridge compound as they passed through a tranquil residential area—a small town, not on any target list, seemingly untouched by a world in turmoil. As shopkeepers pulled down shades and locked their doors, Margaret observed the almost complete absence of damage or evidence of war. It could have been a photograph taken at any time in the last fifty years.

From the backseat, Margaret noticed the large man in the passenger seat and concluded that all the men assigned to the security service were large. She also thought they needed bigger cars since he certainly looked uncomfortable.

Thomas reflected on the other problems he had caused, having achieved his primary objective at the Cabinet meeting. Viktor was out of the picture due to the bombing, but that Yuri person was still out there. Moreover, they needed to ensure Mrs. Somerville was somewhere safe until all this was resolved. He remembered Margaret's narrow escape in her house—their house.

During the contemplative silence, Thomas held Margaret's hand and said, "Thanks for your help back there with Uncle Winnie. It was really important."

"Of course, it was, although I didn't realize it at the time." Did you know all along?"

"Heavens no, but in the last two days, things have become clearer, and just before the meeting, everything came together. I understood why we're together and what was going to happen. I don't think I'll ever be able to explain it, and that's what he'll ask me tomorrow. Hopefully, it's not with a bunch of generals sitting around."

Margaret laughed. "Oh, Thomas, I can picture them now, harrumphing with nervous coughs, crossing and uncrossing their polished boots. God, that's going to be funny.

Thomas looked up. "While you were talking, I had a thought. Churchill could wave his wand, make me a state secret, and avoid dealing with me completely."

"You were thinking while I was talking?"

"Well, not really," he said. "The thought was riding on your words, which I wouldn't have had without your speaking."

"You're so full of nonsense; you're not sure of anything."

"No, that's not true. I am sure of one thing," Thomas replied.

"Penny, for your riding thoughts," she said with a big grin that barely fit on her face.

"That's easy." He squeezed her hand and said, "I love you. Please promise you'll never leave me."

"Oh, Thomas, you can be such a romantic, and girls eat it up, but I'm worried about you. Besides, given your unstable memory and the questionable knowledge that shouldn't exist, I'm not sure what promise I'm making. So the word never is a situation that really can't be..."

Thomas placed a hand on either side of her face, pulled her close, and kissed her until she started to push him away. With her mouth pressed against Thomas's lips, she mumbled, "Ahawwright," and pulled away. "This is the back seat of a car, and I'm not that kind of..."

Suddenly, Glass exploded into the car from the back window. Margaret felt the impact on her hair and face as Thomas violently grabbed her. A second explosion struck the driver's side and front windscreen. Thomas threw Margaret onto the floor between the seats, hearing her make a sound.

"Are you all right?" he asked.

"Yes," she replied. "Thomas, what's happening?"

"I don't know."

Thomas heard the driver react to the impact. The car veered sharply to the left with a violent jolt and crashed through a front display window, careening into a clothing shop on the corner. The vehicle came to a stop deep inside the shop, with more glass raining down onto the car's hood and embedding into the front grille, along with the display dress. As she lay on the floor, Margaret felt blood dripping from her head onto her hand.

The officer in the passenger seat shouted for them to stay down as he tried to open his door. Heaving his weight, he pushed aside a small display case wedged against the door. Drawing his weapon, he half-rolled out of the opening, staying low and close to the car. Thomas heard another series of shots, followed by the metallic sound of the officer's gun clattering to the shop floor. He could hear the officer cry out in pain.

Thomas opened the rear door, which partially shielded the officer. Holding it fully open with his right hand, Thomas reached down with his left to pull the officer closer to the car while trying to remain below window level.

"Thomas," Margaret yelled, reaching out to him from inside the car. Thomas tried to locate the shooter or shooters to determine where they could take cover. Another shot rang out, and he felt the impact against the door he was holding open. He looked out the rear window and saw two men crouched low, running up the opposite side of the street. Thomas reached over and grabbed the officer's gun. The driver was still below the seat, and the officer at his feet was in considerable pain. Thomas glanced at the weapon, recognizing it as a Walther PPK. "Light and small," he thought. "Exactly why the officers carry them." He looked around, listened, and evaluated his options.

Clearly outnumbered and recalling the incident in the park, he made a decision. He grasped Margaret's still-outstretched hand and said, "Stay right here. Don't run or move; do you hear me? I'm the one they want. I can lead them away from here. You call security on the car radio or phone when they follow me. Tell them to come quickly."

"No," Margaret replied.

Thomas pressed on, "When I lose them, I'll return here or call from somewhere to inform you of my location. It will be all right if you follow my instructions."

In forceful tones, Margaret looked up with her usual determined expression and said, "Thomas Watson, there's no way in bloody hell you're leaving me. We're staying together. You can't fight those men. You're a schoolteacher, a professor."

Thomas reached down. Margaret was dumbfounded as he gently placed his finger on her lips, making a hushing sound to signal her to be quiet. This was something only her father had ever done after hearing quite enough from his daughter. Until now, he had been the only one to dare to try.

"You're whip-smart, Hatcher. Now, be sensible. This is the only way." Thomas set the safety on the PPK and dropped the clip from the handgun into his hand. "Full," he thought. Eight are in the clip, and one is in the chamber if he remembers correctly. Seating the clip back in place, he heard its click. He turned the safety off and placed it in his outside coat pocket. He saw the stunned look on Margaret's face.

"Look, I know what I'm doing," Thomas said. "I can't explain now, but I'm sure it's the only way."

Another shot struck his door. "Look, everything will be fine. I'm not going to lose you after finally finding you." Then, smiling, he added,

"After all, I love you, and that's all we need." Along with her fear, Margaret was now confused. "Thomas was looking for me?" she thought.

A new car approached down the street, slowing and stopping right behind the crashed vehicle at the shop. Thomas bolted from behind the car door in the shop, past the new car, and toward the corner just twenty feet away.

Margaret saw four men running and yelling in what she believed to be Russian. She couldn't believe that Thomas was gone. She wiped the blood from her brow. Slowly, she gazed out the open rear window, now devoid of glass. Thomas was right; she felt helpless and hated it.

As he turned the corner, Thomas could feel the gun bounce against his side while he ran. He sprinted as fast as he could, knowing he would become a target the moment they rounded the corner.

As the driver in the new car saw the shooters run past, he glanced into the shop and noticed Margaret peering out from the back of the disabled vehicle.

He shouted, "I'm sure they're gone, but stay down," gesturing with his hand. Noticing the blood on her forehead, he quickly added, "Are you all right?"

Margaret Hatcher was rendered speechless as she recognized the man.

Standing in a sheltered entryway, Thomas waited for the men to turn the corner. He drew the gun from his jacket and remained poised. It took a second or two longer than he had expected, and for a moment, he wondered if they had stayed with Margaret. Eventually, a figure emerged, followed by another, and Thomas, lying in wait, aimed the gun upward and squeezed the trigger.

At the sound of the shot, the men vanished from view. Thomas set the safety. Aware that they were in pursuit, he sped off to the next corner. There were four of them, and one unmistakable authoritative voice yelled in Russian. Strangely, the leader wore several bandages and limped slightly as he attempted to run. Thomas thought he recognized the voice, but at that moment, it didn't matter who was pursuing him. Instinctively, he knew they couldn't take an accurate shot while running. The inevitable solution was that one would stop and take aim while the others continued the chase, rotating positions. Another peculiar detail emerged as the circumstances unfolded. He hoped the group chasing him wouldn't catch on.

Thomas understood that the pursuer was at a disadvantage in a chase like this. They had to advance defensively, cautious of potential hiding spots for the victim. Conversely, the pursued had the upper hand, focused solely on their destination. In this scenario, Thomas kept himself visible to divert them from Margaret. This tactic prevented him from increasing the distance, but he had no other option. The chase continued for several blocks into a residential area, and the exertion began to wear on him. As he turned onto another street, he realized that the tension in his chest would limit his air intake, prompting him to try to breathe deeply consciously.

Now a safe distance from Margaret, Thomas knew he had to change his tactics. He stopped behind a parked car on the street, reached into his pocket, and released the safety. Leaning on the bonnet, he placed his hand on the flat surface and gripped the gun handle. He aimed at the opposite corner, drew a long breath, and slowly exhaled. He shot at the first thing that appeared. One of the men grabbed his thigh and shouted while the others scrambled for cover. With that, Thomas dashed onto the street at the end of the alley. It was now three to one.

Thomas arrived at a row of shops. Several had received deliveries that were resting on the pavement. In front of one shop were large wooden crates, stacked one on top of another, roughly three feet square. They stood about six feet high, providing solid cover and an advantageous angle for firing. He quickly concluded it was the best spot for the next hit-and-run.

Thomas took cover behind the boxes. Hidden from view, he could hear the men turning and walking down the street to his right. Then, he caught more orders shouted from further up the street. In a gamble, they had split up and guessed correctly. There was no way he could have known; now, two were approaching from the left and one from the right. He couldn't move without revealing himself to three guns. Soon, they would begin the search. The options were few, and time was running out.

The Russian commanding officer shouted at one man, gesturing for him to come closer. In a moment of confusion, Thomas recognized the distinctive sound of Viktor's voice, and his heart sank. Viktor wasn't dead.

Thomas thought, "If the Russians want me out of the way, getting me out of the country would be impossible. This meant they would have to kill him.

Leaning against the crates, he crouched low. The shop behind him had three large glass windows. He realized his reflection in the glass could reveal his location, worsening a bad situation, but it would have to suffice for now since he was stuck with his decision.

The shooters were converging on his position, which, in a way, was a welcome sight. It meant, hopefully, that Margaret was safe. He looked at the gun in his hand, knowing it was useless; he could only shoot one or two before the third person reacted. He thought of Margaret and how he would die without seeing her again, and his heart dropped at the thought. He'd promised to meet her later, but he knew things were about to end. What was clear was that dying wasn't as important as losing the love of his life.

Thomas shifted slightly, trying to stay out of direct sight of the three men, but it was increasingly difficult.

He heard Viktor shout, "Find him, you fools. He must be nearby and hiding." Thomas moved again, and Viktor pointed, yelling, "He's behind those boxes!" he exclaimed, gesturing. "Don't shoot. He's mine."

Viktor was now only fifty feet away, recklessly driven by adrenaline coursing through him, his shirt stained with blood and his head wrapped in a bandage. Thomas saw Viktor approach, his face flushed and breathing heavily. Now, just twenty feet away, Viktor pulled the trigger, and Thomas heard the sound of glass shattering behind him. This was followed by another shot, and Thomas was certain he was dealing with seconds until it was over.

He tensed- and nothing. No pain. He waited for a moment, and as he looked around the box, a stunned Thomas saw Viktor's knees buckle. Viktor's gun hand went limp, dropping the pistol, while his other hand clutched the sacred spot above his heart. He fell heavily to the ground, burdened by the weight of his dark past.

The other Russian officers witnessed Viktor fall. Rushing over, one of the officers nervously looked down at Viktor, who lay in the street, moments away from death.

He told the other officer, "Viktor was a fool fixated on death and finally succeeded. That doesn't mean we have to die here."

The sounds of sirens grew closer, and a patrol car appeared up the street.

The officer stated, "We have to get out of here now. We can still follow Moscow's orders, but this situation has become too dangerous."

The other officer replied, "You're right. Let's get out of here."

Lying face down on the street, Viktor knew the direction of the shot. He managed to lift his head and locked eyes with the shooter, realizing the flaw in his plans.

Behind a small mountain of burned and broken debris in the street, Yuri Ivanovich Stakova peered over the barrel of Pavel's pistol, looking into the soul of a man who had played the game and lost. For a brief second, as time slowed before the moment of death, Viktor would realize who had brought him to his end. Viktor struggled to maintain his hate-filled glare for as long as possible. It was the final flicker that illuminated his mind; the gradual lowering of his head marked the drifting away of his life. Battling to the very end, Viktor's face finally met the paving stones, and his body went limp.

Yuri exhaled, saying, "Grant to no one but what you wish." He saw Viktor's officers fleeing. He didn't recognize them, but that wasn't surprising. He had patiently followed Margaret and Thomas, knowing Viktor wouldn't be far behind and would eventually make his move against Watson. Yuri had fulfilled his promise to ensure the couple's safety by protecting himself. That was what a professional would do. Unfortunately, Thomas and Margaret would spend the rest of their lives believing he was the enemy. With a half-smile, Yuri thought of the irony.

For a brief moment, he considered running to check on Thomas, but local officials were getting out of their car. Now, Yuri faced his own set of problems. If arrested, the local officials could notify Moscow, and he would be a dead man. It was time to set his escape plan in motion. A private plane would meet him at an airfield and take him far over the Atlantic to Portugal. He would then transfer to a commercial flight to Morocco, where a neutral freighter would transport him to a safe destination for the remainder of the war. "American food," he curled his lip in a snobbish flair, objecting to the two words being used together. Yuri had made many contacts during his long career and had called in favors. The United States was warm and out of harm's way, but it wouldn't erase the unusual story he would leave behind. The very curious Thomas Watson would haunt his thoughts for a long time.

Before leaving the country, one final loose end needed to be tied up. He had promised Mrs. Somerville that he would return to check on her. After that, he would collect his bags and conclude his career on a positive note. Yuri turned and swiftly made his way up the street to his car.

***

Thomas stood cautiously, peering over the boxes in the direction of the gunshot. He spotted a large man moving quickly down the street. The slight limp gave him away. He was certain it was Yuri, and a wave of confusion came with that recognition. It made no sense; Yuri had saved his life. This was undoubtedly the last thing Thomas would have expected.

Thomas noticed officers approaching Viktor, who was on the ground. After evading Viktor's attempts to kill him, Thomas understood that his priority was to return to Margaret. A few blocks later, he turned the corner and, amidst the chaos, discovered Margaret sitting on a chair in the street, surrounded by police and pressing a bandage to her head.

"Thomas," she shouted, jumping from the chair, pushing aside a warden, and sprinting toward his open arms.

"Oh, thank you for coming back," she said, kissing him repeatedly.

He held her close, examining her forehead. "Are you all right?"

"I am now," she replied. "Don't you ever do that again? Your disappearing is a rather sensitive issue for me."

Thomas glanced over as ambulance attendants lifted the officer he had pulled to safety. His right shoulder was bandaged, and he had a severe leg wound. The driver was already inside.

Thomas said, "That looks bad. How is the driver?"

Margaret replied, "He has a minor injury to the top of his shoulder. Both of them are going to the hospital."

"We need to find out which hospital they are going to. We should visit them; it's the least we can do."

Just then, they heard someone shout, "Watson?"

They both turned to see Officer Handraddy getting out of a car. "Are you two all right?" he asked.

Thomas replied, "Yes, but we're responsible for the injuries to two of your men."

Handraddy's anguish was evident as he passed them. He exchanged glances with the driver inside the ambulance and placed a concerned hand on his unconscious officer while the attendants slid him into the vehicle. Handraddy spoke to the attendant and then returned to Margaret and Thomas. Thomas, still holding Margaret, said, "Four men were trying to kill me, and two got away. One of them had me dead to rights, and someone shot him before he could put a bullet in me."

He turned to Margaret. "I'm not sure, but I think Yuri saved my life."

Margaret replied, "It had to be him since he was following us. After the crash, he drove by and asked if I was all right. Seeing him was shocking."

Thomas knew it wasn't a coincidence. He thought, "Why would he do that? There has to be a reason."

Handraddy declared, "I'm personally taking both of you back to the Hatcher estate." He addressed the men who had arrived with him, instructing, "Load up. We're off."

Thomas observed two cars and six officers getting into the vehicles. Handraddy held the rear door open for them to enter, fully in professional mode.

Chapter Eighty Five

Leyton High Road

An hour later, Yuri, once again reminded of his advancing years, ascended the back stairs to the flat and knocked firmly on the door. “Mrs. Somerville, open the door. It’s Yuri.”

Inside, he heard Somerville’s voice call out, "This place is a bit too busy for a secret hideout. What’s the password?"

Yuri chuckled, “You don’t recognize my voice, then?”

Somerville indeed recognized his voice and the unexpected emotion it created. She felt it all a little confusing.

She said, "What's the password? Stick to the rules," she replied.

“Princess. Now, will you let me in?”

Beth swung open the door, a sly grin tugging at her lips. “I have to say it’s nice to see you in one piece. Come in. We’ve got reason to celebrate."

"Celebrate what?" he asked, brow furrowed.

"Your freedom, of course. Moscow never wanted you dead, so it seems you're useful to me now."

“What do you mean?”

"Well, your friend Pavel came by with a message from the embassy. It turns out that Moscow never ordered that Viktor bloke to take you out. He was acting alone, with his uncle, or something dodgy like that. Anyway, the director at the embassy wants to see you. Official-like, it seems, to let you know himself."

“Pavel’s message sounds awfully vague, and what do you mean of use to you now?”

She ignored his second question and said, "Vague or not, you were going to have to leave the country, and now you’re not. Is that clear enough for you? A tiny part of me is pleased for both you and…"

Yuri raised an eyebrow. “And…?”

Somerville ignored him again. She handed him a glass. "Here. Have a drink."

“What’s this?”

"It's a wine glass. Don't they have them in Russia?"

She turned back, grabbed a bottle, and poured champagne into his glass. "Lucky for us, I have a few connections in the underworld. Champagne is practically impossible to come by these days. I had to be clever to get my hands on it.

Yuri sniffed the air. "Are you cooking?"

"Yes, I did fetch a few things for dinner. Do you mind? You were no help; I only found a bottle of vodka in your cupboards. Now that you're here, I need to heat it all."

"You made dinner?"

Mrs. Somerville gave him a warm smile. The meal seemed to be having the desired effect. She clinked her glass against his. "Don't get used to it, darling."

Yuri chuckled to himself. Once, he wondered if their connection could have grown into something deeper, but his decision to leave the country had closed that door. Yet, amid the chaos surrounding them, she had made him dinner—a simple yet comforting gesture. It unexpectedly opened a window for him to pause, reflect, and reconsider what the future might hold.

Chapter Eighty Six

Hatcher Estate

The drive back to the estate was a welcomed relief—quiet and uneventful, just the kind of peace they had been yearning for. Handraddy was in the car ahead. Long stretches of road unfurled before them, with only the steady passage of memories to break the silence—faint yet sharp reminders of all they had endured.

Thomas glanced at Margaret, her gaze lost in the blur outside the window. That look was all too familiar. It reflected the weariness of someone worn down to the bone, her spirit frayed by the constant strain of the past few days.

After a long silence, Thomas finally spoke, his tone gentle and somewhat hesitant. "When we arrive at your mother's, I suppose we'll have a chance to gather our thoughts. Maybe, just for a little while, we can pretend the war isn't waiting at our doorstep.

Margaret turned her head slowly, her sigh barely audible. "Thomas, the war isn't something we can simply wish away. It has planted itself squarely in front of us, whether we like it or not. True, we've fared better than many—our home is still standing, at least—but it's been one thing after another since you came into my life."

Thomas raised an eyebrow, sensing the awkwardness creep into his words. "Do you regret my being in your life?"

Her gaze softened, and she shook her head with a fond smile. "Of course not, you daft fool. I'm referring to all the scrapes we seem to get into, time after time. And now, thoughts of the future... well, they've begun to haunt me. What does it all mean? What happens next? I'll tell you, right now, I'm imagining a quiet life somewhere up north—Carlisle, maybe—teaching the little ones."

Thomas pondered quietly before replying, "We could certainly do that. I believe we've done our part. Bletchley's efforts are making a tangible difference and will continue to shape the war's course. And don't forget—we were at one of the most crucial meetings of this entire affair."

Margaret raised an eyebrow, unconvinced. "And what good did that do?"

"Well," Thomas said, his voice thoughtful, "I'm not entirely sure. As Churchill remarked, he had made up his mind already. But I suppose, if anything, my words gave him a nudge—encouraged him to push a bit harder. Turing's message, too, arrived at just the right moment. At the very least, the Prime Minister must reconsider how best to utilize me in this fight. It's not a matter of little consequence."

Margaret sighed again, but it was softer now as she turned her eyes to his with an earnestness that made Thomas feel a little lighter. "Those things do matter, no question about it. But Thomas, you matter more. It's all happened in what feels like the blink of an eye. One moment, I was dealing with a complete idiot and the next... I've fallen for you—the truest love of my life." She chuckled softly, then added, "Well, so far, anyway."

"Planning to find someone else, then?"

Margaret grinned, her eyes sparkling. "Oh, good heavens, no! But who knows, you might vanish into some broom closet and never be seen again. I'm simply keeping my options open, my dear."

Thomas laughed warmly, the sound easing the tension between them. "I can't say I blame you, love. Not after everything."

Soon enough, the Hatcher Estate loomed once more on the horizon, grand as ever—too grand, really, for Thomas to feel entirely at ease. No matter how often he saw the place, its imposing presence always seemed just a touch too magnificent for reality.

As the motorcar rolled to a gentle stop at the imposing front doors, he heard Margaret murmur, "Oh my."

"What is it?" Thomas asked, glancing toward her.

She pointed. "It's Mother and Edith—at the top of the steps. The front gate must have sent word ahead."

"She is greeting her daughter," Thomas remarked. "Is that so unusual?" However, as he spoke, he remembered their initial visit when it had seemed she needed an appointment to visit the house where she had grown up.

"Yes," was her brief response." Well then, when was the last time she greeted you outside?" he asked with a teasing lift of his brow.

Margaret placed a hand gently on his knee. "Before the pyramids were built, darling."

That drew a deep, genuine laugh from Thomas, rumbling up from his chest.

The door creaked open, and Handraddy stepped aside smartly to allow them to exit the vehicle.

On the driveway, Thomas turned to him. "We truly can't thank you enough. What was the name of the officer who was badly injured?"

"Anderson," said Handraddy with crisp efficiency.

"Could you call and tell us where he was taken—what hospital?"

"Certainly. I shall see to it at once. For now, I'll take my leave."

But Margaret interjected, her voice warm. "Officer Handraddy, after everything that has happened over the past twenty-four hours, I dare say you've almost become part of the family. I'll take full credit for nudging you from the ranks of 'highly trained officer of mayhem' to—well, still the same, but with a softer heart."

Handraddy offered a rare smile, nodding in response. "Indeed. If such a transformation has occurred, let's hope it remains a family secret—wouldn't want to damage my reputation."

Thomas gave him a firm handshake, and Margaret was already halfway up the steps.

Her mother greeted her with open arms. "Welcome home, darling. I've heard about everything you've been through. Thank heaven you're safe, and that terrible ordeal is behind you."

Thomas watched the reunion quietly, his heart full. So many miles had been traveled to bring them to this moment.

"Edith, how are you, dearest?" Margaret asked, wrapping her in an embrace.

"Oh, all things considered, I couldn't be better," Edith replied cheerfully. "Everyone's been incredibly kind. I'll never be able to thank you enough—but I must apologize as I must leave. I left a number and work calls. War waits for no one, you know."

Margaret said, "You'll stay in touch, won't you? Let's have lunch soon—when you're able. "

"I'd like that," Edith replied with a warm smile.

Just then, a vehicle pulled up. She glanced back. "I believe that's me." With that, she descended the steps toward the waiting car. After one last wave, she entered the vehicle.

Later, they sat in the comfort of the family room in the hush that followed excitement. Margaret spoke first. "We should take some time to regain our footing and ease back into normal life."

"That sounds wonderful, my dear," her mother said softly. "I do hope there'll be more visits. I'd like that very much."

"So would I," Margaret replied. "Now, is there anything to eat? I'm absolutely famished."

"Of course, dear."

At that moment, Marion appeared silently at the door, standing dutifully until Lady Hatcher nodded in acknowledgment.

"Yes, Marion? As you can see, this is a rather significant reunion with my daughter. What is it?"

"Ma'am, I apologize for the interruption, but there's a call for Mr. Watson. It's Mr. Churchill. He claims it's urgent."

Thomas glanced at both Margaret and her mother. With an air of inevitability, he rose from the couch and headed to the hall. The phone rested on a table, and he picked up the receiver.

"Thomas here. Can I help you, sir?"

"Definitely, you can continue to help me win the war. But first, are you and Margaret safe?"

"We are both fine, thank you for asking."

Churchill replied, "Good. Then I'll get right to it. I'm sure you hoped things would settle down, but I have an urgent matter that cannot be discussed over the phone. I need you in London as soon as possible. Can you do this?"

Thomas took a deep breath, overhearing Margaret and her mother continue talking. He knew this news would not be well received by Margaret. Nonetheless, he replied, "Yes, sir, I'm at your service and will be there as soon as possible."

THE END

"The farther backward you can look,
The farther forward you're likely to see."
– Sir Winston Churchill

I live with my family in the Bay Area in Northern California, and writing came to me late in life. It's now something I look forward to doing every day. The comments I receive make it a labor of love. I would be very interested in what you think of this story, and thank you for supporting my writing. You can find more information on my other books and a contact form on my website.

FOLLOW THIS LINK TO MY WEBSITE

https://richardDtaylor.com

Sign up for my newsletter for news and upcoming release dates on my upcoming books.

FOLLOW THIS LINK TO SUBSCRIBE.

https://landing.mailerlite.com/webforms/landing/n0o5d3

Please let your friends know and consider writing an online review or star rating if you enjoyed reading this book. Writers live by reviews as they help us evaluate the writing from the readers' comments, and we get to see what you enjoyed in the story. The market for books is very competitive, so the opinions shared by people are very important. If you would like to write a review or leave a rating, you can select the link below, and it'll take you directly to Amazon and a review form for this book.

FOLLOW THIS LINK TO SUBMIT A RATING

https://www.amazon.com/review/createreview?&asin=%20B09C3ZWNQN

AUTHOR'S NOTE: I sincerely welcome any comments regarding the historical accuracy or the misuse of American and British words, references, or phrases. Thank you and contact me here:

richardDtaylor@gmail.com

Join Margaret and Thomas on their London adventures in the next book, featuring the beloved characters you've come to enjoy.

TARGET LONDON

A New German Secret Weapon
A High Stakes Battle For Survival

In the WWII sequel to *Behind Yesterday*, Thomas Watson, gifted with a unique ability to recall the future, uncovers the existence of a new German secret weapon. This advanced technology drastically increases the accuracy of the already devastating German bombing campaign.

Winston Churchill tasks Watson and a team of top scientists with developing a countermeasure to protect the sole factory producing Spitfires and prevent catastrophic damage to London. The mission, set against an impossible timeline, involves some of the brightest minds in the empire. Failure to succeed would grant the Germans air superiority and lead to Hitler's immediate invasion of England.

This story is a must-read if you enjoy plot twists, suspense, and mystery!

Link to
TARGET LONDON
On Amazon

https://www.amazon.com/dp/B0C2B37RQ3

COMPANION PIECE

Additional information for the book Behind Yesterday

While reading historical novels, I've often felt frustrated by the challenge of distinguishing between historical facts and fictional elements. For readers who value this distinction, I would like to clarify these points. All dialogue in this story, including Churchill's, remains true to the characters but is entirely fictional. Writing any historical novel requires extensive research; often, there is more to the story than what appears in the book. I've compiled additional information to enhance your understanding of the narrative.

Key Events and Places
This section hopes to clarify the historical points for individuals who will find the difference important.

Fictional Story Characters
Personal comments on the characters in the story.

Historical characters
Some information on the characters from history.

Additional Information
This section provides more in-depth research information and descriptions of items relevant to the story and period.

Chapter Comments
This section discusses information pertinent to specific chapters.

Key Events and Places

The historical sections of the book highlight several key events from the Battle of Britain, which serve as the foundation for the story. These events illustrate England's genuine and precarious challenges during that period. While timelines and sequences have been adjusted for narrative purposes, the following is a list of the critical events featured in the book.

Cabinet meeting: Many view Churchill's persuasive argument during a cabinet meeting after he became prime minister as a critical moment in the war. At that time, most cabinet members neither trusted nor personally liked Churchill, and they confronted dire threats to their nation's survival. Among these threats was the looming crisis of the British Expeditionary Force being pushed out of France and off the continent.

Churchill convinced the cabinet to abandon the idea of suing for peace and instead uphold Chamberlain's declaration of war. Just hours after the meeting and vote, Germany invaded the Netherlands and Belgium, and France fell shortly thereafter. Had Churchill not prevailed, England would not have remained the bastion of freedom, defending Europe and the world. Many historians argue that this decision was the most pivotal moment of the twentieth century.

Massive Air Attack: Another pivotal event occurred just months after the Cabinet meeting. As the story recounts, Hitler shifted the bombing focus from airfields to London and civilian targets. If he had continued targeting the airfields, even for a few more hours, he might have eliminated England's ability to repel an invasion. This critical decision ultimately saved the island and paved the way for the D-Day invasion of mainland Europe. I combined Hitler's decision with Churchill's actions for the story's sake.

Bletchley/Ultra: The effort to decode Enigma messages was a top-secret government project. The intelligence derived from these messages, known as Ultra, provided some of the most critical information of the war. However, only a select few in the U.S. and U.K. governments, including top generals and officials, were aware of its existence. In certain situations, they refrained from acting on this intelligence to avoid alerting the Germans to their advanced capabilities.

It is widely claimed that the decoding effort shortened the war by 2 to 3 years. This project led to the development of the Bombe, a machine used for decryption, and its more advanced successor, Colossus. Electric switches were employed to speed up the decoding process, and switch settings were automated using punched tape. A key component of this solution was the conversion board, designed by Gordon Welchman. For more details, see Chapter 34

Fictional Story Characters

Margaret: This character was both the most challenging and rewarding to write. I envisioned a feisty, independent woman born fifty years ahead of her time—sharp-witted, not to be trifled with, yet still holding onto the innocence of youth. Writing her dialogue was initially tricky, requiring thinking from a woman's perspective. However, early in the story, her character seemed to come to life, stepping into the room and taking charge of her own dialogue—a delightful surprise. The process was an incredible journey to a far-off land and back again for me.

Thomas: A highly complex character. His 'knowledge' had to be imparted throughout the story to culminate in the final cabinet meeting scene.

Yuri: Everyone loves a charming spy.

Mrs. Somerville: Initially a minor character, she gradually asserted herself into a more prominent role, much to my satisfaction. The writing process is fascinating in that some characters seem to take on a life of their own—and she was one of them.

Historical characters

Those from history like Hugh Dowding, Turing, Parks, Ismay, Halifax, Colville, Petrie, Mrs. Nell, etc., are true to their roles, with fictional dialog and the following comments:

Sir Winston Leonard Spencer-Churchill:

While the dialogue attributed to Churchill in this story stays true to his manner and character, it is entirely fictional. The only real-life quote from Churchill appears at the end of the book.

As one of the most written-about figures of the 20th century, a wealth of information on Churchill's life is readily available. Here, I've included just a few intriguing highlights:

Painting – Painting was a source of relaxation for Churchill throughout much of his life, particularly when he was out of politics. In 2007, one of his works sold at Sotheby's in London for £1,000,000, which would have been quite helpful given his financial struggles.

Alcohol – While certainly consuming more alcohol than average, it is generally accepted that Churchill was not an alcoholic. In a wager with Viscount Rothermere, he stated he could abstain from all alcohol for a year. He won the bet.

Dardanelles – Churchill was the political force behind and the military architect of the ill-fated Gallipoli landings on the Dardanelles during the First World War. Although a later report attributed the failure to poor execution by the generals, the public continued to hold Churchill primarily responsible, and he never fully regained their trust.

Military Leader

Before leading Britain to its most important military victory, Churchill almost didn't make it into the Royal Military College at Sandhurst. He failed the entrance exam twice and needed a tutor. He did poorly in all of his subjects except history and, of course, English.

Accident Prone

Churchill was accident-prone and, throughout his life, suffered many injuries, including being hit by a car crossing New York's Fifth Avenue. He almost drowned in a Swiss lake, fell many times from horses, and crashed a plane while learning to fly.

Lost Post-War Election

In July 1945, after nearly a decade without elections, Britain held its first general election, and he was voted out of office. The opposition successfully portrayed his party as out of touch with the people's needs. Upon learning of his defeat, he is said to have remarked, *"They have a perfect right to kick us out. That is democracy. That is what we have been fighting for.*

"

Nobel Prize.

He returned for a second term as Prime Minister in 1951. During this time, he received the Nobel Prize in Literature for "his mastery of historical and biographical description and for brilliant oratory defending exalted human values. He also penned a fiction novel that he advised friends not to read.

Famous Quotes – His mastery of the English language was exceeded only by his witty rejoinders. Below is one of my favorites:

> **Lady Nancy Astor:** Winston, I'd poison your tea if you were my husband.
>
> **Churchill:** Nancy, if I were your husband, I'd drink it."

Iron Curtain

"In March 1946, he brought the term 'Iron Curtain' into widespread use—a phrase that became iconic during the Cold War. Churchill introduced it during a speech at Westminster College in Fulton, Missouri, with President Truman seated on the stage. In this address, Churchill criticized the Soviet Union's policies in Europe, a moment widely regarded as the opening salvo of the Cold War."

"From Stettin in the Baltic to Trieste in the Adriatic, an "Iron curtain" has descended across the continent."

Sir John Rupert Colville

I described Jock Colville's character in the story as excessively fussy and tense, but this was not the case. As Churchill's private secretary, he was the low center of gravity and a cornerstone of Churchill's talented staff and advisors. However, this talent tended to make him a bit colorless for the story and in need of some flair.

E. F. L. Wood, 1st Earl of Halifax (aka Lord Halifax)

While Churchill and Halifax never saw eye to eye, they cooperated on many important issues regarding the war effort. Halifax was said to have refused the post of Prime Minister, thinking he could not lead from the House of Lords. Some feel it was a tactical move to avoid facing the lack of support to win the position. The decision resulted in Churchill's election.

Dr. Alan Turing

Alan Turing's development of the exclusion programming method was crucial for rapidly decrypting enemy messages. The machine designed to implement this method, the Bombe, played a pivotal role, while the later refined Colossus is widely acknowledged as the first large-scale digital computing machine.

Due to strict secrecy laws, information about Colossus remained classified until 1974. In its absence, the ENIAC machine built in the United States was commonly credited as the "first real computer." However, in 1995, documents released by the National Security Agency through a Freedom of Information Act request revealed the significance of Colossus and Turing's contributions, solidifying Britain's pioneering efforts in computing history.

Although some of the brightest minds in England worked on cracking the Enigma code, success would not have been possible without Turing's leadership and ingenuity. Many who were aware of his private life feared that Bletchley Park security might discover it and remove him from the project—a decision that, by unanimous agreement, could have cost the Allies the war.

Despite his monumental contributions, Turing faced immense persecution after the war due to his sexual orientation. In 1953, he was convicted of "homosexual acts" and suffered greatly as a result. Tragically, he died by suicide at age 41 in his home in Wilmslow, Cheshire.

In 2009, British Prime Minister Gordon Brown issued an official apology on behalf of the government for Turing's treatment, recognizing his invaluable contributions to shortening the war. Turing's legacy continues to be honored: his image appears on the current Bank of England £50 note, released to commemorate his birthday, and in 1999, *Time* magazine named him one of the 100 Most Important People of the 20th Century.

DOCUMENTS

Sotheby placed some of Dr. Turing's papers from a private collection at an auction in February 2011. Wanting to ensure the documents stayed at the National Museum of Computing, located at Bletchley, the trustees attempted to raise £500,000 to bid on the collection. With fundraising well short of its target, Google made a substantial contribution, making the purchase possible. Google's purchase also created fears the papers would find their way to Silicon Valley, where Turing is a legend and inspiration. Ironically, Google not only made the purchase possible but insisted on keeping the materials at the museum.

Colossus machine

In 1994, efforts successfully reproduced the Colossus machine. It became operational in 2007. It is located at the Bletchley Museum in Hut H.

Additional Information

General descriptions:

Small details such as taped windows, victory gardens, rationing, and brands of products and cars are accurate. Not entirely due to the war, it was a fascinating time of change in fashion, society, and the size of the world.

Kzar Pushka

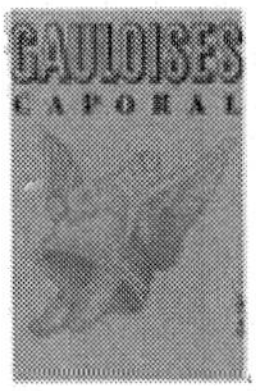

Gauloises

Chesterfield

1939 Lagonda Rapide

Entirely by chance, shortly after writing the book, I went to the Blackhawk Automobile Museum in Danville, CA. I just smiled when I came across the exact same car described in the book. I took this picture, and it's hard to explain something like that.

Fashion

Military uniforms, with their padded shoulders and tailored suit-like jackets, heavily influenced the era's fashion. Women's hats, a staple since the Roaring Twenties, remained a prominent and stylish accessory. This period undoubtedly gave rise to some of the most distinctive styles and innovations, marking a definitive break from the conservative Edwardian traditions of the previous century.

Gabrielle Coco Chanel

Coco Chanel Chanel was a powerful force in fashion, renowned for her clean, almost masculine design aesthetic. During the German occupation of Paris, she was accused of collaborating with the Nazis due to her relationship with a Nazi officer. Despite widespread disapproval after the war, she quickly revived her fashion house, solidifying her lasting influence in the industry.

China Clipper

Before the war, international air travel was just beginning to connect the world. The iconic Pan Am Clipper, a flying boat known for its luxurious experience, relied on water landings since most parts of the world lacked runways capable of accommodating large planes. However, the widespread use of large bombers during the war necessitated the construction of numerous long runways. As a result, the Clipper and its legendary style of travel quickly became obsolete.

Chapter Comments

Chapter 1: Thomas travels back in time and into an alternate reality, carrying knowledge he doesn't fully comprehend. As for the mechanism of his time travel, the mirror felt slightly more plausible than using Floo Powder and a network of chimneys.

Chapter 4: A stray German bomber accidentally dropped its bombs on the Chiltern district, a London suburb, on the day Thomas first arrived in England. The British retaliated the following night. Enraged by his pilots' disobedience of his direct order requiring his approval before bombing civilian targets, Hitler punished them by sending them to the Eastern Front, where they likely met an early death.

Chapter 5:

The war rooms and the prime minister's telephone room descriptions are accurate. After the war, Churchill ordered the lights turned off, and the offices closed, anticipating they would soon be reopened for what he believed was an inevitable conflict with Russia. However, the rooms remained sealed, left exactly as they were, with restricted access. It wasn't until 1984 that Margaret Thatcher, a great admirer of Churchill, opened the war rooms to the public for the first time.

Chapter 6:

Henri Matisse (1869-1954)Femme au manteau violet. (Woman in a Purple Coat.) was painted in 1937. The original was sold at Christie's in 1994 for $22,000,000.

Chapter 14: Siegfried Sassoon (1896–1967, aged 80) was a decorated World War I soldier and poet known for his vivid descriptions of the horrors of trench warfare and his sharp satire of the patriotic fervor he believed fueled the war. I encountered his work years ago and found it more than fitting for this story.

Suicide in the Trenches

I knew a simple soldier boy
Who grinned at life in empty joy,
Slept soundly through the lonesome dark,
And whistled early with the lark.
In winter trenches, cowed and glum,
With crumps and lice and lack of rum,
He put a bullet through his brain.
No one spoke of him again.

You smug-faced crowds with kindling eye.
Who cheer when soldier lads march by,
Sneak home and pray you'll never know
The hell where youth and laughter go.
Siegfried Sasson

Chapter 16:

The iconic Supermarine Spitfire (left) was the most renowned fighter aircraft of the Battle of Britain. With its distinctive curved wings, it is widely regarded as one of the most visually stunning fighter designs in history. It remained the top-performing fighter of the war until the American-built Mustang (right) and the jet-powered German ME262 were introduced.

Chapter 18 Lonnie Garrah was a WAAF Squadron Officer, the equivalent of an army major. Thus, she outranked an Army Sergeant both officially and practically, carrying higher authority, privileges, and responsibilities as a commissioned officer. Fraternalizing between ranks was not prohibited but definitely frowned upon

Chapter 24:

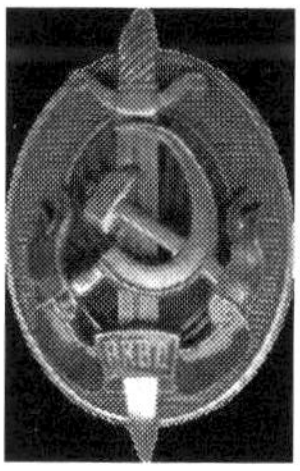

The People's Commissariat for Internal Affairs (Narodnyy Komissariat Vnutrennikh Del), known as the NKVD, was tasked with safeguarding the security of the Russian state and served as the powerful enforcement arm of Stalin's regime. In 1954, it was reorganized into the Committee for State Security (Komitet Gosudarstvennoy Bezopasnosti), commonly known as the KGB. After the fall of the Berlin Wall and the dissolution of the Soviet Union, it evolved into the FSB (Federal Security Service). President Vladimir Putin, a former KGB member, has described the collapse of the Soviet Union as the greatest tragedy of the twentieth century.

Chapter 25:

Uxbridge Control Center

Left picture

This picture shows the upper area where Parks and his staff sat behind the curved glass. To their right was the VIP area where Churchill sat. Directly on the floor below sat the controllers until called into action. In front of them was the irregular map table they used to track the RAF's flights.

Right picture.

The status board at the other end of the room, facing the controllers, was where lights informed them what planes were ready, in the air, or refueling.

Chapter 32:

A distinctively designed former private estate, Bletchley was the center of England's intelligence gathering and a state secret until 1980. All the code-breaking occurred in the surrounding huts and not the main house. All descriptions regarding huts, barns, locations, and the main mansion are correct.

Chapter 34:

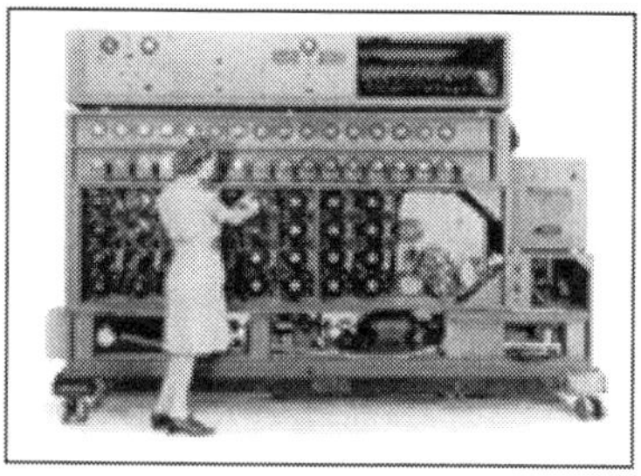

Pictured on the left is a captured Enigma machine used by the German navy to encrypt messages. The original machine, housed in a wooden box, is now on display at the Bletchley Park Museum. Critical to its encryption process, the rotors are visible at the top. The first Enigma machine was captured by a British officer from a German U-boat and retrieved just before the submarine sank—a courageous act that significantly impacted the course of the war.

On the right is the front of the Bombe machine, which uses electrically driven rotors to position the drums and decrypt Enigma messages. The next iteration, Colossus, incorporated vacuum tubes (valves) to enhance decryption capabilities further. While the description of Turing's machine has been simplified for storytelling purposes, many of the elements referenced are accurate. The device's complexity and the contributions of countless individuals to its success go far beyond the scope of this story. I encourage you to delve deeper into one of the war's greatest secrets.

Chapter 40:

The Crown Inn at Shendly Brook. Turing stayed here for much of his time working at Bletchley.

Chapter 56: Frederick Hanover, the Duke of York, owned the estate in Fernhurst, which, like many grand homes of the era, was eventually turned over to the Government. While the Duke did leave an inscription referencing 'King and Country,' all other descriptions in the story are fictional. The phrase 'King and Country' remained in use until Queen Elizabeth II ascended the throne in 1952. Notably, there was a 238-year gap between reigning queens, dating back to Queen Anne in 1714.

Chapter 62: The Germans employed a bombing system guided by radio waves, but as the British improved their jamming techniques, the system became increasingly inaccurate. This often caused bombs to miss their intended targets by significant margins, bringing the war to unexpected places in the countryside. One famous newspaper photograph captured a clock tower in the Richmond district that was mistakenly bombed during the war. The clock's hands were frozen at 11:35 AM, marking the exact moment of the destruction. Ironically, R.V. Jones, the scientist who perfected the jamming system, had to navigate through the clock tower's rubble outside his flat on his way to work that morning.

Chapter 70:

Blenheim Palace, completed in 1724, served as the Churchill family's home for 300 years and is one of England's largest houses.

Facing financial difficulties, Charles, the 9th Duke of Marlborough (1871–1934), resolved the issue by marrying the wealthy American heiress, Consuelo Vanderbilt. Although Winston Churchill was born in Blenheim, he never lived there as a resident. After his father's death, Lord Randolph Churchill, Winston allowed the state to use the palace during the war. Today, the Churchill family still occupies a small portion of the estate.

Chapter 79: Despite their significant contribution to the war effort, WAAFs (Woman's Auxiliary Air Force) were not allowed to be officers and thus could not have a relationship with enlisted soldiers. Lonnie's character is an officer to facilitate her relationship with Paddy and the Sergeant standing guard.

Map of Southern England showing the airbases.

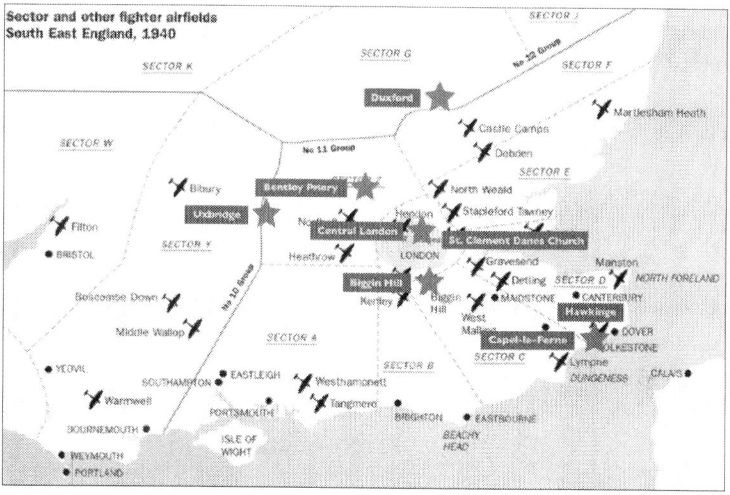

ON A PERSONAL NOTE:

HAROLD TAYLOR 6-10-1924 - 2-26-2010-

"My father was a proud member of the 'Greatest Generation,' serving as a Naval veteran of both World War II and the Korean War, during which he earned several citations and medals. Over eight years of service, he served aboard multiple ships engaged in direct combat in the Pacific. He survived the sinking of the USS Sarsi, spending eight harrowing hours in the water before being rescued the next day.

On August 29, 1945, his ship, the USS San Diego, became one of the first Allied vessels to enter Tokyo Bay following Japan's formal cease-fire. The crew played a vital role in liberating prisoner-of-war camps at Omori, Ofuna, and the Shinagawa hospital. Just days later, on September 2, 1945, he witnessed the Japanese government's official surrender aboard the USS Missouri, marking the end of World War II—all from the deck of his ship, the USS San Diego, a light cruiser."

Significant Duty Stations
USS San Juan CL-54
USS San Diego CL-53
USS Sarsi ATF-111
USS Mender ARS(D)-2
Reserve Fleet, Bremerton, WA

Significant Awards
American Area Campaign Medal
Asiatic-Pacific Campaign Ribbon W18 Stars
World War II Victory Medal
Korean Service Medal With/Star
Philippine Liberation Ribbon With/Star

I live in the Bay Area in Northern California, and writing came to me late in life. It's now something I need to do every day, and the comments I receive make it a labor of love. I would be very interested to know what you think of this story. Thank you for supporting my writing. You can find more information on my other books and a contact form on my website.

Link to visit my website
www.richardDtaylor.com

www.richardDtaylor.com

Oh, this is the most important.

"If you enjoyed this book, please share it with your friends and consider leaving an online review or star rating. Reviews are invaluable to writers—they help us understand your perspective, see what resonated with you, and improve our craft. In today's competitive book market, your opinions make a big difference. If you'd like to leave a review or rating, click the link below to be directed to Amazon, where you can easily fill out a review form for this book."

Link to submit a quick
Amazon star review.
★★★★★

http://www.amazon.com/review/create-review?&asin=B0C2B211RD&

BYCP V8

ADDITIONAL BOOK BY RICHARD D TAYLOR

Enjoy a sample of Geneva Intrusion.

GENEVA INTRUSION

A Kate Adler Book # 1

IRAN WANTS TO START A WAR HIJACKING TANKERS. KATE ADLER ESCAPES AN ASSASSINATION ATTEMPT AND IS RUNNING FOR HER LIFE TOWARD A BIG SURPRISE.

A Cartel thriller delivering constant surprises.
Enjoy a sample of Geneva Intrusion.

CHAPTER—1

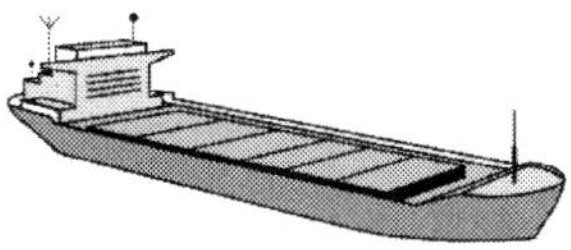

BOARDING THE *MONTCLAIR STAR* — THURSDAY PM

Panama-flagged oil tanker *Montclair Star*

Location: The Persian Gulf, 25 miles off the coast of Iran.

US Fifth Fleet in the area

"Pirates, pirates on port side," Juarez, a deck hand, breathlessly shouted as he careened up the stairs to the bridge.

Standing on the tanker Montclair Star's bridge wing, Captain Carlino Bertucci was aware of the situation. A man with twenty-four years' experience was tracking the pirates on radar and concentrating on the small boat through his binoculars. He lowered the glasses, walked into the wheelhouse, and quickly radioed the US Maritime Administration emergency group.

"Mayday. Mayday. Mayday. This is the *Montclair Star*—hijacking in progress. Request any aid. Coordinates 26 degrees 30 minutes by 53 degrees 15 minutes, course 135, speed 19 knots."

"*Montclair Star*, this is the warship *USS Connolly*. We copy your transmission," said the young ensign on the Arleigh Burke-class destroyer. "Relaying your information to coalition channels now."

"They're on approach, situation is critical, *Montclair* out," Bertucci said, leaving the channel open.

Five men in a small, sea-worn skiff violently attacked the choppy waves, fighting towards the massive oil tanker in the Strait of Hormuz. The leader, a large man, stood at the front with knees bent, absorbing the powerful surges of the bow as it dove deep into the water and then thrust upward. He studied the distance as they approached the plodding behemoth. It required his total concentration to maintain his balance atop the erratically battered boat. Drawing his forearm across his face, he once again failed to wipe away the saltwater stinging his eyes. A fatigued AK-47, whose violent history would never be known, lay at his feet, covered in the spray that filled the air.

"Faster," the leader shouted, "faster." The skiff suddenly shifted starboard under his feet, causing him to slam his foot against the outboard rail to stay aboard. He looked disdainfully at the frail young man soaked to the core, trying to control the screaming outboard motor. "Keep her steady, or we lose speed," he yelled with a wave of his arm. Eyes fixed on the tanker, he waited until the last moment to pick up the semi-automatic rifle.

Bertucci approached the wall speaker and pushed the ship's PA button. "This is the captain, pirates alongside. This is not a drill. Repeat, this is not a drill." With the ship's phone in his hand, he selected the engine room and said, "Banoy, you heard the announcement. Pirates will attempt to board. Give me all the speed you have."

Banoy said, "Do you authorize full ahead?"

"Yes," the captain yelled to his chief engineer, "do it *now*."

The radio speaker came alive. "This is the warship *USS Connolly* to the *Montclair Star*; what is your status, over?"

Bertucci looked over the port side wing and saw a man on the skiff below with a gun pointed directly at the bridge. "Everyone down," he shouted, taking an awkward dive for the floor as bullets pinged off the outside of the bridge.

On the *Connolly*, the ensign turned to his captain. "No response, sir, but I heard automatic gunfire."

The *Connolly*'s captain turned to the executive officer and said, "Get a helo in the air, and you," he pointed at another ensign, "turns for flank speed and, navigator, get me to their position."

"Yes, sir," was the reply from each of the crewmen.

The craft was still trying to gain on the tanker as it fought against the dangerous waves generated off the enormous ship's bow. The leader put down the AK-47 and picked up a Soviet-made grenade launcher. Holding it up to his eye, he observed the larger ship move in and out of the weapon's sight and fired.

The unstable platform on which he stood caused the grenade to errantly head for the upper corner of the superstructure, where it entered the side window of the bridge and went out the front without an explosion. Glass rained down on the *Montclair*'s bridge crew.

Captain Bertucci commanded the helmsman, "Hard-a-port," attempting to run into the smaller craft, making it more difficult to board.

Bertucci's voice was tense as he turned to his first mate. "Let's get those jets on." The man moved swiftly to the control panel and threw the master switch. "Jets on," he shouted as the four-inch water jets around the ship created a non-lethal means of making it more difficult for the pirates to make it to the ladder from their small craft.

Just then, automatic gunfire came through the open door. The captain watched as the overhead exploded in a sequential pattern of bullets above him. He looked at his crew face down on the deck.

"Change that order," he said to the first mate. "Get your men to the citadel. Leave the jets on."

The first mate rushed everyone off the bridge and into the companionway.

"All hands to the citadel — *now*," Bertucci said over the PA. He then picked up the telephone. "Banoy," he said, "shut down the engines and electrical power and get your guys to the safe room."

"Aye, sir," Banoy responded.

Another cartridge full of ammunition came up from below, pinging off the outside hull and taking out more glass. Bertucci, on his knees, could feel his heart pounding as he turned the dial on the ship's safe. He pulled at the door and grabbed the ship's log. Bent over, he exited the bridge, descending five flights of stairs into a room designed to deny the pirates the leverage of hostages. They knew untrained pirates could not start the engines, and short of an explosive charge applied to the hatch, they were reasonably safe. They expected the pirates to leave once they realized time was short, help was on the way, and they could not navigate the ship to a friendly port.

Bathed in the water from the jets, the leader motioned for a crewmember to throw up the ladder. The third try caught the tanker's bulwark. He and his four men ascended the ladder, all barefoot and dressed in the typical Somali pirates' threadbare clothing. Clearing the bulwark, the men took cover behind a raised oil tank access hatch and, from the duffel bag, unwrapped four KL-7.62 semi-automatic assault rifles from their waterproof covers, several flash/smoke grenades, extra ammunition, and a medical backpack. The lead man felt the engine's muted vibration under his feet stop, and the noise generated by the defensive water jets faded as they shut down. The five men moved quickly towards the main superstructure in practiced precision. The trailing two men concentrated on the superstructure's gangways, with the rest looking for any threat at deck level. Silently and methodically making their way to their destination.

Seconds later, the five men stood on the port bridge wing just outside the pilot house. The group leader, gun at his shoulder, nodded as one of his men pulled open the hatch to the wheelhouse. A second man rolled a flash/smoke grenade into the room. Their backs were against the outside bulkhead as it went off. The leader entered, quickly swinging his gun's barrel into the space, ready to open fire. Two men covering the area's right and left sides immediately followed him. It was unoccupied. Unsurprised, the leader knew the crew would be locked away but was trained not to take any chances. The smoke in the air streamed towards the broken windows and outside as if it needed to be elsewhere.

Silently, he pointed at one of the men, who went over to the helmsman's console. Looking at the dark gauges, which showed no damage, the man nodded, indicating everything seemed okay. The leader turned to another man at the console, looking at a sheet with the new coordinates. He motioned for them to stay. Both men pulled on latex gloves before they touched anything. He nodded for the other two men to follow him.

Having previously studied the ship's layout, they proceeded directly down to the engine room, guns raised around every corner, expecting the unexpected. As they approached the engine room, one of the men had another flash-bang grenade ready. The group leader looked through the round window in the hatch and found the room empty. He waved his hand at the grenade, and the man put it away. They entered the dimly lit, pale green engine control room as the door opened. There was a shadowy quiet, and the thick, stale air smelled of diesel. Large windows overlooked the massive, silent engines in the dark room two decks below as the start team technician stood at the engineering console. With an assistant, his job was to start the engines. He surveyed the panel and nodded to the group leader with a thumbs-up.

Finally, the group leader turned to the start team and spoke aloud in a Persian dialect. "Time for you to do your job. Let me know when you're ready." The start team put their guns down, and the still-armed leader moved to the entrance door to protect their position.

The assistant pulled on his latex medical gloves as he approached the thirty-foot-long gray control panel that resembled a lineup of ten tall refrigerators, each with a withering array of gauges and dials. He came to a stop in front of the electrical generator module. He pulled open his vest and extracted two plastic-covered sheets of instructions. As he looked at the papers, he flipped the breaker switches in the proper sequence and watched the red status lights turn green. He pulled down on the master handle and heard the generators restart. Their eyes adjusted as the regular lights took over from the dim battery-powered lights.

"Electrical on," the assistant said.

"Check," said the tech, staring at the control console indicator lights.

The assistant set More switches to bring up the hydraulic and lube oil pressure.

"Check again," the tech said, monitoring the pressure gauges.

Throwing another multi-breaker switch sequence down the control panel started the air compressor. The tech watched the indicator on the control panel rise to 128 PSI. He checked the fuel flow indicator and several other gauges and said, "Check, starting main engine one." He held down the large red button labeled "M/E One Start" until the green light above it appeared. The deck vibrated beneath their feet as the room filled with the groans and deep moans of a mighty giant awakened. The exact sequence was employed on the "M/E Two Start" button until all three engines were idling.

"Normal idle in three minutes," he told the group leader at the door.

"Good," the group leader said. "Full ahead when you're ready. Lock the door behind me. I will be on the bridge. Don't forget, nothing is to be left behind when you leave. Wipe down any questionable areas."

"Yes, Captain," both men said. The tech looked at his assistant and then put his hand on the maneuvering handle that engaged the propeller shafts. He looked at the maneuvering chart that said Max 105, Full 95, Half 65. After four minutes and with full green indicators, he moved the handle slowly, first to 65 RPM. The tech felt the additional vibration on the console and in the room as the noise level rose significantly. The immense vessel was now ready for its new heading.

Get your copy of Geneva Intrusion on Amazon today.

Link to
GENEVA INTRUSION
On Amazon

Manufactured by Amazon.ca
Bolton, ON

46222330R00240